Thomas Lauer

Porting to Win32™

A Guide to Making Your Applications Ready for the 32-Bit Future of Windows™

With 67 Figures
DOS Diskette Included

Springer

Thomas Lauer
Im Bruehl 17
55288 Udenheim
Germany

This is a translation from the German *Die 32-Bit-Expedition: Win 32,*[TM] *Windows*[TM] *4.0 und Windows NT.*[TM] *Leitfaden und Referenz zur Portierung von Windows 3.x-Programmen,* published by Springer-Verlag Berlin © 1993.

Library of Congress Cataloging-in-Publication Data.

Lauer, Thomas.
   Porting to Win32 /
  Thomas Lauer.
     p. cm.
   Includes bibliographical references and index.
   ISBN 978-0-387-94572-9
   1. Application software. 2. Microsoft Win32. I. Title.
QA76.76.A65L37   1995
005.26—dc20   95-23946
                                       CIP

Printed on acid-free paper.

Production managed by Frederick H. Bartlett and Terry Kornak; manufacturing supervised by Jeffrey Taub.
Photocomposed copy prepared from the author's Microsoft Word files.

9 8 7 6 5 4 3 2 1

Additional material to this book can be downloaded from http://extras.springer.com.

ISBN 978-0-387-94572-9   ISBN 978-1-4612-0727-6 (eBook)
DOI 10.1007/978-1-4612-0727-6

Contents at a Glance

Introduction and Overview... 1

1   Fundamental Aspects and Preliminary Considerations 7

1.1 Windows: 3.x (16 Bit) versus NT and 95 (32 Bit) 7

1.2 Win32 and the Competition..17

1.3 Basic Architecture of Windows NT 22

1.4 Basic Architecture of Windows 95...40

1.5 What Changes on My Source Codes are Required to
    Support the Win32 API? 44

1.6 A Look on the Win32 SDK...58

1.7 Is My Application Substantially Improved After Porting
    to Win32? 62

1.8 … And What About the Effort? 66

1.9 The Little Brother: Win32s 71

1.10 Summary 78

2   Strategies to Portable Programming 81

2.1 Starting Points and Objectives 81

2.2 Two Alternatives for Porting..89

2.3 Methodical Advice to Planning a Port 93

2.4 Tools and Other Assistance 98

2.5 STRICT Software, Portable Software 105

2.6 Naming of Variables: The Hungarian Variant...........................113

2.7 Which Platform for Windows 3.1: Win32s or Win16? 122

2.8 Some Hints for Porting OS/2 Programs.....................................126

2.9 Summary 132

3   Portable Programs in C and C++ 135

3.1 Some Fundamental Considerations 135

3.2 ANSI C, What Else? 139

3.3 The C Pre-processor...142

3.4 Simple Data Types 149

3.5 Structured Data 159

3.6 Pointer Subtleties..171

3.7 Coding Practice 175

3.8 Compiler Warnings and Error Messages 178

3.9 And What about C++? 197

Contents

4   Portable Windows Programming **201**

4.1 Some Signposts for Portable Windows Programs 201

4.2 Using the Enlarged Win32 Data Types 205

4.3 WINDOWSX.H: A Way to Portable Programs 212

4.4 Message Processing and Parameter Packing............................ 227

4.5 Portable Macros to Communicate with Child Windows......... 234

4.6 Changes in the Base Functionality 241

4.7 Changes in the Window Management 262

4.8 Changes and Improvements in the Graphics Device
    Interface (GDI)... 278

4.9 The Programming of DLLs 290

4.10 Unicode: Plus and Minus 300

4.11 Some Guidelines for Binary Compatible Win16
    Applications... 309

4.12 A Study Trip: From MS-DOS to Win32.................................... 314

**5   Win32 Development Tools and
    Their Use** **319**

5.1 The Creation of Win32 GUI Applications................................. 319

5.2 Particularities for Text Mode Programs 336

5.3 DLLs: What Has Been Modified?... 339

5.4 What Do the Borland Tools Offer?... 349

5.5 Latest News: Visual C++ 2 and Win32 Enhancements........... 351

Appendices **355**

A1 Important Data Types Compared`... 355

A2 PORT.INI: Enhanced and Clarified 359

A3 The Message Cracker Signatures 369

A4 The Example Program Used to Demonstrate Warnings
    and Error Messages 379

A5 The New __stdcall Calling Sequence.. 387

A6 Some Hints for Pascal and Modula-2 393

A7 The Contents of the Enclosed Disk 401

Annotated Bibliography... **403**

Glossary **409**

Index **421**

Table of Contents

Introduction and Overview 1

1   Fundamental Aspects and Preliminary Considerations 7

1.1   Windows: 3.x (16 Bit) versus NT and 95 (32 Bit)...................... 7
Old: Windows 3.x..8
And new: Windows NT 10
And what about Windows 95?..14

1.2   Win32 and the Competition.. 17
IBM and OS/2...17
X as UNIX..19
The most important technical features in comparison 21

1.3   Basic Architecture of Windows NT 22
The NT executive 23
Basic kernel features 25
The NT subsystems...31
MS-DOS and Win16 support..32
Big boss: the Win32 subsystem 34
Communication with the Win32 subsystem 37

1.4   Basic Architecture of Windows 95 40
Virtual: machine manager and device drivers...............................41
Two personalities: Win95 system DLLs.......................................42

1.5   What Changes on My Source Codes are Required to Support the Win32 API?.. 44
The linear 32-bit address space 45
Separated address spaces, isolated applications 48
User input: Mouse and keyboard 51
GDI coordinates and company 54
MS-DOS and CPU specifics...55
Using undocumented features...55
Difficulties in DLL programming...57
Conclusions..58

Contents

1.6   **A Look on the Win32 SDK**... **58**
     Win32 SDK: a single version for NT and 95 59
     Programming with the SDK 60

1.7   **Is My Application Substantially Improved After Porting to**
     Win32?... **62**
     Just porting? 63
     Or immediately include improvements? 64

1.8   **... And What About the Effort?**... **66**
     Some clues, anyway 70

1.9   **The Little Brother: Win32s** **71**
     What is Win32s and what does it do? 71
     Pluses and minuses for the developer.. 75

1.10   **Summary** **78**

2   Strategies to Portable Programming 81

2.1   **Starting Points and Objectives**... **81**
     Preferably STRICT…... 82
     At the very least, fully protected mode compatible! 84
     K&R or ANSI C?... 85
     And the goal? Either one-way porting…... 86
     … Or programming for Win16 and Win32?.................................... 87

2.2   **Two Alternatives for Porting**.. **89**
     Bottom up 89
     Top down.. 89
     Which method is better?.. 90

2.3   **Methodical Advice to Planning a Port** **93**
     Big projects require some planning 93
     Self-defined guidelines and helper libraries................................. 95

2.4   **Tools and Other Assistance** **98**
     Add-on libraries as helpers... 98
     And what about class libraries for C++?... 99
     More tools: PORTTOOL and the SDK documentation................. 101
     Tools for developers coming from OS/2 103
     CompuServe, a gold mine of information 104

2.5   **STRICT Software, Portable Software** **105**
     Okay, STRICT! But what's the best way?...................................... 107
     Some hints for C++ programmers 111

Contents

2.6   Naming of Variables: The Hungarian Variant.........................**113**
Advantages of Hungarian notation...113
More to the utilization..115
Some suggestions 118

2.7   Which Platform for Windows 3.1: Win32s or Win16?..........**122**
Pro Win32s 123
And contra?..124

2.8   Some Hints for Porting OS/2 Programs................................**126**
Tools and methods of approach...127
Some hints for text-mode programs..129
Porting OS/2 PM applications 130

2.9   Summary..**132**

3   Portable Programs in C and C++..............135

3.1   Some Fundamental Considerations..**135**

3.2   ANSI C, What Else? **139**
The most important advantages of ANSI C 139
A few words about Pascal and Modula-2 140

3.3   The C Pre-processor..**142**
Some simple tricks with #define..142
Complex macro definitions: a dash of portability........................146

3.4   Simple Data Types **149**
Own data type definitions 150
... and related problems..153
About erroneous casts and other wrongdoers..............................154
May I introduce myself: sizeof() 156
Always good for a surprise: BOOL!...157

3.5   Structured Data **159**
Unions: memory economy, shady maneuvers or what?..............160
Structured use of structs 162
Structures and memory layout 166

3.6   Pointer Subtleties **171**
FAR? NEAR? Neither — nor: FLAT! 171
Segment and offset arithmetics: hands off! 173

Contents

3.7 **Coding Practice** 175
Macros, prototypes, and libraries 175

3.8 **Compiler Warnings and Error Messages** 178
Warnings and errors in detail 179

3.9 **And What about C++?** 197

4 **Portable Windows Programming** 201

4.1 **Some Signposts for Portable Windows Programs** 201
Syntax versus semantics: two perfect examples 202
Windows portability: an overview 203

4.2 **Using the Enlarged Win32 Data Types** 205
WORD, the second… 205
Where does the pointer point? 207
New polymorphic types: LPARAM and WPARAM 211

4.3 **WINDOWSX.H: A Way to Portable Programs** 212
The simple helper macros 213
To the fullest: message crackers 215
Examples: WM_COMMAND… 217
… and WM_MOUSEMOVE 221
The most important benefit: portability 224

4.4 **Message Processing and Parameter Packing** 227
The little brothers of the message crackers 228
Helper macros to reassemble the message parameters 233

4.5 **Portable Macros to Communicate with Child Windows** 234
Some common definitions 235
Class-specific macros 236

4.6 **Changes in the Base Functionality** 241
The access to data of preceding instances 241
Memory management: the local and global heaps 245
Solved in a completely different way: shared memory 249
A ticket to the I/O system and back, please! 251
Long or short: the treatment of filenames 255
INI files and registry 258

4.7 **Changes in the Window Management** 262
The calling sequence of window procedures 263
DDE and colleagues 264
Cooperation with other programs 269

Contents

Mouse and keyboard: the local input model 271

Focus and active window 273

The mousetrap...274

Last but not least: hooks..277

4.8 Changes and Improvements in the Graphics Device Interface (GDI) **278**

GDI: nowadays in C++..278

Coordinates in wide-screen format. 279

Packed coordinates 282

Brave, new-world transformation 285

Handles: strictly private! 287

News also for metafiles 288

4.9 The Programming of DLLs.. **290**

DLLs and memory management 291

Initialization and termination 295

Global windows classes 297

4.10 Unicode: Plus and Minus **300**

Well, another layer of macros! 302

The C compiler and Unicode strings......................................304

One character equals one byte?..306

Unicode: Yes or No? 308

4.11 Some Guidelines for Binary Compatible Win16 Applications **309**

4.12 A Study Trip: From MS-DOS to Win32................................ **314**

DOS antiques under Win32...314

Text mode and Win32...315

Sorry: no graphics!..317

5 Win32 Development Tools and Their Use **319**

5.1 The Creation of Win32 GUI Applications............................. **319**

But what is with Win32s?...320

Program creation at a glance 321

The 32-Bit C/C++ compiler 323

News from the Resource Compiler 326

LINK: one does it all 327

NMAKE: complete control 332

The Win32 header files...334

Contents

5.2   **Particularities for Text Mode Programs**.................................. 336
      Text mode: no big differences.. 337
      Example: batch job and MAKE file.. 338

5.3   **DLLs: What Has Been Modified?** 339
      DLLs and data sections.. 340
      The linking of a DLL 343
      Common data sections... 345
      And dynamic memory allocations?.. 347

5.4   **What Do the Borland Tools Offer?**...................................... 349

5.5   **Latest News: Visual C++ 2 and Win32 Enhancements**......... 351

Appendices 355

A1   **Important Data Types Compared`** 355

A2   **PORT.INI: Enhanced and Clarified** 359

A3   **The Message Cracker Signatures** 369

A4   **The Example Program Used to Demonstrate Warnings
     and Error Messages** 379

A5   **The New __stdcall Calling Sequence**.................................... 387

A6   **Some Hints for Pascal and Modula-2**.................................... 393

A7   **The Contents of the Enclosed Disk** 401

Annotated Bibliography 403

Glossary 409

Index 421

List of Figures

1.1:   Windows 3.1 all over! 9   *Chapter 1*
1.2:   Windows NT: Spotting the small differences from Win16
        requires sharp vision. 11
1.3:   The Windows family shown in early 1995 13
1.4:   Windows 95: New look for an old friend? 14
1.5:   The basic structure of Windows NT 24
1.6:   The most important NT executive objects 25
1.7:   Three APIs for process creation, one NT kernel call 30
1.8:   The environment subsystems of Windows NT 31
1.9:   The most important parts of the Win32 subsystem 36
1.10:   Communication between Win32 subsystem and applications 38
1.11:   The virtual address space of a typical Win32 application 46
1.12:   Applications have isolated address spaces — communication
        is possible only through network-like mechanisms. 49
1.13:   The route of input messages in Win16 and Win32 53
1.14:   From source to application: the development process with
        the Win32 SDK. 60
1.15:   The file manager, a complex interface: MDI, drag-and-drop,
        icon and bitmap processing, etc. 67
1.16:   Compared to the file manager, rather easy to port: the PIF
        editor (the window on the right shows the RC file with the
        dialog box resource) 68
1.17:   The integration of Win32s and Windows 3.1 72

2.1:   The four source code categories for Win16 82   *Chapter 2*
2.2:   UAE: an alarming symptom 85
2.3:   One set of sources, but two applications 87
2.4:   Bottom up — from small to big 90
2.5:   Top down: a working center is expanded stepwise 91
2.6:   The components of a self-defined portability library 95
2.7:   The intersection of the three APIs defines the range of a
        really portable class library! 100
2.8:   PORTTOOL at work 102

Figures

2.9: A view into the CompuServe forum MSWIN32, created especially for Win32 developers 104

2.10: Line-by-line copying of function headers 110

2.11: Function names with and without STRICT 112

2.12: The three elements of Hungarian notation 118

2.13: A portable layer of macros for function attributes 121

2.14: The OS/2 API analyzer after the job 128

Chapter 3 3.1: A vicious circle that most developers know only too well! 138

3.2: From macro to program code 148

3.3: The memory layout of the union BAD_TRICK 161

3.4: Direct access to members of structs: simple, but hardly maintainable. 163

3.5: Structured access with a layer of access functions 164

3.6: The memory layout of structure XYZ under Win16 and Win32 169

Chapter 4 4.1: Non-portable access to internal data structures in private Windows segments 208

4.2: NEAR, FAR, HUGE, and flat: the pointer zoo of Windows 209

4.3: Addressing of memory through HUGE pointers 210

4.4: The distribution of data coming with WM_KEYDOWN 217

4.5: Macro expansion and recomposing the message parameters wParam and lParam 224

4.6: Data and their distribution on wParam and lParam 230

4.7: The six control classes and the _Enable-macro 236

4.8: Investigation of casts: from LRESULT to HICON. 237

4.9: Communication and data exchange through private messages 243

4.10: Simple data transfer via window text 245

4.11: The mechanisms for memory management (Win16) 247

4.12: Memory management under Win32 248

4.13: Copying memory areas with WM_COPYDATA 252

4.14: 16-bit registration information in REG.DAT 260

4.15: The Win32 registry 261

4.16: Tasks, messages, and queues under Win16 270

4.17: Processes, threads, queues, and windows under Win32 271

4.18: The GDI transformations of Win32 286
4.19: Two rectangles: Win16 exclusive and Win32 inclusive.................286
4.20: DLL memory management under Win16 292
4.21: The normal case under Win32: one DLL data section
       per client. 293
4.22: One shared section for all DLL users 294
4.23: Win32 applications and Unicode conversion 301
4.24: Too old: the Win32 message box for old 2.x programs. 311
4.25: Lots of enemies, much honor: the Windows platforms. 313

5.1:   WINDBG, the graphical debugger of the Win32 SDK...................323
5.2:   Dynamic stack growth with the aid of the virtual
       memory manager 331
5.3:   The Win32 include files 335
5.4:   The steps to the generation of a Win32 DLL 344
5.5:   Visual C++ 2, AppStudio, under Windows NT 352

Chapter 5

List of Tables

1.1: Windows NT, OS/2, and UNIX compared 21   *Chapter 1*
1.2: Comparison of Windows NT and Win16: CPU properties
and memory management. 26
1.3: Comparison of Windows NT and Win16: kernel. 27
1.4: Comparison of Windows NT and Win16: I/O system
and NTFS. 28
1.5: Comparison of Windows NT and Win16: Win32 subsystem. 34
1.6: New Win32 possibilities: advantages for developers and
customers. 65

2.1: The most important data type conversions for STRICT 108   *Chapter 2*
2.2: Hungarian notation I: abbreviations of simple data types. 115
2.3: Hungarian notation II: type abbreviations for important
data structures. 116
2.4: Hungarian notation III: important qualifications. 117

4.1: Information sent with Windows messages 216   *Chapter 4*
4.2: Messages affected by parameter modifications 229
4.3: Differences and similarities of Win16 and Win32
memory management 246
4.4: INT 21H calls and corresponding Win32 functions 254
4.5: DDE messages and PackDDElParam() 268
4.6: GDI functions returning coordinate pairs 283
4.7: Win32 messages and functions returning packed
coordinates 284
4.8: Constants for DLL initialization and termination 296

5.1: MSC compiler switches compared 324   *Chapter 5*
5.2: The RC switches 327
5.3: The four LINK modes 328
5.4: Important LINK switches 328

Tables

5.5: Options for the selection of the API subsystem 329

5.6: Header files not automatically included 336

Appendix 1.   A1.1: The most important Windows data types in direct
comparison 355

A1.2: OS/2 compatible Win32 data types 357

Appendix 3.   A3.1: The signatures of the message crackers 369

Appendix 5.   A5.1: _cdecl and _pascal calling sequence 387

Introduction and Overview

"Of course I can't say, whether it will become better if it gets changed; but as much as I can say, it must change if it shall become good." Georg Christoph *Lichtenberg*, Sudelbücher

These words were written in the 18th century by a fairly unknown German physicist and writer, yet I think they are amazingly well suited as a description of the current situation of the Windows™ operating system. We're definitely in for a change: new 32-bit systems are quickly gaining importance while the "old" 16-bit environments are still of a certain significance. Two 32-bit products building on the Windows wave of success are fighting for market attention: Windows NT™, available since 1993 and now in version 3.51, and Windows 95, still in the deepest beta stages and not expected to be available until third quarter of 1995.

NT is short for "New Technology."

Much has already been written about these newest Microsoft creations; unfortunately, due the high technical complexity of both systems, the existing material is not always easy to comprehend. The really hard facts for developers about programming and especially porting to the new Win32 API* are not often found. This group at the moment can resort only to the still incomplete and rather dry Win32 API documentation. There are a few more or less usable books about the different Windows 32-bit architectures and Win32 programming [see the Bibliography], concentrating mainly on the new features. What is lacking, however, is a comprehensive textbook to investigate the bells and whistles of the 32-bit Windows API in the light of Win16 programming and, above all, to show *in detail* how to port existing Win16 applications. In comparison with 16-bit Windows systems, quite a few basic design and architectural decisions have led to either a notably changed or even a completely new API. Therefore, some familiar hiking paths have totally gone wild and are nearly impenetrable under Win32, others must first be rediscovered and cleared up a bit, while a third group is safe to hike only with certain security precautions. That brings us to the purpose of this

* API means "Application Programming Interface," a modern buzzword describing the programming interface of a system.

book: to undertake an expedition into these new and to a large extent unexplored territories, explaining along the way what all these things mean to existing programs and their native use under Win32 systems. After all, before putting such nice things as multiple threads or Unicode into their applications, developers have to port them to Win32 in the first place! And this is, in spite of all the promises from Microsoft, somewhat more difficult than I'd expected — at the very least in certain sections. The book is not focused so much on the detailed explanation of all the new functions and possibilities (these won't escape you anyway!); rather, its main concern is to make the transition from 16 to 32 bit as easy and smooth as possible for you as the developer and/or project lead. So, let's have a closer look at the individual parts of the text!

Chapter 1: Fundamental Aspects and Preliminary Considerations

The first chapter is for project leads and developers alike. It gives an overview of the new Win32 systems, describes the most important features, and compares them with Win16 and also with the competition coming along in the form of OS/2 3.x and UNIX. I'll show the important architectural and implementation issues, concentrating on Windows NT and detailing the differences for Windows 95 when required. Since Windows NT is a much more advanced OS than Windows 95 and will be the base for all future Microsoft systems, and since both systems share a common programming model (precisely the Win32 API), this seemed the most reasonable thing to do. Next, the most important areas causing problems when porting a Win16 application to Win32 are divided into six broad categories and accurately explained. In this context I'll briefly

* SDK: Software Development Kit

examine the SDK tools* required for programming Win32 applications. A great deal of discussion is devoted to the question whether and in which form an existing program can benefit from porting and, of course, how much effort the actual port will require. Last, but not least, we'll glance at the somewhat confusing concoction named "Win32s" which claims to make available a subset of the 32-bit API under Windows 3.1.

Chapter 2: Strategies for Portable Programming

In the second chapter we're getting closer to the porting business: here all the questions dealing with planning and realization of large porting projects are treated. I pay little attention for now to the actual changes in specific API functions, but more to general hints and advices influencing the course of the port as a whole. The issues discussed span from the ideal state of the source codes before accomplishing the port to the definition of the goals and possible alternatives for the actual procedure and methodical questions. In this category you'll see, for instance, the utilization of the STRICT option (already implemented with the

Windows 3.1 SDK!) as well as the description of portability helpers such as class libraries or porting tools. Porting OS/2 applications to Win32 is also examined, but here I can give just an overview — a complete and detailed treatment would surely require a book on its own. By the way, this chapter (like the first) is definitely helpful for project leads or managers to gain an overview of the range of problems to expect.

Things get rather technical beginning with the third chapter: ways and means to portable programming under C and C++ are exhaustively discussed — so if your C is somewhat rusty, perhaps a bit of polishing would be advantageous. Beside hints and tips on the use of the C/C++ pre-processor, I look into all important language features in the light of portability. This includes data type definitions as well as pointer manipulations, cast operations, and of course the proper use of all language statements. Another detailed section deals with the most important compiler warnings and error messages for Microsoft and Borland compilers; a glance at C++ and its role in portable programming rounds off the chapter. The major part of all the material in this third chapter is also relevant for Pascal and Modula-2 programmers — I assume just a basic understanding of the C language.

Chapter 3: Portable Programming in C and C++

In the fourth chapter (by far the most extensive of the whole book), we're finally reaching the center of all the good and evil things: building on the six problem categories explained in the first chapter, we will discuss all the important changes between Win16 and Win32(s) as well as their consequences to your source code. First I talk about the numerous Windows data types, as well as their assistance in portability, and which obstacles are to be anticipated. The next three sections concern themselves with the C/C++ header file WINDOWSX.H, first delivered with the 3.1 SDK and now available in appropriate form in the 32-bit counterparts. This file contains about 500 (!) macro definitions that enormously facilitate the portable creation of Windows source code files — unfortunately, they're not adequately explained in the MS documentation. Then I'll dissect the three most important Windows components: all the changes in the KERNEL, USER, and GDI modules are listed and explained. Somewhat more difficult problems will be illustrated through an actual source code example. DLL programming under Win32 shows some peculiarities and subtle traps, as some basic concepts considerably have changed — a separate section deals with that area. Windows NT supports the Unicode character set: what does that mean in detail; in which way can this character set be used transparently; and — the most

Chapter 4: Portable Windows Programming

important question — should you support it? All these questions and then some will be answered in Chapter 4. Finally, we take a closer look at the features that an "old" 16-bit application should have (or not have!) to execute properly under Win32. Windows 95 will be much more accommodating in this respect than Windows NT, but you'll never know under which system users will execute your programs. I'll treat both old MS-DOS and Windows applications at the same time.

Chapter 5: Win32 Development Tools and Their Use

A bit more peaceful is the last chapter, which describes the use of the new Win32 development kits. The SDK tools have not been modified fundamentally (well, as a matter of fact, they have, but their usage is mostly backward compatible), but as usual the devil hides in the details. I describe the usage and all the options of the new tools and compare them, when appropriate, to their 16-bit colleagues. A separate section deals with the generation of DLLs, which have undergone many changes (fortunately for the better). I won't confine the discussion to the Microsoft SDKs, so I'll also take a closer look at 32-bit programming with the current versions of Visual C++ and Borland C++, too.

As well as the seven appendices

Seven appendices with further substantial information about data types, porting details, calling conventions, etc., etc. round off the book. In one of the appendices, Pascal and Modula-2 developers will find some specific hints; Appendix 7 describes the contents of the accompanying disk. A glossary explains some of the more important terms of Windows programming and also deals with the new 32-bit jargon.

A problem with a book such as this is that I have to work with and write about products not yet officially released (I'm writing these lines in March of 1995, so Windows NT 3.5 was just released, but Chicago is still looming in the darkness). Some observations in the text may therefore not be complete, and others may even prove to be inaccurate (but hopefully not too much). I'm planning to release in regular intervals "electronic updates" to the book with information on errors, changes, enhancements, etc. brought to my knowledge. Those will be in a text file and found in several fora on CompuServe (e.g., in the MSWIN32 forum). Later, you'll find more about that online service and accessing these files. However, the single most important requirement for this to work is that you, the reader (yes, exactly you!), inform me of such things if you ever stumble across them!

Address of the publisher: see imprint.

The easiest and quickest way to do so will be with my CompuServe account (my CIS id is 100023, 1554) or via Microsoft Network (my address there is ThomasL@msn.com); an alternate possibility is a written notice to the publisher, c/o Thomas Lauer. And another remark if you are a female reader: I use only male designations in the text such as developer, he, his, etc., but no clumsy things as "he or she" or "his or her." Of course, I realize that female programmers and project leads will read the book, so I simply count on sufficient pragmatism from your side in order not to let this "simplification" become a problem. After all, we will discuss some pretty complicated technical matters, so making the text artificially complex seems unnecessary. If you have any remark about that, just e-mail!

A last comment: I sometimes can't help it and will give a personal statement or share my point of view on things I found really amazing (for better or worse). These are of course seen through my very particular pair of glasses and now and again are a bit provocative or even polemical (deliberately). So for additional remarks or "counter-polemics" I'm always game. The same holds true even more for errors, omissions, and the like that you might find here. These are fully to be entered to my account; at any rate, a short acknowledgement via CompuServe (see above) will help me to improve on these issues in future revisions.

Your input is always welcome!

Enough of this long opening speech: I sincerely hope that this book brings you as much fun and know-how, when porting your programs and working with Win32, as it was fun for me to bash my way through all those impassable or unknown paths and trails! And in this sense I wish you good luck and every success on your own 32-bit expeditions. ¡Vamos!

March 1995   Thomas Lauer

Chapter 1

Fundamental Aspects and Preliminary Considerations

"In the world of operating systems, the wheels of progress turn slowly." Helen Custer, Inside Windows NT

As the last 15 years have shown, this is a very accurate observation. But in the last couple of years the big wheels have completed another full revolution and given us a radically new operating system: Windows NT. *Radically* new? Well, Windows NT can't (and won't) deny its ancestors — quite to the contrary: both the look and feel and the API* definition by Microsoft, conform as much as possible to previous Windows systems. On the other hand, the NT system code *is* all new and is completely 32-bit based; OS design and implementation are quite different from anything else in the ever-growing MS zoo of operating systems.

* API is short for "Application Programming Interface."

And there is yet another system in the makings, officially called Windows 95 and code named Chicago. This is kind of a grown-up 32-bit version of Windows 3.x. Here, we get a new and improved** user interface, but the inner workings are — at least partially — based on ancient (but hopefully stable) 16-bit code. An important observation is that both products share a common programming interface called Win32 API. Before diving into the dark, and still to a large extent unexplored, depths of porting Win16-based programs to this API, we shall first introduce all "family members" and give a short characterization of each.

** improved when compared to Windows 3.x or current NT versions...

1.1 Windows: 3.x (16 Bit) versus NT and 95 (32 Bit)

"Necessity relieves us of the ordeal of choice." Marquis de Vauvenarges, Réflexions et Maximes

On the 16-bit side we have good ol' Windows 3.x, including some near relatives such as PenWindows and Windows for Workgroups (WfW); in the 32-bit category we see Windows NT, currently in version 3.5 (with 3.51 in beta) as well as Windows 95, expected the soonest in August of 1995, a fundamentally renovated and enhanced version of Windows 3.x. The latter two are (finally) real 32-bit operating systems and present the developer a common, and for a large part, similar API. Unfortunately, this programmer's interface is *not* completely backward compatible (after all, that is exactly the reason for this book!).

Old: Windows 3.x

MS-DOS also includes the functionally similar DOSes from IBM, Novell, etc.

Enormously successful since 1990 and now in common use is the MS-DOS-based* operating system extension called Windows 3.x. (Microsoft likes to talk about a full operating system; I won't discuss that issue here. There are good reasons for both opinions.) The current version is WfW 3.11 (see figure 1.1), which features a comparatively well-documented programming model with a very extensive API; in the following I'll designate both together as Win16 for short. Moreover, I'll ignore Windows 3.x operating in real mode; beginning with Windows 3.1 this mode was gone anyway (no, I'm not exactly hopping mad about that). The following discussion refers, if nothing else is explicitly stated, to the 386-enhanced mode.

For reference documentation see [Ref. 1] on page 403.

The Win16 API builds heavily on the design of its real-mode predecessors (which were, by the way, by no means adequate to the protected mode of 80x86** processors) and developed nearly 100 percent backward compatibility over time. This means strength and weakness at the same time: on the one hand, customers and developers alike could profit from a stable API; on the other hand, a lot of stuff that proved inadequate or even counterproductive had to be carried over for the very sake of compatibility. Every new version of Windows has put up some ballast together with new features like TrueType or OLE. The whole thing grew a bit "heavy" — so a consolidation of and some cleaning up of the API seem to be more than in order.

** "80x86" here (and later on) means genuine 32-bit CPUs, i.e., x > 2!*

Win16 is, as the name already shows, a 16-bit system at the API level, both in the standard and 386-enhanced modes. Memory areas larger than 64 KB can be managed only with the help of complicated segment calculations — I'm ignoring the rather difficult to use (and therefore seldom used) 32-bit support via WINMEM32.DLL.*** But after all, 16-bit protected mode *has* removed the annoying 640 KB limit of MS-

*** This dynamic link library (DLL) makes available 32-bit segments to Win16 applications.*

DOS. Assuming corresponding hardware equipment, properly implemented applications can easily access several megabytes of memory. Put clearly, for standard mode this means a maximum of 16 MB being at your disposal; in enhanced mode with virtual memory management enabled (which is realized through the paging logic of x86 processors) you can theoretically allocate up to 4 GB. However, all applications and the Windows system components share this global address space; there exists no access separation between allocated memory areas on a per-process basis. Individual programs and the system itself are barely protected against misfunctioning software and, even worse, against deliberate manipulations! This insufficient protection scheme is one of the main reasons for the frequent system crashes and numerous UAE messages (see figure 2.2 on page 85). With version 3.1, most of the API functions perform at least some parameter validations, but this relaxes the situation only partially (by the way: parameter validation is an achievement also found and even extended in the 32-bit systems).

UAE is short for "unrecoverable application error": in plain language, a severe programming error.

Figure 1.1: Windows 3.1 all over!

Unfortunately, Win16 does not remove the next big hurdle it inherits from the operating system (whose services are still needed for various system-related tasks): in spite of many tricks,* MS-DOS remains a rather

* such as TSR programming or task switchers like DesqView

simple system with only single-tasking capabilities. What is claimed to be "multi-tasking" by Windows or, more appropriately, by Microsoft — namely the capability to work with several co-resident programs at the same time — is actually a feature implemented above the operating system level and requires a lot of implicit synchronization work behind the scenes: so to speak a pseudo-talent. Consequently and a bit shamefacedly Microsoft describes this "ability" as "non preemptive" or "cooperative" multi-tasking, because it assumes and requires cooperative behavior of all involved applications. Somebody constantly working on long documents or recalculating big spreadsheets may often find himself staring at the as famous as notorious hourglass and knows only too well that this (optimistic) assumption is not even true for Microsoft's applications...

But this is not the only place where the insufficient integration of MS-DOS and Windows is noticeable: numerous bigger and smaller edges on which application developers especially can very quickly get a bump (or two) clearly show that Windows is a rather heavyweight superstructure, forcing the aged MS-DOS slowly but surely onto its knees. In this category you can find the extremely complex implementation model for device drivers and VxDs* (many programmers have lost some teeth while biting these) as well as the poor possibilities for exchanging data between DOS and Windows applications. Always a rather fussy subject was the network support: only with Windows for Workgroups 3.1 (WfW) has Microsoft reached an acceptable solution at least for peer-to-peer networks. Incidentally, for our purposes WfW can be seen as Windows 3.1 (as can PenWindows) and is included in the generic term Win16. Last but not least, the proper usage of the Windows SDK tools to create a Win16 application is a weird and secret science in itself — the countless compiler and linker switches for memory models, to DLL building, callback pro- and epilogues, etc., etc., are plainly, but clearly, a real pain in the neck for developers.

VxD is a generic abbreviation for "virtual device driver;" these are used to virtualize hardware accesses.

In a peer-to-peer network, all workstations are assigned equal rights, unlike a server machine in server-based net.

And new: Windows NT

All the above-described problems (and presumably then some) were clearly realized by the people responsible for Windows at Microsoft. And after the alliance with IBM had been broken in such an elegant manner and one could walk unimpeded on one's own paths, the guys in Redmond made a quick decision: the 32-bit operating system called

OS/2 NT or OS/3 already under development was completely overtaken by MS. After some renaming, sweetening and decorating with the Windows look and feel, a new product was born — Windows New Technology, or NT for short (see figure 1.2).

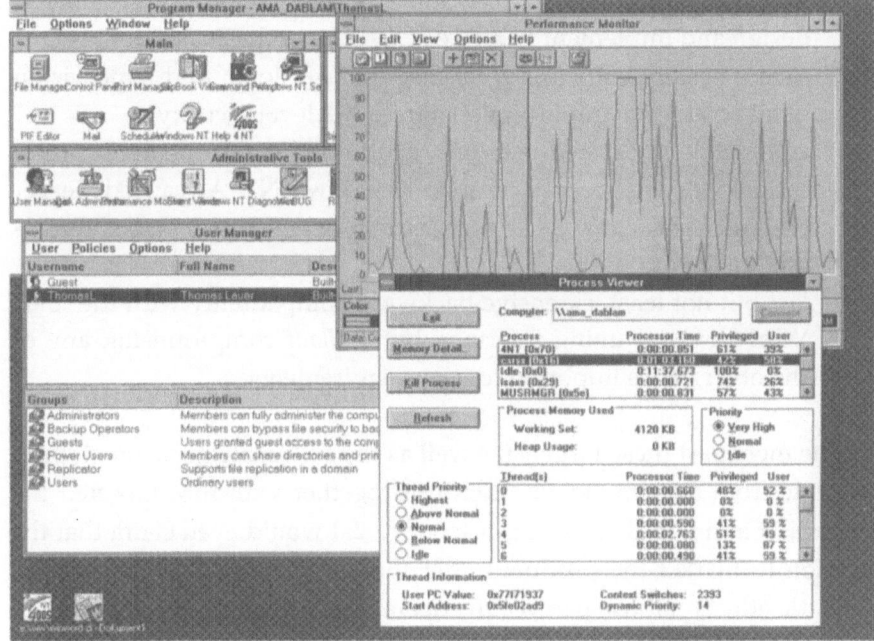

Figure 1.2: Windows NT:
spotting the small differences
to Win16 requires sharp
vision.

The limitations and weaknesses of Win16, as well as the desire to build upon the positive parts of the unsuccessful OS/2 1.x design, dictated the most important system requirements:

The most important design
decisions

- complete separation of all applications from each other and from the OS kernel (making the system suitable for mission-critical applications);
- full support for the 32-bit memory model of 80x86 CPUs, therefore getting rid of separate segments, and access to a full 4 GB virtual memory space per application (aka flat memory model);
- implementation on different hardware platforms and API level portability between these as much as possible (this level is called the Win32 API);

* *Preemptive means that the system gives a process a defined time span to execute, then stops it and activates the next process.*

* genuine preemptive* multi-tasking and multi-threading (the generation of several execution paths — called threads — in a single process);

* support for other important operating systems (MS-DOS, OS/2 1.x, POSIX compliance, to start with) both for executables and on the API level (the latter makes it at least theoretically possible to design and implement POSIX or OS/2 1.x programs under NT);

C2 is one of seven security levels defined by the DoD and means that end users must log in and must be able to protect files, etc., against unauthorized access.

* secure system software with checked user login and supervision of all accesses to important resources (C2 level security);

* completely integrated network capabilities and for complex applications seamless connection to Windows NT Advanced Server (behind which the LAN Manager in an enlarged and NT-compatible form is hidden);

* last but not least, extensive backward compatibility with the "old" Win16 programming interface, but *without* compromising any of the other, more important design requirements.

For the most part these targets (as well as their ultimate implementation) still date from the time when Microsoft together with IBM targeted the NT project as a portable successor to OS/2 2. I would even claim that the decision to market the product under the cover name of Windows NT had little effect on those parts of the operating system independent of the graphical user interface. Probably only the GUI** subsystem had to be changed considerably when translating from OS/2 PM to the Windows programming models and APIs. Be this as it may: Windows NT is for sure a very, very serious candidate for the most important and successful high-end operating system of the nineties. But as this wording shows there indeed remains enough room for (advanced versions of) MS-DOS and Windows 3.x: the low end and mid-range, according to the expectations of Microsoft for the near future, should be served with these two, teamed up as Windows 95 (more on that in the following section). And first steps in this direction were already undertaken in 1993: a Windows 3.1 extension named Win32s is supposed to transport some of the advantages of 32-bit programming "back" to the Win16 platform. The objectives and structure of this strange "hermaphrodite" are discussed in section 1.9 on page 71. So NT (as I'll call Windows NT for convenience from now on) is not at all a complete and comprehensive substitute for Windows 3.x; quite the contrary: it is a top-level extension of the Windows family

* *** GUI — graphical user interface*

* *Win32s is a subset of the Win32 API, hence the name.*

and rounds up the product line. The complete family tree (at least for the time being) is shown in figure 1.3 on the following page.

To me, the single most important fact about NT seems that it is newly written from top to bottom and is a complete system software with a fully integrated graphical user interface. In contrast to the rather wobbly MS-DOS/Win16 combination, Windows NT is made of one piece regarding both the design decisions and the implementation. From what I've seen (including the new 3.5 version) NT is in fact a *very* stable and powerful system. Or to be a bit more practical and less pompous: whenever possible, I prefer to work under NT than with Windows 3.1!

NT: completely new!

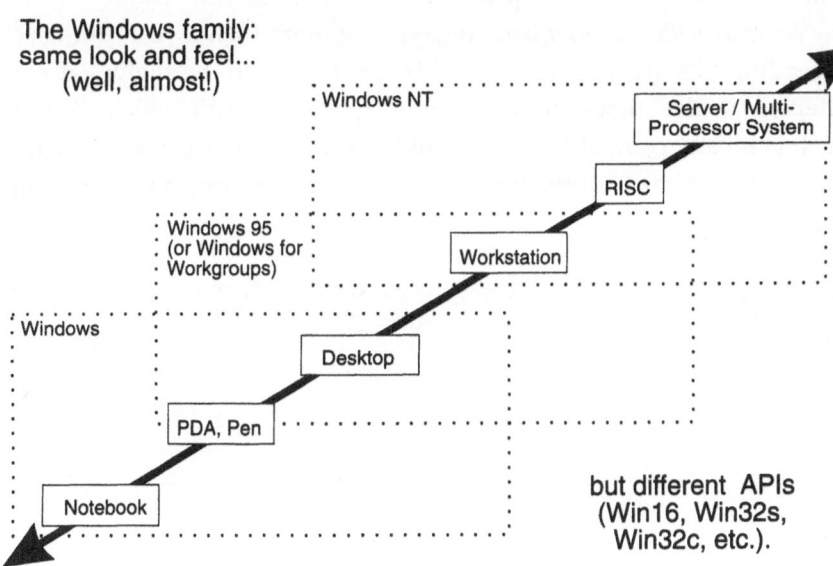

The Windows family:
same look and feel...
(well, almost!)

Figure 1.3: The Windows family shown in early 1995

Alas, the amount of new features indeed has a price: NT has significantly higher hardware requirements than Win16. A completely configured Windows 3.1 system can run on a 286 machine equipped with 2 MB (admittedly at a comparatively low speed) and allocates about 10 to 15 MB on the hard disk (including MS-DOS). NT, on the other hand, requires at least a 386SX, but also runs slowly on such a CPU (actually, very slooooowly). With a 386 and 8 MB main memory, the system works, but not exactly satisfactorily (in this case, getting more memory is premium to upgrading the CPU). NT 3.5 is much better than 3.1 was in this

But there is a price: the hardware requirements.

respect, but still requires at least 12 MB to get some work done in a reasonable amount of time. The hard disk is also allowed to be a bit larger:
the complete operating system allocates about 60 MB, some 20 MB
(recommended minimum) for the system paging file not yet included.
And Win32 SDK developers should just double these figures: *at least* 16
MB memory and 120 MB free space on the hard disk (as well as either a
486 DX/50 or better or a big sack of coffee).

And what about Windows 95?

*Take two: Win32 API, the
second!*

*Unicode is a 16-bit character
set and supports all modern
alphabets.*

Well, that is an interesting question — I was sure you wouldn't forget
it.... Windows 95 has now been delayed by more than a year, but if you
are reading this, the product should be on its way to the shelves at your
preferred dealer (hopefully). Chicago sports an API called Win32c,
which is mostly compatible to the full NT interface but has some significant omissions, such as the missing security checks or no Unicode support.

*Figure 1.4: Windows 95:
New look for an old friend?*

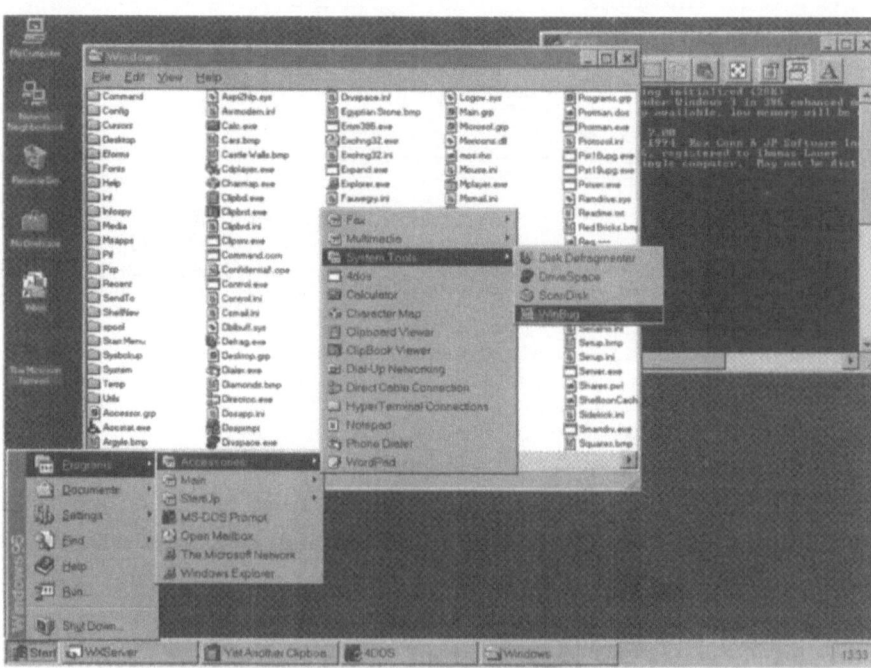

On the other hand, Win32c has some API *additions* to be found only in future versions of NT (aka Cairo). These are mainly concerned with the new look and feel of Windows 95 as shown in figure 1.4. Anyhow, Windows 95 can be seen as a genuine 32-bit system and as such inherits some of the most important qualities of NT. It represents another implementation of the Win32 API: this API simply defines a (common) 32-bit standard to which Windows 95 also has to adhere. 80x86 based NT programs (remember: NT also runs on other CPUs such as DEC's Alpha) should be able to run unmodified under Chicago — the name for 32-bit executables is not "portable executables," or PE for short, by accident. This is also true for source code, which should be portable back and forth between Win32 systems without special requirements. Unfortunately, this bright picture darkens somewhat if you use APIs supported by NT but not under Chicago (e.g., C2 level security) or vice versa. In this case there are three possibilities: the first is conditional compilation, resulting in two different EXE files (static solution). The second strategy compiles one EXE, which performs a run-time check for the actual system type and uses only the supported APIs (that would be dynamic). The third, and the ugliest, is to ignore the differences altogether and to wait and see what happens. Surprisingly, this works well for quite a number of unsupported functions because Windows 95 uses some well-thought-out defaults. You'll find detailed information about these questions and a thorough discussion in the second chapter. What is important right now is the fact that Windows 95 introduces exactly the same porting problems and requires the same adaptations as does Windows NT. In this sense the Win32 API is indeed the determining common factor of both 32-bit systems.

Luckily, 32-bit EXE files are binary compatible.

The 16-bit versions of Windows always required help from the underlying system software (albeit 3.1 does so less than earlier releases). At present I'm not sure whether Windows 95 will include a DOS of its own (a kind of MS-DOS 7.0?) or boot directly into the GUI component as does NT. One thing is sure: even if there is a separate DOS, Windows 95 will not require its services. The system VxDs and DLLs include full 32-bit support for all operating system relevant stuff, so there is no need for a MS-DOS shell. On the other hand, a 16-bit version of DOS will be included for backward compatibility.

Windows 95: on its own or DOS based?

Which brings us to the next important point: Windows 95 will be an *update* to the 3.x versions. It seems to go without saying, but this indeed has far-reaching consequences. Both hardware requirements *and* backward compatibility of a product designed as an update must inevitably show other dimensions than those of a completely new product. Users expect (with good reason) that they can operate Windows 95 more or less with the same hardware equipment as 3.x and that all their "old" 16-bit programs run unmodified and flawlessly under the new system. I even think that these expectations are the main reasons for the delay in the release of Windows 95. Making such a complicated thing like Windows significantly better *and* keeping it backward compatible at the same time gets more difficult with every release. (If you think Windows 95 should be the last "traditional" upgrade, I heartily agree with you. Future Windows version will hopefully be NT based.)

80286 machines: off limits, please!

With the update to Windows 95, all 286-based machines will become useless. This fact is sad enough for users with these machines, but the number of people concerned should be quite small. But can you imagine what would happen if Windows 95 had similar requirements as NT? Approximately 80 percent of all 3/486 machines would require a costly hardware renovation (this is one reason for the small number of NT copies sold). This is, quite frankly, unacceptable for most customers (and, apart from that, of course *reduces* the number of update units). Hence the

So, what is lacking in Windows 95?

requirements won't (significantly) outgrow a 386 CPU, 4 MB RAM and 30 MB free space on the hard disk (the values are just rough estimations of mine). And obviously, a system that has to live in only half of the memory space inevitably *has* to accept some functional restrictions. So some of the key elements of Windows NT are omitted in Windows 95, and a complete discussion of exactly what is missing can be found later in this chapter.

Finally, Windows 95 as an end-user product will be bound to the Intel x86 platform. In practice this restriction will to a large extent become insignificant simply because of the high degree of API compatibility between Windows systems based on the 32-bit API. If Win32 programs can be ported to regular MIPS R4000 or Alpha AXP hardware through (more or less) plain recompilation under Windows NT on that platform, then hardly any developers will have particular difficulties compiling and releasing corresponding EXE files for those machines as well.

Whether porting to Windows 95 or to Windows NT, the problems are the same.

With a single word: Windows 95 will be kind of little brother of Windows NT. The 3.1 developer, however, should see very similar problems whether porting a Win16 application to NT or to 95. But Windows developers will probably arrive in the 32-bit world in much better shape than the DOS gurus: here the changes from the 16- to a 32-bit DOS will be much more significant. But before I'm losing myself in untenable speculations, let's get into another subject also very suitable for assumptions and conjectures.

1.2 Win32 and the Competition

"There should be no technical reason why customers and developers should have to move away from their investments in Windows." Patrick De Smedt, General Manager of Microsoft, in a Win32 developers conference

Microsoft has, as usual, some rather detailed ideas about which Windows system is best suited for what purpose. Figure 1.3, already shown, also reveals how the various Windows systems will be positioned in relation to the underlying hardware. Whether and how far these ideas penetrate the market depends on a whole lot of factors. It seems very important that Microsoft succeed with clearly carving out the actual differences between the individual product lines and platforms. MS tries this in part, not unexpectedly, simply with the aid of price tags: NT is considerably more expensive than Windows 3.1 or its successor will be. Also, the much higher hardware requirements won't miss the desired effect. Only those end users who can really profit from the advanced Windows NT features will perform the necessary system upgrades (at least in the short run). On the other hand, the evolution of Windows 3.x towards Win32 will also result in increasing hardware demands (albeit growing slower than those of NT). A further important reason for the initial uncertainty, especially in big companies with a large installed Win16 base, is the fact that Windows NT requires much more administration than Windows 3.1. The latter is already complex enough for most "normal" users, so only so-called power users or professionals* will be able to install and maintain a Windows NT system. However, NT shares these qualities with its two main competitors, OS/2 and UNIX, which we'll inspect in a moment.

Windows and the various hardware platforms

Windows NT is considerably more expensive than 3.1 or Windows 95.

* elsewhere also called system administrators...

IBM and OS/2

The essential point here is the competition between IBM and OS/2 on the one hand and Microsoft with the Windows NT and 95 combo on the

OS/2: mooooore 32-bit applications are needed!

17

other hand. At present Microsoft seems to have the better deck of cards: regarding just the technical merits, OS/2 Warp is admittedly vastly superior to Win16 but can't keep up with NT (at least in some areas). Moreover, and *really* importantly, it lacks the application variety that first led MS-DOS and then Windows to commercial success. So, two things are urgently needed: a couple of programs in the kind of (in-) famous killer applications (whatever that means nowadays) and, even more important, a comprehensive range of capable standard products (native 32-bit of course) for word processing, drawing, and the like. The current version contains at least a surprisingly complete Windows 3.x emulation, including OLE and TrueType; obviously IBM even plans to support Win32s (see section 1.9) under future versions of OS/2. Since IBM had unrestricted access to the Microsoft source codes (for Win16 only, of course!) at least until the end of 1993, all improvements to the Win16 API will probably also appear in OS/2. Unfortunately, without *native* applications the system is downgraded to an improved DOS and Windows multi-tasker and does not at all benefit from its doubtless existing technical potential. But things can worsen for Microsoft because of the ever-growing delay in the Windows 95 release. If OS/2 can gain enough customers and market acceptance before the Windows 95 launch, and if application support gets a bit better, IBM has quite a good chance of establishing OS/2 as a stable and reliable platform in addition to Windows.

Particularly the fact that Windows NT and 95 have to a large extent a backward compatible API and can more or less directly access a huge base of potentially easy (and therefore fast) to port programs might prove to be one of the main arguments for their long-term success. Apart from that, NT already supports text-mode-based OS/2 1.x applications, and future versions will probably include Presentation Manager support (but Microsoft has needed more than two years in order to realize that PM support is not at all a sign of weakness, but simply a *conditio sine qua non* for a number of users). Many a competitor has underestimated IBM's capabilities at the wrong moment and later paid dearly for the consequences: IBM now prepares a full line of OS/2 products including a portable high-end version of OS/2 (called Workplace OS) supporting symmetric multi-processing; it has a personal edition running on standard 4 MB desktops at the low end and will supply everything in between. The advanced version is an especially interesting step: compared with the essential NT features, it seems to be very competitive. This

Under Windows NT, OS/2 programs are executable (at present 16-bit text mode only).

comes as no big surprise since IBM had enough time to think and included the Mach 3.0 kernel as OS base (interestingly enough, the NT kernel itself was once a possible candidate, too). The OS realizes complete API support for all OS/2 versions, Win16, and MS-DOS. This portable OS/2 version will probably also include a Win32 emulation. Or put differently: both the Win32 API and the OS/2 API will at some time in the future contain mutual support. And for reasons of backward compatibility all today's projects, only perceptible in shadowy outlines, such as Cairo and Pink, won't be left uninfluenced by this development — and then Microsoft might again team up with IBM.

Mach is a portable UNIX derivative, supporting different UNIX API "dialects."

In this case, the customers (as usual) have paid the bill (pun intended). First they were completely bewildered about what company and OS to choose, then essential or appropriate applications couldn't run on the selected platform (due to either lack of programs or lack of 32-bit support; ironically Win16 had applications but no 32-bit support and IBM vice versa). In the end nobody will know what good the whole trouble and waste of effort were (well, a glance at the balance sheet of Microsoft will probably answer at least *that* question...), not to mention the numerous software publishers who listened to the glib talk and enthusiastic assertions of IBM and Microsoft in the late eighties and fully got on the OS/2 bandwagon as the future high-end platform in order to design corresponding products (which afterwards couldn't be sold because of lack of audience). But enough of this blasphemy, let's address the second big competitor in the high-end OS market — the somewhat aged, but nevertheless lively, UNIX, obtainable in numerous more or less compatible versions.

X as UNIX

Here a similar statement as for OS/2 is valid: with POSIX emulation NT attempts to poach in foreign properties and Bill Gates* has already unambiguously stated that NT is designed and implemented as a direct competitor to UNIX. As far as I know, there are no Microsoft plans to build a UNIX-like user interface such as Motif or Open Look into NT. But this only means that this won't be available directly from Microsoft: third-party manufacturers will probably take advantage of every weak point of the system, genuine or not, and build corresponding products.

* Original words: "NT is UNIX!"

And in its well-established manner, Microsoft will purchase the most successful company in the end.

My prognosis is that UNIX will have to satisfy two crucial requirements in order to compete with Windows NT as a mainstream system: first, a standardized, low-priced, and not too resource-hungry implementation must catch on. In this context non-UNIX supplements such as a complete and fast MS-DOS emulation (of course also on non-Intel platforms) are certainly not to be neglected. Second, all standard applications that have acquired a certain importance (and those aren't few) must be available in correspondingly powerful versions for this system. And there you have it — again: in order for commercial success an operating system needs useful applications. But software developers do write applications only for systems that are commercially successful; that's the way it is. Whether a UNIX version in the future will be able to break this vicious circle* (which already broke OS/2 1.x's neck) I have to doubt after all the experiences I had in the last few years with X systems. Table 1.1 compares the most important *technical* features of Windows NT/95, OS/2 2.x and UNIX and is found on the next page.

Possibly the strongest argument for the long-term success of Windows NT against UNIX is the fact that the complete Windows product line, beginning with Windows for Workgroups 3.11 to Windows 95 to Windows NT and Windows NT Advanced Server, is the brain child of only one company, in a sense even of one man. Bill Gates is already gloating over the uncontrolled growth of UNIX-like systems, the long reaction times of IBM,** as well as the lack of business success of the NT competitors. In his view the Windows evolution is defined and controlled by only one person (at least basically): Gates himself. From a technical point of view this doesn't inevitably produce optimal results. But it safeguards that further development is not discussed (and talked crack) in numerous committees and manufacturers, but to some extent advances smoothly and consistently. At least this will make possible (partly) reliable assessments of products and strategies of Gates/Microsoft (which, however, can just as fast change, as the 1990 big bang between IBM and MS has shown).

NT competitor in the UNIX world: UnixWare from Novell? Or possibly Linux?

* also known as the chicken-and-egg syndrome

** ...indeed, Microsoft is often not too much faster!

The most important technical features in comparison

The following table sums up the most important technical criteria of our three nominees. The table is not exhaustive nor can it replace detailed considerations about weighing the important factors and then choosing the most suitable operating system. It just creates a frame in order to show the basic capabilities and to judge which of the three systems meets certain requirements. The ranks range on a five-point scale, starting with ++ (meaning very good support) to +, 0, - and -- (for no support at all).

Hardware basis is an appropriately equipped 80x86 machine.

Feature or characteristic	NT	OS/2	UNIX
32-bit flat memory model, separated address spaces	++	++	++
Genuine ("preemptive") multi-tasking	++	++	++
Multi-threading	++	++	--
Multi-user support	-	-	++
Seamless Windows 3.1 Support	++	++	0
Windows 3.x source code compatibility	++	0	--
POSIX compatible	+	-	++
SAA compatibility	+	++	0
DDE and OLE	++	+	--
Structured exception handling	++	-	-
Installable file systems	++	+	0
Simple model for device drivers	+	0	++
Protection and security	++	0	+
Available for numerous hardware platforms	0	-	++
Standardized and portable system	++	-	+
Graphical user interface (GUI)	++	++	+
Built-in network support (peer-to-peer)	++	0	++
Hardware requirements	++	+	+
Symmetric multi-processing (SMP)	++	--	0
Stability of the system ("system crash resistant")	++	+	+
Unicode and internationalization	++	0	-
DLLs or shared memory libraries	++	++	+
Mature IPC mechanisms	++	++	+
Remote procedure calls (RPC), distributed processing	+	0	++

Table 1.1: Windows NT, OS/2 and UNIX compared

It certainly would be wrong to simply balance the plus and minus marks of all three systems to select the "best" system. This approach leads (possibly) to the technical superior system; whether this product is automatically suitable for your special needs is at least questionable. First, the above-mentioned characteristics are completely unweighed: the simpler model of device driver development when measured on a absolute scale is surely not as essential as multi-tasking capabilities (unless you happen to be a device driver programmer, of course). On the other hand, the suitability is crucially influenced by the environment in which the system is used. This is valid not only for technical evaluations, but for the entire data management policy (at the very least in bigger organizations). For example, a true-blue-colored company will hardly go without complete SAA compatibility — in spite of all the technical advantages of Windows NT. In this case the frame of the overall PC strategy will probably be based on OS/2. On the contrary, very heterogeneous DP landscapes (e.g., those found in research areas) will profit from the good UNIX connectivity. But in the long run, Windows NT will presumably also penetrate these markets (forcefully supported by Windows 95) — Bill Gates has already announced corresponding intentions....

1.3 Basic Architecture of Windows NT

"If we do not start at the beginning, we have no hope to arrive." Johann Gottfried Seume, Apokryphen

Now the time has come to look at what happens under the surface. I'll give a short overview of Windows NT's basic structure and architecture, thereby comparing the most important Win32 features to Win16. For completeness I will also point out when a specific Win32 functionality is not found (or is modified) in Windows 95. The main reason why I'm concentrating on Windows NT here is because this system is the most advanced implementation of the Win32 API — Dave Cutler, the "man behind NT," has already said that in his opinion Microsoft will build future systems more and more on the code basis laid by NT. Nevertheless, some basic remarks specific to Windows 95 will follow in the next section.

NT was designed and implemented from the beginning as a portable and extensible operating system.* These requirements dictated some basic preconditions for the overall system structure:

* From now on, I'll abbreviate "operating system" as OS.

- Processsor or hardware-dependent code must be minimized as much as possible and should be isolated in a separate code layer.
- All the remaining OS parts are implemented in a portable high-level language like ANSI C.
- The different OS levels should be mirrored in a layered model for all system modules.
- Device drivers as well as installable file systems must be re-configurable at run time and may be replaced even dynamically.
- The OS kernel must be small and flexible enough to support different programming models and APIs (quite like a chameleon). Future API layers should be able to be attached easily to the system.

Well, this short list of requirements resulted in a system structure as depicted in figure 1.5 on the next page. Most remarkable is the explicit separation between the protected kernel-mode code and the "normal" user-mode parts. Quite large parts of the system code do *not* run in kernel mode, as is the standard case with most other OS implementations; instead they execute as autonomous user processes (i.e., they *are* executable programs) that make available OS services to other programs.

Kernel mode allows unlimited access to all resources of a machine, while in user mode all accesses are performed under OS control.

These OS parts are therefore called servers (and the user of a server, e.g., an application program, is of course a client; NT is in fact an exemplary implementation of a client/server architecture on a single machine). The server processes are also called protected subsystems; they are, among other things, responsible for the realization of different API shells.** More about the subsystems follows later on; first I'll take a look at the kernel functionality.

** i.e., POSIX, OS/2, or Win32

The NT executive

This layer of code is also called NT executive: here the real OS work is done. The executive supplies a full set of low-level OS calls to the subsystems. Some important points can be noticed: the separation between HAL*** and the layers above; basically HAL is for NT what the BIOS was

*** HAL has nothing to do with IBM, it means Hardware Abstraction Layer.

for MS-DOS: it shields the upper layers from hardware dependencies. The executive itself is split into separate modules that use their services among themselves and export them to the subsystem level. The modules are completely isolated from each other and communicate only through clearly defined interfaces.

Figure 1.5: The basic struc-
ture of Windows NT

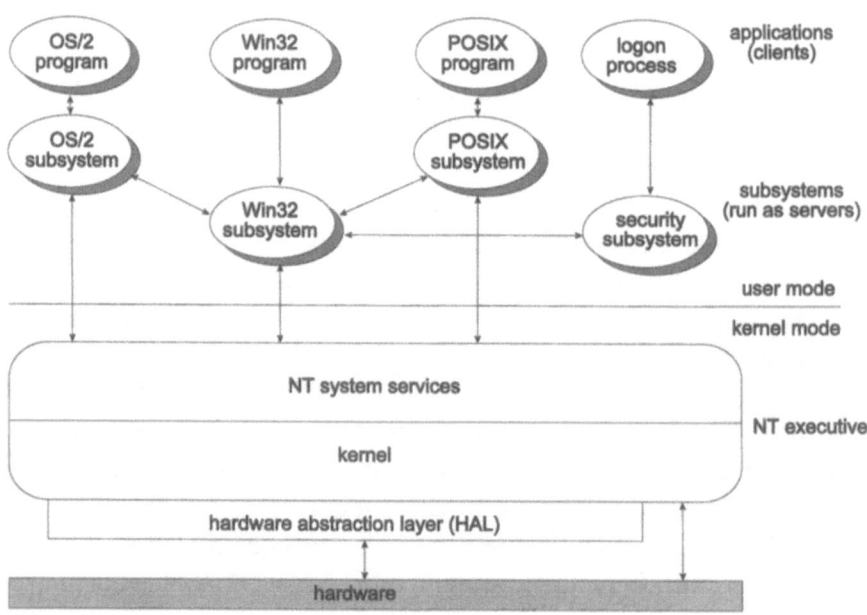

The crucial mechanism here is object orientation: everything important to the executive, whether memory areas, files, threads, or events, is defined and implemented as a separate object. These objects can be manipulated *only* through explicitly exported methods; hence the developer has complete control over the use of the object. Executive objects normally are based on (or even combined from) simpler kernel objects, and generally the latter are not seen in the subsystems. The various security mechanisms of Windows NT are for the better part already implemented on this level; hence, they are fully integrated and not a later addition. Figure 1.6 on the following page shows the most important NT executive objects.

NT executive objects are
based on kernel objects.

Device drivers and installable file systems (which are just another variety of device drivers as far as the kernel is concerned) are fully separated from the rest of the executive. They are handled exclusively by the kernel I/O manager through a uniform protocol. Drivers can build one upon the other and create a layered structure: on top is a file system driver (e.g., for NTFS*) conducting all the installed device drivers for storage devices. In this layered structure new device drivers can be added (and old ones can be removed) dynamically; so a running NT site must not necessarily be shut down when a new or enhanced device (or file system) is becoming available.

*NTFS is short for New Technology File System, a new and enhanced file system supplied with NT.

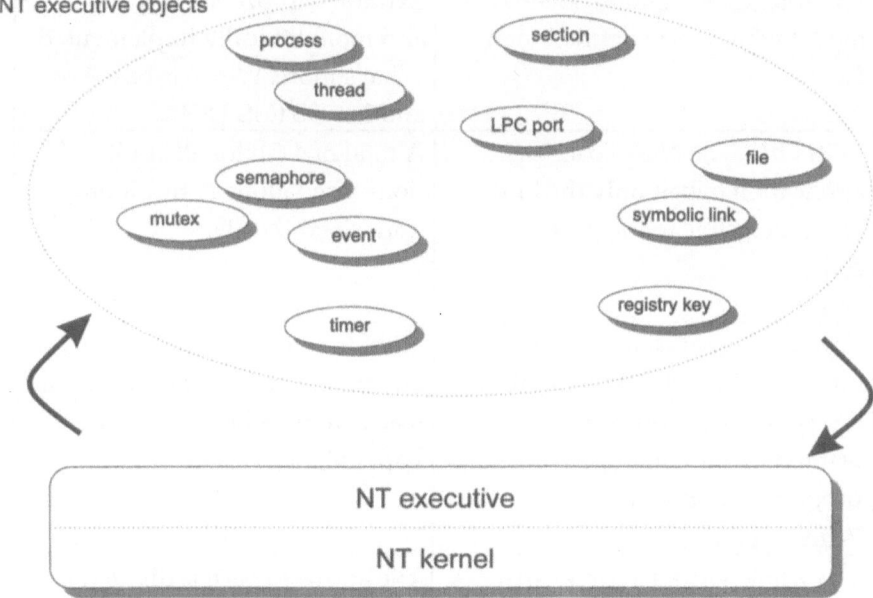

NT executive objects

Figure 1.6: The most important NT executive objects

Basic kernel features

The important targets for NT have already been mentioned, and so now a more detailed discussion of the resulting technical product features is illuminating and for our purposes significant. Tables 1.2, 1.3, and 1.4 show related characteristics grouped together; a comparison with Windows 3.1** shows the differences and enhancements of NT. Wherever possible I have included the Windows 95 mark to indicate which features are supported there too. Let's first review the basic CPU properties and the memory management.

** If nothing explicitly stated for enhanced-mode Windows

Table 1.2: Comparison of
Windows NT and Win16:
CPU properties and memory
management.

Windows NT	Win16
Genuine 32-bit system (CPU registers, flat memory model, etc.), support for 64 bit is planned. **Win95! (partly)**	16-bit processing; only a few non-standardized (and therefore non-portable) methods for 32-bit processing exist.
Support for multi-processor systems (aka symmetric multi-processing, SMP for short).	Here, alone the idea seems quite strange.
Portable implemention, layered model with clearly defined interfaces.	Extremely processor dependent and monolithically implemented. What's more, Win16 is based on another OS (MS-DOS).
4 GB virtual address space per application (albeit only the lower half is accesible to the program's code). **Win95!**	A total of 4 GB for *all* applications, used globally by all programs and the OS.
Complete separation of all applications from each other and the OS; so neither erroneous nor wanted manipulations of other programs are possible. **Win95! (partly)**	No safe separation at all, hence at any time malfunctions or security leaks are possible (and actually happen!).
The whole virtual address space (4 GB) can be addressed with a single 32-bit offset, so no manipulations with segments are necessary (or even possible!). **Win95!**	The address space is divided into chunks of 64 KB; this results in a difficult and not exactly efficient memory management.
Demand paging and virtual memory management can be used to control the attributes of all pages of a process (e.g., guard pages, copy-on-write). **Win95!**	Paging is used, but only to supply virtual memory; programs don't have full control over their memory pages.

Some fundamental features of the executive (which have partly even influenced the design of the subsystems) are discussed in the next table.

Windows NT	Win16
Object-oriented design: OS objects like files, processes, memory areas, and the like are created, manipulated, and destroyed as objects in the kernel.	A relatively unordered collection of functions and variables, which time and again had to be hacked and patched (partially also because of dubious design decisions). The code is full of hair-raising tricks, exceptions, and the like.
Full preemptive multi-tasking and multiple threads including all required synchronization objects and efficient IPC mechanisms. **Win95! (partly)**	Cooperative multi-tasking, single threaded. IPC support only through DDE or OLE (complex and slow).
Portable and structured exception handling makes possible a more efficient and safer implementation of the OS and applications as well. **Win95!**	No comparable mechanism exists; exceptions and errors must be processed individually.
The kernel uses Unicode as the native character set. All alphabets and special symbols currently in worldwide use are available and can be used. The adjustment of applications to national or cultural peculiarities is eased. The Win16 ANSI format is fully and transparently supported.	The ANSI character sets and code pages are employed (which is, alas, not compatible to the OEM (IBM-ASCII) character set). Windows documents need conversion if to be used under DOS, this has to performed manually.
Every process receives a limit for its resource consumption (called a quota). The quotas are under system control and take memory allocations, kernel object usage, etc., into account.	Win16 has no control at all over the resource allocation of applications. Noncooperating programs ("hogs") can easily affect other applications and even the system.

Table 1.3: Comparison of Windows NT and Win16: kernel.

Okay, let's leave the kernel and have a look at the attributes of the New Technology File System (NTFS) which is loosely based on OS/2's HPFS and was introduced with Windows NT.

Table 1.4: Comparison of
Windows NT and Win16: I/O
system and NTFS.

Windows NT	Win16
Device drivers and file systems (FAT, HPFS, NTFS) can be loaded and removed at run time. They can be implemented in a portable way with a high-level language. Hence they should be easy to port and maintain. **Win95! (partly)**	Complex driver model, may even require bimodal implementations (for DOS/real mode and Windows/protected mode). Most often drivers have to be written in assembly language. The only supported files system is FAT.
Disk files can be treated as memory mapped files, where the file is mapped into the virtual address space of a process. This allows shared memory as well as easier and more efficient file I/O. **Win95!**	No similar mechanism; files are always disk based. The global address space is one giant, shared memory arena (with the well-known consequences).
Integrated support for CD-ROMs with a separate file system called CDFS. **Win95!**	Device drivers and DOS utilities simulate a FAT compatible system.
Asynchronous I/O operations are possible (but not mandatory). Hence, suitable programs might run much faster.	All I/O is synchronous: the application has to wait until the operation is complete.
NTFS files can be as large as 2^{64} bytes. Extremely large hard disks (and further mass storage media still in experimental state) can be supported.	MS-DOS is only able to support files with a maximum of 2^{32} bytes (and even this took much pain and several years to show up!).
NTFS is transaction based and saves system information redundantly. Safe and fast repair of the file system is possible.	MS-DOS saves two copies of the FAT, but other vital information for rebuilding a destroyed disk is missing. Transactions are unheard of.
To a certain degree NTFS employs fault tolerance (e.g., through disk striping and mirroring and the like).	Nothing similar is available. As with transactions, only dedicated network software achieves this level.

Windows NT	Win16
Through NT security all files on NTFS volumes can be protected against unauthorized access.	MS-DOS supports only the most primitive protection mechanisms which can be easily circumvented by experienced programmers. Again, third party products must be employed.
NT Workstation directly supports peer-to-peer networking. The networking code as well as the required utilities are fully integrated. NT Server implements a full server network.	MS-DOS has some rudimentary networking built in, but no full support. At least with Windows for Workgroups, a level similar to NT Workstation can be achieved.

The NT executive makes available all the necessary building blocks to the subsystems (albeit in rather primitive form). The latter implement the corresponding API calls with the help of these components. As an example I'll show the creation of a user process (see figure 1.7): POSIX applications need a call named fork(), which creates a new child process and initializes its address space with the contents of the parent's memory. A Win32 program, on the other hand, calls CreateProcess(); this creates a new process and initializes its memory with an executable file from disk. No relationship whatsoever exists between creator and created program. Finally, OS/2 with its DosExecPgm() call is a mixture: here a program is always loaded into the address space (like NT), but the two processes share an explicit parent-child relationship (like POSIX).

The NT executive is the basis for the subsystems.

And nobody knows how another API, possibly to be supported in the future, might implement this call. Therefore the NT executive builds and exports only the most basic functionality and mechanisms for process creation and manipulation (e.g., NtCreateProcess()). These calls are indeed (and by purpose) very simple, but they allow the API subsystems to define the exact behavior through explicitly coding in a fashion specific for the corresponding API.

These building blocks are called primitives.

In this sense the executive can be seen as the motor of the operating system: which body is actually used (so that the final car looks like a Porsche or a Landrover) is decided by the API subsystem. Therefore we can notice that the NT functions are only of secondary importance for application programmers (i.e., there are only very few places where the NT kernel functionality is used directly). Much more important are the

APIs exported from the various subsystems: they define how the system looks to the developer and they decide about the portability. That's exactly why the Win32 API is so important!

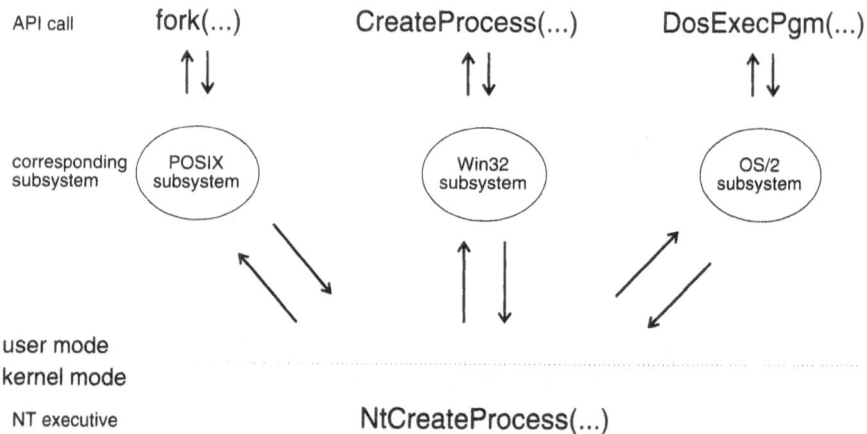

*Where is information and
documentation about the
kernel?*

Nevertheless, I am not completely happy with that state. The main problem is that Micsosoft doesn't make available a complete documentation of the NT kernel functions. Instead they refer the developer to the Win32 API. Admittedly, almost everything can be done with its help; but I feel this mystery-mongering is not really adequate. Why shouldn't other people besides Microsoft's engineers have the possibility to access kernel functionality? Surely one or two useful (or even necessary?) functions *are* in the box! And if MS applications are finally nicer, faster, better than those of the competition, this might not have to do only with the genius of Gates or his developers. (Should you feel that the insinuation behind this is not justified or too far-fetched: Andrew Schulman and his co-authors have written some interesting stuff that might be meaningful in this context; see especially Chapter 1 in [Ref. 3]. And the FTC and other authorities also have had some not-so-nice things to say about the practices of Microsoft (even more interesting would be what the authorities were *not* allowed to say...). So watch out!)

The NT subsystems

After this short side trip, let's get back to reality: knowing the NT kernel *is* important, yet knowing the subsystems and their APIs in general and the Win32 subsystem and the Win32 API in particular is simply more important — at least for application developers. So, let's have a look at this part of the NT architecture. The overall structure is shown in figures 1.5 and 1.8; as you can easily see, the Win32 subsystem (or Win32sub for short, but it has nothing to do with Win32s!) is at the center of it all. Indeed, almost all subsystems at one place or the other have to access functionality in Win32sub, so beside the kernel this is really the single most important OS entity!

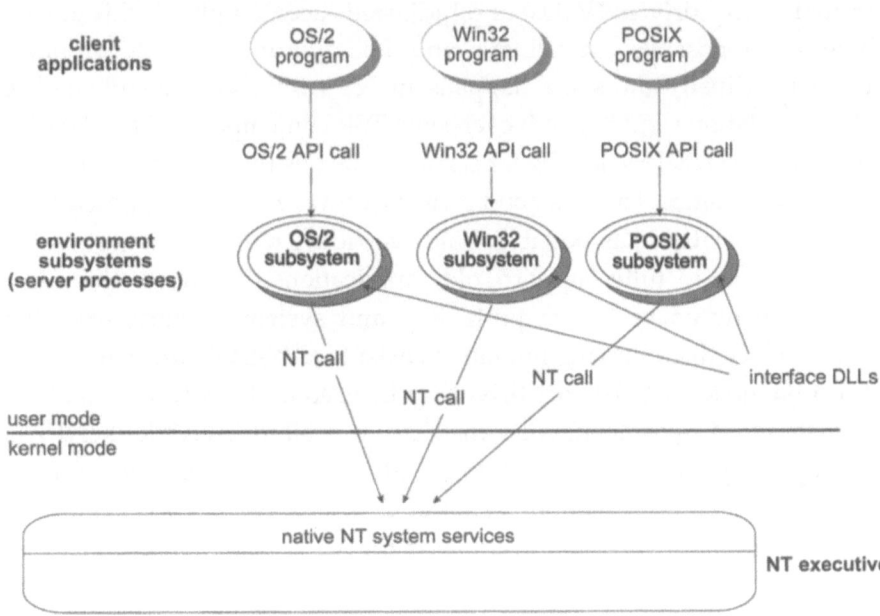

Figure 1.8: The environment subsystems of Windows NT

Basically NT knows two different kinds of subsystems: the first are the so-called environment subsystems that implement and export a specific OS API. Examples are Win32sub or the POSIX subsystem. In the second category are the integral subsystems, which are implementing specific system services beyond the OS APIs. An example for the latter is the security subsystem (see figure 1.5 at the right) responsible for logon and adherence to the security rules. Network servers could also be imple-

Environment subsystems

Integral subsystems

mented as subsystems (or alternatively as an installable file system in the I/O manager).

MS-DOS and Win16 support

Two subsystems not shown explicitly in the figure play a special role: the subsystems for MS-DOS and Win16 support. They are based on the virtual DOS machine (VDM) model already known from enhanced-mode Windows. Applications loaded into a VDM run in the virtual 8086 (V86) mode and believe to have complete control over the machine. Accesses to I/O ports, software interrupts, access to the memory area below 1 MB (including video memory and the BIOS data area) are caught by several virtual device drivers (VxDs) and "adjusted" accordingly. (If this adjustment is not possible, the call fails, and the application doesn't run properly.) Principally the same happens in NT's MS-DOS subsystem. The DOS emulation is quite good; even such TSR contemporaries as SideKick

DOS emulation is limited by NT's security requirements.

do run. Nevertheless, it is by far not as perfect as the emulation found in OS/2 for instance. This has good reasons, however: NT is supposed to be as stable a platform as possible. This overriding requirement just makes it impossible to fully support "old" applications. Whenever there is a conflict between backward portability and system stability, the latter wins. Hence the following limitations exist for MS-DOS programs under NT: first, no MS-DOS device driver can be used under NT, so if you have non-standard equipment, you either have to wait for an NT kernel driver or buy compatible hardware. Second, all attempts to access (or change) system-relevant information is subject to NT's security checks; most often this means they're just disallowed for MS-DOS programs. Here we find things like directly accessing the disk controller or other important hardware resources as well as trying to change the system time if the user logged in does not have sufficient privilege to do so.

Problems with hardware-specific programs or applications using undocumented features

Programs using undocumented back-doors or side-traps (DOS and BIOS, it doesn't matter) are also good candidates for failure. However, there are two categories of "undocumented" functionality: the first is everything really undocumented, such as relying on a specific version of COMMAND.COM because code *inside* the file is patched (even better are programs that actually patch DOS itself!). This behavior will almost certainly lead into deep trouble under NT. These are cases of what I'd call "hard" use of undocumented features. Then there's the soft case: facts that actually are formally undocumented* in the strict sense, but that are so well known that everybody (more or less) uses them. This is true for quite a lot of system calls as well as DOS variables. In this case Microsoft faces an interesting dilemma: the feature *is* undocumented, yet everybody knows it, everybody likes it, everybody uses it. Therefore it has to be put (even with bad grace) into the system. In this sense the MS-DOS subsystem supports most of the "soft" undocumented features (well, as long as they don't compromise system security, of course!).

Officially, MS doesn't know anything about that feature; internally, they use it heavily.

Basically the same observations are true for the Win16 subsystem,** which is required to execute old 16-bit applications. Inside the WOW layer all old programs run exactly as they would under Windows 3.1 — the deciding issue here is that WOW *only* supports cooperative multi-tasking. WOW itself can be seen as a single-threaded virtual machine that only allows one Win16 task at a time to execute. (Of course, WOW is fully integrated into NT's preemptive multi-tasking, so a hanging Win16 task only halts the WOW layer, but not the system. This was the reason why NT 3.5 introduced the possibility of starting separate copies of WOW: if all Win16 applications are run in a separate VDM, they can't crash the other 16-bit programs.)

** *This subsystem is called WOW, which means Windows On Win32.*

WOW supports almost all Win16 programs, as you'd expect only very hardware-dependent stuff or code heavily using undocumented features might experience some problems. Certain programs that violate the basic rules for binary compatible Win16 apps under Win32 (see section 4.11 for more about these rules) also won't run properly — or even at all (earlier versions of CorelDRAW are well-known culprits). In newer versions of WOW, Microsoft has partially programmed around some of these things to increase backward compatibility. The Win16 subsystem currently supports only enhanced mode; whether there will be a standard-mode version is very unclear (as a matter of fact, some network drivers as well as application programs *require* standard-mode Windows). Yet Win16 programs requiring VxDs (e.g., some debuggers) do *not* run under NT, in this respect they're similar to MS-DOS applications requiring a DOS device driver.

WOW (on Intel hardware) only supports 386-enhanced mode.

Win16 programs can exchange data (via clipboard, DDE, OLE) with *all* other applications running on the system, including all 32-bit programs. The necessary translation is automatically performed in the WOW layer. Alas, a 32-bit DLL is not allowed to call 16-bit code directly, an IPC channel must be used for this. The other way, however, is possible with the help of the so-called generic thunks. These allow 16-bit programs to load and access code located in a 32-bit DLL.

Interestingly enough, both 16-bit subsystems are also available on the non-Intel NT platforms (e.g., Alpha AXP or PowerPC). The implementation has to deliver an x86 emulator, which is used as the basis for the MS-DOS and Win16 subsystems (currently only the 286 CPU is emulated, so on *non*-Intel hardware WOW is actually running in *standard* mode!). Support for DOS specialties is amazingly good — the emulators can even run programs like the Microsoft Flight Simulator, an application often used in the past to check for IBM compatibility. The performance is not too bad, on a newer DEC Alpha the speed is about the same as on a 486DX2/50 (I don't know what conclusions *you* draw on the speed of the CPUs concerned).

DOS and WOW under MIPS, Alpha, etc.

Big boss: the Win32 subsystem

Let's get to the 32-bit stuff: next on the list is the Win32 subsystem. Before I discuss the internals, another table to compare the features of Win32sub with good, old Win16 is in order (again the Win95 symbol shows up when a feature is also found in Windows 95).

Table 1.5: Comparison of Windows NT and Win16: Win32 subsystem.

Windows NT	Win16
Subsystems (MS-DOS, WOW, OS/2, etc.) supply an environment suitable for executing corresponding programs.	Win16 doesn't make available further APIs. The DOS emulation could possibly be classified as a nice try in this direction.
The Win32 susbsytem exclusively handles the user interface. All other subsystems can access the screen, keyboard, etc., only under its control.	Win16 tries to achieve this goal with the help of VxDs, but often doesn't accomplish this because of conceptual weaknesses in Win16 and the VxD definition.
DLLs can use global and per-instance data. **Win95!**	DLLs can use only global data.
Windows messages have a 32:32 format (i.e., the type WPARAM was widened to 32 bit). **Win95!**	Messages have the good, old 16:32 format.

Windows NT	Win16
GDI supports three levels of co-ordinate transformation: device, logical, and world. Scaling, shearing, rotations, and the like are fully device independent and easily implemented.	The Win16 GDI supports two levels of coordinates, world is missing here. Much more effort on the developer's part is required for device independent drawings.
GDI coordinates are 32 bit; the device level supports a fixed point format.	Coordinates are just 16 bit; this often leads to difficult code, with rounding problems and errors.
GDI supports paths, bézier curves, and several other enhancements. **Win95! (partly)**	GDI supplies mostly simple drawing operations.
The concept of metafiles has been enhanced significantly. They're more device independent and can be used more consistently. **Win95!**	Metafiles can be output without distortions only on the device they were originally created for. By far not all GDI calls lead to metafile output.

So far, we've had an overview of the most important Win32sub features. Now I'll take a closer look at the actual implementation of this OS component. We will definitely get some good ideas about how our programs put Win32sub to work. This subsystem is worth studying for more than one reason: first, it defines the native API of Windows NT (and Windows 95 as well!). Second, it is the basis for all other subsystems when it comes to user I/O. And third, its integration into the system is an interesting approach in OS design. Besides the standard components found in Win16, Win32 has two interesting enhancements: on the one hand are all new text-mode-based functions (called console API); on the other hand is a full and complete shell of system services for process management, multi-tasking, file I/O, and the like. Whatever you would like to see in an OS but missed in Win16, Win32 probably has it in one form or another (see figure 1.9).

The Win32 subsystem under examination

Win32sub is not some OS code sitting in a DLL and waiting to be called. No, it is a real executable, a running program like your programs. The subsystem is loaded late in the boot process and takes over full control of the user interface. Although Win32sub is a normal executable with

Win32sub is an autonomous application.

all the necessary attributes (e.g., separate address space, resource limits, etc.) there are some quite significant differences to ordinary applications like Winword:

- Win32sub cannot be terminated (actually it can: but only if the OS is shut down), nor does it have its own windows or produces other visible output.

Figure 1.9: The most important parts of the Win32 subsystem

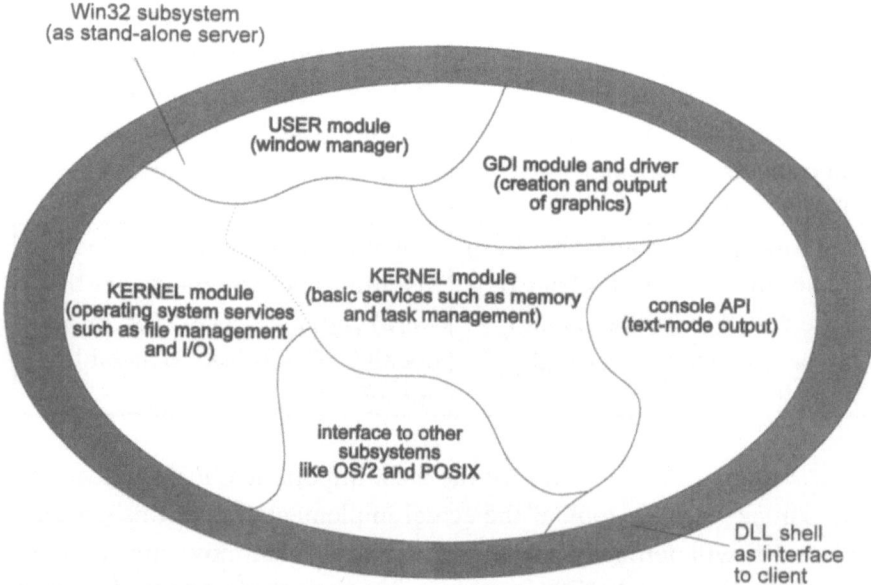

- Instead it makes available a complete set of services to other applications. This includes full windowing and graphics capabilities as well as a shell for the system functionality exported from the NT executive. Native NT functions are called only as an absolute exception by other applications. (Why that? In principle every program should be able to call into the NT kernel. The answer is simple: because....)

NT handles are not Win32 handles!

- Win32sub moves between kernel and application as a filter or an intermediary and another abstraction level is introduced. In general, Win32sub objects (e.g., a file handle) are not directly mapped to the corresponding NT executive objects. An example: Create-File() returns a file handle, but this handle only makes sense in the context of Win32sub, but not in the kernel. The necessary mapping and translation is performed automatically in Win32sub. Hence, the developer is normally confronted with an all-or-nothing approach: either he uses Win32sub concepts, functions, and data types or he works with the simpler kernel objects and has to build all the Win32 functionality himself.

- As a matter of fact, this additional abstraction level has a distinct advantage: this separation allows the kernel developers to modify and enhance the NT executive without the fear of breaking existing Win32 applications. As long as Win32sub exports the same interface (namely the Win32 API) to applications, things are fine.

An additional shell between developer and NT executive

- Win32sub is designed as a server, and the interaction with other programs is carried out according to a client/server relationship. This is used by other subsystems as well: the VIO interface of the OS/2 subsystem is not implemented in the OS/2 part but is based on Win32sub functionality.

- Last but not least, Win32sub is responsible for enforcing the kernel security policies, so that no application is able to break into the system. In a sense Win32sub is a moved-up defense line of the kernel.

Communication with the Win32 subsystem

All that is nice and well, but it leaves one big question: how does an application actually *use* the services of Win32sub? The model is quite different to Win16, where services were simply implemented in DLLs and could be called as normal functions. Put differently: how is the communication between subsystems on one side and application programs on the other accomplished? I don't want to go into too much technical detail here, but a short rundown of the communication channels is in order. The mechanism employed is called LPC, which is short for local procedure call. The LPC protocol is a special case of RPC (or remote procedure calls) that is used to implement distributed computing. LPC works only on a single machine (hence local), and the basic function is as follows (see also figure 1.10):

- First, Win32sub creates for every client (application) needing services two communication ports (simplified, you can think of two mailboxes). One of the ports is given to the application, and the other remains with Win32sub. The ports are actually located in the upper half of the application's 4 GB address space and are basically a shared memory section.

- To access a specific Win32sub function (e.g., CreateWindow()), the application creates a memory block with all the required parameters and a code for the function to be executed. This block is copied to the communication port. (This is done with kernel help, because the application can't directly access the upper half of its address space.)

- Win32sub is constantly monitoring the port and if it sees a request a thread in the subsystem is awakened, which decodes the stored parameters and performs the actual function call. This requires a context switch and now another program is actually executing.

- After the call is finished, the results are again packed and copied to the second communications port, the application wakes up (another context switch), reads the memory block, and continues execution.

Figure 1.10: Communication between Win32 subsystem and applications

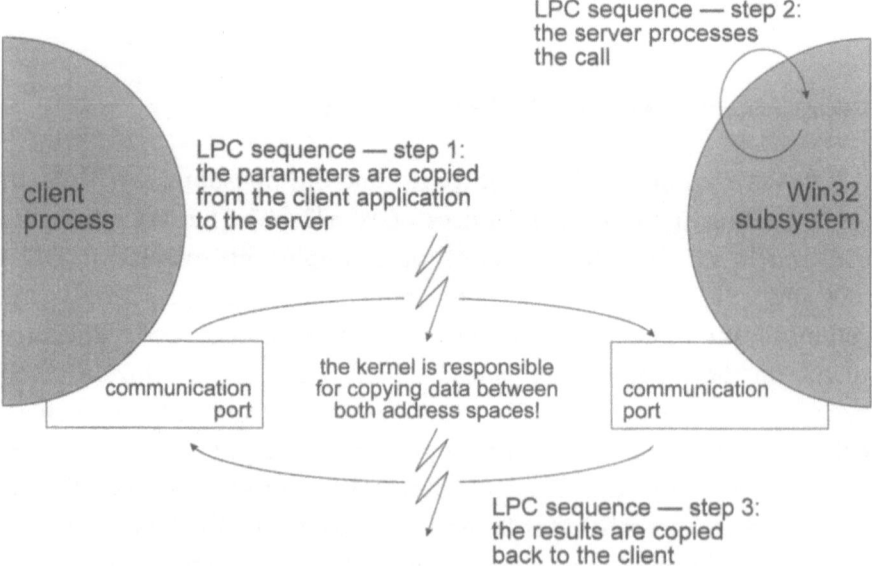

This sounds pretty complicated compared to a simple DLL call in Win16. This is even true in *two* respects: first, the performance might suffer badly; second, all the parameter packing and unpacking looks like a lot of work for the application programmer. Well, the latter problem is easily solved: Microsoft simply invented some helper DLLs that implement all the nitty-gritty details of the LPC protocol. The net effect is that you just call (as you did in the past) a function like CreateWindow(). This function is located in a DLL (USER32.DLL) loaded into your address space and does all the magic of getting the call to Win32sub and back. Much more difficult was the performance problem. Here several mechanisms are used to achieve an acceptable level:

What about performance?

First, many calls can be coded completely on the client-side DLL. This is obviously not true for all calls changing the global system state (e.g., creating a window), but it's valid for many simpler calls like PtInRect() or lstrcmp(). This saves (especially for simple functions) a lot of effort, because they can be handled without actually activating Win32sub.

Optimization 1: local calls

The second optimization builds on the first: if calls *changing* the global system state can't be perfomed on the client side, what about functions *querying* the system state? The client side tries to buffer (like a cache) as much information about the system as possible, so that if some information is queried, a call to Win32sub is not necessarily required. Examples might be the current focus window or the mouse capture. Another possibility is to store systemwide information in kernel objects. These can be secured in such a way that applications can only *read* them, while Win32sub actually modifies them.

Optimization 2: caching of data

The third optimization is used mainly for GDI calls and has the prosaic name of LPC batching. The trick is simple: the client-side DLL doesn't send every LPC in the very moment of creation but stores them in an internal queue. If this queue gets full, or if certain other, precisely defined conditions are met, all batched LPCs are sent in one big chunk and can be executed very fast in the subsystem. Of course, the main problem here is the "precisely defined conditions"; if these are not very well balanced, the output may become irregular and bumpy. Fortunately, Microsoft has put some effort into the design of LPC batching, so adverse effects are to be observed only in the most contrived circumstances (or on very slow machines).

Optimization 3: batching LPC calls

To conclude: Win32sub functionality comes in two parts; either it is contained in the Win32 subsystem itself, in which case the client-side

DLLs do the required packing and the actual call. Or they're fully contained in the client-side DLL, in which case there is no big difference from the way things worked in Win16. Both cases are not easily distinguishable for the application programmer, because the client-side DLLs shield him from these implementation details. The whole concept and its realization are a very good example for the already cited backward compatibility of Windows NT: the underlying implementation is vastly different from Win16, yet the APIs are largely compatible. The internals are different, yet the surface is (almost) the same.

Changes to the source code

This observation is to a large extent also valid when it comes to porting Win16 source codes. Of course, extending such a complex system like Windows to 32 bit makes some significant changes on existing sources unavoidable. But as long as the to-be-ported source code adheres to some basic portability criteria (which will be detailed in the second chapter), porting an application is not as difficult as one would think at first. Another possibility could be the parallel maintenance of two applications from a single set of sources, one for Win16, the other for Win32. While this requires more effort than a simple port, under specific circumstances it might prove to be the better solution. This issue, too, is discussed in the next chapter. Now I'd like to give some *very* basic remarks about the architecture of Windows 95 — mostly to show the elegant consistency and homogeneity of the Win32 API while the two underlying implementations are more different than even the most pessimistic would have believed.

One source file, but two
executables!

1.4 Basic Architecture of Windows 95

"De nihilo nihil. (From nothing comes only nothing.)" Lucretian, De rerum natura

To declare Windows 3.1 as "nothing" is certainly far from the truth. The somewhat sarcastic citation is (in this context) more directed towards the *technical* nature of Win16 (and the Windows 95 product). In a certain sense the Win95 developers *have* done an incredible job: to create a Win32-compatible system like Windows 95 while keeping so much backward compatibility definitely requires much more work and technical wits than having the freedom to build a brand-new system like NT from scratch. Yet Win16 is a hack on a hack of hacks — and Windows 95

32 bit and backward compatible?

is even worse. Basically Win95 is Windows for Workgroups enhanced with a 32-bit kernel handling the new system services (32-bit memory management, threads, etc.) — so most of what you've learned about Win16's architecture can be applied. Actually, a lot of the work necessary for the enhancements is not done in any Windows DLL module: the virtual machine manager and the layer of virtual device drivers are greatly enhanced in Win95 and now supply most of the basic functionality for system services. Just as NT is divided into two very different OS parts (i.e., executive vs. subsystems), so is Windows 95 (albeit on another level of "integration"). So let's start with the virtual "things."

Virtual: machine manager and device drivers

The virtual machine manager (VMM) is the basis for the system. As in Win16, its main purpose is to create and manage the virtual machines (VM) of which there is one for every DOS box and another one as the system VM. The system VM runs all Windows programs (16 *and* 32 bit) and like NT sports an address space of 4 GB, but with an unusual memory layout. On the one hand, *all* 16-bit programs are located somewhere in the 4 GB space and of course can see each other — like they could under Win16. On the other hand, the address space is page-switched with respect to the executing 32-bit programs. To put things into perspective: take one of the separated Windows NT virtual address spaces, map all running 16-bit modules (EXEs and DLLs) into strictly defined places in the 4 GB area, *leave the 16-bit parts in place* whenever you page-switch address spaces for 32-bit programs — and you have the Win95 model. The net effect is that the 32-bit programs can't see each other's memory, but they can access all of the memory for 16-bit applications. Analogously, all 16-bit components can see each other, but they can access *only* the currently executing 32-bit program. From the viewpoint of the 32-bit applications, all 16-bit memory can be viewed as genuine shared memory mapped into the address space of all 32-bit programs.

The memory layout of the system VM

All that juggling around with memory pages is done in the VMM with the help of some virtual device drivers (VxDs); this code is hidden in the file VMM32.VXD. Compared to Win16, these beasts have gained importance, because they supply more and more of the basic OS functionality (e.g., the preemptive multi-tasking in VWIN32 or the 32-bit file system with long filenames in VFAT which already appeared in WfW);

VxDs: more important than with Win16!

41

yet they are (like the NT executive) off limits for the application developer. Consequently, the documentation for VxD programming is still found only in the device driver kit (DDK). Around the base OS (the VMM and system VxDs) a layer of system DLLs is provided as an interface — very similar to Windows NT separation into executive and subsystem (in principle, of course, not in implementation!). So, in a sense the VMM/VxD shell plays in Win95 exactly the same role as the executive under NT.

Two interesting features of VxD are notable: first they can be loaded, removed, and configured dynamically; this greatly helps to reduce the memory requirements of the system and furthermore is one the requirements for plug and play (interestingly enough, the VxD responsible for this, called VXDLDR, was already present in WfW). Second, Win32 VxDs can be created with high-level languages like C; so implementation and debugging should be much easier than under Win16. Yet in the long run it is questionable whether VxDs calls are the way to go: whenever you can do something with the Win32 API, use that call first! Only resort to VxD programming if there's *definitely* no other way to go. (After all, VxDs are Win95 specific and their use is not portable at all!)

VxDs are dynamically configurable.

Two personalities: Win95 system DLLs

All Win32 API calls enter one of the 32-bit system DLLs (i.e., KERNEL-32.DLL, USER32.DLL, GDI32.DLL, etc.), yet this does *not* mean that the actual work is done there. As said, a lot of the base OS functions are located in the virtual layer, so quite a few calls into KERNEL32.DLL are just wrappers around the corresponding VxD call. On the other hand, the VxDs don't export the windowing or graphics capabilities, so these *must* be implemented in some system DLLs. Actually they are, but to a large extent not on the 32-bit side! Since Windows 95 has to be 99.99 percent backward compatible, a full Win16 API implementation was required anyway. So in an attempt (successful, I feel) to combine the best of two worlds, the Win95 developers decided to leave the windowing and most of the graphics functionality in place (i.e., in USER.EXE and GDI.EXE), so for Win16 programs nothing changes. Win32 code, on the other hand, calls into a translation layer (mostly in USER32.DLL and GDI32.DLL) which hands over the call to the Win16 module responsible

16-bit DLL vs. 32-Bit DLL

and the action happens there. This hybrid architecture opens three possibilities for the final destination of a Win32 API call: the first is in a system VxD, the second is in a 32-bit DLL, and the third is in a 16-bit DLL. The important fact is that, if at all possible, the 32-bit application doesn't notice this strange arrangement. There were some compromises to be made (the most famous and over-discussed one being probably the Win16Mutex), but compared to all the constraints (the two most important being the Win16 compatibility and the ability to run in 4 MB RAM) the Win95 designers have done what could be achieved with a *reasonable* amount of work (by the way, this much work was reasonable *only* because there are some 70 million copies of Win16 in the field; any other measure (including slipping release schedules) would show that the amount of work they had put into Win95 is just unbelievable, exorbitant, and greatly excessive).

It is easy to see that most of USER's and GDI's calls end up in the 16-bit modules — just compare the sizes of the files: USER32.DLL is about 43 KB, USER.EXE is a whopping 450 KB; for GDI the ratio is somewhat more level: 126 KB for GDI32.DLL vs. 307 KB for GDI.EXE. The question now is, how does this translation actually work? In a nutshell, sandwiched between the 16-bit and 32-bit components is a code layer, called the "thunking" layer, which transparently translates all parameters, messages, memory pointers, etc., between the two sides of the fence. As a matter of fact, thunking works in both directions: some GDI calls are in fact implemented in 32 bit, so the 16-bit code can thunk up and use this functionality. (Whoever recognizes this from the Win32s extension is not far off: the principle is very much the same, more on that can be found in section 1.9 about Win32s).

Translation and thunking layers

The conclusion of this short discussion is that in theory Windows 95 is an almost complete implementation of the Win32 API, but in practice the system's ability to really fulfill the promises of Win32 is somewhat hampered because of the need for full Win16 support and the strange hybrid implementation resulting from that need. On the other hand, the enhancements *are* remarkable compared to Win16 (yet in comparison with NT they're not so breathtaking). But not only the technical brilliance of an operating system counts — more important is its market share: it is here where Windows 95 will be much stronger for some time to come than Windows NT. For the Win95 developer, however, the porting issues (and effort) are very much the same as for NT; the Win32 API hides almost all peculiarities of the corresponding implementation. In this sense

Windows 95 is a hybrid implementation.

the following section about the necessary changes is valid for both systems: it doesn't matter whether you plan to port to NT or 95 — in *this* respect they're the same!

1.5 What Changes on My Source Codes are Required to Support the Win32 API?

"Here is, I believe, the fundamental rule of all being: Life is not at all like this. It is completely different." Kurt Tucholsky, Schnipsel

The fundamental properties of the NT design essentially define the basic differences between the Win16 and Win32 APIs (and so NT even influenced Windows 95!). The necessary changes to 16-bit sources in order to render them Win32 compatible can be summed up in the following six main categories:

These six categories cover nearly all necessary changes.

- using the virtual linear 32-bit address space;
- the strict separation of all processes from each other (or their address spaces, respectively);
- the global changes at the conceptual model for user input with keyboard and mouse;
- the enlarged GDI coordinate system and further changes in graphical output;
- the removal of MS-DOS and 80x86 specific calls or features;
- and finally the (mis-)use of undocumented Win16 features.

Additionally, some words about dynamically linked libraries (DLLs) are in order. Some of the changes in the six areas mentioned above have some special (and rather tricky) consequences on DLL programming. DLL developers probably can't avoid some significant and time-consuming changes. You'll find more about that at the end of this section (see page 57).

Finally, there is a rather long list of Win16 functions that require only small and easy-to-handle changes — either in the parameter list or, in very rare cases, also in functionality. All these simple modifications *Appendix 2: Expanded* are not listed here (mostly because of space constraints), instead I'll refer *PORT.INI with lots of addi-* you to Appendix 2. As a matter of fact, the compiler gives an error or *tional information* warning on most of these issues, so the necessary adjustments are easily identified and even more easily carried out (see also section 3.8, page 178, for important compiler diagnostics).

The linear 32-bit address space

So, let's address the first issue on our list! In nearly every Windows program the consequences of the unsegmented and widened address space will require more or less important changes. The fact that all Win32 programs run in a virtual linear address space of 4 GB directly leads to the extension of the most important data types from 16 to 32 bit. In this category we find signed and unsigned integers, nearly all handle types, and the ubiquitous NEAR pointers. Under Win16 an unsigned int (in C parlance) suffices to walk through a segment byte for byte (since 16-bit segments have a 64 KB limit). The restriction to 16 bit was easily acceptable, because larger memory areas could be addressed only through rather strange segment arithmetic anyway. The *reasonable* addressing of a linear 4 GB address space with 16-bit integers is impossible.

Data type extensions: from 16 to 32 bit.

The obvious consequence: 32-bit C compilers define ints and all data types building on an int with a width of 32 bit. Exactly the same consideration leads, willy-nilly, to the doubling of all NEAR pointers: while these are (in Win16) just an offset into a specified segment with its maximum size of 65,536 bytes (for instance the data segment of an application containing the local heap), under Win32 they represent an offset into the virtual, linear address space with its maximum size of 4,294,967,296 bytes. And in order to address these, well, I'm sure by now you already know how many bits are needed.... Figure 1.11 shows the memory layout and organization of a typical Win32 process.

NEAR pointers grow a bit (or 16?) fatter.

And here we find the underlying reason why nearly all data types representing handles are also widened to 32 bit under Win32. For us ordinary mortals, a windows handle (of type HWND) is simply a "magic" number used as an argument in numerous functions calls (at least as long as you don't read "bad books"; see [Refs. 3 and 4]). Windows itself interprets this same HWND as a NEAR pointer to an (internal) data structure that describes all the attributes of the corresponding window. (Hadn't we noticed just before that a NEAR pointer is always an offset into a specific segment? So into which segment, please, "points" an HWND? A very legitimate question whose detailed answer would lead us far, far into Windows internals. At least I can state that the individual Win16 system

Handles: Of course 32-bit wide, too!

See also figure 4.1 on page 208.

components, such as USER.EXE or GDI.EXE, possess data segments on their own, local heaps included. A variable of type HWND is nothing more than a NEAR pointer into a USER data segment; an HBRUSH refers to a GDI segment, etc. More about these definitely not portable, but nevertheless interesting, internals may be found, for example, in [Ref. 3].)

Figure 1.11: The virtual address space of a typical Win32 application

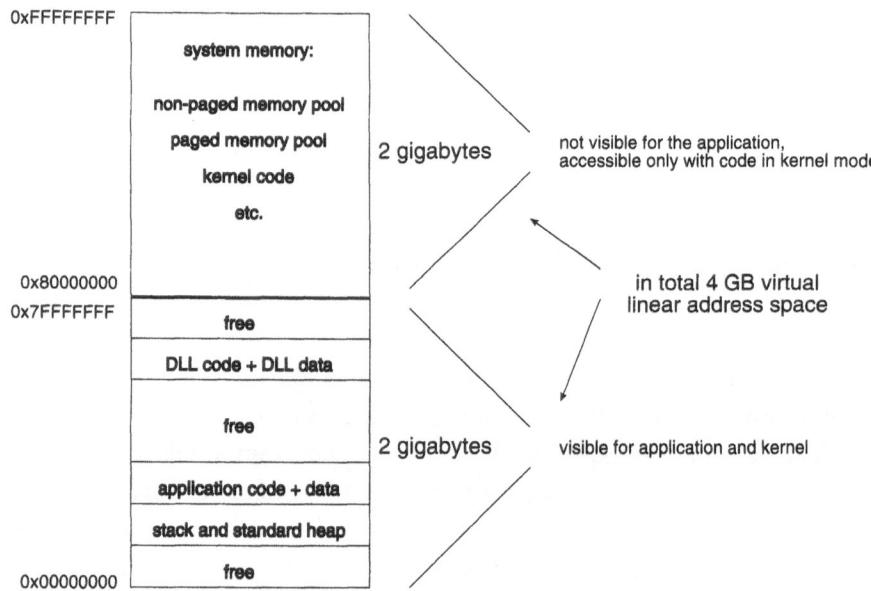

As you'd expect, the widening of the basic data types has some far-reaching consequences: assignments of HWNDs to WORDs and vice versa are quite common under Win16. On a Win32 system this will lead almost certainly into some sort of GUI nirvana, since there a WORD is still defined as just an unsigned short and therefore persists on being 16-bit wide. In order to enable portable source code construction, the Windows 3.1 SDK introduced a new data type named UINT (short for unsigned int). In contrast to WORD, this data type grows under Win32 to 32 bit. Most of the other relevant data types are also defined through corresponding typedefs, so when you used them consistently (!) and properly (!) changes to the source codes should be necessary only in special circumstances. You'll find a comprehensive overview and comparison of all basic data types for both APIs in Appendix 1. By the way,

UINT: rescue in an emergency!

data structures using the enlarged data types of course allocate correspondingly more memory (see section 3.5, page 159).

Finally, the parameter types of the various callback procedures (WNDPROC, DLGPROC, etc.) have also changed. The fact that an HWND and the message value itself (a UINT) are now 32-bit wide isn't of further disturbance: if the corresponding data types are used properly, this change is fully transparent, so in this respect the window procedure's code doesn't require any modifications. And the fourth argument was, is, and remains a LONG with 4 bytes (even if recently renamed to LPARAM). Only argument 3 causes some difficulties, growing from a 16-bit value (WORD) to 32 bit (WPARAM). WPARAM is defined in both systems the same way: as an unsigned int (and is therefore *not* of the same size!); this unfortunately produces all sorts of trouble. The change became necessary, however, because a number of messages — prominent examples are WM_COMMAND or the WM_[H/V]SCROLL duo — are packing several data items (e.g., HWNDs and notification codes) into parameters 3 and 4. And since this information requires more room under Win32, the format of the affected messages was eventually changed. Alas, this leads to different packaging of those data items under Win16 compared to Win32, as illustrated by the example of WM_COMMAND:

New data types for message parameters 3 (wParam) and 4 (lParam): WPARAM and LPARAM.

```
// WM_COMMAND (16-bit case):
idItem=wParam;                     // item, control, or accelerator ID
hwndCtl=(HWND)LOWORD(lParam);      // handle of control
wNotifyCode=HIWORD(lParam);        // notification code


// WM_COMMAND (32-bit case):
idItem=LOWORD(wParam);             // item, control, or accelerator ID
hwndCtl=(HWND)lParam;              // handle of control
wNotifyCode=HIWORD(wParam);        // notification code
```

The unpleasant news about these changes (which involve approximately two dozen messages as well as all control notifications*) is that clear and portable source code is considerably more difficult to write. Depending on the target system, different strategies to access the data in the message parameters are necessary, calling either for conditional compilation (ugly) or separate source files (unclear). The pleasant news is that some Microsoft employees thought the same and searched for a solution: a partial approach involves the so-called message crackers that perform

* Examples for control notifications are BN_CLICKED, LBN_SETFOCUS, or EN_VSCROLL.

the portable decomposition of all information contained in wParam and lParam. We shall cover them in more detail in Chapter 4 (see section 4.3, page 212, as well as section 4.4, page 227).

Separated address spaces, isolated applications

The introduction of a flat memory model is not the only item that forces certain differences between the two APIs. The second issue on our list, the complete separation of all address spaces, can also trigger some important changes (although not as extensive as the widening of the most important data types to 32 bit). Now, what exactly does "complete separation of all address spaces" mean? In a nutshell: each Win32 program runs in a completely private memory space without any possibility for other processes (including the Win32 subsystem) to *directly* read or write its memory. And analogously an application can no longer access the memory areas of other programs (not even child processes). There are of course "safe" capabilities to do this under system control, because otherwise no debugger or similar program may be implemented, but even there significant restrictions exist.

No access to memory areas used by another process!

This statement has some far-reaching consequences that are definitely not to be comprehended in a few seconds: no common HGLOBALs anymore — not even when allocated with GMEM_(DDE)SHARE; locked global memory areas remain strictly private; no shared memory accesses via FAR pointers, etc., etc. Only DDE messages (sent completely under system control) can be used as before to exchange memory handles between different processes — here the OS performs the necessary magic silently, behind the scenes. In principle we can compare the situation under Win32 to that in a network. On a single machine (which may even contain more than one CPU: as is well known, NT supports SMP*) several processes are running much in the same fashion as they would on different workstations in a local network, isolated from each other through real physical separation. In a network, data exchange is possible only under full system control through explicitly defined communication channels (see figure 1.12 on the following page). Two processes running on the same Win32 machine are isolated from each other in respect to direct memory accesses, as they would be on two different machines running in a network. So, for communication between the two a form of IPC is definitely required. One of these IPC mechanisms was already

* SMP means symmetric multi-processing.

mentioned in the discussion about communication between applications and the Win32 subsystem: LPC as a special case of RPC, a network protocol for distributed program execution (distributed computing). Fortunately, Win32 puts a vast array of other methods at our disposal.

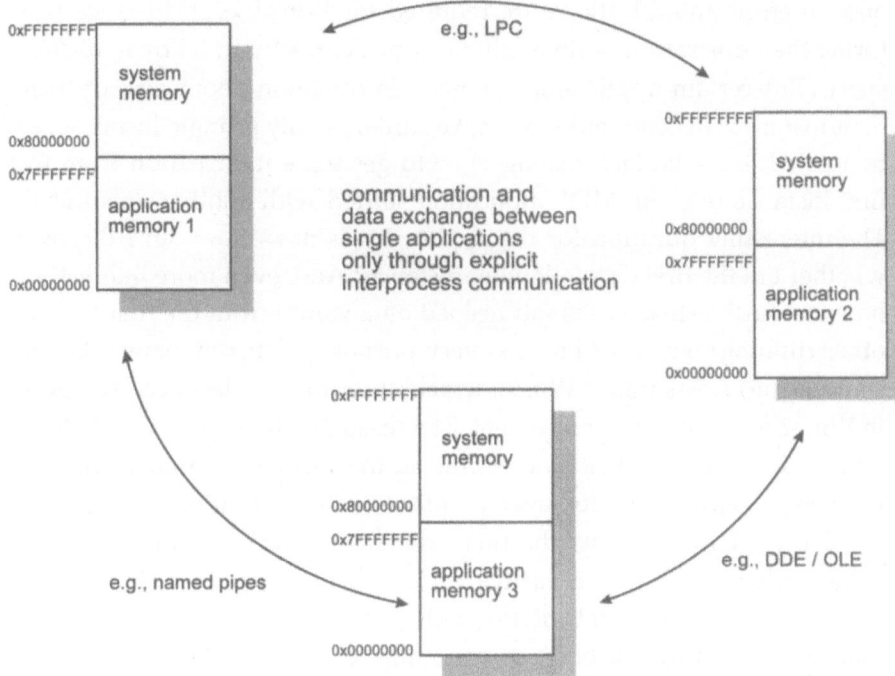

Figure 1.12: Applications have isolated address spaces — communication is possible only through network-like mechanisms.

Actually this conceptual change probably had the largest overall impact on me when I started development under Win32. I was so accustomed to the global memory model of Windows 3.x that some barriers in my head broke down only after much thought. Nevertheless, this process produced a great deal of true "Oh-I-see" experiences. The complete separation of all process-owned memory areas has some rather unexpected practical consequences, which I'm going to describe now in detail.

For starters, the second argument of the WinMain() call (an HINSTANCE normally named hPrevInstance) always equals 0 under Win32! This is true even for further instances of the same program. This interesting fact of course has consequences: each application believes that it is the first started instance. Even if it is actually the second or third instance, because of the value 0 for hPrevInstance, it will nevertheless reregister all local classes, private messages, or clipboard formats, etc. In a certain sense this is a necessary and even desired result of separating the

There is no second instance anymore (means: hPrevInstance is always 0).

address spaces: each application must register all needed classes and further local data itself before these can be used — simply because there is *no* way to access data items and window classes in other programs (previous instances *are* other programs). If a Win16 application evaluates hPrevInstance just for the purpose of performing these registrations only once, then no modifications are required for Win32: each instance performs the necessary one-time initializations correctly in its own address space. But certain applications *do* need information about already running instances in order either to make sure that only a single instance can be loaded (e.g., the task manager) or to get some information from the first instance (e.g., an MDI application started with another document). The interesting question for the application is now, how can I discover whether I'm the first or a following instance? And, even more interesting, how can further instances read needed data values from the first (or any other running) instance? For that very purpose a function named GetInstanceData() exists under Win16, which unfortunately has been removed in Win32 without any replacement. The reasoning behind this is obvious: such code would implicitly access the address space of another program (namely, an already loaded instance of the same application).

Now for the remedy: the first problem — whether other instances are already executing — is easily overcome with a simple FindWindow() call; the exchange of data items with previous instances on the other hand is more difficult: here we can either employ a DDE conversation (brrrr!) or use some of the new shared memory mechanisms (e.g., memory mapped files). You'll find more about the two possibilities, including some code samples, in section 4.6 on page 241.

Remedy: use either Find-Window() or standard IPC mechanisms such as DDE.

The strict separation of processes from each other has further implications: global window classes (under Win16 simply registered with the flag CS_GLOBALCLASS) are still possible but are somewhat more costly to implement than under Win16, because the code has to be moved into a separate DLL (that's true: no global classes in EXE files anymore!). DLLs pose problems anyway: Dynamically linked libraries are loaded and mapped completely into the address space of *just the calling process* — but nothing more! Therefore, loading a DLL doesn't mean that this DLL is now accessible systemwide. Beside other things, this means that all data sections of a DLL (what was called its data segment under Win16) will be allocated and initialized *anew for each application* — actually in the application's address space! That contrasts sharply with Win16, where each DLL is a (single-instanced) module on its own and therefore has a single

Data sections in DLLs

data segment for all global variables and its own local heap. In order to use global variables in the Win16 sense in a Win32 DLL, the standard attributes of the corresponding data sections have to be modified in the DEF file used for linking the DLL (see more on page 57 and especially in section 5.3 on page 339).

Here's another change: a popular practice of various graphics programs (sometimes even necessary because of memory restrictions) was to create frequently needed GDI objects (pens, brushes, etc.) only once, but use them later in several instances or modules. This method is of course absolutely impossible under Win32 (because a Win16 pen is simply a data structure located in the GDI data segment shared by all programs; under Win32 the pen data and handle are allocated in the private memory space of the application).

Basically all approaches to access or copy private memory areas of another process, even tricky ones (especially tricky ones!), are not portable, period. The only exception is DDE conversations since the utilized memory areas (represented by global handles) are dispatched with DDE messages; these are sent under control of the Win32 subsystem, so the handles (and memory areas) are automatically translated into the address space of the receiving application (which means that global handles employed for process communication purposes are only usable in conjunction with DDE messages but not in any other way, e.g., privately defined protocols). Communication via clipboard is also performed under full system control and therefore completely portable.

No shared access on global handles or memory areas

Only exception is DDE and clipboard!

User input: Mouse and keyboard

The third point on our small list is concerned with user input through the mouse and keyboard. In order to be able to describe the changes necessary for Win32, I'll have to go into some detail. Under Win16, every user input leads to the generation of a hardware interrupt that is immediately handled by the Windows kernel. The interrupt handling creates an input event (which ultimately becomes a message such as WM_KEYDOWN or WM_MOUSEMOVE) and stores this event together with the window handle of the affected window in a systemwide input queue. Some time later, the application to which the window pertains reads its private message queue with a GetMessage() call. And sooner or later an input event for this program will be on top of the system queue,

The making of an input message like WM_KEYDOWN

51

so this event is fetched from the system queue and delivered to the window within normal message loop processing. So far, so good. The crucial disadvantage of this procedure becomes apparent if a program does *not* serve its message loop regularly. Then the input event waiting on top of the system input queue blocks the reading of any other input event and we have the well-known "hourglass" effect: the Windows message processing comes to a halt, and the system appears blocked or even crashed. (You see why Microsoft calls Windows 3.x a "cooperative" multi-tasking system?)

Unfetched input messages block the system queue under OS/2 as well.

This (annoying) problem seemed to be solved in modern operating systems with their utilization of preemptive multi-tasking. Alas, that's a fallacy, as a quick glance at the OS/2 Presentation Manager shows: in spite of multiple threads it's still possible that (admittedly rather clumsily implemented) programs hinder or even totally suspend other running applications. How come? On top of the system input queue (under Win16 and OS/2 alike) an input message is sitting destined for a specific window. And as long as this information hasn't been read by the responsible application, all further input message processing is stopped — even under OS/2. All messages in the system input queue behind the first one are blocked and can't be read by other applications, even if these get activated and try to poll their message loop. Or put differently: a program not serving its message loop (either because of a lengthy calculation or simply a crash) can't read its input messages off the system queue, so consequently the queue gets jammed. Under OS/2 this effect is easily prevented through the creation of two (or more) threads: the first thread is responsible *only* for message loop processing; all time-consuming calculations are carried out by a second thread (even so, in that scenario no crashes in the first thread should ever occur!). However, for this preventive work the application developer is responsible, not the operating system.

Remedy with OS/2: an own thread.

A blocked queue is not acceptable in the light of the NT design.

The fact that a clumsily implemented program (as formulated above) can block the execution of all other applications is totally unacceptable for Windows NT, precisely since one of the main goals for an improved system was absolute stability and reliability. A single program can absolutely bump or even fail altogether (e.g., because of erroneous implementation), but *under no circumstances* should this affect the operability of all other running applications, including the operating system itself. So an improved input model was necessary, which became known as localized handling of user input. Somewhat simplified, this model

Remedy here: local input state.

52

requires that each process has its own local input state including input messages, which is regularly and automatically updated by the system. This means that all input messages will be put into the local input queue of the corresponding process practically in the moment of their creation — and not later, when the program processes its message loop. Because these messages are not dumped into the system queue, they can't block it anymore, as figure 1.13 shows.

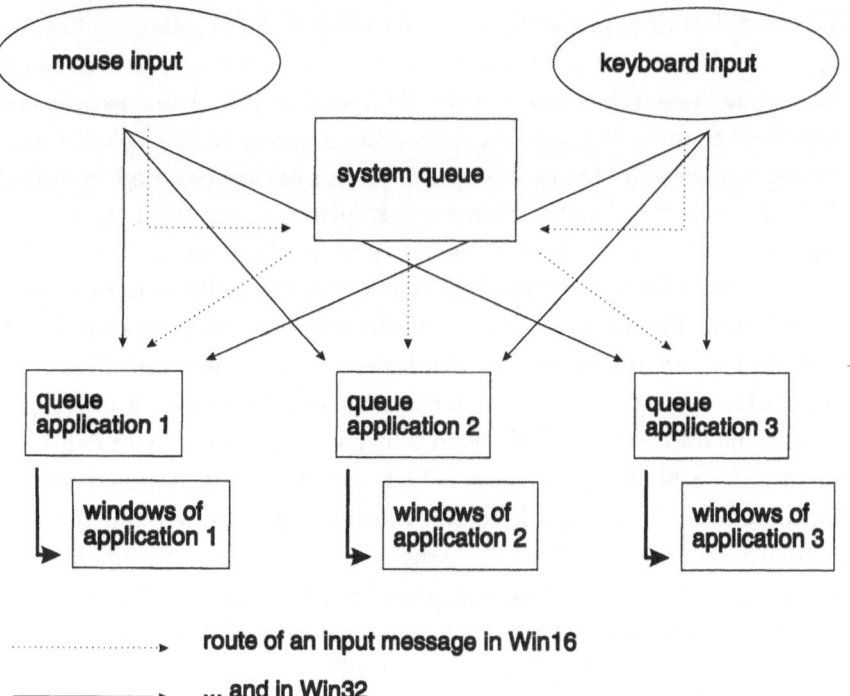

route of an input message in Win16

... and in Win32

Figure 1.13: The route of input messages in Win16 and Win32

Evidently these changes in the treatment of input messages have consequences for developers, otherwise I wouldn't discuss them at such length. So what exactly happens? As one perhaps might assume, the handling of input messages in your window procedures is not touched at all; this area remains essentially unmodified. Rather, some of the functions concerned with administration and changing the input state are involved. In this category we find the pair [Set/Release]Capture() used to capture all mouse messages into one window. Here the calling sequence hasn't changed, but the functionality has. Other spots touched are the management of the active window as well as the meaning of the input focus: GetFocus() doesn't necessarily return the window handle of the actual focus window. The obligatory changes in the source code are

Local input state concerns mouse capture and focus.

53

found in comparatively few areas; however, depending on what your code does, they can be quite costly to implement. More on these problems is found in section 4.7, starting on page 262.

GDI coordinates and company

The fourth item, the widening of GDI coordinates to 32 bit and further GDI modifications, is a rather simple subject. Most places where the larger coordinates are used can be modified transparently, since the corresponding data types such as POINT, RECT, etc., have experienced equivalent changes too. Specific difficulties are only to be expected when x/y coordinate pairs (as two separate 16-bit ints) are handled in a single DWORD or LONG (such as functions returning a position). A good example is MoveTo() returning the previous position in a packed 32-bit format. Since a DWORD with its 4-byte length is exactly as long as an int under Win32, this packing doesn't work anymore. Work-around: for the most part these functions are duplicated in an enhanced form (e.g., MoveToEx() instead of MoveTo()) carrying an additional argument. This is either the address of a POINT, in which case the coordinate values are returned or a NULL pointer, in which case no value is returned. This indeed requires many small changes to the source codes, but these are not overly complicated. And since the new, enhanced ...Ex functions are already available under Win16 (beginning with Windows 3.1), it is quite easy to write portable sources (or to change existing programs).

Minor graphical differences may result from the GDI (in contrast to the window manager) being completely recoded for Windows NT (by the way, the recoding was done for the most part in C++). Luckily this didn't change the arguments or calling syntax of GDI functions; instead the new, enhanced algorithms and their implementation may produce slightly altered screen or printer output when compared to Windows 3.1. These differences should indeed be very marginal and not visible to the naked eye on high-resolution graphics adapters. Another small alteration will lead to problems only in very extreme cases: the already mentioned batching of LPC calls to the GDI server (see section 1.3) can theoretically produce some bumpy or jolting output (but as far as I have seen, only under unfavorable circumstances or on very slow machines).

Under Win16: 2 * sizeof(int) == sizeof(DWORD).

No packing of coordinates under Win32!

Luckily, the enlarged GDI functions, such as MoveToEx(), are available under Win16.

The Windows NT GDI was recoded in C++, so very minor differences in the graphical output are possible.

MS-DOS and CPU specifics

The fifth area: the Win32 API *completely* abandons MS-DOS or 80x86 specific functions. Most likely, Windows 95 will be at first a bit less exacting than NT, but in the long run Win32 programs shouldn't make any use of hardware-specific code. This can mean significant changes to your code depending on which DOS and CPU specifics you've actually used and also on your way of implementation. For most INT 21H subfunctions there are named replacements in the Win32 API which work in a more or less compatible way. An example: in order to discover the free space on a disk drive, a Win16 program uses INT 21H, AX == 0x0036 (or a function in the run-time library of your compiler, which normally is likewise nonportable).

Instead of INT 21H, subfunction 0x36 we now have to call GetDiskFreeSpace().

Under Win32 there exists a similar function named GetDiskFree-Space() with the added advantage of being portable to all Win32 platforms (therefore also callable on MIPS or Alpha AXP implementations). BIOS calls under Win32 are just as impossible as the use of EMS or XMS interfaces and the like. (Well understood: this restriction is valid only for true Win32 applications! "Old" 16-bit MS-DOS programs, running within their subsystem in independent VDMs, can of course take advantage of all those features as well as nearly all other x86 specifics — at least on Intel platforms.) The NT subsystems are a bit stricter in this respect (because of OS reliability and security checks); the backward compatibility of Windows 95 for old apps — including Win16 programs — is definitely better.

CPU-specific Win16 calls as the selector API or various MS-DOS related functions for global memory management (such as GlobalWire() and GlobalUnwire()) are for the most part removed without replacement. The whole field is not exactly crystal clear because of the multitude of involved functions, so for detailed information and an enumeration of the functions, respectively, I refer you to section 4.6, page 241 and especially Appendix 2 showing an enhanced version of PORT.INI.

The selector API includes such beasts as SetSelector-Base() or SetSelectorLimit().

Using undocumented features

Regarding this sixth (and last, phew) item, intricate studies are neither necessary nor possible. If you're using an undocumented Win16 feature (hasn't Mom told you not to do so?), there are just two possibilities: the

Some undocumented Win16 features are actually documented under Win32!

55

feature exists in Win32 (and is perhaps even documented). Or plainly and simply, you're out of luck (well, Mom warned you!). It is impossible, however, to predict reliably which undocumented features actually were saved and carried over and which were left behind en route. Microsoft has always warned with raised forefinger against such vicious deeds (alas, as a brief glance at the import lists of Microsoft programs shows, this warning never reached the application programmers in Redmond). Fortunately, the probability that undocumented functionality exists under Win32 in very similar form is comparatively high. The 16-bit sources of the windowing component were (in contrast to the Win32 GDI) not completely rewritten for Win32, but were pulled up nearly identically to 32 bit. And so some of the undocumented features simply travelled with the sources, that's perfectly understandable.

But certainly not the use of internal Win16 data structures!

On the other hand, accessing undocumented or internal Win16 data structures is probably a real dead end: the widening of nearly all basic data types to 32 bit and, moreover, the separation of address spaces render some really nice Win16 gimmicks impossible. A certain compensation might be the fact that a whole list of Win16 internals is now officially documented under Win32. This includes various messages (e.g., WM_[GET/SET]HOTKEY), a lot of functions (such as keybd_event()), but also some data structures and constants.

TOOLHELP.DLL and STRESS.DLL ...

A word about TOOLHELP.DLL: though the functions exported through this DLL are for the most part documented, it is still unclear how and when those will be supported under Win32 systems. This has two main reasons: first, many TOOLHELP functions are x86 specific and simply had to be deleted. Second, at present there is still no 32-bit version of TOOLHELP available (in fact, there *is* something for Windows 95, but its use is discouraged because the calls are not portable). From what I hear from Microsoft, they are indeed working on a replacement for the

"... but we're working on it! No, really!"

Win32 API (and for quite a while now!), but when this will be available and which *portable* functions will be included have not yet been fixed. The same holds true for STRESS.DLL, so these functions aren't portable either. In a sense this is evident: most of the STRESS functions were designed to thwart the efforts of the operating system to check and limit the resource consumption of applications.

Difficulties in DLL programming

As if all this is not yet enough DLL developers especially should expect some further complications. First of all, DLL initialization and termination are now performed in a more systematic way than under Win16, but this will probably be a comparatively simple modification. Second, DLLs under Win32 are not globally known modules (as already mentioned), but will be mapped locally into the address space of the process loading the DLL. This fact has several consequences: 32-bit DLLs don't have a data segment in the 16-bit sense and therefore no local heap of their own. They instead have to allocate memory in the address space of their client. Static DLL data sections (e.g., global and static variables) are in the default case allocated and initialized from scratch for each and every process in its own memory area. Provided a DLL needs global variables for coordination and administration of several client processes, changes are most supposedly necessary.

Initialization and termination

Access to DLL data sections

Moreover, each process must load all needed DLLs into its private address space, either implicitly (with activation through the program loader) or explicitly via LoadLibrary() calls. It doesn't suffice to load a DLL once into the system in order to make it visible and accessible to all other applications. Or put differently: DLL mapping is no longer systemwide, but now occurs in the private address space of the process loading the DLL. (I'm repeating this to really bang it into your head.)

Another big problem that affects DLLs more than full applications is the fact that a call into a Win16 DLL is under normal circumstances completely executed (a so-called atomic function call). Because of the nature of cooperative multi-tasking, the developer of a DLL could be sure that a call into the DLL was performed completely, before a switch to another process could happen. And because these occur only in message loop processing or when voluntarily calling Yield(), the programmer always had full control over the execution path. Of course, this assumption isn't true under Win32 with its preemptive multi-tasking. Therefore, especially those DLLs that simultaneously support several clients *must* include proper synchronization mechanisms at critical spots to ensure secure manipulation of shared data structures. This problem is often of a non-trivial nature and requires an intimate knowledge of the DLL's implementation and the source codes!

Preemptive multi-tasking can easily implicate synchronization problems.

Last but not least, the developers of custom controls or other global window classes will have to perform some elementary changes in order

Global classes with CS_GLOBALCLASS?

57

to get things going: the class flag CS_GLOBALCLASS doesn't operate as expected under Win32. More about this and all the other DLL changes mentioned is available in sections 4.9, page 290, as well as section 5.3, page 339. In the latter section you'll also find some examples.

Conclusions

Summary of changes

The six categories described plus the difficulties with DLL programming can't include all possible problems that may arise when porting code to the Win32 API. A whole bunch of Win16 functions only have negligible modifications; some stuff isn't easily categorized; under certain circumstances the heavy use of multiple threads (e.g., preemptive multitasking) makes further adaptations necessary. But at least 95 percent of all necessary source code changes can be classified into one of the six (plus one) categories.

Unfortunately you're not yet done with just the adaptation of the source codes (although these probably will cause most of the trouble). The sources are not yet an executable: only through treatment with the SDK development tools you will get an application. And not unexpectedly, there also are various changes to record. I'll give an overview of the

* also Win32 SDK, for short

Win32 software development kit* in the next section. Detailed discussions of the required changes, including some examples, are found in Chapter 5. There you'll also find some hints for other 32-bit development systems such as Borland's C++ 4.x or Visual C++ 2.x.

1.6 A Look on the Win32 SDK

"Who looks under the surface does so at his own risk." Oscar Wilde, The Picture of Dorian Gray

The Win32 software development kit is the key to programming under and for Windows NT and 95. As the name already indicates, it delivers

Win32 SDK — only for
Win32 subsystems

just the tools needed for producing software to be run in the 32-bit subsystems of either system (well, the very latest release didn't even contain a C compiler and linker, so you are more or less required to get VC++ 2 or another development system). What I searched for in vain were informations and interfaces to the NT kernel itself as well as to the POSIX and OS/2 subsystems (this is only partially available). This will hopefully change with a future release. For Windows 95 somewhat more information is made available about the low-level workings; but in both cases system-related programming such as kernel drivers (NT) or VxD programming (95) requires the respective device driver kit (DDK).

Nevertheless, the SDK is impressive: the still-not-completed manuals alone reach about ten kilograms on my scale (*not* including the C/C++ manuals); a kilogram SDK manual corresponds to approximately 620 pages. The Win32 header files for C/C++ programming with over 4 MB size have about 10 times (!) the volume of all Windows 3.1 headers together.

Win32 SDK: a single version for NT and 95

I'm currently working with the released Win32 SDK for Windows NT 3.5 and the beta SDK for Chicago. Since I don't know what version* of the Win32 SDK you have (if you currently have one at all), possibly some of these hints are not valid for your version. However, such deviations should be rare and easy to identify, since the Microsoft documentation discusses important changes relative to previous versions. To my knowledge, the final version of the Win32 SDK for Chicago should be available when the product is released, but I don't expect any significant changes. By the way, the same is true if you prefer Visual C++ 2.x.

* The final version for Windows 95 is expected shortly after the first public release of the OS.

No, not only the hardware requirements of NT are a bit barbaric (apropos: as a developer you should allow for a fast 486DX machine with at least 16 MB main memory and some 120 MB free space on the hard disk — a CD-ROM drive is also necessary); also the demands on patience, recollection, and comprehension too achieve new record marks for the typical developer. Nevertheless, even Rome wasn't built in one day: the SDK material arrives rather reasonably structured and can easily (well, for an experienced Win16 programmer) be digested piecemeal. Moreover, most of the basic concepts, models, and features are inherently identical to Win16 and require just a short lookthrough. And concerning the new capabilities: you can include those at any time, as the mood takes you (or necessity dictates…).

Hardware requirements for a developer's machine

Programming with the SDK

Many changes in detail

The development process under Win32 is fundamentally the same as with Win16, although a sharp glance shows some significant changes and even some new features. Figure 1.14 on the following page gives a schematical overview of the involved source files, the tools to treat them and the way to building a working 32-bit application. The format of Win32 EXE files (also named "portable executables" or PE for short) is completely different from the old SE (or NE*) format of Win16 programs. This is hardly astonishing, since the concept of segmentation is finally buried with Win32.

* SE: segmented executables; NE: new executables.

Figure 1.14: From source to application: the development process with the Win32 SDK.

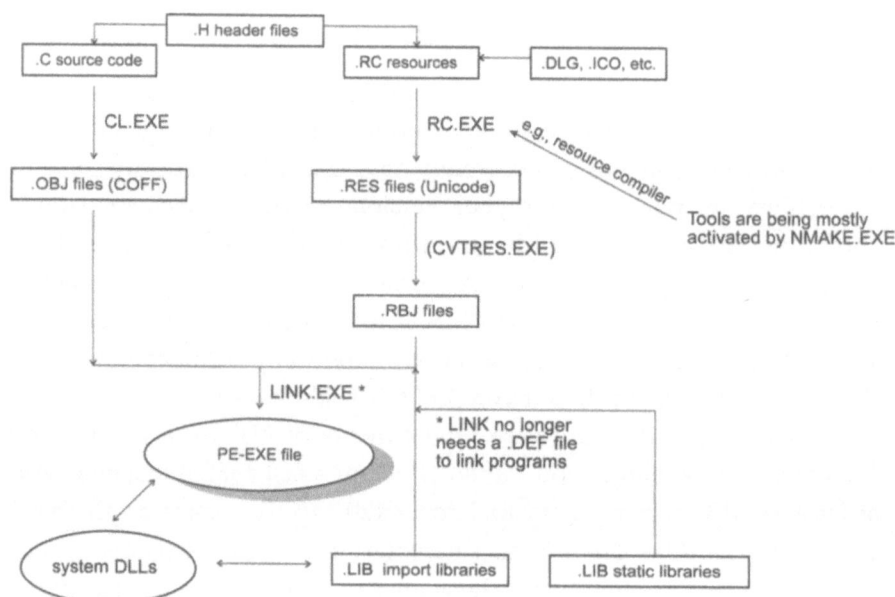

The following, not unimportant, differences to the Win16 development environment are most notable:

CL (formerly CL386) is based on C/C++ version 7.0.

- Many tools (e.g., the linker) have completely new options and switches. This doesn't mean that the existing switches experienced some changes — no, the option names and their usage are completely different. The C/C++ compiler is based on version 7.0, but has undergone (beside the 32-bit code generation of course) a lot of small changes. The number of switches has significantly decreased to a sensible level (what a joy!); the remaining options are much better organized (according to my theory: "The more stupid the system software, the more compiler switches and options are needed.").

- The library manager LIB and the EXEHDR utility are no longer independent programs, but are built into the linker LINK.EXE. This program (formerly called LINK32) includes these (and several additional) utilities.

- Resources are still compiled with RC, the resource compiler from RC into RES files; however, the binding to the corresponding EXE file is now done with the linker (exactly as if they were object files). The RES files are a straightforward enhancement of the old 3.x format and must be converted into a LINK32 compatible RBJ file (a hybrid of RES and OBJ) with CVTRES before being handed over to the linker. This step seems unnecessary in the latest SDK releases.

  RC is now a pure compiler.

- IMPLIB isn't needed anymore, as its functionality is taken over by LIB (and therefore the linker). DEF files are not needed for the linking of executables; all the details about the application previously recorded in DEF files (stack and heap size, etc.) are now transmitted as linker options. For the generation of DLLs the linker still reads DEF files to produce an EXP file with the required export definitions.

  IMPLIB and EXEHDR are omitted.

- A debugger (based upon the QuickC Debugger) named WINDBG is running as a GUI program and replaces CodeView. Two additional debuggers, namely NTSD, with remote resemblance to SYMDEB, and I386KD (MIPSKD and ALPHAKD for the other machines, respectively) for kernel debugging are better left to spartanic command line guys or people who have to debug kernel mode code.

  NT symbolic debugger
  KD — kernel debugger

- PORTTOOL is a relatively simple-minded (and as a matter of fact rather buggy) program that claims to help with the porting process. The heart of PORTTOOL is an editor with the ability to search for non-portable constructions (or what it thinks to be non-portable...) in your source code. The search is based on a freely editable text file (named PORT.INI) with API information (an enhanced version of that file processing many more portability is-

  PORTTOOL and PORT.INI

sues is shown in Appendix 2 and is also found on the accompanying disk).

- On MIPS machines two C compilers are available: the first originates from MIPS and is a pure ANSI C compiler; the second is a joint venture of Microsoft and MIPS and therefore strongly resembles C 7.0 and compiles C++ code, too.

Profiler and working set tuner

- Two profilers, both for API calls and for the measurement of execution time needed by your code, are also contained in the SDK. Moreover, various tools are supplied to optimize the loading time and memory usage of programs and DLLs.
- Otherwise you'll find mainly the same stuff as in the Windows 3.1 SDK in more or less adapted form (the dialog editor, for example, runs under Windows NT, but still produces RES files for Win16 to be converted with CVTRES. Sigh...)

The handling of the Microsoft SDK tools, as far as changes or enhancements must be observed, is shown in detail in Chapter 5, especially section 5.1, page 319 (GUI programs) and 5.2, page 336 (text-mode applications). The 32-bit development tools from Borland as well as Visual C++ 2.x are treated in sections 5.4 and 5.5.

We turn now to a completely different but not less important subject: In which ways does an existing Win16 program improve when ported to Win32? This question is answered in the next section.

1.7 Is My Application Substantially Improved After Porting to Win32?

"This, after all, was the poodle's heart!" Johann Wolfgang von Goethe, Faust, First Part

Well, a question such as this one reminds me of Radio Eriwan (a legendary, extremely dull radio station somewhere in the former USSR trying to answer the listener's equally dull questions). So here is a suitable answer: in principle yes, but.... The diversity of software running under Windows today makes a simple yes-or-no answer impossible. On the

The kind of the program is crucial.

one hand, the question itself has several facets and implications; on the other hand, the answer depends obviously on the character the application, and its intentions. Let's first redefine and clarify the question a bit:

which improvements can you anticipate in your ported program without *explicitly* supporting new Win32 features? Or asked differently: if you want to invest only the absolutely necessary costs of porting, what advantages are to be expected from 32-bit Windows?

Just porting?

This issue has — nearly independent of the kind of program in question — the following answers:

- The virtual address space as well as the flat memory model allow simple and fast access to very large memory areas. The segmentation of code or data and all related problems are obsolete.

  Flat memory brings simpler and faster memory accesses.

- The long filenames under Windows 95 and the New Technology file system (NTFS) under NT allow for superior performance, bigger files, better security and fault tolerance.
- The program is protected from unauthorized accesses (whether abusive or inadvertent) through strict address space separation.

  Greater application safety through separated address spaces

- The response behavior is improved and more predictable through the genuine preemptive multi-tasking capabilities and desynchronized input queues.
- After a successful port, in principle the application can be recompiled and run on other NT platforms too (MIPS Rx000, DEC Alpha, Power PC, etc.).

  Portability to other 32-bit platforms

- Completely transparent access on all network resources is possible through the I/O manager.
- And last but not least: system resources used by the program (e.g., NTFS files) are, assuming a proper NT installation and administration, safe from tinkering or unauthorized accesses.

Another "benefit" materializing both for the end user of the program as well as for the developer: while porting you'll normally find the opportunity to correct a lot of more or less important errors; moreover, in a sense the source code will become safer because questionable cast operations, dubious 16-bit constructions, and the like are fixed almost mandatorily.

And the source code can improve as well...

Almost all ported software will profit from these enhancements; but which of these advantages (and to what extent) improve the 32-bit version mostly depends on the overall character of your application. A numerical program handling large, scarcely filled arrays (e.g., sparse matrices) will benefit greatly from the linear, virtual 4 GB address space. An application processing sensitive data (e.g., the database of a marriage bureau) presumably gains more advantages from the safe execution and the security checks. And if your software has to manage an exorbitant amount of full-text data (such as would be the case with a world-wide database for unfulfilled election promises), NTFS' big files come in handy. But even a simple auxiliary program such as the calendar supplied with Windows can win through Win32: with the aid of preemptive multi-tasking you will never again miss a date only because another application blocked the system queue and "hourglassed" the whole system.

As a matter of fact, you will observe that many of the above-mentioned "automatic" improvements also include Win16 programs all of which immediately run as binary compatible applications under NT (via WOW) and 95. (Well, "immediately" is only theoretically true; in reality things often look somewhat different: even a Win16 program has to satisfy *some* NT-specific conditions.*) Apart from the enlarged linear address space and the global input model that are still valid for Win16 programs (as you'd expect this can result even under NT in a crashed or blocked Win16 application, but such a program renders inoperable only the WOW layer it is executing in, not the system itself), most Win16 applications are thankful beneficiaries of the discussed enhancements.

See also section 4.11, page 309.

Or immediately include improvements?

Here is another (and probably more exciting) facet of the question regarding the improvements a ported application can expect: which new features (whose inclusion, alas, will cause — partially considerable — additional effort over the pure porting work) can be used in an existing program and on what advantages can developers and users alike count? Before getting into this, here is an important warning: you have to realize that the use of really new Win32 features (such as threads) considerably restricts the backward compatibility to Win16. Unfortunately, this observation is to a large extent independent of the question of whether the program actually runs under Window 3.x as a genuine Win16 application or as a crippled Win32 app under Win32s (see section 1.9 for more

*New features: good for the program, but **very** bad for portability!*

facts about Win32s). This issue will be of interest in several sections to come.

Anyhow, the survey contained in table 1.6 gives you a first, rough overview of the enhanced Win32 possibilities and their advantages for both developers and end users.

Win32 feature or functionality	Advantages for the developer	... and the program (or the enduser)
Multi-tasking and multi-threading	Code is easier to structure.	More efficient, improved response
Structured exception and error handling (SEH)	Simpler, more complete and consistent error handling	Solid, shorter, faster
IPC support	Safe multi-tasking, simple data communications	More communicative, better integration of applications
Memory mapped files	Simple, efficient access to files	Faster; less I/O-oriented
Unicode	Smooth file transfer	Usable worldwide
Long, descriptive filenames		Intuitively usable
Asynchronous I/O operations		Efficient, swift to handle
32-bit GDI coordinates	No rounding problems, no special coordinate space required	Exact representations, even on high-resolution displays
Bézier curves and paths	Complex drawings and special effects without too much programming effort	Quick and spectacular graphical effects even in simple products
World coordinates	GDI code will be simpler and clearer	
Security checks		Guarded before misuse
Network API	Portable network code	Inherent network functions
Per-instance data in DLLs	Simpler, more efficient use	

Table 1.6: New Win32 possibilities: advantages for developers and customers.

Most of these possibilities can be added after a successful port step by step as necessity demands (or deadlines allow). Admittedly — and to calm your enthusiasm a bit — you'll have to take into consideration that such an enhanced Win32 program is not (easily) recompilable under Win16 or for Win32s. The development and maintenance of an application available for both platforms is of course much more costly and complicated than pure one-way porting. Besides a careful and well-planned design maintaining a multi-platform program requires above all a disciplined implementation.

The second chapter will deal in detail with the practical questions of planning and executing a porting task. Basically, so much can be said here already, the number one rule is: *first* port the already existing functionality of the program completely and have it execute errorfree on the 32-bit environment; *after that*, in a second step, additional Win32-specific features should be built in. Certainly there are exceptions: for example, long filenames are a feature that has to be taken into account while actually doing the port. In the same way, 32-bit GDI coordinates automatically get in underway. The situation is different for multiple threads, new IPC mechanisms, and structured exception handling, for example: including these requires some real work. And that brings us to the next section!

First port — then improve!

*As usual, the exception
proves the rule...*

1.8 ... And What About the Effort?

"The idea doesn't replace the work." Max Weber, Science as Profession

Even more so than for the subject of possible improvements, the reply to this question depends on your application. And that's true in two regards: first, said a bit sloppily, the more complex the user interface, the more costly the port. It should be obvious that a program where 80 percent of the code is required for a complex and intuitive user interface (a good example might be the file manager as shown in figure 1.15 on the next page) essentially needs more porting work than a simple application with only 20 or 30 percent of the code for the user interface and the bulk of the code for calculations or the implementation of complex algorithms (these things are normally much easier to port).

*Complex user interface
means huge porting effort.*

Figure 1.15: The file manager, a complex interface: MDI, drag-and-drop, icon and bitmap processing, etc.

An example for this second category is the Windows PIF editor: if only the main dialog box (see figure 1.16) is ported, the rest of the effort is a child's game. From this follows the first rule: normally GUI-intensive software requires much more porting effort than do calculation-bound or algorithmically complex programs.

Second (and I know from personal experience that I'm touching a sore point here), the source codes are not always in a state that makes porting big fun. The endless pressure of deadlines, continuing design changes, flaws in the compiler, plain laziness or sloppiness, lack of information, indifference or non-interest: there are literally thousands of good reasons* why existing source code is often not as clearly structured as it should be according to textbook fashion. Experience teaches that duration and effort of a port depend at least logarithmically, in worse cases quadratically on the "chaos coefficient" of the sources. So if you're still expecting an exact estimation of the time frame or even a formula to calculate the time required, I unfortunately have to disappoint you. But undeniably there are some rules and hints that at the very least could facilitate an estimation:

And what about the state of the sources?!

* ... as well as the second main law of thermodynamics

Modular sources

- The better your source code is modularized, the easier one source file after the other can be adapted and compiled in order to resolve the compiler-generated errors and warnings. Clear separation between code for the user interface and the actual implementation of the employed algorithms facilitates this step-by-step transfer.

Pay attention to compiler warnings!

- The fewer warnings the compiler presents *before* starting the port (i.e., still under Windows 3.x) at the highest warning level, the simpler the port will be.

Figure 1.16: Compared to the file manager rather easy to port: the PIF editor. In the window on the right the RC file with the dialog box resource is shown.

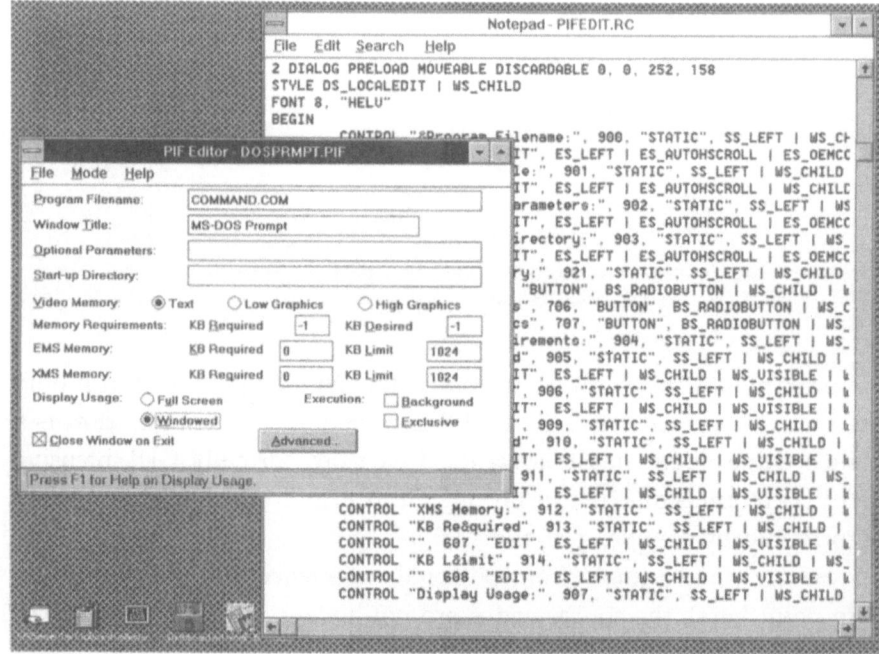

Activate the STRICT option.

- If you can compile even in "#define STRICT" mode (see section 2.5 on page 105) and get no or only very few warnings, then things aren't too bad at all (but Murphy doesn't sleep…).

Hands off obscure maneuvers!

- On the other hand, whoever has silenced the compiler through the help of dubious casts and other grasps into the unholy bag of C tricks and believed things sorted out forever, now has to pay for his carelessness (following the motto "late revenge of the compiler").

Use undocumented features only sparingly…

- The nonchalant use of undocumented features is indeed often unavoidable, but seldom advantageous for portability. Anyhow, in Win32 a large group of 3.x internals are now, all officially, documented; probably Microsoft has silently (or with some teeth-gnashing?) implemented many others. Yet there is *absolutely* no guarantee that any undocumented 3.x specialty will work properly after the port. Under Windows 95, ported programs are probably better off than under NT, since the first represents a direct update path and Microsoft has (nay, must) put special effort into maintaining backward compatibility.

- The same is valid for the undisciplined use of MS-DOS-specific characteristics (BIOS, INT 21H etc.). If absolutely, positively (!) unavoidable, you should at least isolate such code in separate functions that are easily replaced or adapted. As much as possible combine all these functions into a single portability layer.

  ... and isolate these as well as other non-portable constructions into a separate code layer.

- Many techniques used in Win16 to circumvent the numerous Windows and DOS restrictions such as HUGE pointers or mixing of several memory models (mixed memory model programming) have to be removed or adapted for Win32. Ironically, these problems are aggravated by the fact that several of these techniques are very difficult to localize in separate modules but spread over the whole program text.

  Abandon 16-bit tricks.

- Comments could aid with tricky or sophisticated parts of a program that might even run unmodified under Win32 — if you would only understand the hack.... They are especially important if a team is involved or if the original author of the sources isn't identical with the person responsible for porting or maintenance.

  Comments in the sources can help.

- Finally, it should be clear that one can port successfully and with estimable effort only such software whose internal working is understood. What in the first instant sounds like a bad joke is unfortunately too often a sad fact: some (Windows) developers "recycle" code fragments from third-party sources (e.g., books, periodicals, examples that came with the compiler, etc.) — but without analyzing the code or understanding how the fragment works (a procedure known as "copy-paste-edit programming"). This seems okay as long as the resulting program operates (more or less) correctly. But when the code needs to be ported to another platform, then things can get very, very unpleasant.

  Source codes should be not only edited, but also understood!

On the other hand, there is assistance: books (like this one) and tools (such as the fabulous PORTTOOL from Microsoft) can facilitate the task considerably. The most important requirement for the job is a thorough

Well, the Win32 API is not for Windows greenhorns.

knowledge of the object — someone who is about to understand his very first Windows program shouldn't meddle with porting to Win32 for a good while. And a clear overview of the project to port is very desirable too (more about that in the second chapter). The motto of section 2.1 should be taken to heart: it is wise first to gain a clear understanding of the starting point and the final target as well as the means and efforts required to reach it before beginning the actual port.

Some clues, anyway

Overall about 15,000 lines plus/minus 30 percent

So not to leave you without at least some concrete information, let's look at the following example: a normal (meaning neither especially well structured nor extraordinarily slipshod) program with about 15 to 20 source code modules (all in the order of 500 to 1000 lines) has to be ported by the developer who wrote it in the first place. Adjusting the

Making things STRICT: a week.

sources so that they can be compiled in STRICT mode without warnings — but still under Windows 3.x — takes even with slightly messy sources probably less than a week. Two further days I would expect for master-

Mastering the SDK tools: two days.

ing the Win32 development tools (compiler, linker, etc.) including the necessary changes to the makefile(s). Sure enough, most of this effort only applies for the first project and just disappears for the next proj-

Adaptations required for the Win32 API: another three days.

ect(s). Then the individual source files have to be (re-)compiled under NT (or 95); by the time they get through without severe warnings surely another two or three days have passed. From experience, the debugging is expensive only if the application had unidentified, flagrant errors that first show up under the 32-bit environment. However, if this happens,

Debugging: An open-end festival...

the time needed for debugging is impossible to estimate (unfortunately, this is true for catching bugs under every OS...). Overall and as a rough guess: two (maximum three) weeks if the application doesn't show un-expected errors. This is for a simple port only, it will take somewhat

Grand total: two weeks.

longer to change the sources, so that they are still suitable for compila-tion under both 16- and 32-bit platforms (which is for some time to come probably the default case). In this case some additional effort has to be invested to take conditional compilation (#ifdef, etc.) into account. How-ever, to ease this, Microsoft has defined numerous macros and portabil-ity functions that remove most of the rough edges (see section 3.3, page 142 as well as the discussion of WINDOWSX.H in Chapter 4).

If the sources are already available for STRICT mode under Windows 3.1, the porting process is considerably faster and easier. About half of the stated time (reaching a good week) seems realistic. Please note that this estimation can deliver only rough ideas: numerous factors* not universally classifiable can lead to a considerable increase or decrease in the time required. If a great deal of programs are to be ported, the average number of ported lines per day will probably increase considerably and proportionally to the experience of the programmers (especially because the more mechanical parts of a port can be carried out relatively quickly by inexperienced helpers).

such as the memory model or the use of assembler or inline code

Another important observation: the order of the individual porting steps in the above shown "abridged" version is not essentially the optimal procedure for porting a non-trivial program. They were ordered and described in that manner solely to build a base for a rough time estimate. Rules, advice, and hints for the actual realization of a port, including planning and preparation, are found in the second chapter.

More on the overall procedure in the second chapter.

1.9 The Little Brother: Win32s

"Win32 is defined as 'portable enhancement of the Win16 API plus new functionality'. Now, Win32s is simply the following: Win32 without the 'new functionality'." Alistair Banks, Microsoft, in a file with explanations to Win32s circulating in CompuServe

Well, well! I honestly have to admit that to me, in contrast to Mr. Banks, it was not immediately clear what is meant by Win32s** and above all, for what purpose it was invented. (But Microsoft mimics with the multitude of Windows APIs only what Intel has successfully demonstrated with the 486 DX, SX, OverDrive, DX2, DX4, etc., etc.). Or is there more than first meets the eye? In order to answer this pressing question, we first should have a glance at Win32s: what, in the world, hides behind this nebulous expression?

*** "s" for subset or for sandpit?*

What is Win32s and what does it do?

Win32s (requiring a 386 processor or better) is a collection of DLLs, a virtual device driver (VxD), and an executable file that are simply installed on top of a running Windows 3.1 system. Ah, first point: Win32s

Win32s leans on Windows 3.1...

71

sits on Windows 3.1! After the Win32s installation is completed, native Win32 programs can be executed under the control of Windows 3.1 (principally each 32-bit application written for the graphical user interface of Windows NT or 95 is supported, though no text-mode — or console — application). Here follows the second observation: Win32s enhances 3.1 in such a way that it can load and run 32-bit programs as well as the usual 16-bit applications (and therefore Win32s requires at least a 386 processor). For the end user the whole thing is (as usual) entirely hasslefree: he simply installs a product — which itself silently installs the Win32s files if required — and normally doesn't even realize that he is now working with a genuine 32-bit program. Everything necessary to execute the application is performed transparently by the Win32s components under the direction of Windows 3.1. Win32s just sits between the 32-bit application code and Windows 3.1 as an additional layer. Hence, seen by light Win32s is nothing more than a Windows extender (funny enough, Windows itself is a DOS extender...). So is Win32s a thing on a thing on a thing? Will there ever be an end to that card-house-like construction? Anyway, figure 1.17 schematically shows how the individual Win32s components and Win16 work together.

... and expands the system to 32-bit processing.

Figure 1.17: The integration of Win32s and Windows 3.1

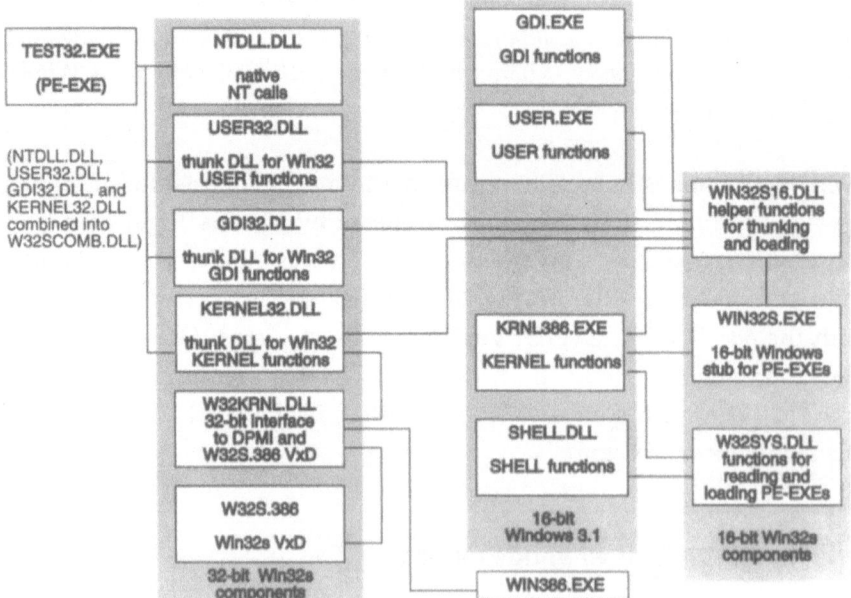

But what happens under this attractive facade in terms of technical requirements? The loading, activation, and (hopefully) flawless behavior of a Win32 program in a 16-bit world require both changes to Windows 3.1 and energetic help from Win32s:

- The Windows 3.1 loader recognizes that the program is not a normal segmented executable (SE) for Windows, but a so-called portable executable (PE), and therefore a 32-bit application. In this case it decides it is not competent and hands the program over to a Win32s DLL. The system extension necessary for this neat trick first became available with Windows 3.1 (and therefore Win32s won't run under 3.0 or any previous version of Windows).

    The 3.1 loader recognizes Win32 PE programs.

- The Win32s DLL now allocates all necessary memory areas for the code and data sections of the program in a 32-bit segment, thereby relying completely (!) on the virtual memory management of Win16. This means that a 32-bit program running under Win32s shares memory in the Win16 manner with all other applications: there are no separated address spaces like those in genuine 32-bit Windows implementations. The individual code and data sections are then loaded from the EXE file into memory and the program is started.

    No separated address spaces under Win32s!

- Sooner or later the program calls a Windows function such as RegisterClass() — but of course with 32-bit parameters and addresses. All those calls are intercepted by the responsible Win32s DLLs (for RegisterClass() that is USER32.DLL). This DLL transforms numerical arguments as required into 16-bit format; memory addresses are mapped to 16-bit segments. Now, with these values the original function (RegisterClass() in Win16 USER.DLL) is called, which does what it is supposed to do and returns to the 32-bit Win32s DLL. Here, possible return values are converted back to 32-bit fashion and finally passed on to the application. This additional layer of translation code is called the "thunking" layer, or thunk for short.

    Thunks trap the 32-bit calls.

- Message dispatching is handled in a similar manner: filters that transparently carry out the necessary translation processes are sandwiched between Win16's USER module and *all* 32-bit window procedures. So, for Windows 3.1 and all other running 16-bit applications, the 32-bit program looks just like an ordinary 16-bit Windows program. On the other hand, the program believes it's

    Window messages are translated, too.

executing in a Win32 environment and sees only 32-bit programs. Thunks (for functions and messages) also support system hooks and subclassing.

*32-bit resources are trans-
formed automatically.*

- Of course, all resources to be loaded from the executable file are stored in 32-bit format, so the resource loader of Win16 can't load them into memory. Again a translator moves in between program and Windows in order to take care of the conversion from Win32 to Win16 resources on the fly.

*No direct calls into private
16-bit DLLs, only with the
detour of universal thunks!*

- The Win32s thunking layers support all standard 16-bit Windows messages and functions but no calls into third-party DLLs. This means that a call from 32 bit into a 16-bit DLL not included in the default Windows implementation (e.g., a database manager) is not directly supported. With a bit of thinking, the reason becomes clear: every thunk is a special entry point for one and only one function. Even if Microsoft could have delivered thunking layers for some important external DLLs, they would not be able to provide a thunk for each and every function in a private DLL somewhere in the world. As the developer who needs that specific 16-bit function, you have two possibilities: either you get a 32-bit version of the DLL in question or you must grin and bear it — namely write your own thunking layer. Microsoft has indeed invented a concept (named "universal thunks," UT for short) with whose aid these restrictions can be circumvented. Unfortunately, UTs are not at all Win32 compatible, hence implementing *and* porting universal thunks to a "real" Win32 system require considerable additional effort.

*The message order is
identical.*

- The order in which the window procedures receive messages is of course the same for a Win16 and a Win32s program. Thunking just translates values or memory addresses but doesn't change the messaging order. Since the exact same Win32s executable can be run under Win32 (either Windows NT or 95, because the EXE file is in fact a genuine 32-bit executable), this implicitly means that the message order must remain unaltered in all Win32 environments. In a sense, this is an undocumented behavior that is completely backward compatible.

*DPMI: DOS protected mode
interface*

- All Win32s memory requirements (e.g., via GlobalAlloc()) will eventually be passed on to DPMI. The application sees just a linear 32-bit address space; shared memory for the 16- and 32-bit environments is made available via segment aliasing.

- The Win32s VxD supports the structured exception-handling model (SEH), which therefore can be used unchanged in Win32s programs (beside the use of the flat memory model, this is the second real improvement over the Win16 API).

So far, so good. What does a Win32s program look like for the developer? The answer is quite simple and should not be very surprising after the previous discussion: it is plainly and simply a regular 32-bit Windows program! Admittedly, some specialties have to be taken into account. But in principle each Windows 95 or NT program can execute through Win32s under Windows 3.1, too. Neither the programmer nor the compiler or linker has to perform any Win32s-specific steps when creating a 32-bit application. All data types, macros, functions, etc., exhibited by the Win32 API are available and callable. But sadly, and now we come to the restrictions, the Win32 function CreateThread() (for example) returns just NULL if called under Win32s, indicating that no new thread could be created. Since Win32s is just a 32-bit interface to Windows 3.1 (which has only very unclear ideas about multi-tasking and absolutely no idea about multiple threads), this isn't exactly surprising.

A Win32s EXE is a normal NT EXE (and vice versa)!

And so the earlier quotation from Mr. Banks hopefully gets a bit clearer: Win32s is just a thin coating around Win16 in order to pretend that there's a convenient atmosphere for Win32 applications. It delivers no further Win32 functionality beyond Windows 3.1 (apart from the 32-bit memory model and structured exception handling). No Unicode, no multiple threads, no enhanced GDI with Bézier curves and paths, no NTFS either? Not even a bit? Exactly, all that and then still some features are not at all compatible with Win32s. The supported subset will in the long run include some other parts of the full Win32 functionality, namely those that are relatively easy to implement under Win16. In the makings are memory mapped files, various IPC mechanisms such as named pipes, etc. But a lot of what makes the Win32 API so attractive is just impossible with Windows 3.1 (even with the greatest effort, Win16 really *is* very limited). So, let's wait for Windows 95….

Win32s: only a coating — no new functionality.

By far, not all Win32 functions can be used.

Pluses and minuses for the developer

What does Win32s mean for the developer? First of all, a lot of additional work! No, seriously — Win32s has some distinctive advantages: above

Advantages: flat memory model, 32-bit processing.

all the availability of the Win32 API under Win16 as well as the linear 32-bit memory model with its performance gains are very attractive arguments (the latter is especially important for applications to be ported from 32-bit systems such as UNIX). As said: Win32s works principally like a DOS extender but is more a kind of Win16 extender. And certain classes of very memory-hungry applications were possible only through the help of these products. Also, at first glance, the capability for sharing only one source code base and EXE file for Win16 and Win32 systems appears to be a big advantage.

Unfortunately, there are important drawbacks as well: the performance gain is at least partly eaten through the thunking and other layers that have to move between 32-bit application and Windows 3.1. An extremely memory-intensive program with "little GUI" will profit more from Win32s than a program with many, many Win16 functions calls. I've seen programs running five to ten times (!) faster under Win32s; on the other hand, I know some user-interface bound programs losing about 20 to 30 percent of their performance. (The most extreme case I've ever seen was a graphics application where some parts slowed down as much as 50 percent! But this was an exception.) Furthermore (at present), a Win32s program can be neither developed nor debugged stand-alone under Win16. For development you need a machine with a real 32-bit system. Part of the problem is that the Win32 SDK tools (or a 32-bit version of Visual C++) are necessary for development — but these do not run under Win32s (frankly, it's a pretty stupid idea to produce a 32-bit compatibility layer for Win16 which is not able to run its own development tools). For this you need Windows NT or 95 and, yes indeed, a corresponding hardware equipment. Admittedly, Win32s makes 32-bit programs available under Win16: but this is true only for GUI applications, not for text-mode (command-line) programs such as a compiler and or a linker…. Luckily, the 32-bit tools of Borland and other third-party manufacturers *are* able to work under MS-DOS (see section 5.4, page 349). And additional utilities to talk the MS tools into running under Win16 are available too (see section 5.1, page 319).

*#2: The developer requires
NT or 95 and the Win32
SDK.*

As if this were not unpleasant enough yet, another significant problem rears its ugly head: even with Win32s it's difficult to write source code in such a fashion that no precautions for Win16 specifics are necessary (for real-world programs, not toy apps). Admittedly, proper coding assumed, only one application and one set of sources have to be maintained, but the source codes must take into account some quite odd idiosyncrasies of the Win16 API (or its conversion to Win32s, respectively). The extent to which special coding for Win32s is necessary depends heavily on the type of the application. Under certain circumstances the creation of two separate EXE files (a genuine 16-bit program for Win16, the other as a 32-bit EXE for the true 32-bit OSes) from one set of source codes may be less expensive than doing the job with just a single executable. The latter means that the so implemented application must discover the actual system software (NT, Chicago, or Win32s) at run time and *dynamically* adjust to it. Section 2.7 illuminates this realm in more detail.

Finally, my last criticism, the already mentioned "shaky" DOS/Windows combination does not exactly become more stable through Win32s. The more code layers piled one upon the other, the greater the probability of crashes, malfunctions, or incompatibilities appears to me — for instance, the incomplete integration of Win32s applications in special situations such as the use of the TOOLHELP function NotifyRegister(). Or to quote a "musical layer model" for the sake of comparison — MS-DOS, Windows 3.1, Win32s, and all the above floating applications remind me of a fairy tale from the Grimm brothers, presenting in fact a fine allegory: at the bottom stands the aged DOS donkey, carrying the not exactly fresh Windows dog, then the Win32s cat, and on top the application rooster, all four crying like mad to frighten some robbers (yeah, this gang of four has acquired world-wide fame under the name "Bremer Stadtmusikanten"). The whole party seems indeed rather wobbly and finally collapses with the appropriate hullabaloo, but (at least in the fairy tale) the objective of the show is nevertheless reached — the robbers run away.

And what about stability?

All things considered, I am not totally convinced that Win32s is actually a general requirement. Rather, it conceals some of the doubtless existing weaknesses of the aging Win16 environment, so the comparison with Win32 and, even more important for Microsoft, with OS/2 is not overly unfavorable. Otherwise some customers for whom NT's hardware requirements are a bit too large would perhaps change sides and migrate into the OS/2 camp.* On the other hand, and this seems the only real argument for Win32s, it *can* serve as a vehicle to give potential Win32 developers an incentive to develop today, even with significant restrictions, Win32 applications that can be sold under Windows 3.1 (with its umpteen million installations) — following the motto "32-bit program can bring 16-bit turnover." In this sense Win32s seen from the technical

Win32s: necessity or just a Microsoft trick?

* "s" for safeguard?

side is as necessary as a goiter, but it can be a decisive Microsoft move to establish Win32 as the No. 1 API and Windows NT as the most successful high-end operating system. As mentioned, software producers prefer to write programs for systems already successful on the market, than for newcomers. And Win32s elegantly combines the pleasant elements (for Microsoft) with the useful ones (for software developers). Moreover, a manufacturer may not implement and support yet another 32-bit version (namely for OS/2) — and this is surely a not unwillingly seen side effect.

Anyway, Win16 (and with it Win32s) will die a smooth death in the not-too-distant future, simply because it will be replaced by a genuine 32-bit version (namely Windows 95). And then at the latest the whole Win32s hocus-pocus is just as superfluous as are certain Intel processors today. But I'll get into the technical matters as well as important questions about the programming of Win32s programs in the remaining chapters, as required. The issue of correctly working applications for all 32-bit platforms must especially be investigated in detail. After all, you can't be sure that your fine 32-bit program won't be used on a Win32s platform somewhere — even ten years from now (actually, I know some people who still work with Windows 3.0…).

1.10 Summary

"What is the short meaning of this long speech?" Friedrich Schiller, Wallenstein

Whew! Here we are at the end of the first chapter! The quintessence of all this summed up in few words:

Windows NT is an enhancement to the Windows family in the high-end area and has the following strengths: it is extensible, scalable, portable and to a large extent backward compatible (on the API and application level). It makes available MS-DOS and Windows 3.x emulation, POSIX and OS/2 support, as well as C2 level security. Further catch-words are flat memory model, symmetric multi-processing, preemptive multi-tasking, and multi-threading. NT is at least competitive in comparison to OS/2 3.x and UNIX (alas, that's also true for the hardware requirements); a lot of technical advantages even put it at a somewhat better position than its main competitors. Nevertheless, it is a brand-new system that still has to go though its childhood diseases (to a lesser extent this is also true for the 3.5 release of NT).

Windows NT is a state-of-the-art system, into which was rushed much experience with other modern operating system projects. It is built in modular and layered fashion and permits nearly arbitrary changes of system components at run time. The extensible subsystems communicate with applications through a client/server model and permit the execution as well as creation of programs not native to Windows NT through API emulation. The Win32 subsystem under Windows NT was the first available implementation of the Win32 API.

Windows NT is a modern, powerful high-end operating system.

Windows 95, not to be expected before the second half of 1995, will also realize an implementation of the Win32 API (to a large extent complete). The programming concepts and models are therefore identical to NT except for some specialized areas like security. The backward compatibility of Windows 95 will be much better than NT's, and the hardware requirements will be moderate but will nevertheless continue to increase in the future. Whether Windows 95 will be nearly as stable as NT has proven to be an interesting question. My expectations are not very high, simply because 95 has to care too much about compatibility with old applications and therefore heavily builds on the roots of an aged system. Anyway, both systems exhibit the Win32 API, so nearly all important criteria of portability for NT will be valid for Windows 95 (or vice versa).

The utilization of the Win32 SDK tools has not been modified substantially compared to Win16, although the devil hides in the details (where else?). The most important changes are attributed to the widening to 32 bit as well as to the separated and enlarged address spaces. A major advantage of this change is the fact that the API indeed became much more consistent and logical than Win16. A whole bank of nonportable, hardware-dependent 3.x functions was removed without replacement. So you should expect Win32 source code to be nearly 100 percent portable between x86 and RISC CPUs.

The Win32 SDK

All types of Windows applications can profit from Win32 API improvements: the least binary compatible Win16 programs (in which case the cost of porting happens to be extremely low indeed, if at all necessary); a lot more, fully ported applications, completely adjusted to the Win32 API, will benefit (the effort here is not to be neglected, however); the most advantages software will experience when taking advantage of certain advanced Win32 features like multiple threads or long filenames

What advantages does Win32 bring to your programs?

(this of course means still larger efforts and severely restricts backward compatibility to Win16).

And Win32s? Win32s is a 32-bit enhancement of Windows 3.1 and offers properly implemented Win32 applications the capability to execute on a Win16 platform, thereby profiting especially from the linear 32-bit memory model. Of course, the Win32s programmer has to port his sources from 16 to 32 bit; the necessary adaptations are to a large extent identical to those for "genuine" Win32 applications. Unfortunately, a great deal of important advantages of the full Win32 API are not supported under Win32s and, even worse, a whole lot of 16-bit specific programming anomalies have to be observed. All that doesn't exactly simplify programming for Win32s. Provided that 32-bit programs pay attention to several rules, they certainly can be written as binary compatible executables for Windows NT, Windows 95, and Windows 3.1 plus Win32s. Win32s seems only relevant for a transitional period and will become more or less superfluous when Microsoft releases Windows 95. Then Win32s should slowly vanish in the depths of 16-bit programming — nevertheless, we will have to support its idiosyncrasies for at least the next few years. In the long run, even Windows 95 will disappear and give room to an NT and OLE 2 based, object-oriented operating system. Well, our correspondent in Cairo will keep us abreast of further developments....

Strategies to Portable Programming

Okay, now starts the serious part: in this second chapter we'll deal with porting a Win16 application to Win32 on a project-related level. An application doesn't consist of tens of thousands of lines of source code (or more); it (hopefully!) has some organization and structure, therefore exhibiting certain global features that certainly could influence the conversion to another operating system. We could use a military but not completely inappropriate analogy and compare our position for this chapter to that of a general on his hill, trying to evaluate the military situation in order to use the existing troops in the best way possible. Of course you can't win a big battle without fighting the usual countless small skirmishes: you'll find lots of specific and detailed hints for portable programming and the proper use of individual data types, functions, messages, etc., later in Chapters 3 and 4.

A successful port requires careful planning and a complete project overview.

2.1 Starting Points and Objectives

"If one does not know the objective, not a single way will be the right one." The Koran

Obviously, our starting point is an existing and working Win16 application. But this is by far an insufficient description, since the source codes of Win16 programs can nowadays be classified broadly into four different standard categories (and innumerable varieties of those):

Our starting point: a Win16 program — but in four possible variants.

- either antique 2.x code, which has never been adapted to Windows 3.0 (not to mention 3.1…);
- or you have to deal with a 3.0 application which you couldn't convert to the enhanced 3.1 API yet (perhaps because of time constraints);

- the third category is probably the most common: code recompiled for and running under 3.1 (which may even support some of the newer 3.1 features);
- last but not least: programs designed for 3.1 and compiled with the STRICT option without producing any serious compiler diagnostics (see section 3.8, page 178, for a summary of the important warnings and error messages).

For more about STRICT see
section 2.5 on page 105.

Preferably STRICT...

As you must surely have noticed and as shown in the following figure 2.1, these four source code categories strictly build one upon the other:

Figure 2.1: The four source
code categories for Win16

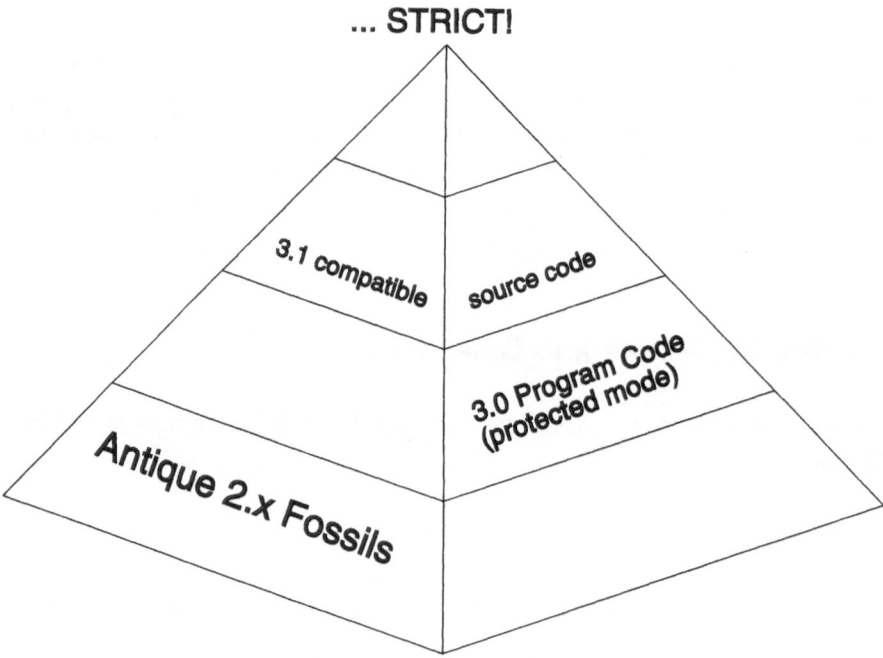

Well, the top variant seems particularly nice as starting point for a Win32 port. You'll still have to pay attention to many small changes and to carry them out, but STRICT compliant sources fulfill an important assumption: in terms of the utilization of the numerous Windows-specific data types, they are syntactically correct (as far as a C/C++ compiler can determine, of course) and should contain only very few points to be improved because of the widened or modified Win32 data types. So, here is a valuable hint for developers who don't need (or want) to port immediately but have in mind some medium- or long-term porting projects: convert your source files to STRICT. Provided you don't work with C++, you should be able to do this step by step, adapting one C file after the other, when you have the time and opportunity to do. Very good candidates are sources that you have to change often (and naturally those you have to create completely anew). Stable code should only be converted to STRICT when you have enough time to accurately investigate the resultant compiler warnings and error messages and to correct them accordingly (unless you have to modify it anyway for some other reasons, such as debugging or maintenance).

Even when not porting immediately: STRICT helps!

Unfortunately, C++ users must grin and bear it and will usually have to convert all source files of a given project in a single step. The reason behind this: a C++ compiler attaches textual information concerning parameter types and function results to the function names in the created object files. This process is called "name mangling" and enables the distinction of overloaded functions; furthermore, those modified names are used later on for implementing typesafe linking. When calling a specific function, two C++ modules — one compiled with STRICT and the other compiled traditionally (that's how I refer to those files that have been translated without "#define STRICT") — will not work with the exact same type definition for HWND (for instance). This is precisely the primary purpose of STRICT: only an accurate definition of all used data types enables the compiler to perform a stricter type checking. The object files exporting the (then different) names of external functions can't be linked correctly to an application anymore. The linker gives error messages concerning external functions not found ("unresolved externals"). A detailed example in section 2.5 will give you more information on this problem.

STRICT is not as easy to implement for C++ sources.

The cleanest and most successful approach to a port is therefore in a first step to make older 3.0 codes (or normal 3.1 sources, respectively) STRICT compatible and then to tackle the port. This two-step method (kind of a "divide-and-conquer" strategy) is easier to master and rarely forces ad hoc solutions that can render big projects disordered and more difficult to maintain. However, considering merely the duration of the port, this approach will usually cost you some more time.

STRICT is best to start with.

At the very least, fully protected mode compatible!

Any developer wishing to get (or needing) fast results may wonder whether it is worthwhile to make his sources STRICT compatible under such circumstances. In spite of my fondness for this starting point, conventional source codes can of course be ported as well — to be honest, STRICT compatibility is *by no means* a Win32 precondition! It is difficult to give an appropriate answer: on the pro side is the fact that STRICT programs show much better type checking; the changes made by the developer render the code more accurate and automatically more portable. On the other hand, the time spent to make those changes and the fact that some of them are necessary for STRICT compatibility but not at all required for porting may be a good reason not to do so. Furthermore, the use of STRICT is of course not sufficient to detect and remove all possible portability problems.

Strictly speaking, STRICT is not a necessity.

The variant of STRICTifying source codes *during* the port should be the exception. My main objection to this method: since you'll have to deal with two processes at the same time, chances are that you'll lose the overview and fail to reach both goals in the scheduled time. I'd like to emphasize once again: STRICT is indeed highly preferable but not at all mandatory!

No multi-tasking, please!

At any rate, before beginning a port, I would expect *one* fundamental feature from my Windows 3.x sources: the program should run *absolutely errorfree* in the standard and enhanced Win16 modes (and preferably under Windows 3.1 because of the better run-time checks). Errorfree in this context doesn't mean bugfree, but without system crashes. I'd like to go even one step further and set as a further condition that the program should execute correctly under the debugging version of Windows 3.1.* Since the debug kernel is only included in the Microsoft SDK and many developers don't have access to it, I can only recommend using the debug kernel warmly to those who have installed the SDK. (I can't help it, so here is my personal opinion: Microsoft would do better to supply *all* developers with a free copy of the debugging kernel — via CompuServe, for instance. Since many application errors are identified as system errors (at least by inexperienced users), Windows has gained an even worse reputation than it deserves. But as long as MS doesn't achieve this remarkable feat, you'll possibly better have a go and purchase the Win16 SDK...)

* This special version offers numerous additional diagnostics for developers.

... the debug kernel is in fact indispensable for professional development.

As said, errorfree or correct means that the program runs without any UAEs (as shown in figure 2.2), general protection violations, or similar charming bugs. Faulty real-mode programs showing such symptoms under the Windows 3.x protected modes are *guaranteed* to fail after being ported to Win32. Since you are better acquainted with your 3.x development environment and have all the tools you need, it seems more logical to adjust old real-mode code to protected mode with Win16. The Win32 port should be done in a separate, second step.

UAE is the infamous "unexpected application error" (by the way: does anybody have an idea of what might be the opposite, namely an "expected" application error?).

I would give similar advice to all collectors of antiques who still have to fight with prehistoric 2.x remnants: first and foremost, make your program Windows 3.1 compatible with the familiar tools (think, for instance, that since 3.0 the system font is proportionally spaced!) before satisfying your 32-bit cravings. Don't underestimate the advantages of having mastered the environment and the tools, particularly in this case!

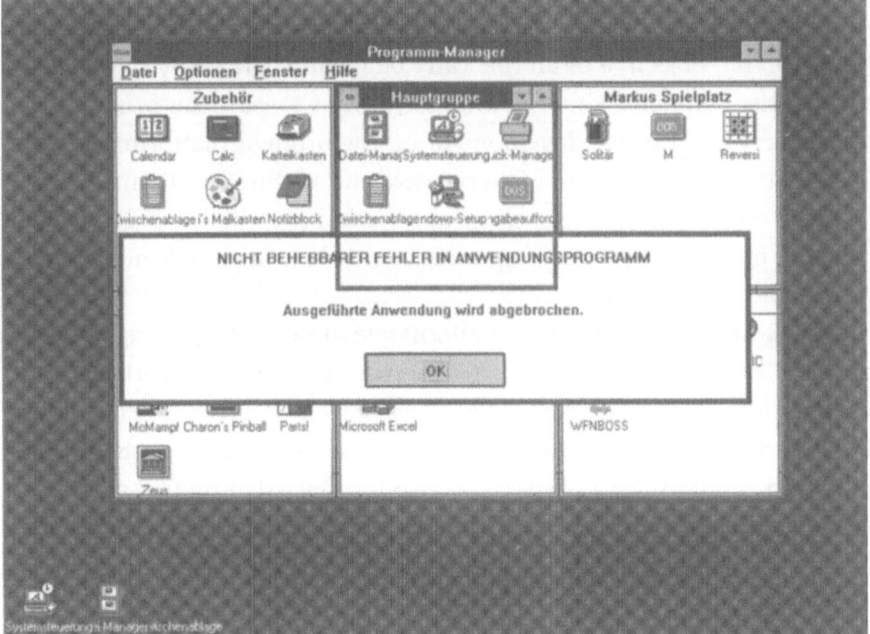

Figure 2.2: UAE: an alarming symptom.

K&R or ANSI C?

Here's another complication: what to do with remains of old code that are K&R C compatible but don't use the opportunities allowed by ANSI

Prototypes are essential.

C, for instance function prototypes? You should convert at least all function headers to ANSI C: working on a complex project (especially under Windows) without persistently using ANSI C prototypes shows much bravery indeed, but only a little insight. Also, observe the hints given in Chapter 3 to write portable source codes in (ANSI) C or C++.

Let's proceed to a first summary: the best starting point would be ANSI C prototypes combined with the STRICT option of Windows 3.1. In any case, errorfree code under 3.x in protected mode is better than nothing. If you happen to have enough time: first convert the sources to STRICT before porting to Win32. If not, do the best you can without STRICT. The knights of the pre-3.0 era have by far the worst position: they first have to adapt the application to 3.1 before even starting to think about Win32.

And the goal? Either one-way porting...

Just one Win32 EXE file?

Likewise, the objective of all this can't be formulated easily in one short and precise sentence: either you literally want to port the program and won't carry out further development on the original platform anymore. Or (what is probably more often the case and pictured in figure 2.3) you want to write and maintain your application for Win16 and Win32 in parallel, meaning that the program is available as a Win16 and a Win32 executable.

Or two: one for Win32, the other for Win16?

Let's first address the easier alternative of one-way porting. Here regardless of all the antiquated Win16 customs you can work and add changes just as you like: forget old non-portable 16-bit code, and replace it with adequate Win32 program text. On that occasion, you should look into your program for 16-bitisms — also for those that on first sight don't seem to affect its operation. Some examples: array indices and loop counters in short or WORD variables, code and data segment divisions as well as the alignment of self-defined data structures, including character or short components. Sooner or later, these constructions will become a nuisance: even if your application compiles perfectly and seems to run errorfree under Win32, some very serious traps could be hidden. Be aware that porting is completed successfully only when the whole application, including all options, was tested with a complete set of data (especially boundary cases) and operates errorfree. The fact that the 16-

Test, test, test!

bit implementation of an algorithm compiles cleanly and seems to work under 32 bit doesn't mean it is automatically flawless.

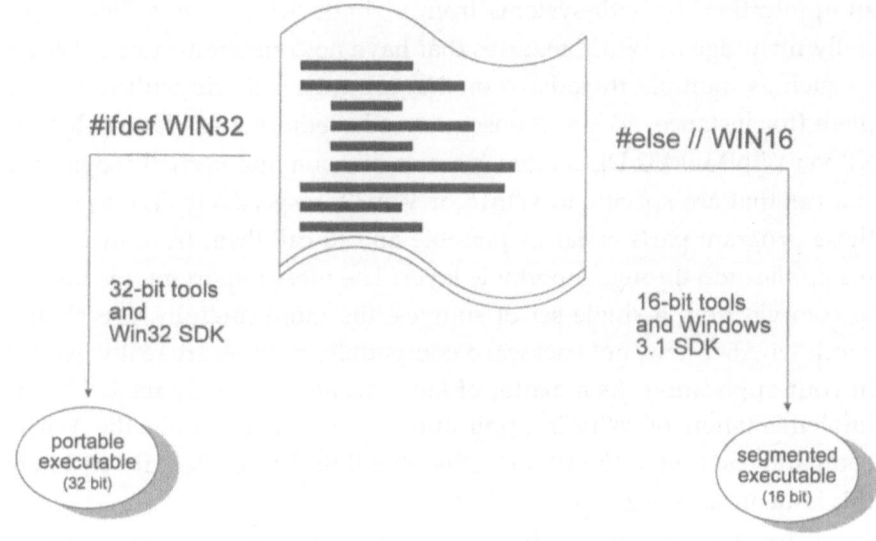

#ifdef WIN32

#else // WIN16

32-bit tools
and
Win32 SDK

16-bit tools
and Windows
3.1 SDK

portable
executable
(32 bit)

segmented
executable
(16 bit)

Figure 2.3: One set of sources, but two applications

... Or programming for Win16 and Win32?

The second alternative, namely producing a Win16 as well as a Win32 executable from one set of sources, is a bit more difficult to implement. You can find assistance for this task with three mechanisms: first, conditional compilation (via #ifdef and company), which unfortunately can become very complex and even counterproductive in lengthy program files. The second possibility may be more helpful: skillful macro definitions in the header files can elegantly be employed to hide many portability problems in the actual sources. This solution especially allows you to pack regularly used #ifdefs once into a separate macro definition (and remember: macros can easily be longer than one line). The third mechanism goes still further and isolates non-portable code in an independent function that has the same calling parameters (syntax) and the same functionality (semantics) under Win16 and Win32; the implementation, however, can be totally different. By consistently putting all port-

One set of sources — two executables

Conditional compilation

Portable macro definitions

A layer with helper functions

ability functions occurring during a porting project into a library of its own, you can make future porting work much easier.

In spite of all these measures, you won't always be able to compile an application for both systems from a single set of source files. Especially the usage of Win32 features that have no counterpart under Win16 — such as multiple threads — or that are extremely difficult to realize there (for instance, access to unsegmented memory areas larger than 64 KB via WINMEM32.DLL) often forces a division into partially separated sources that are specific to Win16 or Win32, respectively. Try to isolate those program parts as far as possible and to call them from the rest of the application through a portable layer. The more important it is for you to compile from a single set of sources, the more carefully you should check whether new, not backward compatible, features are really needed in your application. As a matter of fact, this area is closely related to the implementation of Win32s applications that can use only the Win16 compatible subset of the Win32 APIs. You'll find a detailed discussion of this issue in section 2.7, page 122.

Advanced Win32 features are bad for backward portability.

Corresponding to the two different objectives, you can recognize two independent problem areas: the first deals with the pure port, the other with portable programming and maintenance of two applications. While the first means an unique endeavor which will be finished by the end of the porting process (just a simple one-way port), the latter requires regular efforts to be done after the initial port in order to guarantee the compatibility with all target platforms. For the second I'll coin for want of a better word the name "portabilization." In any event, portable programming in the Windows environment must take into account two different levels: on the one hand, you have of course to fight the differences in the respective APIs, which are to be resolved through adequate formulation of the program texts. On the other hand, and this aspect is often underestimated, the pure transition from a 16-bit to a 32-bit system (that is to say, independently from the specifics of the underlying operating systems) demands certain features in the source codes. I'll discuss the problems associated with this question and give you some general advice and detailed hints in sections 3.4 to 3.7.

Just porting...

... or keeping sources backward portable?

2.2 Two Alternatives for Porting

"Whatever you do, do it wisely and consider the end!" Gesta Romanorum

Okay, so you are about to start your first porting project and want to create a working Win32 application from your Win16 source code base. How and where to start? Basically, you can choose one of two different ways: the first starts with the details to slowly climb to an ever-higher level (therefore called bottom up); the other is exactly the other way around: first the center or the most important part of the problem is identified and then broken down step by step to its finer details. This approach is, not surprisingly, called top down.

Either bottom up...

... or top down!

Bottom up

To port bottom up means that you adapt one source code file after the other to the Win32 API as far as possible and with the aid of the hints given in Chapters 3 and 4. Then you compile the file and according to error messages and warnings proceed to further changes, recompile, etc., until everything compiles and an object file is created. All source files are treated in this way (including the needed resources). Finally, all object files are linked, possible errors are removed, and the application is tested (presumably with the aid of a debugger). Each error found leads to new changes and to the recompilation of different source files until the program runs errorfree on all platforms it is designed for. Figure 2.4 on the next page shows the fundamental process.

First make all changes, then compile and debug!

Top down

Top down follows a totally different strategy: the first step is to realize a minimal running 32-bit program. You can do this by porting just the file containing the WinMain() function to Win32, so that it can be compiled and linked without errors. All function calls into other, not yet translated modules must therefore be either commented out or replaced by calls to empty functions (stubs). This procedure works best with a relatively clear modularization of the source codes — the extreme negative case here would be having only one giant, totally unstructured C file, thousands of lines long: in this case top down degenerates to bottom up.

First build a working nucleus and then enhance it.

*Figure 2.4: Bottom up —
from small to big.*

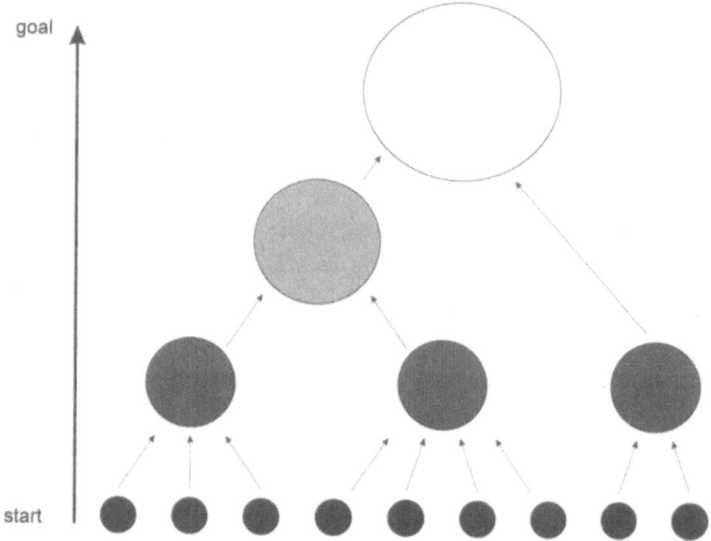

When the main program is done (it doesn't need to do much more than
create the top-level window and display the main menu),* the further
functionality of the application can be added step by step — in the ideal
case, one source code file after the other. The corresponding function
calls are added (or decommented) in the main file, the new program
code is tested and debugged, etc., until the whole application is ported.
How things happen top down is shown in figure 2.5.

* But it works at least!

Which method is better?

Of course, both solutions are greatly idealized cases: in real life each port
will have to combine elements of both strategies. But before starting,
you'll have to decide whether you first want to adapt your source code
files one after the other and then test the program as a whole or, the
other way around, if you wish to fill a working structure step by step
with life. My own experience shows that the top-down solution is best
fitted for a one-way port (e.g.,when you don't have to worry about
backward compatibility). There are three reasons for that: first, it enables
a controlled and stepwise adaptation of the program, which is very im-

*Top down — for three
reasons!*

Simpler debugging

portant for testing and debugging. Once a part of an application has been ported and debugged, it doesn't have to be considered later on (under normal circumstances). The developer can thus pay full attention to the next program part coming up, in order to implement it errorfree. This step-by-step approach corresponds more to the human way of thinking than does the rather stubborn and somewhat machinelike bottom-up method.

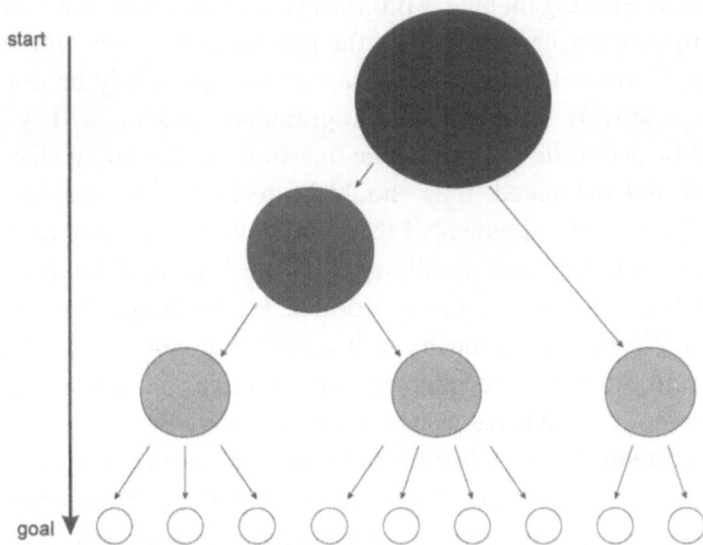

start

goal

Figure 2.5: Top down: a working center is expanded stepwise.

Second, top down has an important psychological effect: you don't fight for weeks and weeks as against windmills without a visible result. Instead quite rapidly you get your first success: a program that might not do much, but at any rate it is Win32 and it works! And every new feature built in, each successful debugging session puts you into an even better mood. The importance of such motivation can't be stressed enough!

And success is motivating!

Finally, top down also has advantages when porting extensive projects: once the main program shell and its interfaces have been defined and ported, a team of developers can port and debug each part rather independently from each other. Furthermore, the experience gathered during porting and especially testing of the very first program parts will be very valuable during further stages of the project.

Top down promotes teamwork and eases experience exchange.

But bottom up can have advantages...

The situation may be somewhat different if you have already gained some experience with the Win32 API and if you need the application for both Win16 and Win32: that means your source codes have to be backward compatible and you therefore have to "portabilize" them. In that case, bottom up definitely can have some advantages: with this method experienced developers can detect repeating code patterns in the sources much easier than with top down. Those should be isolated in a portability library or treated with conditional compilation and/or macro definitions. When working on bigger projects, you'll find another advantage of

... for instance with very large projects.

bottom up: the mechanical parts of the porting work — the monotonous changing of always similar code sequences — can easily be done by a group of relatively inexperienced programmers as long as they are supervised by senior developers. Once the source codes are in shape to be compiled and debugged, they should be rechecked by the developers who designed and implemented them in the first place. Due to the close interaction of testing and modifying, it is much more difficult to imple-

Define intermediary milestones!

ment such a division of labor top down. Try to design the bottom-up port of a Win16 application in such a way that certain milestones are defined and can be reached step by step. As already was mentioned, the positive effect of visible results is extremely motivating.

As you surely can tell from the preceding remarks, I clearly tend towards top-down porting. It can convert smaller projects orderly and

The proper mix is the trick!

very fast and eases the porting of bigger projects. However, a certain touch of bottom up can be very valuable depending on the circumstances and the developer's experience with Win32. A last piece of advice for the

First a simple project "to practice"...

first time: don't take a real application for your first porting project. Play with a simple and maybe even useless test program with perhaps two, at most three, modules and no more than about 1000 or 2000 lines (if you don't have such a small project at hand, just use one of the larger example programs that — hopefully — came with your development system).

Such a warm-up program can be carried out within a few days, even by developers who never worked under Win32 before. The experiences gained with the new 32-bit tools and the necessary changes made in the source codes do not only facilitate the porting of a bigger application but also enable you to accurately plan a real project and use a well-thought-out strategy.

2.3 Methodical Advice to Planning a Port

*"The trick is not to rush your head through the wall, but to find the door —
with your eyes." A saying attributed to Georg von Siemens*

If your application is a rather small project (about 5 to 10 source code
modules with a total of 5000 to 15,000 lines maximum), you won't have
to deal with the preparation and the planning of the port extensively.
Presumably, the simplest and quickest procedure will be the top-down
technique: first make the source codes STRICT compatible, then convert
the main program, make it work, and add the remaining program parts.
However, any other approach would be successful as well without a big
difference in the required effort.

Small projects: ready, set, go!

Big projects require some planning

Things look slightly different if you have either a big application or several small programs to port. In that case, you'd better think of an order,
some milestones, and a method of approach before you start with the
actual porting work.

- A clear strategy helps you to get the priorities right: it is best to
  implement program parts essential for the port (e.g., the code for
  the user interface, which normally involves most of the work) before the less difficult code (that is to say, code independent of the
  user interface).

  What's important?

- The complexity of the individual modules might also play a role in
  the porting order. Some developers like to begin with the heavy
  work, to get it done as fast as possible, some others solve the simple problems first before taking their time to tackle the real ones. It
  is certainly easier to convert some simple graphics routines than to
  port a complete window class that must be added to the dialog
  editor as a custom control. You should expect some difficulties,
  especially in the following cases:

  First the easy...

  ... or the difficult parts?

  - DLL programming including global window classes;
  - applications using their own (private) methods to communi-
    cate with other programs instead of standardized mechanisms
    such as DDE or OLE;

  Particularly nasty problem cases

- programs strongly tailored to the segmentation of Intel CPUs;
- applications written in system-specific ways (e.g., with heavy use of TOOLHELP functions).

What about helpers?
- Certain less complicated program parts can be isolated and translated by inexperienced helpers. This can save significant time in the project, especially with very big applications.

- Clearly defined milestones are very important, because they are (or should be!) comparatively easy to reach and are extremely motivating when achieved. That's also the main reason why milestones should be easy to visualize ("you have to see something").

Try not to be too perfect!
- During the porting of a program part, it is often better to choose a quick and temporary acceptable approach instead of wasting time with the search for an optimal solution. You should try to enhance your program only when it has been ported and proved to work correctly. You'll have a much better overview on the project and much more experience at that time, which will enable you to perform a quicker and more efficient reworking.

Regular exchange of information and experiences
- If several developers work together on a project, they should meet regularly to exchange information and experiences, especially at the beginning. Difficult problem cases can then be discussed and solved together.

- You should define confining guidelines and recommendations concerning repeating problem cases before starting the port in order to ensure uniform handling. These should be controlled and adjusted during the project.

Along the way, the sources can be improved.
- Last but not least: use the necessary source code renovations during porting, and try to integrate some basic improvements and changes to the sources, when they appear to be useful ("I've always wanted to change this..."). For instance this can result in a better modularization of the source code or a more consistent enforcement of specific programming guidelines, etc.

Translate the resources in the very first step.
In the very first stage of top-down porting, besides conversion of the main program, I would already make all the resources available, even if they are needed only very much later. Since the Win16 resource files are nearly 100 percent compatible with Win32, this way you can use all resources without big effort from the beginning and resource handling remains fully transparent throughout the rest of the project.

If the application to be ported still has to be available under Win16, you should work from the beginning on a mechanism in order to create and enhance a portability library. Such a library can save much time, especially when it is maintained and used by several developers working on the same project (however, this requires regular discussions among, and the consent of, all team members). Self-defined libraries have a further advantage: they contribute to making the source codes clearer, more uniform, and more consistent.

Extremely important: a portability library!

Self-defined guidelines and helper libraries

Besides genuine functions that deal with the portable use of certain areas of the Win32 API, portability libraries can also provide developers with macro definitions adapted to the actual target system. In a similar approach, global guidelines and requirements for the modification of certain constructions should be integrated into the header files as simple textual comments (see figure 2.6).

Figure 2.6: The components of a self-defined portability library

A rather convoluted example would be the possibility of designing the message handling in a more consistent and portable way through the strict use of a new macro layer (for C) or a class library (for C++). Actually, there *are* macros for this very purpose already defined by Microsoft — you'll find more information in sections 4.3 to 4.5 concerning WINDOWSX.H. With big projects, it is worth studying the basic concepts underlying these macros before starting the port and to adapt or enhance them for your own purposes. Of course, the same principle holds true for MFC, if you're developing in C++.

A cooking recipe

You should use the following outline in the form of a cooking recipe as a basis for your own planning. It does not consider any special adaptations and will certainly have to be modified or enhanced to cater for the circumstances of your project. Anyhow, this will give you a useful starting point:

#define STRICT

1. If at all possible, stay under Win16 for a while to make the application STRICT compatible and to remove all compiler diagnostics referring to portability problems (see also section 2.5, page 105 and section 3.8, page 178).

Adapt the main module.

2. Convert the main module: first the WinMain() function, then the windows procedure of the main window. When doing this, you should ignore messages or program parts that seem difficult or take too much time to convert. Comment all calls into other modules that have not been ported yet, or replace them with dummy functions. If necessary, make sure that all your changes are Win16 compatible (for instance, by using #ifdefs or by isolating in portability functions). Use this stage of the project to make all resources available.

Adjust your makefile and compile.

3. Adapt the makefile (when available) or the batch jobs, respectively, to compilation and linking with the Win32 tools. Now you can create the main module. Use the debugger to get an idea of whether or not the application operates correctly within the changed program parts. Identify and modify problem areas, change, and recompile the whole stuff. You'll have to repeat this procedure until the main module runs errorfree.

Add the remaining files stepwise.

4. Next, you'll have to add the missing modules and program parts in the order you think is best for your project. I would be especially cautious when adapting window or callback procedures, respectively, with all *global* memory management calls and non-

standard approaches to interprocess communications. Operate gradually and complete one job after the other. Areas that cannot yet be converted optimally should be modified at least in such a way that you can continue the port and marked for easy pick-up and optimization later on (for example: "// !!! Here, the problem is ... "). At really critical points use explanatory comments: often after porting the easier stuff, I found places marked with only one or two rather cryptic statements (e.g., "// !!! transformation?"). Then again, I had to brood over the source code for quite a while before I found out what was meant....

5. Very important: regularly check whether the program is still running errorfree. Make extensive tests after the actual porting job is finished. Doing that, you should pay particular attention to boundary cases or special boundary conditions. New features resulting automatically from the port (such as long filenames) should be checked very carefully. Extremely important is testing on all possible 32-bit platforms. If the program doesn't run properly on a particular system (e.g Win32s), then at any rate check the actual system at start-up and disable the execution under this platform!

   Regular testing

6. Wait before you integrate really new Win32-specific features until the program is completely ported and runs errorfree. When enhancing the program and writing new source code, keep in mind that certain features may not be available under Win32s or Win16.

   Include Win32 enhancements only after completing the port!

7. If necessary, make sure that the ported application also works correctly under Win16. Most of the time, an iterative component is necessary to have the program run equally well under all platforms.

   Check backward compatibility.

Conclusion: before you start to port larger projects, built a "road map" in which you can divide the whole project into several maintainable single steps. Set binding guidelines for the most important (about 95 percent) of the problem areas (see Chapters 3 and 4 for a detailed description). Bare in mind that the program functionality should *only* be enhanced if it doesn't influence the porting process negatively. And last but not least: if you meet a difficult problem, don't strive for an immediate perfect solution, just look for a momentarily acceptable one. You have enough time to improve the program after the porting process has been completed. In

Perfect — or just acceptable?

a sense this realization is just another consequence of the top-down method!

2.4 Tools and Other Assistance

"Why isn't software more like hardware? ... There should be catalogs of software modules: when we build a new system, we should be ordering components from these catalogs and combining them, rather than reinventing the wheel every time." M.D. McIllroy, Software Engineering Concepts and Techniques

Until now, this piously — already in 1968! — expressed wish withstood its realization very successfully. Real recycling of program code is winning importance only very slowly and until now has not been very effective. However, in the last few years, one branch of the industry has experienced what we could classify as a real boom: the market of add-on libraries trying to support the developer by dealing with certain clearly defined programming tasks. After all, Windows itself was also designed as an (admittedly giant) extension library, a simple (?) tool for easier (??) programming of graphical user interfaces.

Reusability of source code?

Add-on libraries as helpers

What does all this have to do with porting and portability? Very much indeed: in the tool market you can find an assortment of products promising help: they give you add-on functions as well as source code portability between different platforms. The same source code is assumed to be compilable and to work under MS-DOS, Windows, OS/2, UNIX, Macintosh, and who knows what else. Meanwhile, the manufacturers of the various development systems also offer additions — more or less abstracting from the Windows API (e.g.,Microsoft's Foundation Classes or Borland's ObjectWindows). These, to a certain extent, also enable portable programming. Alas (unfortunately, good things always have an "alas"), all this benefits only the (object-oriented) C++ developer. I don't know yet of any really usable and portable GUI library for C developers. There have been a few starts, but most manufacturers of add-on tools concentrate on the supposedly more attractive C++ market. I have to admit that C++ is gaining (justified) importance; I also realize that this

Portability as product?

C? What's that?

language is better suited for the creation of portable class libraries than C. But yet, most companies on the tool market ignore the fact that the prevailing part of all applications is written in C code and naturally has to be maintained in this form. Even a completely revamped and new coded system as our study case Windows NT is still written mostly in C. The only considerable exception is the Graphics Device Interface (GDI) which was almost completely written in C++.

Microsoft itself missed out on this opportunity; with the great success of Windows 3.0, a systematic shell around the Windows API would have greatly eased development, especially for C programmers. There are very few, very tentative approaches into this direction: on the one hand, you'll find the Hungarian notation (see section 2.6 on page 113), on the other hand, we have the macro definitions in WINDOWSX.H that first appeared in Windows 3.1 and were in fact created only as an aid to porting to the Win32 API!

And what did Microsoft do?

Not enough!

If your programs are mainly written as C source, you presumably won't profit much from C++ class libraries easing portable GUI programming. You have to carry the main work of porting to Win32 (or of portabilization, respectively) on your shoulders. Nevertheless, you can try to adapt parts of your application to C++ step by step and to incorporate a useful class library. However, the effort for such an adaptation (including learning C++) can be much more significant than just porting your application from Win16 to Win32!

Porting is easier than recoding in C++ classes.

And what about class libraries for C++?

How does the situation look for C++ developers? I will give some basic information on the subject "class libraries for portable programming," but space doesn't permit me to explain in detail technical finesse or to discuss actual class libraries.

Some basic observations

For most products, the more or less noticeable benefit of portability is achieved at the expense of flexibility. A portable tool can really adequately support only the smallest common denominator of all supported systems. The more features two different systems have in common, the better they can be integrated under one (portable) roof. However, the more differences they show, and the more systems you have to support, the smaller will be the library core that is really 100 percent portable — even when the product tries to emulate certain features. (I won't mention

Portability gain — loss of flexibility

here such basic structural differences as multi-threading: the portable implementation of threads under standard UNIXes and Win16 alike should prove pretty exciting.) Therefore, if you need some standardized elements of a specific user interface outside the scope of the class library you are employing, you'll have to leave safe grounds (see figure 2.7 farther down).

Mixing of portable classes and low-level calls?

Furthermore, not all libraries support the unrestricted use of low-level system calls or the mixture with their own high-level portable classes, respectively. Apart from that, all system-specific program parts must be isolated from the portable rest of the program on a somewhat modular basis.

Steep learning curve

Second, learning the underlying development and class model of your tool is often quite difficult and costs much in time. This statement is of course also valid for the Windows API as such and for OS/2 or UNIX programming. However, there you can find a wide variety of helpers: books, example programs, articles in computer magazines, etc., on the market which make life much easier. You might often have difficulties finding similar information or advice for a relatively infrequently used add-on library or tool.

Figure 2.7: The intersection of the three APIs defines the range of a really portable class library!

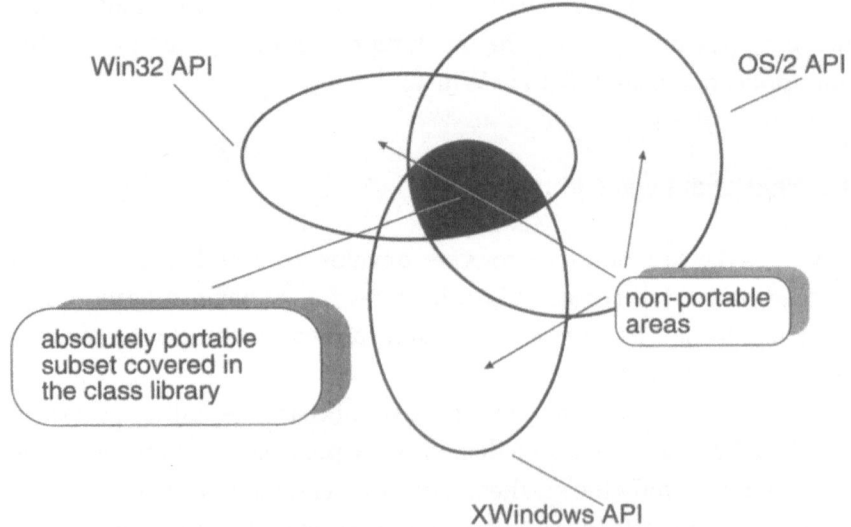

Third, to promote portability with a class library often means to get dependent on a certain manufacturer — and this in two ways. On the one hand, you are limited to their user interfaces or supported APIs, respectively. If your end users or market pressure ever requires another system which is not readily supported, you are left alone with your porting problem. On the other hand, you should choose an economically healthy manufacturer in order to be able to maintain updates of your products for the latest systems in the future.

Dependence from the manufacturer

Fourth, even the best library is not exactly of great help if you have to maintain and/or port an already existing application. Depending on your target platform, it might turn out to be much easier to simply port the application rather than convert to a class library, which as shown in the first point might not solve all the problems of portable programming either. This is the case with relatively similar systems such as Win16 and Win32. But when the particular APIs simply differ too much, the gap between simple porting or converting to a class library may be reduced so much that it can be worth converting to C++ classes because of the higher degree of portability. (By the way: the C++ language itself is by no means more portable than ANSI C. The whole discussion relates to the use of portable class libraries under C++.)

Always troublesome: adaption of existing programs.

Net result: in spite of all these critical remarks, I'd like to stress the fact that class libraries can make porting and especially portable programming *much* easier. Their optimal use in an actual situation depends on your ability to find the most suitable tool for your task. Ah, you mean, this is a truism? Well, just ask yourself how much time you invested to select your specific development system from all the others available for Windows. Or to put it differently: can you explain, based on a trustworthy product evaluation with clearly defined objectives, why you are working with this certain compiler, editor, class library, or linker? The often helpless shoulder shrugging* when asked these questions proves that this "truism" is still too often ignored….

Class libraries can be extremely useful.

** … or even worse:
"Because it was the cheapest product!"*

More tools: PORTTOOL and the SDK documentation

Back to the tools: besides numerous add-on libraries, you can find many other tools facilitating porting and portable programming. A special Win32 helper program from Microsoft may be somewhat important: it is called PORTTOOL (see figure 2.8), is supplied with the Win32 SDK, and

PORTTOOL searches for non-portable code.

supports more or less effective porting of Win16 applications to the Win32 API. The program (whose source code is even found on the SDK CD-ROM) enables loading a source code file into a simple text editor. This editor has only one unusual characteristic: it can detect all kinds of non-portable constructions or other things seemingly suspect in the source code. But don't believe that Microsoft has invented a clever algorithm! No, very much in the usual style of the company, brute force is used: PORTTOOL only searches the source code for certain keywords, and the editor window displays the found places with an informative comment. The developer (you!) still has to do most of the job. Unfortunately, this tool quite often finds issues that are entirely correct and do not need to be changed at all. Furthermore, its implementation is quite erroneous.* Alas, the name PORTTOOL promises much more then the implementation can realize.

* Possibly this is the reason for making the sources available!?

Figure 2.8: PORTTOOL at work

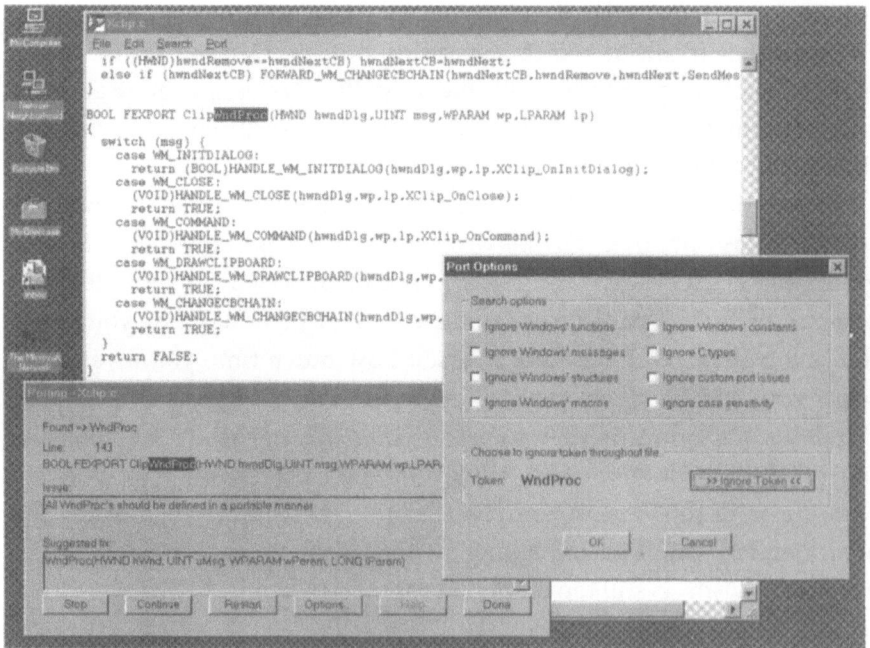

At least the detection of critical spots is based on a freely editable text file, which is read in by the program at the beginning. This file is named PORT.INI and is located in the subdirectory X:\MSTOOLS\BIN\).** PORT.INI contains the literal names and further information concerning most of the important non-portable constructions. You'll find a much

** "X:" is the drive where you installed the SDK tools.

enhanced version of this file in Appendix 2 and on the enclosed disk, including all the advice, tips and tricks given in Chapters 3 and 4.

A small booklet supplied with the Win32 SDK documentation with the very promising title "Programming Techniques" (especially Chapters 1, 5, 6 and 7) can also be considered a tool. You won't find anything new in that booklet after reading this book, but it's nevertheless a pleasant reading, particularly because the author(s) are sometimes unintentionally comical: "Although not absolutely required you should name the parameters in your function prototypes. This improves the readability of header files and introduces a certain amount of self-documentation as well." Even a very cautious look into various Microsoft header files demonstrates that some MS developers haven't yet read this breathtaking advice...

SDK documentation

The whopping 30+ MB WinHelp files describing the Win32 API are another important source of SDK information (you'll find it under X:\MSTOOLS\HELP*.HLP). Compared to the printed documentation, they have the advantage of being up to date; the search for certain information is considerably faster, and access to the Win32 API is eased thanks to many introductions — called overviews — to new or enhanced features.

A BIG help: the WIN32 API help.

Tools for developers coming from OS/2

Microsoft is *much* more concerned about OS/2 developers than about Win16 programmers when it comes to porting. In order to have the OS/2 group jump onto the 32-bit Windows bandwagon, the company has provided a whole collection of free utilities and support information as well as a separate section in the CompuServe forum for Win32(s) developers only dealing with OS/2 porting problems (see next paragraph for more information about this forum). Part of the tools needed for OS/2 programs are indeed superfluous for Win16 programmers (e.g., a tool to translate the different resource formats), but I can't help it: Microsoft undertakes huge efforts to win as many OS/2 developers for Win32 as possible. Section 2.8 will give you a detailed overview and some hints concerning the porting process of OS/2 programs to Win32 (text mode and Presentation Manager). The Microsoft tools are briefly described there, too.

For detailed information, see section 2.8.

CompuServe, a gold mine of information

I already mentioned the online service CompuServe as a further source
of information and support (see figure 2.9).

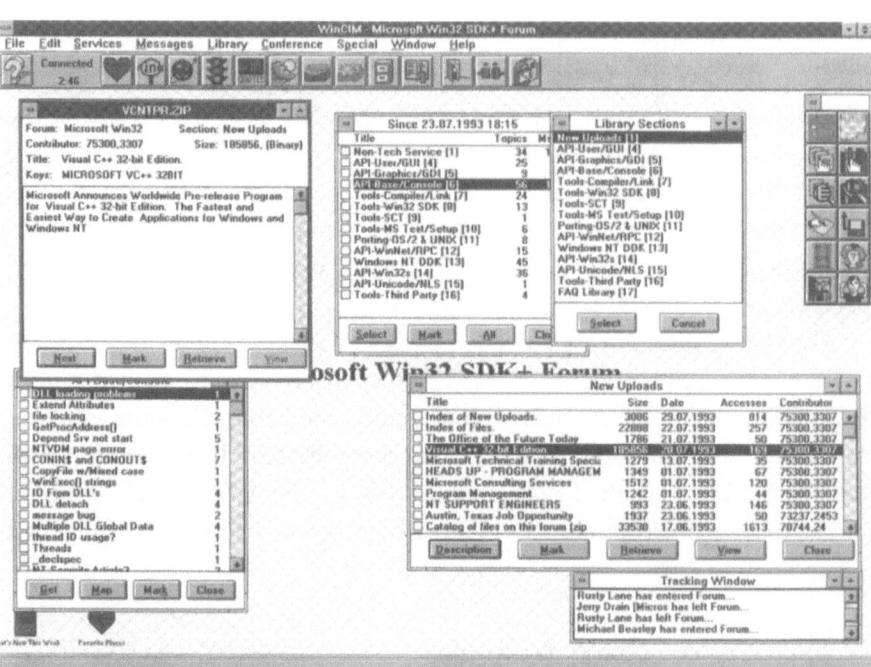

Figure 2.9: A view into the CompuServe forum MSWIN32, created especially for Win32 developers.

Get in touch with other developers and the MS staff. If you're not yet a member, I would strongly advise to subscribe as soon
as possible. CompuServe has many advantages for Win32 developers:
the connection to the Win32 support group in Redmond is much faster
and more direct. By attending the public CompuServe discussion fora,
you can get in touch with Microsoft employees and other developers
worldwide and exchange information, views, and opinions. You can ask
questions, and most of the time, there will be someone able to give you
tips or advice (or somebody knows someone, who knows somebody...).

Furthermore, most important manufacturers feed those fora with
significant information and hints about their products (in some cases
Important fora: MSWIN32 even updates are available). As far as we're concerned, the following
and WINNT. Microsoft fora are particularly interesting: WINNT is for all questions
and problems concerning Windows NT as an end-user product, and
MSWIN32 is for developers dealing with Win32 programming (there, in
library #10 "Porting — OS/2 and UNIX," you'll find the above mentioned

OS/2 tools). If you happen to get stuck, you'll (almost) always find an open ear with the mostly competent Microsoft employees as well as other forum members. And still another advantage: new drivers, product updates, and even patches for developer's tools, etc. occurring between the different SDK releases are distributed basically via MSWIN32, library #6 "Tools — Compiler/Linker" as well as library #7 "Tools — Win32 SDK." Okay, since I'm not a sales representative of CompuServe, I'll interrupt this advertisement now…

2.5 STRICT Software, Portable Software

"#define STRICT" Anonymous, in numerous Windows source code files

After praising the various advantages of the STRICT option in several places, in this section I finally want to describe what you can expect from this important "tool," how you can use it, and what you have to pay attention for.

STRICT was unfortunately not introduced until the release of the Windows 3.1 SDK; it enables a C/C++ compiler to perform a much more accurate and thorough type and error checking during function calls, assignments, etc. For this purpose, lots of Windows-specific data types and a bunch of function prototypes are defined completely differently than without STRICT. The option is switched on when the constant STRICT is #defined just before the first Windows header file (usually WINDOWS.H) is #included:

Exactly what does STRICT do?

```
#define STRICT  // this simple #define activates STRICT
// and after that the usual #include:
#include <windows.h>
// as well as additional header files
#include <ddeml.h>
```

A specific example for a redefinition through the use of STRICT: in Windows 3.0 (and 3.1 without STRICT), an HWND (handle to a window) and an HINSTANCE (an instance handle) are defined simply as an unsigned int. Thus, the compiler has not the slightest chance to warn you if you (erroneously or not) try to fake a function like DestroyWindow() by calling it with an HINSTANCE parameter instead of an HWND. Now,

For instance HWND and HINSTANCE

switching to STRICT means that instead of a simple unsigned int, a whole C structure is defined and a NEAR pointer type to this struct is used instead as the handle type. And with the help of these typed pointers, which indicate different struct definitions, the compiler can easily detect that an HWND has nothing to do with an HINSTANCE and with a warning will bring your attention to the improper use.

Prototype redefinition
Some function prototypes are defined differently with STRICT; the most prominent example is probably WinMain():

```
#ifdef STRICT
    int PASCAL WinMain(HINSTANCE,HINSTANCE,LPSTR,int);
#else
    int PASCAL WinMain(HANDLE,HANDLE,LPSTR,int);
#endif
```

Pointer or handle?
The more specific HINSTANCE is used instead of the generic HANDLE for the two first parameters. Here is another, more interesting case where you can observe that an HHOOK (STRICT) is in reality a pointer to an HOOKPROC (traditional):

```
#ifdef STRICT
    HHOOK   WINAPI SetWindowsHook(int,HOOKPROC);
    LRESULT WINAPI DefHookProc(int,WPARAM,LPARAM,HHOOK FAR*);
#else
    HOOKPROC WINAPI SetWindowsHook(int,HOOKPROC);
    LRESULT WINAPI DefHookProc(int,WPARAM,LPARAM,HOOKPROC FAR*);
#endif
```

Typed callback functions
The callback function types like WNDPROC, DLGPROC or (as already shown) HOOKPROC are another area where STRICT leads to numerous more appropriate type definitions. While those callback types are normally defined as FARPROC (and therefore would accept anything as arguments), in the STRICT world they get defined with all parameter types spelled out. This enables the compiler to check if any incoming callback function has the correct number, order, and type of parameters.

The COMSTAT and DCB structs ANSI compatible
The COMSTAT and DCB structures are not ANSI C compatible in the 3.0 version of WINDOWS.H (what a horror!); this also changes STRICTly with the 3.1 version. And after various tries, Microsoft finally achieved a *truly remarkable* feat: at last I'm able to compile their own

header files (but only those in the 3.1 SDK) *without any annoying warning
diagnostics* at /W4 (the highest warning level). Unfortunately, the newer
Win32 header files are not that far yet: the 32-bit compiler keeps spitting
out bunches of warnings with /W4 as it always did before....

It is very interesting and can also be useful for your porting work to
inspect the Windows header files (both in the 16- and 32-bit versions) for
places where STRICT is used. In this way you can discover, for instance,
that there are two macros to define specific handle types: the first, DE-
CLARE_HANDLE, creates a plain 16-bit handle; the second, DECLA-
RE_HANDLE32, (not surprisingly) a 32-bit handle (which in most cases
will be a FAR pointer to an internal data structure). Depending on the
setting of STRICT, these macros automatically define a handle, either as
an untyped scalar data type (UINT or DWORD, respectively) or as a
pointer (NEAR or FAR, respectively) to an internal structure. If you wish
to define more STRICT handle data types for your own purposes, you
should definitely use these macros.

*The two macros DE-
CLARE_HANDLE and
DECLARE_HANDLE32*

Okay, STRICT! But what's the best way?

What's the best way to render a source file STRICT compatible? Unfortunately, a bit more than what you and I would presumably like to do. But
nevertheless, your program will become much safer and more portable
with STRICT. Beside that, the conversion to STRICT helped me to detect
some genuine programming errors, which sooner or later would have
caused me some severe headaches. A word of advice: if you decide to
port your source codes to Win32 and want to make them STRICT compatible at the same time, I would strongly recommend doing so under
Windows 3.1, as you are acquainted with that system, know your tools,
and won't have to ruminate for ages over some strange, cryptic error
messages just to discover that you forgot the compiler switch
/QZrt%4!@axy ....

*STRICTifying is better done
under Win16.*

The conversion process itself can be divided into five single steps.
Steps 1 (not necessary if you worked with the highest warning level al-
ready), 2, and especially 5 will cost you relatively much time and effort.
So, let's go!

Five single steps

1. Modify your makefile(s) in such a way that the compiler uses the
    strictest possible warning level (Microsoft C: /W4, Borland C: -w).

*Compile with the highest
warning level.*

107

Recompile your application and save the resulting diagnostics in a file. Examine the warnings and error messages and modify your source codes accordingly, so that all messages indicating errors based on dubious constructions or non-portable code disappear (see the hints in section 3.8, page 178). Make sure that your application still runs correctly after that step!

Replace all usage of generic data types.

2. Replace all generic data types, such as HANDLE, LONG, WORD, etc., both in your C source files and in the function prototypes (provided there are some; see next issue!) with the new, more specific types. This doesn't mean that types such as LONG, WORD, etc., should disappear from your source code at all. All places where a LONG or WORD variable is really needed will of course remain unchanged. But certain places have to be changed in any case. The list in table 2.1 gives more information on the most important modifications:

Table 2.1: The most important data type conversions for STRICT

Original	Depending on the situation, may be changed to
HANDLE	HINSTANCE, HMODULE, HGLOBAL, HLO-CAL, HTASK, HMENU, HPEN, etc.
WORD	WPARAM (if third argument of a WNDPROC)
WORD	UINT (if not third argument of a WNDPROC)
LONG	LPARAM (if fourth argument of a WNDPROC)
LONG	LRESULT (if result type of a WNDPROC)
FARPROC	WNDPROC, DLGPROC, WNDENUMPROC, TIMERPROC, HOOKPROC, etc.

Three possibilities for type WORD:

WPARAM

UINT

WORD

Here, a comment about the (overused) type WORD is in order: you have to distinguish among three different situations. Either it describes the third argument of a windows callback function, in which case you should use a WPARAM instead. Or a WORD variable is used as counter, index, length specification, etc. In this case, you'll replace it with a UINT (which is 16 bit under Win16 and 32 bit under Win32). The third, rare case would be that you effectively need a 16-bit variable under Win32 too: then you just continue to use the type WORD (since WORD remains an unsigned short). Here is another consideration: the replacement of LONG with LRESULT (or LPARAM, respectively), and of WORD with WPARAM in window procedures can possibly be delayed, as the concerned data types are identical under Win16 even with STRICT. Under Win32 this is quite different: there WORD and WPARAM are not identical anymore! In this context, I'd like to refer you to Appendix 1, where you'll find a summary of the most important data types in the Win16 and Win32 APIs and their changes (also taking STRICT into account).

3. You should provide ANSI C compatible prototypes for all functions, even those that are called in one module only, *without a single exception*. In the case of statically declared (local) functions it is sufficient when the prototype appears at the beginning of the C module in which they are defined; prototypes for externally known functions should be isolated into a header file that can be read by all source code modules. You should *never* copy the required prototypes out of header files into your C source files: each future change has to be repeated in dozens or even hundreds of files, which could very well end up as a nightmare.

Consistently use prototypes!

The Microsoft C compiler offers an option (/Zg) to extract function prototypes from a C file, which I don't believe to be of great value, however. Since the prototypes appear without the names of the function parameters, you only see the pure type information; this is of course completely sufficient for the compiler to check the parameter types. But as even the Microsoft documentation guys know (see above) the expressiveness of a function declaration depends not only on the types but also on the parameter names. This doesn't help the compiler, but it is extremely convenient for the developer! And to make the whole situation even more convoluted, the compiler reduces all parameter definitions to their individual basic types! This too is formally correct and doesn't disturb the compilation process any further, but as a result, the mechanically produced prototypes can't be decrypted by any normal human being. The following comparison (with STRICT switched on) shows you what to expect:

Better create prototypes "by hand" than with compiler aid.

```
// Without parameter names, but at least comprehensible
HWND WINAPI CreateWindowEx(DWORD,LPCSTR,LPCSTR,DWORD,
    int,int,int,int,HWND,HMENU,HINSTANCE,void FAR*);


// With option /Zg: have fun with the decoding...
external const struct HWND__ near *CreateWindowEx(
```

```
unsigned LONG,const char FAR*,const char FAR*,
unsigned LONG,int,int,int,int,
const struct HWND__ near*,const struct HMENU__ near*,
const struct HINSTANCE__ near*,void FAR*);
```

As a matter of fact, the "manual" creation of prototypes with a *real* programmer's editor (does mean: *not* something like Windows Notepad...) can be done without problem simply by copying line after line into the header file (see figure 2.10). By definition a real editor is able to process several files simultaneously. In this way the declarations remain readable and self-documenting:

Figure 2.10: Line by line copying of function headers

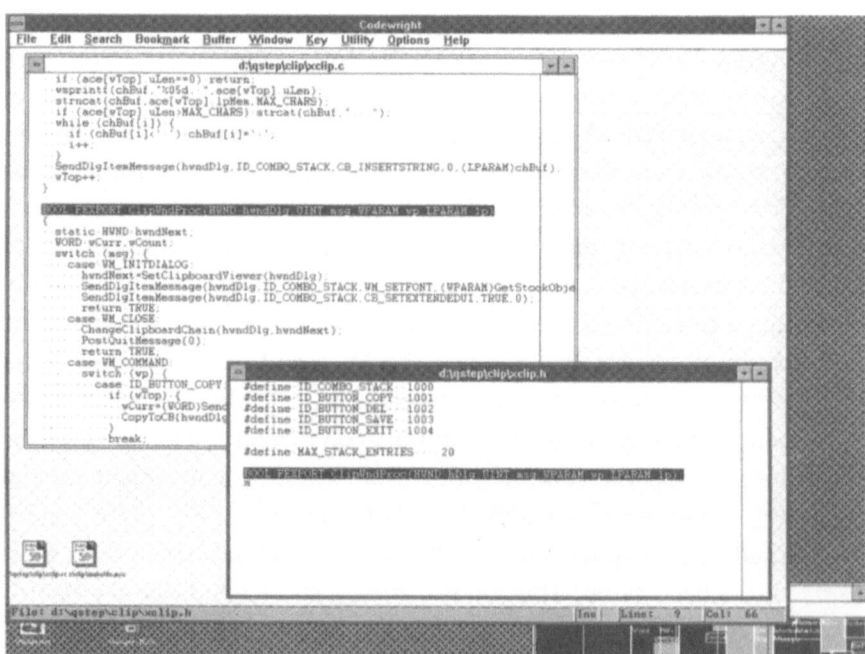

Recompile again.

4. The application is completely recompiled once more (still without STRICT) and possible warnings (which should be very few by now) are eliminated. Make sure that the program still operates correctly.

Now the goal of all the work: #define STRICT.

5. Now, you have to define STRICT either in all modules simultaneously or, what seems more sensible, in one C module after the other. After recompiling a file, remove all errors and warnings until you get an object file without any serious warnings. After

having done that for all files, check once more to see if the application is running properly. If everything works, you are finished; otherwise you'll have to start the debugger.

Some hints for C++ programmers

As already mentioned above, C developers don't have to modify all their source code files to use STRICT. Some files can be converted later on, some only partially or even not at all. Alas, it is mostly true that in contrast, C++ sources have to be converted at once — *all* modules in a single step. But there is one exception: all functions explicitly defined as ' extern "C" ' can be called from files compiled with STRICT or from conventional files alike. The reason is the different generation of external function names: normally, a C++ compiler will append some character combination to the actual source code function name, indicating the number of parameters and the parameter types. This feature is used for the implementation of overloaded functions and for typesafe linking and is known as "name mangling." The linkage statement ' extern "C" ' tells the C++ compiler simply to forget about this nice modification. A simple example says often more than a thousand words:

C developers can STRICTify file by file.

C++ programs on the other hand have to be converted in one step.

Exception: ' extern "C" '.

```
// first function regular (with normal C++ linkage)
LONG FAR PASCAL Proc1(HWND hwnd,WORD msg,WORD wP,LONG lP);
LONG FAR PASCAL Proc1(HWND hwnd,WORD msg,WORD wP,LONG lP)
{
   return DefWindowProc(hwnd,msg,wP,lP);
}
// second function with external "C" (C linkage)
extern "C" LONG FAR PASCAL Proc2(HWND hwnd,WORD msg,
   WORD wP,LONG lP);
extern "C" LONG FAR PASCAL Proc2(HWND hwnd,WORD msg,
   WORD wP,LONG lP)
{
   return DefWindowProc(hwnd,msg,wP,lP);
}
```

The source code is first compiled without STRICT and contains two externally known functions with absolutely identical parameters. The only

"name mangling" live

difference is found in the linkage statement ' extern "C" ' used by Proc2().
And here are the compiler-generated names: function Proc1() gets
@Proc1$QUIUSUSL (Borland) or ?Proc1@@YAJPAXGGJ@Z (Microsoft),
respectively, where the lengthy string after PROC1 represents the type
information mentioned (as you can see, the details of name mangling
aren't exactly standardized). On the other hand, the second function is in
both cases simply called PROC2, which, apart from being in capital letters (caused by the PASCAL calling sequence) is the same name as the
one appearing in the source codes. The whole thing starts to get tricky
when this file is recompiled with #define STRICT.

The resulting names: Proc1() is changed into the Borland tapeworm
@Proc1$QPX6HWND_USUSL, and Microsoft is even worse with
?Proc1@@YAJPBUHWND_@@GGJ@Z. Proc2() stays the same and is
still called PROC2 in both cases. Figure 2.11 explains how the names are
formed:

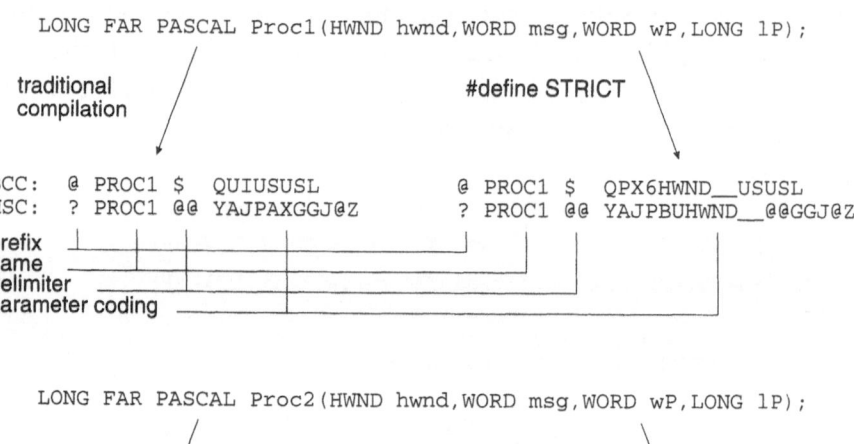

*Figure 2.11: Function names
with and without STRICT*

Now at last it should become obvious why ordinary C++ functions (or
function calls respectively) cannot be compiled and linked in one file
with and in another without STRICT: the external names generated for
the function and placed in the object files are completely different! But,

as already said, all functions defined as ' extern "C" ' can be called by C and C++, while using STRICT. This means that all Windows functions are no problem (luckily...) because they are all defined with ' external "C" ' (as shown in WINDOWS.H). So, if you want to make your C++ source code STRICT, you can concentrate on your own function declarations.

A last word to conclude this: if at all possible, start a Win32 port with STRICT source codes. The change may sometimes be very laborious, but it essentially eases the port because it enables you to concentrate later on the really important differences, while the compiler will deal with the gory details of data type compatibility.

First get STRICT sources, then port.

2.6 Naming of Variables: The Hungarian Variant

"You may also notice that some of the variables in HELLOWIN.C have peculiar-looking names." Charles Petzold, Programming Windows 3.1

Yes indeed, Charles, we have noticed. And we've noticed even more: this somewhat strange naming scheme is also used throughout (nearly) all example programs and some function prototypes as well as in the SDK reference manuals. If you are already working with this methodology, also called Hungarian notation,* you can just browse through this section or even continue immediately with the next one. If not, I would advise you first to study the following explanations and examples attentively, and second to implement them consistently in your programs: you'll get *much* better program code! Really!

* Named after C. Simonyi, a Microsoft programmer born in Hungary

Advantages of Hungarian notation

Briefly explained, the Hungarian notation is a (partially) formalized method to name program items such as variables and (to a lesser extent) functions in a consistent way. It has the following advantages:

- Through the uniform use of the same or very similar names, your program code will become much easier to read, to comprehend, and to maintain. This is especially important for source code, which has to be understood and maintained by other persons than the original creator or team workers.

Improves readability and eases maintenance.

113

- The variable name, consisting of several parts, informs you about its type and purpose, which improves the readability and, above all, enables error prevention and recognition.
- As it is nearly always the case, using an effective and consistent methodology saves time and thinking effort and enables the developer to concentrate on the essential things.
- The porting process is also eased: a "Hungarian" will detect much faster critical spots where a variable is used inconsistently to its Windows type definition (for example an assignment like npString = wOffset, which under Win32 actually is dangerous).

Alas, using such a scheme has some (minor) disadvantages: it has to be learned at first, the typing work is slightly increased, and if some global types happen to change (which, nevertheless, happens seldom), you may have to change whole batteries of variable definitions. The naming scheme is also not precise in the scientific sense: a compiler wouldn't cope very well with the somewhat informal definition; furthermore, many developers have modified or enhanced the scheme in the course of time to adapt it optimally to their needs.

However, I think that this system is one of the (very few) useful approaches to ease and systemize Windows programming for C developers. The times are gone when we could hack in a 100-line program quickly; nowadays, with exorbitantly complex and broad-ranged APIs such as Win16 and even more so with Win32, the developer should use any chance to structure his program texts and, in order to save brain work, thereby utilize a well-thought-out methodology to consistently prepare his source code (in the ideal case, such a scheme would not only cover the naming of variables). Unfortunately, in this respect Microsoft has not exactly been a champion and has never originated a really comprehensive and useful methodology. Anyhow, there are some basic regulations and conventions to make Windows programming easier: Hungarian notation is probably the best known and most important of them.

The best sign to show the significance and purpose of this naming scheme could be the fact that most developers I know have fully accepted the Hungarian notation (after initial skepticism) and most use it now even in their non-Windows programs, too. I never heard of a developer abandoning this scheme after having experienced its advantages. So, how does this strange but powerful method really work?

More to the utilization

According to Simonyi, a variable name consists of three parts: an optional qualification (array, pointer, counter, etc.), a standardized type abbreviation, and the actual name of the variable, which in simple cases can be omitted (figure 2.12 on page 118 shows the naming scheme and some examples). The following important type abbreviations have been defined by Microsoft:

Three-part variable names: qualification, type abbreviation and the actual name.

Abbreviation	Data type	Explanation
b	BYTE	Unsigned 8-bit value
ch	char or CHAR	Single character, 8-bit value signed
dw	DWORD	Unsigned 32-bit value
f	BOOL	Boolean value (FALSE or TRUE)
fn	FARPROC, etc.	Pointer to a (callback) function
fs	short or int	Value with a maximum of 16-bit flags
fl	LONG or int	Ditto with 32-bit flags
h	HANDLE, etc.	Base type for various handle types
hwnd, hdc	HWND, HDC	Handle types: window, device context, etc.
i, n	int or INT	16- or 32-bit integer, depending on system
l	LONG	Signed 32-bit value
sz	char[] etc.	Zero-terminated character string
u	UINT	Unsigned 16- or 32-bit value, depending on the system
v	void or VOID	Typeless (untyped) variable (for pointer use)
w	WORD	Unsigned 16-bit value
x, y	int or LONG	X/Y coordinate for graphics output

Table 2.2: Hungarian notation I: abbreviations of simple data types.

The entry for HWND and HDC in table 2.2 represents a series of handle types such as HMENU, HICON, etc., which have respective abbreviations. The actual part of the name describing meaning and purpose of the variable is attached to the type abbreviation with mixed use of capital and small letters. Here you can indulge in flights of fancy. Some examples:

The name part describes meaning and purpose.

szFilename	character string, contains a filename
fQuit	BOOL, indicating the end of the program
flWinCreate	flags (overall 32) for CreateWindow()
xCntr, yCntr	coordinates for the center of a circle
hwndDlg	window handle of a dialog box
hdcPrint	device context for the printer
chLast	last character read
lParam	LONG parameter of a windows procedure

Besides these standard abbreviations for simple data types, Microsoft has also determined some short cuts corresponding to structures. The list in table 2.3 shows some of the more important C structs, you can easily get more details from the Windows header files.

Table 2.3: Hungarian notation II: type abbreviations for important data structures.

Abbreviation	Based on following data structure
dlit	DLGITEMTEMPLATE
msg	MSG
ps	PAINTSTRUCT
pt	POINT
rc	RECT
tm	TEXTMETRIC
wc	WNDCLASS

Local variables   Just locally defined variables are often used without a name part of their own (e.g., HDC hdc; PAINTSTRUCT ps;). Here too are some examples:

wcMyClass	window class structure
ptCntr	POINT for the center of a circle
rcClientArea	RECT to describe the client area

We still have to discuss the optional qualification, placed in front of the type abbreviation and indicating, for example, whether the variable represents a NEAR or FAR pointer or an array. Additionally, qualifications for specific purposes have been defined. Table 2.4 contains an overview of the most important:

Qualification	Meaning
a	Array
c	Counter
i	Index value (e.g., into an array)
lp	FAR pointer (4 byte under Win16)
np	NEAR pointer (2 byte under Win16)
p	Pointer (size memory model dependent under Win16)

Table 2.4: Hungarian notation III: important qualifications.

A few explicit examples (based on the simple definitions given above) certainly won't do any harm to our understanding:

lpszFileName	FAR pointer to a character string
lpfnWndProc	FAR address of a windows procedure
achFilename	character string (by the way, szFilename has a slightly different meaning)
npfQuit	NEAR pointer to a BOOL
ahwndDlg	array of dialog box handles
iLast	index on the last character read
cx, cy	width or height of a window

You can make quite complicated and incomprehensible names by (recursively) mixing qualification, type abbreviations, and the part of the name (e.g., ialpalpszFilename,* all clear?). Furthermore, these abbreviations are not always unambiguous — chMem is either a character (ch-Mem) or a handle counter (c-h-Mem). But most of the time, you can immediately tell from the naming part and/or the context which data type is hidden behind an abbreviation. If you haven't tried to implement the Hungarian notation in your own programs yet (possibly only because it is not anywhere properly explained in the Microsoft SDK docs), you should test it in a pilot project. I'm sure you won't want to miss it, once you get used to its advantages and comfort. And as already said, it is very useful to force programs you have to port to be easier to maintain and understand:

* For the tireless: index into an array of FAR pointers pointing to an array of FAR string pointers to filenames...

First test, then judge!

```
ClientArea=TopLeft+BottomRight;        // Well, maybe...
rcClientArea=ptTopLeft+ptBottomRight;  // Complete nonsense!
```

117

Figure 2.12 summarizes the three elements of a Hungarian named variable and shows (with the help of some examples) how the final name is built.

Figure 2.12: The three elements of Hungarian notation

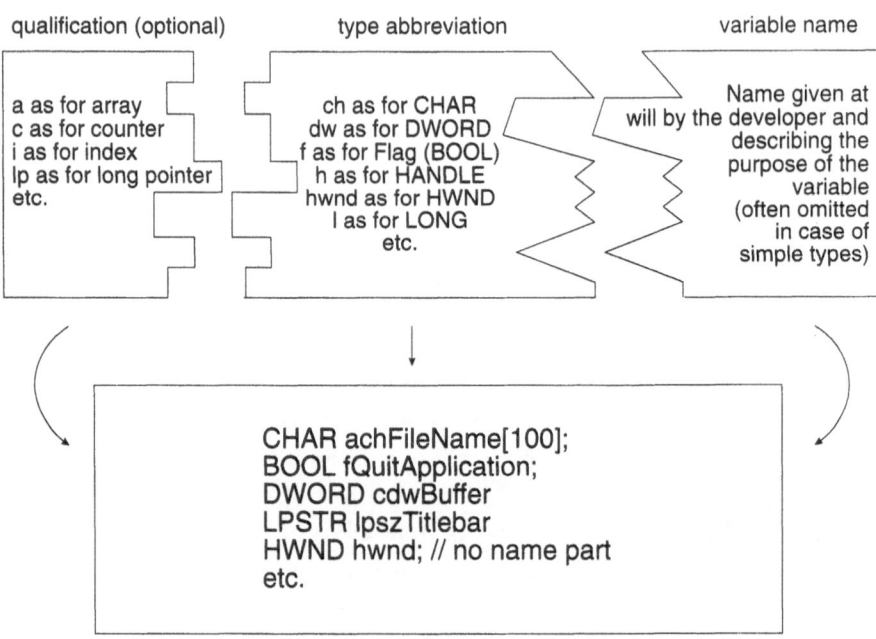

Some suggestions

The Hungarian notation is presumably the only procedure for methodical program development under Windows which has spread over a wider range of developers. Most major projects could be easier to handle and to maintain if some strictly defined and consistent procedures and guidelines were introduced. Unfortunately, since Microsoft has not set any common standard or given at least firm suggestions (except for very *Enough room for individual* few points), you have here a wide playground at your disposal for un- *activities!* restricted fun and activities. I can just give you a few suggestions, which I conceived by myself or took from other developers, as examples for an igniting impulse:

Macros and type definitions are written in capital letters without exception. Especially with constants, I use an unambiguous but consistent naming technique:

```
// resource IDs for dialogbox controls
#define ID_EDIT_DIRECTORY    ...
#define ID_LISTBOX_FILENAME ...
#define ID_BUTTON_LOAD       ...
#define ID_BUTTON_SAVE       ...
#define ID_BUTTON_QUIT       ...
// etc.
// resource IDs for menus: File menu
#define ID_MENU_FILE_NEW     ...
#define ID_MENU_FILE_OPEN    ...
#define ID_MENU_FILE_SAVE    ...
#define ID_MENU_FILE_QUIT    ...
// menu IDs: Edit menu
#define ID_MENU_EDIT_CUT     ...
// etc.
```

Admittedly, you'll have a bit more typing work at the beginning. But on the other hand, you can immediately detect what kind of object or menu you're dealing with. If you want to find out the name of a constant, very seldom will you have to look into the header files: when creating the names following a strict methodology, in most cases you can mentally recompose them easily.

The introduction of functions named according to a unique naming technique (as far as possible) is another very useful point when I have to structure my programs. Most of the time, for certain groups, I use a three- to five-letter prefix indicating the affiliation of the function to this group (a good idea that is assiduously used in the OS/2 API, but was unfortunately skipped by Microsoft). The parameter naming is also as uniform as possible. This has the added advantage that on pointers to complex structures I can easily work with a set of global access macros. This can save a lot of work:

Coherent function names

```
FEXPORT BOOL InputDelChar(LPINPUTFIELD lpInput,int nCount);
FEXPORT BOOL InputDelWord(LPINPUTFIELD lpInput,BOOL fLeft);
FEXPORT BOOL InputDelLine(LPINPUTFIELD lpInput,int nCount);
FEXPORT BOOL InputInsChar(LPINPUTFIELD lpInput,char ch);
FEXPORT BOOL InputInsString(LPINPUTFIELD lpInput,
  LPSTR lpsz);
FEXPORT BOOL InputSaveText(LPINPUTFIELD lpInput,
```

Functions for an input control: prefix Input.

```
    LPSTR lpszFilename);
FEXPORT BOOL InputLoadText(LPINPUTFIELD lpInput,
    LPSTR lpszFilename);
// etc.
// LPINPUTFIELD is a pointer on the structure INPUTFIELD,
// I use the following macro within all functions to get
// access to all individual components:
#define IF(member) lpInput->member
```

Consistent return values

You may notice two further trifles: first, all functions have the return type BOOL; this reflects another iron rule of mine, namely that all functions indicate their success or failure by returning a BOOL value. I make an exception only in such cases where the function does nothing more than return a value without any possibility of an error:

```
FEXPORT int InputTextLength(LPINPUTFIELD lpInput);
```

Self-defined shell of macros

The second interesting point might be the utilization of the macro FEXPORT. Compliant with each system, I have defined three macros in order to describe the possible calling sequences of functions. In the definition I use already existing macros of the respective API, provided this is possible:

Win32

```
#ifdef Win32
    // layer of macros for Win32 function attributes
    // exported functions
    #define FEXPORT CALLBACK
    // globally known functions in the program
    #define FPUBLIC WINAPI
    // local functions used in a module
    #define FLOCAL  static __stdcall
```

Win16

```
#else
    // same layer of macros for Win16 function attributes
    #define FEXPORT FAR PASCAL _export
    #define FPUBLIC FAR PASCAL
    #define FLOCAL  static near PASCAL
#endif
```

This method of an additional layer of macros for the calling sequences enables me to perform the most simple adaptation of the prototypes in a modified environment. This is shown in figure 2.13, which illustrates the example of FEXPORT:

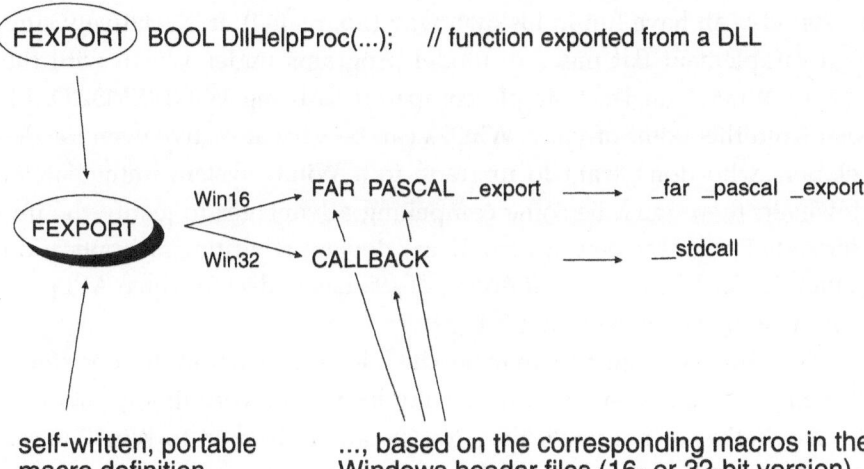

Figure 2.13: A portable layer of macros for function attributes

Of course, these rules and guidelines are by no means binding and subject to continuous evolution. They are certainly not suited to each developer and every project. But if you have to deal with major programming projects, a set of rules and its consistent usage can be enormously helpful. This is even more important if several developers work in a team: then certain rules and standards quickly become essential. Therefore, consider sections 4.3 to 4.5 concerning the macros included in WINDOWSX.H!

Consistency and methodical approaches are especially important when working in a team.

2.7 Which Platform for Windows 3.1: Win32s or Win16?

"In my country each one can reach the blessed state the way he himself wants to." A phrase attributed to Frederick II of Prussia, called The Great

What the "old Fritz" was already propagandizing in the 18th century is also true for the stressed software developer: in the Windows world, everybody can have fun in his own way (no, really!). It is relatively simple to implement flat memory model programs under Win16 with the help of Win32s (at least simple compared to using WINMEM32.DLL). Seen from this point of view, Win32s can be very attractive even for developers who don't want to upgrade to a Win32 system immediately. However, there must be some compelling advantages to justify the implementation for the new system. Every developer writing an application in parallel for Win16 and Windows NT/95 has to decide which API platform he will use for Windows 3.1.

32-bit apps under Win16?

So a few basic remarks to make the relevant factors to this decision a little bit more transparent won't do any harm. The very first question to ask is whether or not you'll have to port an application to Win32 in the short term. If the answer is no, Win32s won't make any sense as a platform for the time being. You can possibly postpone any 32-bit activities until a complete implementation of the Win32 API is realized under Windows 95 (and, more important, has spread widely enough). Then you won't have to bother with any of the various Win32s idiosyncrasies and ugly special cases. The only exception could be if your applications can gain so much performance and/or potential from the flat memory model and 32-bit processing that it is worth changing the operating system anyway. To say it a bit sloppily: if you mainly operate with HUGE pointers on megabyte memory areas, changing to Win32s could possibly be interesting for you. But don't misunderstand me: the Win32s memory management is working on the basis of Win16 (or DPMI, respectively). This means that your program does not become faster just because the memory management it is based upon has become more intelligent (it hasn't). The performance benefit lies solely in the fact that the whole brain-damaged segment arithmetics with HUGE pointers can be omitted. And whoever has looked into the assembler code produced by the C compiler for this will know that this omission is very advantageous (without even mentioning the continuing segment reloads...).

If you're happy with Win16 and don't need to port right now: ignore Win32s.

Exception: very memory-hungry programs.

Pro Win32s

How about programs that have to be available under both Windows 3.1 *and* a Win32-based system? Since they'll have to be ported anyway, shouldn't we do things properly and make the whole project Win32s compatible? The answer is definitely yes if you don't need enhanced Win32 functionality (like threads, IPC, etc.). Because you have to become familiar with the new 32-bit development tools anyway, you might as well take Win32s into consideration. As long as you'll only use the supported parts of the Win32 API (e.g., those that can be emulated by Windows 3.1), this subset will be a very atttractive alternative to the simultaneous maintenance of two executables. The file WIN32S.DAT in the SDK subdirectory X:\MSTOOLS\BIN\ can be of great help here. If you rename it to PORT.INI, you can load it into PORTTOOL, so the utility can search in your 32-bit source code for non-Win32s compatible functions, messages, etc.

Can you do without new Win32 features?

WIN32S.DAT and PORT-TOOL

Things get a bit more complicated when you (or your customers?) decide that your application would run even better with multiple threads. Or if you want to use NTFS features. Or, or, or... There are so many new and important features in Win32 (or could I say it the other way around: MS-DOS/Win16 is so limited?) that you won't escape the corresponding enhancements very long. And this is precisely the snag: each extension used without the explicit blessing of Win32s necessitates some precautions in your source code in order to keep the program working under Win32s and the real 32-bit Windows systems. *Theoretically*, you could load every 32-bit application under Win32s, but the unsupported function calls always return with an error code. This should help you a bit to implement an alternative function. Alistair Banks, already quoted in section 1.9, says it concisely but not exactly helpfully: "So you could develop a Win32 application which for instance creates a thread. Under Windows 3.1 [plus Win32s] CreateThread() will return an error, then you simply employ ›Plan B‹; under Windows NT on the other hand, the call will succeed, here you go... Error messages will be returned for all the functionality above Win16, including béziers, paths, memory mapped files, semaphores, etc., but exactly because of the clear error returns it will be possible to create a single binary file that works under Win3.1 and nevertheless can use all the new features of Windows NT."

Program parts especially tailored for Win32s

So, what is plan B?

Dynamic reconfiguration at run time!?

In my opinion Microsoft makes a comfortable life for itself: in its enthusiasm about 32 bit it seems to have forgotten that using "plan B" in a Win32 application means dynamic reconfiguration of the application at run time for each and every unsupported Win32 feature — and this opens the door to all kinds of subtle bugs. If the famous plan B is as simple as just removing the whole functionality under Windows 3.1, the effort to be invested is surely limited (a good example might be the conversion of a text document from ANSI to Unicode: the corresponding menu item can just be disabled or even removed under Win16). But plan

An unpleasant example: Bézier curves.

B can become very awkward when you need Bézier curves in a graphics program: either you can emulate the functionality for Win16 (my condolences) or you manage somehow to create the object with the existing means (that approach might even yield some acceptable results — at least from time to time...). Or as a third solution: Bézier curves cannot be drawn under Win16. At first the latter alternative seems pretty good: anybody wanting Bézier curves should run the program under a true Win32 system, please! Unfortunately, in real life things are not so easy: what would happen, for instance, to a file created with that program under NT (possibly including Bézier objects) if loaded and processed with the Win16 version of the application? Just deleting the Bézier curves is out of question. That means you'll somehow have to drag them along and resave them correctly in the file at the end. As already said: the interdependencies of program parts, when they are not implemented in a completely identical way, can result in rather tricky and very difficult to

Interoperability between platforms

track errors. And this last example shows one more problem: just checking the application exhaustively under Win16, Win32s, and the Win32 platforms isn't enough; above all, you must define most accurately the interoperability between these systems.

And contra?

Two sets of sources?

Can two partially different sets of source codes and/or conditional compilation really be a useful alternative? In my opinion yes. After all, in spite of the differences of both systems, it is possible to write most of the user interface (not to mention the program parts doing the real work, i.e., the non-GUI code) in an absolutely identical way, provided that you use portable macros and all the other mechanisms shown. Larger program parts that differentiate between 16 and 32 bit are placed in separate source code files. This code is certainly easier to write, maintain and understand as a source code file that has been designed to be compilable under both systems, and therefore contains many peculiar features, specialties, and #ifdefs. After all, the whole discussion can be tracked down to this simple question: how can a developer get acceptable results (that means working programs and maintainable sources) within the shortest time? Considering complex programs using largely new Win32 features not available under Win32s, I pretend that a certain separation of the source code files promotes a better understanding of the program code.

At last, there are some more points where the use of Win32s as a platform for ported Win16 programs is impossible anyway. This is the case when:

Win32s? Impossible, if...

- your application is based on a 16-bit device driver which is not (yet) available under Win32, or,
- you are using DLLs of a third-party manufacturer, which are not yet supplied as 32-bit DLLs (since Win32s doesn't support calls into 16-bit DLLs outside the Win16 kernel). Universal thunks are in both cases a possible but costly (in terms of implementation effort and loss of portability) way out.
- you extensively use non-portable APIs such as the segment and selector API or direct INT 21H and BIOS calls,
- you still (must) work with Windows 3.0. Win32s assumes that you have at least Windows 3.1, a 386, and a 4 MB machine.

Net result: Win32s is certainly usable if you don't need or want those 32-bit features that can't be emulated under Windows 3.1. Win32s is very helpful when your application benefits from the flat memory model. Win32s is necessary if you want to create only one EXE file for 16- and 32-bit systems. However, because of the special cases of Win32s programming, this can damage the maintainability of your program code. On the other hand, the preparation and maintenance of portable source codes for both systems is not so difficult that you should abandon the idea of a common set of sources altogether. On the contrary: Microsoft has made a recognizable effort to make the Win32 API backward compatible (within the bounds of the underlying operating system design).

The net result of all this

2.8 Some Hints for Porting OS/2 Programs

" 'Rin in die Kartoffeln, 'raus aus die Kartoffeln. (Into the job, out of the job.)"
Friedrich Wülfing, Vom Manöver

1989: Gone OS/2!
1994: Gone Win32!
1999: Gone Crazy!?

Here we are in 1995, and believe it or not, I know a bunch of people who, some five years ago, were indeed thinking of porting their Windows programs to OS/2. Nowadays, some of these developers are thinking of porting their OS/2 programs (back) to Windows.... It is true, the spoiled one doesn't have to care for mockery anymore! But perhaps this might cheer you up: the desolate to and fro of both elephants between 1985 and today has affected me fairly well, too.

Is a changeover worth the effort?

The most important question to be asked should be: is it worth changing over to Win32? An existing OS/2 1.x program (whether text mode or Presentation Manager, short PM, doesn't matter) can actually be ported to OS/2 2.x relatively easily. From the technical side this system absolutely is an acceptable standard (see also section 1.2, page 17), so you won't find here any real good arguments for a changeover. The following considerations could be more convincing:

What about market size?

- What about market capacity? There are many more Win16 than OS/2 installations, and the former should be able to execute 32-bit GUI programs thanks to Win32s (in principle). Furthermore, Windows 95 should cause a rush for 32-bit Windows.

Portability, e.g., to RISC?

- Depending on the requirements, portability to RISC environments can also be a powerful advantage of the Win32 API. IBM indeed plans a portable OS/2 version, but when it will be released and how it will look are still only to be found in the stars.

Family vs. single system

- Windows is a complete family, OS/2 a lone wolf. Here too, IBM visibly strives to release slimmed-down variations and systems adapted to certain environments such as Pen Computing for example. But while IBM only promises, Microsoft can deliver: beginning with modular Windows and Windows for Workgroups

* Well, almost...

  through Windows 95,* up to Windows NT and NT Advanced Server. In addition, an NT installation can easily be scaled thanks to symmetric multi-processing: if the existing hardware is too slow, just throw a few more processors in....

OLE 2 and successors

- With OLE 2.0 (and dependent products like Chicago and Cairo), Microsoft has developed a key technology that it has to a large extent under complete control. Whether and how far IBM is able (or wants) to catch that train cannot be said at the present time. Obviously the OpenDoc group (which includes IBM) is trying hard to establish yet another standard for object-oriented architectures. Whether this will be of great success is still not clear. It is also impossible to make any concrete statements about the plans of IBM and Apple concerning Taligent for the time being.

To conclude, a switch to Win32 should be a very well-planned decision, all the more because porting from OS/2 to Win32 is much more difficult than just from Win16 to Win32. Nevertheless, in order to seduce the developer (or to irritate IBM?), Microsoft has developed a few tools that are able to convert OS/2 source code and resources at least partially (these tools are available and can be downloaded from the CompuServe forum MSWIN32, library #10 "Porting — OS/2 and UNIX").

The high cost of porting isn't outweighed by the MS porting tools.

Tools and methods of approach

I want to consider the most important problem areas when converting from OS/2 to Win32 and along the way explain the tools available. Let's start with the API analyzer, which is the first tool you'll use during a port. This program analyzes the source files of an OS/2 program and records all function calls into the operating system (including the number of calls). Based on this file, an Excel spreadsheet is built to calculate a rough first estimate of the required porting work. Figure 2.14 on the opposite page shows an example: the value in the column "Total" means that the analyzed program performs in total 3,301 OS2/2 API calls. The column "Dos Time" tells you that porting this project will cost you about 93 labor-days and the value 180 in "Used" means that the program uses in total 180 functions of the OS/2 API, knowing that 110 (column "Auto") of them can be converted automatically by another supplied tool. This conversion concerns 2,324 (column "AutoApi") of the 3,301 calls and helps you to save about 28 labor-days (column "AutoTime"). Then a list follows, displaying each single call for a better understanding of the general results: here you can see that the function DosAllocShrSeg(), used 9 times and rated as medium, is estimated to take 1.125 labor-days while DosAllocSeg() (used 12 times, but requiring only 0.05 labor-days) seems quite easy to port. The summary in the lower half ("Aggregate API Us-

API analyzer

age") shows how the calls are distributed to the different API groups
(Dos…, Win…, Gpi…, etc.).

Of course, all this is not of any help for actually porting the source
code itself, but at least it enables you to gain quite a good appreciation of
the total work required as well as that in different parts. A small disadvantage of the API analyzer is the fact that it supports OS/2 functions
only, but no PM messages at all. For instance, experience has shown that
a program happily working with sub- or superclassing can be quite difficult to convert: however, the analyzer does not take this fact into consideration (porting WinSubclassWindow() is supposed to be of an average
difficulty…).

*Takes only OS/2 functions
into account, no PM mes-
sages.*

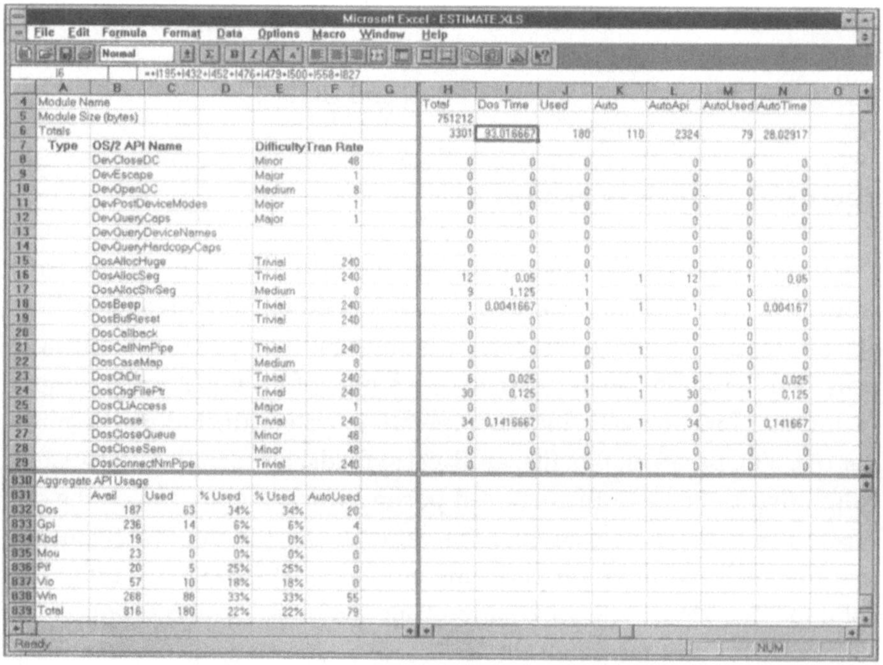

*Figure 2.14: The OS/2 API
analyzer after the job*

Once you have seen the dreadful truth about the efforts a port will need,
you search for relief with the next tool: the API converter already mentioned, which does nothing more than take a C source file and perform
simple textual changes in it. For instance, DosAllocSeg() becomes a function called HP_dosAllocSeg(), which is implemented within a Win32
helper DLL (named HOLEPORT.DLL, available also as source code).
Basically, the converter operates in two different ways: either it replaces
a OS/2 function directly with its Win32 counterpart (including data

API converter

types and constants), so DosClose() becomes CloseHandle(), or it changes to a call of a helper function that is located in the Win32 support DLL. However, the overall conversion is quite ineffective, as it concerns only functions that are easy to port (mentioned as "Trivial" in the Excel spreadsheet). Nevertheless, it will save you 10 to 25 percent of the total porting work — certainly better than nothing!

After that, the OS/2 porter should run another program to convert the resource files into Win32 format (this means text format, since OS/2 RC files have a totally different syntax than Windows resource files). This program is quite effective and normally enables nearly 100 percent conversion of the RC files (except some OS/2-specific controls such as spinbuttons, for example). Unfortunately, from this moment you can no longer escape the really difficult part of the exercise: you have to change the makefile to Win32 and then check and adjust one source file after the other (here, the top-down solution seems even more important than for porting Win16 applications). And as already mentioned, my advice to perform a small training program before your first real porting project is even more valid for OS/2 developers: the overall porting process is so difficult that you shouldn't waste your time and efforts with the tools and the way to use them, so learn this beforehand!

RC translator

And then: DIY!

Absolutely, positively begin with a simple test project.

Some hints for text-mode programs

Another important question: is the application to be ported "only" a text-mode application or a PM program? Since NT has a subsystem supporting OS/2 programs directly (but only 1.x, without PM API), you won't need to port at all if your program uses just the OS/2 1.x API. One of the most successful products in that respect was the OS/2 version of the editor Brief, which in the beginning, when practically no real native editor was available, was often used under NT. Currently, there are still no developer tools available from MS (not exactly astonishing, or is it?) to create OS/2 applications under Windows NT, but this could change soon. On the other hand, OS/2 1.x programs are by definition 16-bit applications, and one could wonder if his program wouldn't be much better off in a 32-bit version. As shown, porting to Win32 can be rather complicated. You have nearly all the possibilities of the OS/2 API under Win32 (after all, NT was once planned as a successor of OS/2!), but too many differences are found in the countless small details, which can

Shall you port text-mode applications at all?

Text-mode: only "procedural" adaptations.

make an adaptation very expensive and very frustrating. Luckily, a text-mode application requires only "procedural" changes: the OS/2 function and possibly the arguments must be replaced with the proper Win32 variant. This indeed causes many, but for the most part simple, changes, which are easily performed by the automatic API translator:

```
// From OS/2:
SEL selBuf;
DosAllocSeg(2048,&selBuf,SEG_NONSHARED);
... // further work on selBuf
DosFreeSeg(selBuf);

// To Win32:
HGLOBAL hBuf;
hBuf=GlobalAlloc(GMEM_FIXED,2048);
... // further work on hBuf
GlobalFree(hBuf);
```

Porting OS/2 PM applications

PM: all the text-mode stuff plus messages.

Considerably more complex is the conversion of PM programs. On the one hand, you also have to adapt the message processing — that can at times get a bit troublesome. This is true mainly because the OS/2 PM windowing model is built somewhat differently than that of Windows — just think of the difference between frame and overlapped windows. What's more, GUI applications are normally much more costly in the implementation of the user interface than text-mode apps. A single text-mode call is often replaced by a sequence of four or more Win... and Gpi... calls. And Gpi... functions, to make things even worse, aren't exactly compatible with the Windows GDI model. All these reasons lead to the fact that porting a user-interface-oriented PM app is something like the "worst case" of an OS/2 to Windows port.

Worst case: OS/2 PM to Windows port.

The most difficult areas

So, which areas pose the largest problems for the developer? You should refer to the Excel spreadsheet shown in figure 2.14, which at least can provide a rough idea of the difficulties to expect when porting specific OS/2 APIs. The grades shown present a more or less realistic level of effort. They can, however, also lead to serious misunderstandings:

according to this list DosGlobalAlloc() is one of the more trivial functions. This is certainly true if the call just deals with an ordinary memory allocation, but it is totally bogus if "giveaway" memory segments for shared memory accesses are to be allocated. I'll enumerate some of the areas that (as my experience shows) are especially prone to be the cause for difficulties:

- Shared memory accesses under Win32 are implemented completely different than with OS/2; most likely, considerable adaptation work will be necessary here. There is a helper DLL named SHRMEM.DLL available which solves at least some of the problems. *Shared memory*

- The synchronization of multiple threads and IPC communications is at least partially different under Win32: in most cases you have simply to choose the corresponding Win32 mechanism and change the sources accordingly. An important exception is critical sections, which work completely differently under Win32, so for these there is no simple 1:1 translation. *Thread synchronization*

- Win32 doesn't know signals, but uses structured exception handling instead for the treatment of error conditions and exceptions. *Signals and exception handling*

- The treatment of dialog box functions is somewhat different in Win32: they return a BOOL value showing whether the actual message was handled in the callback. Under OS/2 you have to call the default function for dialog boxes (i.e.,WinDefDlgProc()) to process all unhandled messages. *Dialog box functions*

- The differences between frame windows on the one hand and overlapped windows on the other can also require some costly changes. The fact that PM child windows can have different owner and parent windows sometimes is a real brain twister. The complete WM_CONTROL handling must be changed to WM_COMMAND or WM_NOTIFY. *Frame windows and WM_CONTROL*

- In the same category falls the fact that PM menus are realized as separate windows with their own set of control messages (e.g., MM_SETITEMATTR). Under Win32 there exists an entirely different approach based on a simple procedural interface. *Menu messages (MM_*)*

- In the default case, graphics coordinates refer to the upper left-hand corner under Win32, not, as with OS/2, to the lower left-hand corner. *The graphics coordinate system*

Message structure and order

- Both the structure and the order of window messages are different. Tricky code built on a certain order or similar undocumented behavior evidently needs some reworking.

DLL initialization and termination

- The initialization and especially termination of DLLs is in most cases not directly portable. First, Win32 DLLs should have corresponding functions (such as LibMain32()), even if these remain empty. Second, a DLL function under OS/2 can be appointed as an "exit list" function to perform the necessary clean-up when the DLL shuts down. Under Win32 this list is neither necessary nor possible; the DLL initialization function takes that responsibility too and jumps in here (for more information see section 4.9, page 290, and for an actual example, see section 5.3, page 339).

A big step back!

Another global problem causing all sorts of difficulties is the reluctance of Microsoft to classify API functions into named groups. Someone who has worked a lot with the OS/2 notation where each and every function is strictly identified through its prefix (Win, Gpi, Kbd, Vio, etc.), probably gets confused very soon with the extremely chaotic naming scheme of the Win32 API elements (admittedly, to that end Win16 is even worse). This "abstinence" results in a genuine backward step for OS/2 developers! But someone who is *really* sure he must port his application will accept that for better or worse....

2.9 Summary

"Enough words are exchanged, let me finally see deeds, too!" Johann Wolfgang von Goethe, Faust, First Part

Starting points and aims

In the sentiment of the above citation, both of the next chapters will deal with the concrete and detailed transformation of all general hints and advice to porting and portable programming already given. Yet it seems important that before starting an actual project the questions of selecting suitable starting points and goals are fully investigated. Especially the state of the source code and the question whether the application shall be available for just one (Win32) or several platforms (Win32 and Win16) have to be examined.

Planning and approach

Bigger projects should not at all be started without a sufficient planning phase. I would generally prefer the top-down technique, but also include elements of bottom up depending on the type of the application, the state of the sources, and the level of Win32 knowledge of the developers who actually perform the port. Particularly with big projects and when teamwork is involved, the creation and continued maintenance of self-defined libraries with portability functions and guidelines is an important contribution to maintainable source codes and portable programs. Besides these (self-made) aids further tools are available: above all, the usage of corresponding C++ class libraries can be a very efficient assistant to portability. Unfortunately, for existing programs in most cases this means that the sources are to be completely rewritten in C++ and have to be adapted to the class library. This effort is almost always much higher than a simple port. Therefore, existing C source codes will profit more from the somewhat simpler but C "compatible" techniques — here two prominent examples are the STRICT option and the Hungarian notation, both of which are unfortunately not of sufficient assistance. Nevertheless, these two basic approaches are based on concepts and ideas that can indeed help you when defining your individual porting guidelines to form the base for the already mentioned portability library. However, for new projects the question about the "best" implementation language is very simple to answer: a C++ program written with the aid of a useful class library with consistent use of its abstracting features is portable to Win32 or any other supported GUI with considerably less effort than its C counterpart.

Suitable resource use

The question of which system is better suited for 16-bit applications — the original Win16 API or the enhanced Win32s add-on — doesn't have a universally valid answer. If both systems need to be supported, and if the program can be implemented *without* using advanced Win32 functionality, then a single executable for Win32s and the true 32-bit OSes is a viable alternative. This is also true for applications gaining so much performance in 32-bit mode that changing to Win32s is justified. On the other hand the maintenance of two executables (16 bit and 32 bit) from one set of sources, to a large extent identical, is easy to handle and (when considering some elementary rules) surely not more costly than catering for all the Win32s idiosyncrasies. Since under 32-bit systems the program has to discover under which platform it is actually running and then reconfigure appropriately, some complex code might be necessary. In contrast a set of sources to be compiled for the two systems can mask many differences relatively easly and clearly through the use of suitably defined macros and conditional compilation.

Win16 or Win32s?

And last but not least, from
OS/2 to Win32

OS/2 programs are unfortunately much more costly to port than Win16 apps. A corresponding activity should only be started with clear and detailed awareness. Text-mode programs are especially good candidates for direct execution under the NT OS/2 subsystem — then a port isn't necessary at all. If you are convinced that porting is indeed unavoidable, then definitely make use of the tools available from Microsoft. Of course, these won't solve all problems, but for certain porting steps they can help you enormously. This especially holds true for many of the routine and "boring" changes which can be performed mechanically, generously leaving you with the more difficult (but as a matter of fact, also more interesting) pieces.

Portable Programs in C and C++

This third chapter will illuminate all those areas of portable (Windows) programming that are mostly independent of specific operating systems details or development tools. Portability of an application (and hence the porting effort) depends not only on the homogeneity of the application programming interfaces offered by the underlying operating systems. It is also a feature that characterizes your source code more or less independently from the actual target system. You can get very complex, yet structured Win16 programs working under Win32 with surprisingly small effort, while other, often shorter but more "chaotic" ones, run only after extensive modifications — if at all. In our case, the effort to be invested for porting depends mostly on the backward compatibility of the Win32 APIs. Fortunately, Microsoft is responsible for this part, which is the subject of the following chapter. On the other hand, the folks in Redmond can invest incredible effort in creating a compatible API; if some basic portability principles are not taken to heart while writing program code assumed eventually to be ported, the porting endeavor can become a rather difficult exercise for the person(s) actually carrying out the port.

Portability and the creation of your source files

Some basic portability principles

3.1 Some Fundamental Considerations

"Vagueness is the empire of error." Marquis de Vauvenarges, Réflexions et Maximes

In the preceding chapter, we extensively discussed which *globally valid* properties your source code or projects had to fulfill in order to ensure maximum portability in the ideal case. The following sections will deal in detail with the questions and features of C/C++ portable programming (well, at least as those are relevant for porting from Win16 to Win32). All the individual points, however, are mostly independent of actual Win16/Win32 API differences, but rather mirror the changed processor architecture (16 vs. 32 bit) or hardware environment (RISC vs. CISC).

Questions related to programming-language specifics

After all, you can't avoid some of the more basic characteristics of 32-bit programming even when you only want to run a simple text-based MS-DOS program with the aid of the "console API" under Windows 95. And it is precisely these fundamental, rather language-related questions that are the main focus of the next sections. However, to illustrate the discussed material, I will of course revert to actual Win32 data types and their APIs.

Of course, you can anticipate fewer hurdles when moving from your trusted 16-bit Microsoft or Borland compilers to their 32-bit equivalents than to an R4000 machine with the MIPS compiler (not to mention the AXP or Power PC machines). Some of the following hints are hence not (immediately) relevant for developers wanting to stay on the x86 side of the fence. On the other hand, on MIPS and DEC hardware, Windows NT is implemented nearly 100 percent source code compatible to the x86 platform, so a (later) porting to the RISC platforms should never be ruled out.

Windows NT runs on non-Intel machines, too.

Before you start to rush into the concrete conversion of your source code with big enthusiasm but perhaps little effect (and in order to get acquainted with the following), you should pay a few minutes' attention to some very simple questions which could possibly have some serious consequences on your programming style:

Some thinking before coding can't do any harm.

- Which data types do you use mostly? And why these and not others?
- What changes (*not enhancements!*) would you like to carry out if you had the possibility of working on your source codes for two or three months without a specific purpose and without time pressure (deadlines)?
- How many rules do you know to keep your source code consistent, readable, and maintainable? Do you really use some of these — and which ones?
- How often have you noted "underway" that a certain approach would indeed be very sensible, but ignored it or did not apply it to your sources further on because of *seemingly* compelling reasons (for example, lack of time)?
- The list of these questions that I often ask myself is easy to extend but always revolves around the basic questions concerning the art of programming.*

* And this wording is not at all accidental!

The crux with developing complex software is the fact that the development process as a whole is inherently iterative. This is true for all parts of the programming environment: programmers' knowledge about the system gets better as time goes by (hopefully...); the programming project itself is subject to continuing design changes; compilers, linkers, etc. are also regularly brought up to date and so on.* And even more problems are created when a system is improved with a significant and often complicated new technology (e.g., Windows and OLE 2). This phenomenon can be summarized under the collective term "ad hoc programming" since often only momentary circumstances count and may lead to elementary design changes (which, a bit later, are revealed as being insufficient or, even worse, incorrect...). This observation applies for trifles and for far-reaching design decisions alike. And in this on-going chaos we are expected to write correct and (at least partly) structured software, not to mention portability? The whole matter results in a vicious circle par excellence (also shown in figure 3.1 on the following page). I have the feeling that every now and then developers should lean back in theirs armchair, stop caring about Captain Gates and his ever-growing fleet of API inventors, and think about the basic principles of writing *good* program code. Developers, especially those permanently catching the latest developments and technologies, simply require some time to digest all those new ideas and concepts in order to use them in a consistent and effective manner in new or existing applications. And constant pressure through deadlines or "featuritis" only serves to make this vicious circle worse — instead of automatically leading to timely, let alone reliable results. These remarks shall definitely provoke a thought process for project managers, too: a program seldom becomes better if the developer keeps fiddling around with it (or its symptoms, respectively) instead of having the responsible persons thinking about ways to master the deep-rooted causes of all this (partly superfluous) maintenance effort.

* Not to mention their errors and "features," which make programming so much fun...

Instead of investing money and time in a never-ending debugging struggle, project managers should consider whether appropriate education and training of developers on the one hand and reasonable planning, the creation of consistent programming guidelines, and the sensible conception of basic features on the other hand wouldn't lead to better products (in the long run). In other words and to illustrate my thoughts with another profession: if the medieval architects and master-builders had built their buildings in the way most software projects are designed and implemented nowadays, no human being could have lived in the

And the remedy?

resulting ramshackle huts and they would all have fled back into the caves. (And who contradicts me by pretending that master-builders had a few centuries' time to "exercise?" I would reply that they could not use any debuggers for their work: thus, if they happened to fail, the resulting fiasco was to be seen and heard for miles and miles, not to speak of the necessary work for cleaning up....)

Figure 3.1: A vicious circle that most developers know only too well!

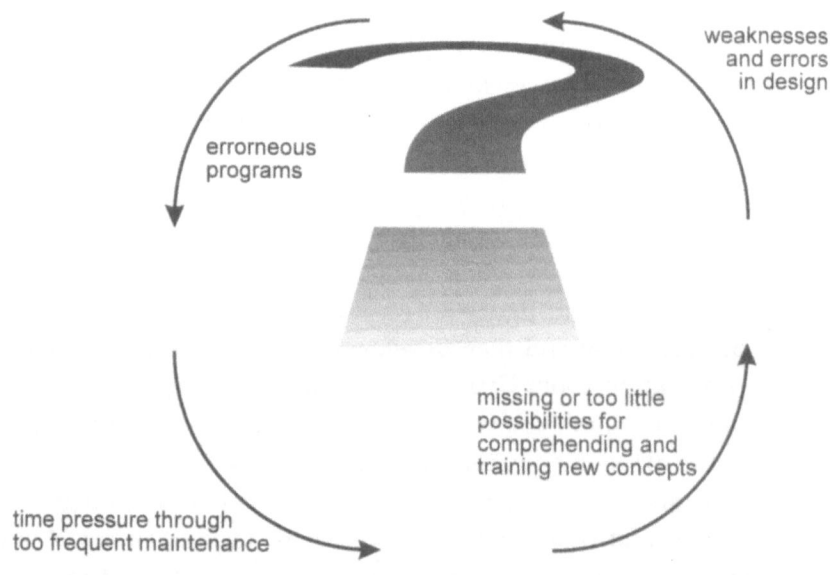

weaknesses
and errors
in design

errorneous
programs

missing or too little
possibilities for
comprehending and
training new concepts

time pressure through
too frequent maintenance

* ... and for ultimate disposal, not recycling!

To say it in a drastic (and surely somewhat too generalized) way: in an ideal world we ought to throw all the "old garbage" into the trash,* then think calmly about the whole thing and get a clear picture of the goals to be set and the proper ways and tools to reach them. Doing that, we should stress more than ever the creation and consistent utilization of well-thought programming concepts (after all, there *is* a kind of "state of the art" in designing and writing programs) and avoid getting involved in a hopeless guerrilla fight against all the innumerable details of a major project from the very beginning. Once there is a useful and supporting frame, those are much easier to categorize and to master.

** but sadly not too often practiced...

This process is surely a feasible beginning** for completely new projects. But unfortunately most of us have to maintain the gigabytes of code already existing today whose further functioning is imperative.

And we have to admit that some programs in very bad condition are not necessarily improved by rescue operations at all but will still cause as much effort and problems as one likes. Be this as it may: at any rate the following hints can help you to improve existing software (with a certain effort) and also to design new projects (with quite a smaller effort) in a portable fashion. Nevertheless, they are guaranteed to be only as half as effective without some reflection and thinking on your side! To support this process, I have included a book dealing with these questions in the annotated bibliography [see Ref. 9].

More facts in [Ref. 9].

3.2 ANSI C, What Else?

"Whether you do not know C at all or are familiar with an older dialect, [with ANSI C] you'll have to learn a completely new language." P. J. Plauger and J. Brodie, Standard C

Well, if you already know and use C, I'm sure it won't be that bad. Nevertheless, ANSI C differs from K&R C* in a few very important and many less significant areas. Most of these changes serve either the better portability of C programs (this exactly interests us primarily now) or the safer and correct use of a language that is notorious for (sometimes even unwanted) abuse and the complexity and illegibility of the resulting source code (and those features won't do any harm either).

* also known as classic C

The most important advantages of ANSI C

Now I'm not going to give an introduction to using ANSI C because there are enough authors who deal more or less successfully with this subject. You'll find a small selection of some useful (in my opinion) books about ANSI C programming in the Bibliography [Refs. 5 and 6 as well as possibly 13]. No, this section shall clarify that the use of a programming language that is defined according to an acknowledged (and useful) standard is an unconditional necessity for portable programming. In the meantime, ANSI C compilers are available in a good to very good quality both for PCs and workstations — also in terms of the speed and optimizing capabilities. Besides a precise language definition that depends on the actual implementation in only a few and clearly identified issues, they provide a standardized and comprehensive run-time

A standardized language is a must for portable programming.

library, which covers most of the basic areas (for example, file I/O, string handling, memory allocation).

When properly using this library, obeying the ANSI C language rules and consistently observing certain portability guidelines, you'll find it relatively easy to port your programs to other platforms, provided that you have access to a (useful) ANSI C development system there. Various providers compete under the MS-DOS platform; I will consider mainly Microsoft and Borland since both have developed full-fledged Win32 development systems and have already issued beta versions for Windows 95. Borland currently limits itself to the x86 platform while Microsoft provides Visual C++ 2.x, a nearly fully compatible C/C++ 7.0 system for MIPS machines and DEC's Alpha (in the future, rumor has it, VC 2 will be available for other NT platforms — e.g., Power PC — as well). However, for NT some quite good self-engineered C development systems already exist from the various processor manufacturers.

Under DOS: Microsoft and Borland.

There is another important reason for the use of ANSI C instead of K&R C as the base language: a lot of new language attributes support the creation of safe (well, safe in comparison to classic C!) and (at least formally) correct C code. Those are, for instance, the use of ANSI C prototypes or the application of const objects as well as stricter rules for the conversion of data types. And in this sense you'll find something true in the above-mentioned quotation: one must have to work with all those new features for quite a while before knowing how to use them correctly and how valuable they really are (frankly: I positively don't know how I managed to live without ANSI C function prototypes before). But that's the way it goes with every new thing: first comes skepticism (and maybe even rejection) because of the changes required and the related learning efforts; however, after a while and once you get used to the improvements, it seems you can't live without them anymore.

What's more, ANSI code is also safer.

A few words about Pascal and Modula-2

Hence, if you want to write portable C programs (no matter in which context), then go on with an ANSI C system. Should you prefer Pascal or Modula-2, you probably won't have another choice than to wait until your compiler manufacturer decides to supply a development system on or — at least — for the target platform. Unfortunately, the standardization of both languages is pure theory, so changing the system is not as easy as with ANSI C. True, there is indeed an ISO standard for Pascal, but it is so inadequate that nearly every manufacturer inflates it with numerous enhancements.* Most likely — because of its large installed base — I'd rather consider good old Turbo Pascal (recently known under the alias Borland Pascal) as representing a certain standard. But this won't be a big help for porting your programs until Borland issues a genuine 32-bit version. On the other hand, I can well imagine that at the very moment I am writing this, Anders Heijlsberg is working on his (remarkable) code generator to get it to 32 bit and to the flat memory model.

... which by no means are compatible to each other, of course!

The situation is hardly better for Modula-2. The language definition may be quite standardized, but in that case too, most manufacturers considered some enhancements as being necessary. This doesn't prevent you from writing portable programs but makes their creation a bit more difficult. In this respect the absence of a useful macro pre-processor is a very annoying problem (this is also a major drawback for Pascal). A powerful macro management is *extremely* helpful (in fact it's indispensable) for writing code that will be run on different platforms. Some compiler suppliers may have equipped their systems with rudimentary macro processors,** but first, those are not really the true McCoy, and second they are, haha!, not portable at all....

*** shall read: conditional compilation.*

A further proven disadvantage is the fact that the Modula-2 language doesn't foresee any comprehensive, commonly accepted and implemented standard run-time library. Except for a few standardized modules (like InOut or Math), there is no support that could be compared to the ANSI C standard library. And so each manufacturer is still preparing his own soup.

Although the ensuing discussion refers to ANSI C, most of the information will be relevant also for Pascal and Modula-2 developers. After all, the concept of a RECORD in Modula-2, for instance, doesn't differ much from structs and unions in C. Generally, the simple data types also have direct counterparts; the same is true for actual language constructions like *if/else* and *while* or *for* loops, etc. You'll find some basic hints and advice in Appendix 6, which specifically deals with questions concerning portable Pascal and Modula-2 programming for Windows developers.

However, much of this chapter is also relevant for Pascal and Modula-2 programmers.

3.3 The C Pre-processor

"You only know the things you have tamed..." Antoine de Saint-Exupéry, The Little Prince

No, no, the ANSI C pre-processor is not *such* a terrible beast. But besides the "normal" possibilities such as simple text replacement or conditional compilation, some tricky applications can ease portable programming considerably — here you can do a few quite remarkable things with it that will surely amaze some programmers (especially those with not much C experience or Pascal programmers). But first, we will illuminate the simpler, obvious possibilities and give some advice regarding their usage.

Some simple tricks with #define

#define constants Use #define as often as possible when you have to use numerical or string constants, which are not supposed to end up in RC files. You should introduce a named constant the latest when the same value is being used at two different places. But most places where constants are being used only once may also gain clarity and readability through the use of an explicit name. Which of the following definitions appears to be clearer?

```
char chBuf[80];    // ???
// Or:
#define MAX_FILENAME_LEN  80
...
char chBuf[MAX_FILENAME_LEN]    // Oh, I see!
```

Similar observations apply to frequently repeating complex expressions: wherever it makes sense, it is better to use an appropriately defined macro. For instance, if you create some windows with a bunch of standard attributes, combine all the WS*_ flags into a single constant:

```
#define MY_WS_FLAGS  ((WS_OVERLAPPEDWINDOW)|(WS_VISIBLE))
```

This has two distinct advantages: it economizes the amount of typing and eases later adaptations (for instance, if all these standard windows require another flag later on). If necessary, you could introduce several such constants for different window classes (WS_OVERLAPPED, WS_POPUP, WS_CHILD, etc.). And a remark about how the preceding macro definition was written: the flags were put into parentheses, joined with the or operator (|) and then once again put into parentheses. Why all this stuff? Well, the strange bracketing ensures that the macro STD_WS_FLAGS can be correctly evaluated in each and every context and will always produce the same result. A (negative) example to illustrate (and to deter you):

Saves some typing work and eases adaptions.

Bracketing because of C's precedence rules!

```
#define SHL_WRONG(a,b)        a<<b
#define SHL_NOTSOWRONG(a,b)   (a<<b)
#define MULT_WRONG(a,b)       (a*b)
#define MULT_RIGHT(a,b)       ((a)*(b))
...
z=SHL_WRONG(1,2)+3;       // Z == 32 instead of 7
z=SHL_NOTSOWRONG(1,2)+3;  // Z now indeed == 7, but ...
z=MULT_WRONG(1+2,3+4);    // Z == 11 instead of
z=MULT_RIGHT(1+2,3+4);    // Z == 21
```

An example

The incorrect evaluation of these macros can evidently be attributed to the fact that macro expansions can easily mix several operators with different evaluation priorities. So when working with complex macro definitions, always pay attention to the precedence rules of C operators and the correct use of parentheses.* It is better to use parentheses too often than too seldom. Writing macro definitions in capital letters (or another specific style) eases future recognition. Programmers will see when using them that they are now dealing with a macro and not a function call. This signaling effect is significant because of the side effects macros may have due to repeated evaluation of their parameters.**

* Motto: "Too many parentheses is better than spending two hours with the debugger."

** See the pair min/max (unfortunately in lower case) in WINDOWS.H for an example.

Size and length values (for buffers or filenames, for instance), ID values for resources and control windows or self-defined flags are particularly good nominees for replacing constant expressions with macros (in many cases even a definition as an enum type may be worth considering). Also, the use of non-standard compiler key words (such as __based, __segment, etc.) is much easier to adapt to other development environments with some cleverly designed macros. Here again I can only re-

#define BASED __based

commend browsing through the header files supplied with the Win16 and Win32 SDKs!

#ifdef eases portability.

The pre-processor statements for conditional compilation are of paramount importance when writing portable source code. First, they enable the implementation of skillful system-specific macro definitions that can conceal API differences from the sources; they also facilitate the portable use of compiler-specific #pragmas and the like. On the other hand, you too can easily distinguish 16-bit from 32-bit code at any time. The following code fragment illustrates both variations:

The constant WIN32 is automatically #defined for any compilation under Windows NT/95.

```
#ifdef WIN32 // first the Win32 specific code
   #define GET_ CTRL_ID(hwnd)   ((HWND)GetWindowLong(hwnd,GWL_ID))
#else // then good old Windows 3.x
   #define GET_CTRL_ID(hwnd)   ((HWND)GetWindowWord(hwnd,GWW_ID))
#endif
...
VOID StartBackgroundProcess(...)
{
   if (GET_ CTRL_ID(hwndMain)==ID_EDIT)
     ...
#ifdef WIN32
   HANDLE hThread=CreateThread(...);
    ...
#else
   UINT uTimer=SetTimer(...);
...
#endif
}
```

The WIN32 constant used in this example is always predefined when a C/C++ program is compiled for the Win32 API. Besides, you'll also find other macros like _X86_, _MIPS_, or _ALPHA_, which indicate the target platform. For more information on these macros see section 5.1 on page 319.

Macros as pseudo functions...

The preceding example shows that the definition of pseudo-functions as macros can be a great time saver, too. Many things that you have to cover with a complex function call can be done much more easily and clearly with a smart macro. Here is another example:

```
#define WS_STD_FLAGS ...  // See above
#define MAINWIN(class,title,menu,inst) CreateWindow(class,\
   title,WS_STD_FLAGS,CW_USEDEFAULT,0,CW_USEDEFAULT,\
   0,NULL,menu,inst,NULL)
```

The creation of top-level windows with the help of this macro is clearer and less subject to typing mistakes than direct calls to the SDK routine. The occasional definition of pseudo-functions which occurs in WIN-DOWS.H falls into the same category:

```
#define MAKEINTRESOURCE(i)  ((LPCSTR)MAKELP(0,(i)))
#define UnlockResource(h)   GlobalUnlock(h)
#define GlobalDiscard(h)    GlobalReAlloc(h,0L,\
   GMEM_MOVEABLE)
```

Moreover, macros can be a big help with type conversions: first, they ease the consistent use of casts; second, there is no need to remember every time what the correct cast operation has to look like; third, such a macro can be quickly updated when the underlying data types change. This single change is certainly much more pleasant than having to browse through some 10,000 lines of source code in order to change maybe 100 items manually... The OS/2 header files have always been exemplary in this respect: there, a lot of conversion macros are defined in order to convert to and from the polymorphic data types of a window procedure (called MPARAM in OS/2 and WPARAM and LPARAM under Win16/32). A few examples to illustrate this spirit:

... and for type conversions.

```
// Macros for type conversion:
#define HWND_FROM_LRESULT(lR)   ((HWND)(UINT)(DWORD)(lR))
#define PTR_FROM_LPARAM(lP)     ((LPVOID)(lP))
#define HWND_TO_LRESULT(hwnd)   ((LRESULT)(UINT)(hwnd))
#define PTR_TO_LPARAM(lP)       ((LPARAM)(lP))
// etc.
```

LRESULT to HWND...

...HWND to LRESULT

It would be a considerable help for the whole matter of porting if Micro-soft decided to supply a complete set of helper macros to convert the most important data types. The header file WINDOWSX.H can be con-sidered a certain step into this direction, so you'll read more about this in the next chapter (see sections 4.3 to 4.5).

Complex macro definitions: a dash of portability

Let's continue: both the macros DECLARE_HANDLE and DECLARE_HANDLE32, already mentioned in Chapter 2 in conjunction with the STRICT option, nicely demonstrate how the definition of portable data types can be accomplished with the help of macros (even if they're a bit complicated). You probably won't need to define such complex macros too often, but they prove that (and how) it works and bring us to the subject of "creative macros"! What about the following set of macros for the portable handling of (additional) window information (i.e., extra bytes) with the aid of the [Get/Set]Window[Long/Word]() APIs?

Portable data type definitions

MEMBERSIZE just calculates the size of a struct member.

```
// A helper macro, so the rest remains (halfway) readable
#define MEMBERSIZE(s,m)   (sizeof(((s NEAR*)1)->m))
```

Read extra bytes...

```
// Macros to access the extra bytes
#define GET_EXTRA(h,s,m,t)   \
  ((t)(MEMBERSIZE(s,m)==sizeof(WORD)?\
  GetWindowWord(h,FIELDOFFSET(s,m)):\
  GetWindowLong(h,FIELDOFFSET(s,m))))
```

... and write them.

```
#define SET_EXTRA(h,s,m,i)  (MEMBERSIZE(s,m)==sizeof(WORD)?\
  SetWindowWord(h,FIELDOFFSET(s,m),(WORD)(UINT)i):\
  SetWindowLong(h,FIELDOFFSET(s,m),(LONG)i))
```

Read standard information...

```
// Macros to access the standard information
#define GET_STDINFO(h,m,t)   ((t)(m==GWW_HINSTANCE||\
  m==GWW_HWNDPARENT||m==GWW_ID?\
  GetWindowWord(h,m):GetWindowLong(h,m)))
```

... and write it.

```
#define SET_STDINFO(h,m,i)   (m==GWW_HINSTANCE||\
  m==GWW_HWNDPARENT||m==GWW_ID?\
  SetWindowWord(h,m,(WORD)(UINT)i):\
  SetWindowLong(h,m,(LONG)i))
```

All these macros and then a few are found on the accompanying disk (see Appendix 7).

```
// Self-defined struct for accessing the extra bytes
typedef struct {
  UINT uInfo;
  LONG lMoreInfo;
```

```
  HWND hwndFirst;
} MYEXTRABYTES;

// Later, when registering the window class:
wc.cbWndExtra=sizeof(MYEXTRABYTES); ...; RegisterClass(&wc);

// And in WinMain():
HWND hwnd=CreateWindow(...);
SET_STDINFO(hwnd,GWW_ID,MY_WINDOW_ID);
SET_EXTRA(hwnd,MYEXTRABYTES,hwndFirst,hwnd);
```

As shown above, you now have portable access to the standard window WORDs and LONGs of a window with the help of the [GET/SET]_STD-INFO macros and the constants GWL_* and GWW_*, respectively. [GET/SET]_EXTRA, on the other hand, ease the access to information in the window's extra bytes with the help of an explicitly defined structure. (To be able to use the extra bytes, the required memory space has to be reserved in the WNDCLASS member cbWndExtra when registering the class.) Because these macros automatically calculate the correct offset and the length of the data type, they have the added advantage of being more transparent; furthermore, it is very simple to change the basic data types (such as a 16-bit HWND widened to 32 bit) since only the MYEX-TRABYTES struct and (if at all necessary) the macro definitions have to be adjusted accordingly. But all the places where the macros are actually used don't need to be touched at all!

So, what is the net effect of these complicated definitions?

Of course, we could have defined equivalent functions instead of a set of macros. In a very similar manner, this approach leads to portable programs, too; the answer to the question about the preferred solution first depends on the size of the macros or functions (the more code being generated by the same macro used over and over again, the bigger the program code section gets). However, short and clearly defined macros can sometimes even *save* space in comparison to function calls (especially when the optimizer of the compiler is doing a good job).

Macro or function?

Also, performance considerations can play an important role in this respect. The above-mentioned macros are very suitable to illustrate this effect: although their definitions seem to be quite "cumbersome" and even implicate a run-time test to determine the size of the data type or the GW[W/L]_* constants, the macros can be evaluated even by average C compilers in such a way that actually only the call to the correct

A complex macro doesn't necessarily mean a lot of code.

[Set/Get]Window[Long/Word]() function appears in the generated code (see also figure 3.2). The evaluation takes place in all macros, of course, but the compiler can discover the result during the translation process (i.e., at compile time), so only the absolutely necessary part of the macro must be compiled to code. As already mentioned, if your compiler is good at optimizing and if you can operate with expressions that are evaluated during translation, it is not that difficult to write complex, yet efficient macros.

Figure 3.2: From macro to program code

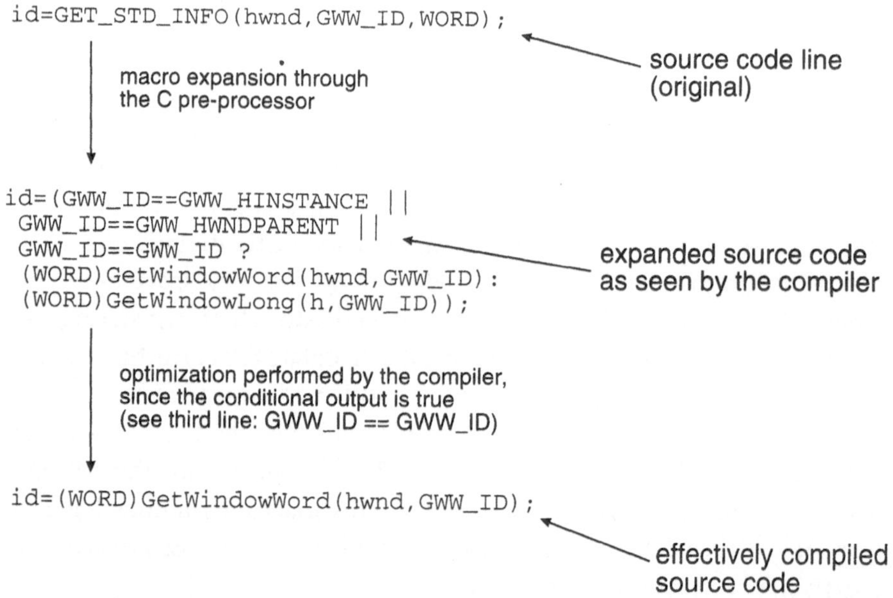

```
id=GET_STD_INFO(hwnd,GWW_ID,WORD);
```
source code line (original)

macro expansion through the C pre-processor

```
id=(GWW_ID==GWW_HINSTANCE ||
 GWW_ID==GWW_HWNDPARENT ||
 GWW_ID==GWW_ID ?
 (WORD)GetWindowWord(hwnd,GWW_ID) :
 (WORD)GetWindowLong(h,GWW_ID));
```
expanded source code as seen by the compiler

optimization performed by the compiler, since the conditional output is true (see third line: GWW_ID == GWW_ID)

```
id=(WORD)GetWindowWord(hwnd,GWW_ID);
```
effectively compiled source code

To conclude this section, let's have a look to another, somewhat simpler example that might serve as an inspiration. It shows a macro used to ease the work with modal dialog boxes, by replacing the bracketing with [Make/Free]ProcInstance() still needed (unfortunately) in the Win16 version.

Observe the block defined through { .. } in the 16-bit fork!

```
#ifdef WIN32
    #define DLGBOX(hi,lpTemplate,hwndP,Proc1) \
        DialogBox(hi,lpTemplate,hwndP,Proc1)
#else // Alas, we're at 16 bit...
    #define DLGBOX(hi,lpTemplate,hwndP,Proc1)  {\
```

```
      DLGPROC p=(DLGPROC)MakeProcInstance((FARPROC)Proc1,hi);\
      DialogBox(hi,lpTemplate,hwndP,p);\
      FreeProcInstance((FARPROC)p); }
  #endif
```

Last but not least, I don't want to withhold two serious drawbacks of using macros: since they only serve as text replacement *before* the actual compilation, they are not included with the debugging information the compiler stores in the object files. Hence you can't access constants which have been created with #define during testing or debugging. (Interestingly, this is not true for C++ type consts which play a similar role: these constants *are* seen in the symbol table. Another reason for C++?) Second, of course, the replacement text will get compiled instead of the calls to the macro pseudo-functions. So, what you see in the debugger as source code is *not* the code the compiler has effectively seen and compiled (a good case of WYSINWYG). To be able to see the real thing, you'll have either to descend to assembler level or to study the pre-processor output. But in spite of these drawbacks, macros simplify the creation and maintenance of portable programs to such an extent that (in my opinion) they are definitely fundamental to the process. Their absence in Pascal and Modula-2 is particularly painful (but perhaps Niklaus Wirth will at last design a language with a macro processor included? Nope, even Oberon, his newest creation, is still far off in this respect...).

Where there's a lot of light, there's some shadow too.

3.4 Simple Data Types

"Words, words, words..." William Shakespeare, Hamlet

Well, obviously already Hamlet (or better, his creator) had to fight against them: WORDs. This quotation suits Windows developers particularly well, because WORD, of all the simple data types, is the one creating the largest portability problems. Using simple C data types always ends up in a mess when the source code depends implicitly on certain assumptions that are different from one platform to another. Even the same processor can establish different sizes for simple data types:* 386 code in a 16-bit segment implies 2-byte ints, in a 32-bit segment, the "natural" length will double (caution: this also affects data

Unfortunately, even with ANSI C the simple data types are platform specific.

* Well, at least if the CPU comes from Intel...

149

types you wouldn't think of in the first place, such as enumerations introduced with *enum*).

Since ANSI C unfortunately leaves the size of all simple data types to the implementation (one of the rare, but serious, weaknesses of the definition), an int will not be the same size everywhere! You'll find a table of all basic Win16 and Win32 data types in Appendix 1; furthermore, section 4.2 on page 205 deals with the most important subtleties. In the following, I won't discuss the features of the various data types defined differently in both APIs, but I'll give some details on basic hints and observations concerning the correct use of simple data types to allow maintainable and portable source codes. So, we won't deal with the difference between HWND and WORD but instead with the correct utilization of the fundamental data types for different processors (or processor modes). Or put into one sentence: what do you have to pay attention to when you want to use simple data types in order to make your programs as portable as possible and in such a way that they can be adapted to other CPU architectures with a minimum of fuss?

See appendix 1 and section 4.2 for more information.

Own data type definitions

Use additional levels of indirection as much as possible.

The most important rule, already suggested by the numerous Windows data type definitions, seems obvious, yet is often overlooked: whenever necessary, introduce a new indirection level between the built-in data types and their utilization, for example, in struct definitions or function prototypes. The following simple example will illustrate what I mean. Imagine you have a globally defined and frequently used data structure (on a 16-bit machine such as an 80286 AT) in which several unsigned ints are used for all sorts of things. One may be an index into an array of doubles, another serves to store flags or bitwise information, a third one will have to deal with the result of a numerical calculation:

```
// A self-defined structure
typedef struct {
    unsigned int Index;
    unsigned int Flags;
    unsigned int LastResult;
} MYOWN_STRUCT;
```

These three members together have a length of 3 * sizeof(unsigned int) == 6 byte; with their use, you can address an array with 65,536 double elements maximum (which, for its part, ought to be defined as HUGE), store up to 16 single flags bit by bit, and keep numerical results up to and including 65535. If you recompile this structure for a real 32-bit processor without changing anything (i.e., sizeof(int) == 4), the length will double and the structure will have a size of 12 byte. Now your array can have over 4 billion values (but strangely isn't HUGE anymore...); calculations comprise values from 0 to 4,294,967,295. And of course, you'll be able to save up to 32 flags. If all this is necessary or at least makes sense under a 32-bit system: congratulations — you'll have little need to change things. But suppose you only have four flags to store, or that the array which is addressed by the member Index can never contain more than 512 entries. In these cases the structure will consume much more memory space than needed (especially if used often). What to do? Well, that's easy:

After recompiling on a 32-bit machine

```
typedef struct {
    unsigned short Index;
    unsigned short Flags;
    unsigned int lastResult;
} MYOWN_STRUCT;
```

sizeof(MYOWN_STRUCT) now == 8 (32 bit) or 6 (16 bit)

A single small change in the header files, and here we are! Are we? Not completely, as is shown in the following code extract from one of the numerous C source files in which the structure is used:

```
MYOWN_STRUCT myown;

void SetMyOwnStruct(unsigned int newIndex,unsigned int
    newFlags,unsigned int newResult)
{
    myown.index=newIndex;
    myown.flags=newFlags;
    myown.lastResult=newResult;
}
```

In the best case such code will generate some compiler warnings; in the worst case it can conceal some devilish problems. The solution seems evident: you simply change the prototype and definition of the function. But then, you'll notice corresponding warnings at all the places where this function is being called. Then you'll start to modify all those places, which will lead to myriads of other rough edges. At the end and three weeks later, you will finally be at a point where you can approach the next of your umpteen data structures... (this scenario is only a bit exaggerated; especially large projects pressed with great difficulties into the 16-bit restrictions of the segmented Intel world might be even worse!). And the moral of the story? Well, the already mentioned introduction of another level with indirect type definitions:*

* No, the real moral of this story is: be very prudent with Intel programmers, because they're mostly masochists.

```
#ifdef Win32 // in a 32-bit system
    typedef unsigned short INDEX;
    typedef unsigned short FLAGS;
    typedef unsigned int   RESULT;
#else // Win16
    typedef unsigned int INDEX;
    typedef unsigned int FLAGS;
    typedef unsigned int RESULT;
#endif
...
typedef struct {
    INDEX index;
    FLAGS flags;
    RESULT lastResult;
} MYONW_STRUCT;

void SetMyOwnStruct(INDEX newIndex,FLAGS NewFlags,
    RESULT newResult);
```

Another level of typedefs

As you can see, using a self-defined level of typedefs combined with conditional compilation leads to the transparent use of all three members and enables them to be used in the sources without major changes (in a sense, a typedef is just an elaborated form of a macro definition!). The reasonable organization of the standard data types used into "logical" classes or categories and the creation of corresponding type definitions are extremely helpful to prevent wasted porting efforts. The main difficulty here is to keep the balance while designing your data types: too careful application of this abstraction mechanism can lead to programs difficult to maintain. On the other hand, using it too heavily can result in complex and puffy sources that some time later can't be understood by anybody — not even by their original creator. As a rule of thumb, I would say that all categories used globally* in your application are good candidates for type definitions of their own.

*or at least in more than one source code module

... and related problems

Unfortunately, it's not that easy to steer clear of all traps related to using simple data types. A good example could be the utilization of printf() or wsprintf() to print formatted values. We'll stick to the above two (system-dependent) defined structures. The following simple printing of the member values will fail under Windows 95, since the sizes of myown.index and myown.flags match the format string only under Win16:

Alas, a type layer alone is not a perfect solution.

```
printf("index:%u,flags:%u,lastResult:%u",
    myown.index,myown.flags,myown.lastResult);
```

Either you help yourself with #ifdef, which unfortunately will be required with each printf() and will render your source code quite unclear if used too much:

```
#ifdef WIN32
    printf("index:%hu,flags:%hu,lastResult:%u",...);
#else
    printf("index:%u,flags:%u,lastResult:%u",...);
#endif
```

Or you remember all the stuff concerning the pre-processor in the preceding section, which ends up to be helpful here:

The pre-processor helps!

```
#ifdef WIN32
    #define PF_INDEX  "%hu"     // printf flag unsigned short
    #define PF_FLAG   PF_INDEX  // ditto
    #define PF_RESULT "%u"      // for unsigned int
#else
```

```
        #define PF_INDEX   "%u"        // printf flag unsigned int
        #define PF_FLAG    PF_INDEX    // ditto
        #define PF_RESULT  PF_INDEX    // ditto
    #endif

    ...

    printf("index:"PF_INDEX",flags:"PF_FLAG",lastResult:"\
    PF_RESULT),myown.index,myown.flags,myown.lastResult);
```

Such a tricky usage seems justified only if the function concerned is called often. Here again, you'll have to balance the ease of your work with the readability of the source codes.

Cast operations

Defining all important data types with typedefs in their own shell, adjustable at any time, is extremely important for portability; however, clearly and correctly defined cast operations must also be defined. Carelessly (or not at all!) implemented type conversions will quickly cause big problems, so I can only refer you to the corresponding compiler warnings!* If you have to perform a lot of repeating cast operations with Windows and/or self-defined data types, you should think about a group of macros that will make the whole matter first simpler and second more transparent. Hints and examples to that subject can be found in section 3.3 on page 142 concerning pre-processor usage.

* See also section 3.8 beginning on page 178.

About erroneous casts and other wrongdoers

Never write code based on implicit assumptions about size or other properties of a specific data type! Someone who trusts that an unsigned int will overflow after 65535 and restart with 0, or who packs two Win16 NEAR pointers into a single LONG or even simply equates HWND, short, and WORD, will get the shock of his life when trying to port his programs. Of course, certain assumptions concerning the data types used are necessary and permissible. They'll start to become a problem only when you don't apply them consistently or when you use one of their basic features unchecked. Two deterring examples shall demonstrate this:

```
    hIcon=(WORD)SendMessage(hwndStatic,STM_GETICON,0,0);  //Brrrr!
```

Such (or similar) code starts with the idea that an HICON corresponds to a WORD. Regardless of whether and in which Windows implementation this might be true, the code above is simply extremely poor programming practice and can only be attributed to thoughtlessness or grubbiness. If the cast (WORD) were simply replaced with (HICON), the compiler would go with it and the resulting code would also run correctly when sizeof(HICON) != sizeof(WORD). But again, Microsoft goes ahead as a shining example: *many* places in the example programs supplied with its C compilers* contain bad code as shown above — which allows us to draw interesting (if not to say alarming) conclusions about the quality of the Windows source codes…. Most basic types are represented through 4-byte entities under Win32, yet a lot of programmers seem to use (WORD) as a magic "cure-all" cast — and that way the stumbling stones are literally preprogrammed!

HICON == WORD?

* which, I thought, were assumed to have some pedagogical value?

The ironclad and second best rule for the utilization of simple (also self-defined) data types: check if the cast is really necessary and always (!) work with the correct typedef. And here you have the other example I promised:

Is a cast really necessary?

```
WORD wTextLen=strlen(S);
```

I can almost hear you screaming, "What?? Such a harmless statement, used a thousand times and obviously correct!!" But hold on a moment before you start believing I am losing my mind: unfortunately, you can find such statements in my source code and not too rarely.** This is the force of habit! But based on the surely unsuspicious Kurt Tucholsky: "Never believe an expert who maintains to have done something this way all the time: one can easily make the same mistake for 20 years!" True, but luckily one can realize that one has done things wrong some time and do it right afterwards! So, let's have a look at the prototype of strlen() in STRING.H: you'll quickly notice that the return value of the function has the type size_t, which is defined in ANSI C as unsigned int! Everything's just fine as long as you write the above statement in Win16. But what happens under Win32, where an unsigned int suddenly contains 32 bit? Then, you'll have a WORD variable (16 bit) on the left and a function call result with 32 bit on the right. You'll have luck if you happen to work only with strings smaller than 64 KB. Even if you ignore the inevitable compiler warning, it can't happen too much. But things can get much more unpleasant, for example, if your code looked like this:

** to my regret…

size_t == unsigned int

```
// Suppose the string in lpszTextBuf has 66000 characters
WORD wTextLen=strlen(lpszTextBuf); // Now wTextLen == 464!
HGLOBAL h=GlobalAlloc(GMEM_MOVEABLE,wTextLen);
LPSTR lpsz=GlobalLock(h);
strcpy(lpsz,lpszTextBuf); // GP fault or worse
```

Admittedly, this scenario is unlikely in a 16-bit environment (this is exactly why code like the one shown above worked correctly for years and

which can easily handle
more than 64 KB of text...

years). But with the enlarged Win32 edit controls,* such code is surely
not off the mark.... But that's the way it is and the type size_t that is used
quite often in ANSI C run-time functions (and unfortunately too seldom
in other programs) is just incompatible with a 16-bit unsigned int. In a
sense, the infamous 64 KB limit is not only valid for segments and (often)
length, width, or height of any object, it also has (re)shaped our thinking
and the programming models in our minds. The porting process (and
subsequently programming under Win32) will be easier, the faster you
succeed in forgetting this way of thinking and consequently the more
your source code reflects those changes. In this sense, it will surely be

Conceptual differences
between 16 and 32 bit

beneficial to the whole business of porting if you spend one (or several)
hour(s) thinking about basic conceptual differences between 16- and 32-
bit environments before starting concrete work with the Win32 SDK.

May I introduce myself: sizeof()

Back to the subject: one of the frequently made implicit assumptions that
quickly turns out to be disastrous under Win32 is the utilization of nu-

How to get the size of a data
type?

merical constants in the sources in order to describe the size of certain
data types, according to the motto: an HWND or a NEAR pointer is
clearly 2 byte long, a LONG or FAR pointer of course 4! Having this in
mind (see above) is unfortunate enough, but that's the way it is. Things
begin to get very dangerous when these assumptions make their way
into your source code, as shown in the following example, which, compiled under Win32, can create all sorts of bad things:

```
// Allocate memory for 8 HWNDs
hahwnd=LocalAlloc(LMEM_FIXED,16); // Under WIN32
// sizeof(HWND)*8 isn't exactly 16!
// Or slightly better, but at the end just as disastrous:
```

```
hahwnd=LocalAlloc(LMEM_FIXED,sizeof(WORD)*8);
...
pahwnd[7]=hwnd7; // either GP fault or,
// more probably, uncontrolled access into the
// application's address space
```

As already mentioned, *all* numerical constants should be replaced by adequate #defines (especially if you can't remember a few months later why all of a sudden the number 42 appears at a certain place...) or in this case by the sizeof operator:

```
hahwnd=LocalAlloc(LMEM_FIXED,sizeof(HWND)*8);
// or, often even better:
#define CHILD_WNDS  8
...
hahwnd=LocalAlloc(LMEM_FIXED,sizeof(HWND)*CHILD_WNDS);
```

Incidentally, the two standard ANSI C header files LIMITS.H (for integers) and FLOAT.H (for floating-point types) make interesting reading matter concerning the size and range of the available basic types!

See also LIMITS.H and FLOAT.H.

Always good for a surprise: BOOL!

The following comment is relevant not only for porting to Win32 but for Windows programming in general; it concerns a particular nasty data type: BOOL and the two related constants FALSE and TRUE. In C, as you certainly know, a condition is false if it has the value 0. It is true, however, if the value is distinct from 0. And here is the problem: the definition "#define TRUE 1" is certainly distinct from 0; but a logical true doesn't necessarily mean the same as the constant TRUE. This confusion is caused by various Windows functions whose return value of type BOOL has been defined in a somewhat inconsistent manner: they should return either FALSE (0) for an error or TRUE (1) for success, but in fact return any value distinct from 0 to indicate the success of the operation. The frequently used RegisterClass() function, which (up to and including Windows 3.0) has been defined with a return type of BOOL, is one of the many exceptions. In this case, the return value of FALSE really shows what the (naive?) programmer assumes: failure. On the other hand, suc-

Therefore "#define FALSE 0"

One of the exceptions: RegisterClass()

cess will not be indicated by TRUE (or the value 1), but by a value distinct from 0 (namely the atom value for the class name, which happens to be somewhere between 0xC000 and 0xFFFF). The following statement is guaranteed to end up in a mess:

```
if (RegisterClass(&wc)==TRUE) ... // Oh no, not that way!
```

Oh, I can hear all the C gurus groan and moan: "A *real* C programmer would *never* write such stupid code." They are likely to be right in this admittedly simple case. But a presumably harmless and correct statement can be very quickly expanded through the extensive use of macros,* so "behind the scenes" code similar to the one above may very well result. The function GlobalUnlock() with the following prototype demonstrates another tricky example:

* or code generators

```
BOOL WINAPI GlobalUnlock(HGLOBAL); // TRUE == success?
```

The return value of this function under Win16 is the current value of the lock counter!** And this sets the stage for two subtle traps: first, a typical developer when confronted with a prototype like this will (rightfully) think that the return value indicates the success of the operation: FALSE == object not unlocked, TRUE == object unlocked. Not at all: the return value is to be interpreted in exactly the opposite way — a fine example of careless API design on the part of Microsoft. (A Windows developer encounters so many exceptions over the years that the rules are becoming the exceptions. Long ago, when the Win16 API had only a few hundred functions, these exceptions were just annoying. Nowadays, we're supposed to deal with *thousands* of functions, so we can expect a somewhat more consistent API design, can't we?! Is somebody in Redmond hearing this?)

** This definition is truly a masterpiece in API design, even for Microsoft circumstances!

Second, and here comes the really tricky point, the return value is the actual value of the lock counter. And so the function can easily return values other than 0 or 1! This becomes quite nasty when you write program lines like these:

```
if (GlobalUnlock(hMem)==TRUE) ... // Well, and now?
...
if (GlobalUnlock(hMem)) ...        // Not much better!
```

Whatever the developer had in mind with these lines, the expected result can definitively be obtained only on the day when Christmas and Easter coincide. Conclusion: first, double-check (especially with functions you are not using frequently) whether your "intuitive" understanding of the return type BOOL corresponds to the understanding* of the function's developer. Second, make sure that explicit comparisons on TRUE (or the value 1) won't occur at all or only with functions definitely delivering a "real" BOOL. The following simple macro can be used as a shell around function calls where this isn't the case:

or non-understanding?

```
#define TO_BOOL(fPseudoBool)   ((fPseudoBool)?TRUE:FALSE)
```

Fortunately, we don't have to care about some other *very* unpleasant features of simple data types while porting Win16 programs. I am thinking of the portable utilization of bit fields and of course of the different byte order of (for example) Intel CPUs and Motorola processors. This spares us some really nasty traps (but Windows NT has a portable design; and I have heard something about it being ported to Macs...). Nevertheless, it is prudent to use access macros as much as possible to access certain parts of a variable or, vice versa, to assemble various parts to obtain a value. For this purpose, WINDOWS.H already contains some macros (see for instance [HI/LO]WORD, MAKELONG etc.), which you can complete with your own add-ons at any time. But if you do so, use the Microsoft macros as a guide: using an incorrectly defined macro over and over again is much worse than using no macro at all!

Little endian vs. big endian

3.5 Structured Data

"Though this be madness, yet there is method in 't." William Shakespeare, Hamlet

It seems that Shakespeare also has a suitable comment for the definition of self-defined complex data types, which is made possible in C with the help of structs and unions. If you took the advice and hints of the preceding section to heart, you shouldn't expect too many problems here. But there are still a few special cases to observe. Let's start with unions, which, fortunately, are not used that much (a little hint for non-C programmers: a C struct roughly corresponds to a RECORD in Pascal or

struct and RECORD

Modula-2; a union is a variant RECORD without an explicit CASE variable).

Unions: memory economy, shady maneuvers or what?

There are mainly two reasons to define a union: either you want to save some memory space and overlap several variables of different types or you need some very tricky type conversions that are not (easily) possible with casts. The first case is not so important here: there are no objections to this way of type definitions and utilizations as long as the underlying base types have been defined correctly. You just might want to invest some time investigating the question of how far the alignment of the various members can influence memory allocation and performance if the union is being used in other structs. You'll find some tips about this subject later on in the discussion about structs.

Unions and tricky memory manipulations

Things are quite different if you want to (mis-)use a union for some *really* smart type manipulations: those definitions will surely have to be adapted. You should enjoy the following (to some extent contrived) delicacy with full attention (see also figure 3.3 on the following page about the memory layout):

```
typedef struct { WORD ofs,seg } OS;
typedef void FAR* LP;
typedef struct { VOID NEAR* np; WORD ds; } NP;
...
typedef union {
  OS os;
  LP lp;
  NP np;
} BAD_TRICK;
...
BAD_TRICK bt; // global variable (stored in the
// application's data segment)
...
bt.lp=&bt;
printf("seg:ofs = %x:%x\n",bt.os.seg,bt.os.ofs);
printf("data segment: %x",bt.np.ds);
```

First, you can see that the creator of this union assumed that the segment (or selector) and offset of an address could be located in 16-bit values each. Second, he thinks that a FAR pointer consists of a segment and an offset. Third, the programmer makes the best use of his knowledge that global variables in a data segment can be split into a NEAR pointer and the data selector (DS) as base register. Last but not least, he is sure that a NEAR pointer combined with a selector results in a FAR pointer. True, all these assumptions are completely valid for Win16. Unfortunately, with Win32, all four are either bogus or at least unusable because of the entirely different memory layout!

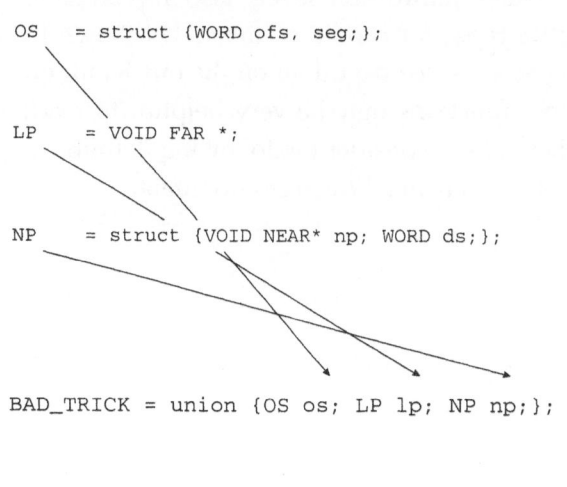

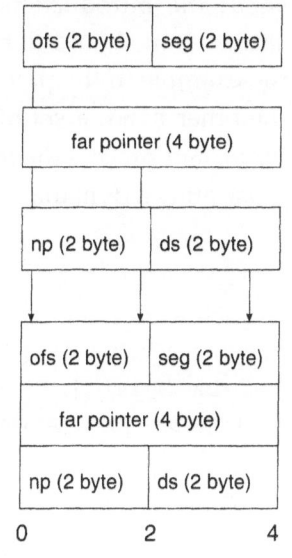

Figure 3.3: The memory layout of the union BAD_TRICK

As shown in the example, such "smart" defined unions are *guaranteed* to be non-portable. BAD_TRICK cannot be used in a satisfying way under Win32 because of the completely different address space concepts. Even less extreme cases normally make use of non-portable information concerning the included data types* — unions are so exposed to CPU changes that you should only use them if you haven't found after much thought, a better way to solve the problem in a portable manner. And if it's *really* necessary: limit the use of those unions to very few modules and create, if at all possible, a macro or function layer for member access

*Somewhat obvious — otherwise we won't need a union!

161

instead of directly fiddling around with them just because this is slightly more convenient (or efficient).

Structured use of structs

An important abstraction mechanism

Now let's have a look at structures: you should use them as often as possible in conjunction with the necessary functions for processing since they are one of the most important abstraction mechanisms available for C/C++ programmers. Even if a C struct doesn't nearly reflect the class concept of C++, it enables you to realize safe and easy maintainable, yet complex, data types (at least if you work methodically and with some self-discipline). It will be beneficial to employ the hints mentioned above about the introduction of further indirection levels also for creating structs. You should define data types for certain members (as shown in the example in the preceding section, see page 150) on the one hand; on the other hand, a set of helper functions may be very helpful (to read, write, and process the members). Let's consider the following definitions illustrating a dynamic array of integers in a Win16 environment:

```
typedef struct {
   HGLOBAL hMem;
   int iCount;
   int iArray[1];
} IARRAY, FAR* LPIARRAY;
...
hTmp=GlobalAlloc(GHND,sizeof(IARRAY)+sizeof(int)*100);
lpia=(LPIARRAY)GlobalLock(hTmp);
lpia->hMem=hTmp;
lpia->iCount=100;   // 100? Or 101!?
lpia->iArray[352]=42;   // Good grief!
```

* At least, this is better than the other way around...

The code is all right (except the last two lines) but still improvable: a constant could be defined for the size of the array to be allocated; you should take into consideration that one more element is allocated then a first glance at the code might suggest.* As far as I'm concerned, the big disadvantage seems to be that each user of the IARRAY struct has to be informed about its internals in order to be able to use them correctly (see figure 3.4). This has two major drawbacks: first, you can make mistakes (such as allocating 101 elements and setting lpia->iCount to 100, for example); second, all source files using the type IARRAY have to be adjusted if the definition of the structure happens to be changed sometime. And often changes are inevitable with the transition to a new operating system!

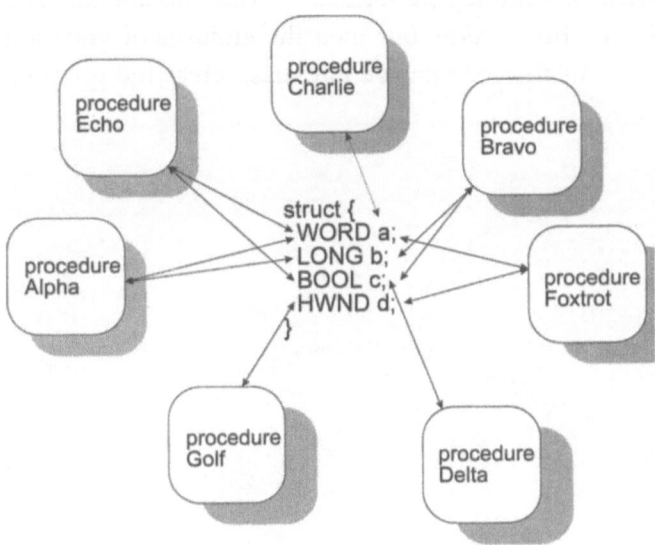

Figure 3.4: Direct access to members of structs: simple, but hardly maintainable.

The following model definitions kill two birds with one stone:

```
#define STRICT          // Always!
...
typedef struct {...};    // As above!
DECLARE_HANDLE(HIA);     // a self-defined STRICT handle...
HIA AllocIA(int iCount); // allocates iCount ints
BOOL FreeIA(HIA hIA);    // deallocates array only, if
// hIA==lpia->hMem
int GetBound(HIA hIA);               // delivers iCount
int SetElement(HIA hIA,int el,int val); // writes or ...
int GetElement(HIA hIA,int el);          // reads an element
```

I'll skip the implementations of the five functions, as they are evident. After what has been said, the advantages of this approach should be obvious (and are illustrated in figure 3.5); admittedly, the deciding drawback catches your eye immediately: code written with the aid of these functions is of course safer, easier to maintain, and easier to port; alas, it is also slower (particularly when frequent accesses to IARRAYs with [Get/Set]Element() are performed). A classical dilemma: either you write good, structured code, but then the enduser of your application may nod off — or the code is fast, but, alas!, gives the programmer the creeps ....

Figure 3.5: Structured
access with a layer of access
functions.

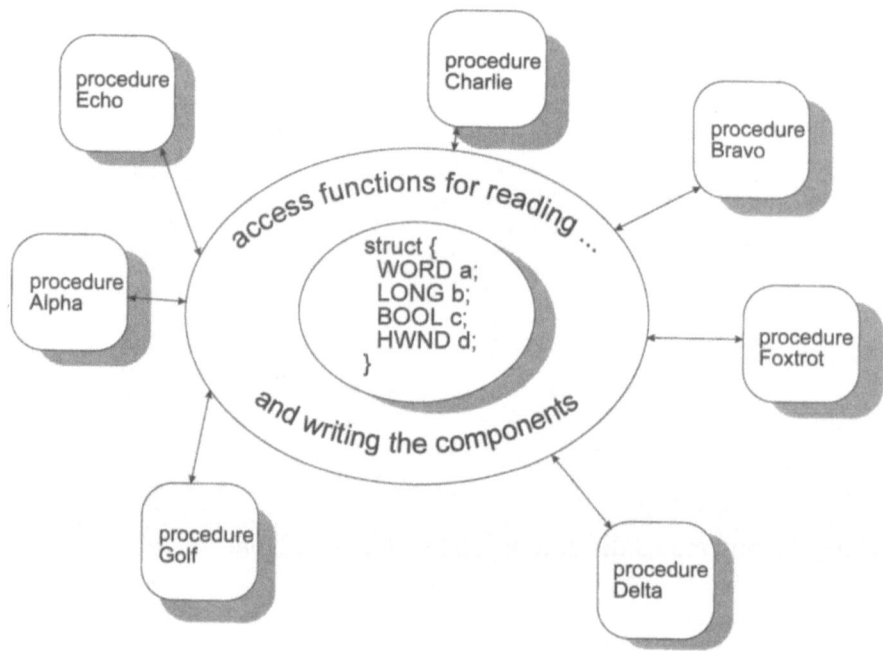

Performance?
Or maintainability?

Unfortunately, once on the horns of a such dilemma, one tends to draw the wrong conclusions and fundamentally prefers the performance of a program to its maintainability and safety. But why throw in the towel so

Or both?

quickly? Before making hasty decisions, think a moment about the whole thing:

A profiler may help!

- OK, the maintainable code *may* be slower. But how much slower? And can you exactly tell where? Often only very few places in a program are performance bottlenecks. And they are easy to find with a profiler and to optimize accordingly. Non-specific statements complaining about (too) great speed losses are of doubtful quality.

- Couldn't you pack at least those parts into separate access functions that are either infrequently called or whose internal overhead is so large that the additional function call to be made wouldn't have serious consequences anyway? *How large is the function overhead really?*

- Are you sure there are no other ways and means to achieve the desired effect? You could define [Set/Get]Element() as macros. Or *Macros?* you may use the capability of defining (small) functions inline. The latter solution is an elegant one, but unfortunately not portable (ANSI C doesn't know inline functions); still, you can use it with a lot of C compilers. The critical question here is probably to which platforms the code is likely to be ported: if you want to port a Win16 program to x86 Win32 by using the Microsoft or Borland C compiler, then there is no problem in using inline functions. On the other hand, if the target platform is a totally different system, it can cost so much effort to port that it could be better to rewrite certain parts of the project in C++ (where inline functions are part of the language definition). *Or inline?*

- In fact, this solution is also worth being considered: C++ offers (if *Or C++?* mastered) extremely powerful mechanisms for the structuring and abstraction of data. It may be better to implement parts or even the whole program in C++.

- Finally, it is debatable whether slower code (as long as it is not too slow...) is not justified by higher crash security and better maintainability. To be very clear about that: many users *indeed* prefer working with a reliable program than with a superfast one! Or to say it in a provocative way: if I realize that a definitely indispensable program is too slow on my hardware, then I know that a CPU upgrade is due sooner or later. But if the application keeps crashing, there is no other alternative than to accept it (with moaning and groaning). Of course, it is not always feasible to purchase new hardware, but this point of view carries a certain logic: why should only programmers pay the bill for the hardware engineers? If the latter built better processors,* then our programs could be more structured — the 8088 vs. 80386 clearly demonstrates what I mean! (And since this remark will earn me a

* For example, a CPU with so large a cache that the whole run-time library can be stored in optimized microcode.

165

"beating" from the hard guys anyway: section 4.6 on page 241 has some more polemical remarks and assertions on this subject...)

But back to the structures! A summary of all this: most of the time you will access structures in C in the traditional way — that means directly. This doesn't necessarily adversely affect the portability, but it is certainly not the recommended practice as far as software engineering (and portability) is concerned. Unfortunately, most efforts to change this will apply to new projects rather than to existing code....

Net result: direct accesses show room for improvement.

Structures and memory layout

I'm afraid this observation is not true for another issue associated with structures to which you should definitely pay attention and which can provoke quite a few changes even in existing source codes. I'm talking about the packing of individual components in structures, also called structure alignment. Until now the Windows versions just had to take the (mostly rather dumb) Intel processors into consideration and therefore could use the densest packing in order to save some memory space. This is not portable at all since most *reasonable* CPU architectures require that all data types with a certain length can only be used with a certain memory layout, therefore an alignment is needed. Not observing this rule will cause either slower code* or, worse, the program won't run at all. (Actually this is true also for the 386 class of CPUs.) Generally, the "natural" register size of the underlying processor defines the alignment of variables in memory. Plainly spoken: for x86 CPUs with access to n-byte long integers in 32-bit segments, the variable has to be aligned on an n-byte boundary ($n = 1, 2, 4$). This is also true for the MIPS R4000 and DEC's Alpha processors, even if the latter also know 8-byte integers. So, an unsigned short can begin at any 2-byte boundary (offset 0, 2, 4, etc.), while an unsigned int should be aligned at a 4-byte boundary (offset 0, 4, 8, etc.).

* because the processor has to deal with bus exception all the time.

An x86 will "punish" the attempt of accessing incorrectly aligned variables just with some wait states while both RISC processors are a bit more ruthless: they trigger a processor exception that must be caught and processed by the system software. The responsible exception handler normally will deal with the error and makes the desired memory item available; however, there could be an enormous performance loss.

And who knows whether other architectures for which NT may be available one day won't be even more restrictive….

Of course, this has some consequences: first in line is the compiler, which has to build aligned struct members through the insertion of filling bytes ("structure padding") in order to ensure the fastest possible access. But since nowadays each and every compiler feature has a switch (and/or #pragma),* the programmer can disable, enable, or switch this activity at will. Because of its denser packing, Win16 even *requires* the explicit use of a compiler switch (or a #pragma) in order to switch off the normal compiler padding to 2-byte boundaries (and many programmers, forgetting this, have spent sheer endless nights in debugging sessions…).

Actually, at least one!

Generally, under Win32 the following rule applies: keep off these switches! Structures have to be correctly defined if they are to be used properly by the various processor types. And this job is better left to the compiler! What does that mean for the Win32 developer? First of all, you should take a closer look at the memory layout of your Win16 structures and take the size and alignment of the basic types into consideration (see also Appendix 1 on page 355). Then you can try to eliminate all cases with an incorrect alignment to optimize the size of the struct. To do so, simply observe the above-mentioned rule: data types with a length of n bytes are aligned on an n-byte boundary. If possible and if the sources don't have to be adapted too much, don't be afraid to change even the placement of certain members. An example for clarification:

Check the memory layout of your Win16 structs.

```
// Win16 with byte packing switched on
typedef struct {
  WORD wSizeXYZ;    // Offset : 0, OK
  char chX;         // 2, OK
  WORD wXLen;       // 3, would be non-aligned, improve!
  Char chY;         // 5, OK
  WORD wYLen;       // 6, OK
  char chZ;         // 8, OK
  WORD wZLen;       // 9, would be non-aligned, improve!
  LONG lSum;        // 11, ditto
  DWORD dwXYZ;      // 15, ditto
} XYZ; // sizeof(XYZ) == 19
```

As indicated by the offsets, the members wXLen, wZLen, lSum, and dwXYZ would not be properly aligned under Win32. So, recompiled

Not properly aligned

without any further alteration under Win32, this structure would be
internally changed by the compiler as follows:

```
typedef struct {
    WORD wSizeXYZ;      // Offset : 0, OK
    char chX;           // 2, OK
    char Filler;        // 1 byte for padding, done by the compiler
    WORD wXLen;         // 4, OK
    char chY;           // 6, OK
    char Filler;        // again 1 byte as padding
    WORD wYLen;         // 8, OK
    char chZ;           // 10, OK
    char Filler;        // and a third byte as padding
    WORD wZLen;         // 12, OK
    char Filler[2];     // LONG requires a 4-byte alignment,
                        // therefore 2 bytes as padding
    LONG lSum;          // 16, OK
    DWORD dwXYZ;        // 20, OK
} XYZ; // sizeof(XYZ) == 24 -- 5 bytes more than Win16!
```

Align and optimize! In order to minimize these five bytes by which each XYZ is larger (see
also figure 3.6 on the next page), you could easily modify the structure as
follows:

```
typedef struct {
    WORD wSizeXYZ;      // Offset : 0, OK
    char chX;           // 2, OK
    char chY;           // 3, OK
    char chZ;           // 4, OK
    WORD wXLen;         // compiler will insert a byte before,
                        // therefore 6, OK
    LONG lSum;          // 8, OK
    DWORD dwXYZ;        // 12, OK
    WORD wYLen;         // 16, OK
    WORD wZLen;         // 18, OK
} XYZ; // sizeof(XYZ) == 20
```

Just one byte larger, yet This last optimized definition is only one byte larger than the Win16
optimally aligned! original and yet is optimally aligned for 32-bit CPUs. (Admittedly, you

pay for the memory savings of 4 bytes per structure with a definition that is optimized for 32-bit processors but not necessarily for other CPUs, for example, a 64-bit CPU. But if the structure is used often, the saved-space argument will have more weight than a possible later processor change.) If you want to experience this place-changing of elements "live," then just take a look at the TEXTMETRIC definition in WINDOWS.H (Win16) or its counterpart TEXTMETRICA in WINGDI.H (Win32), respectively.

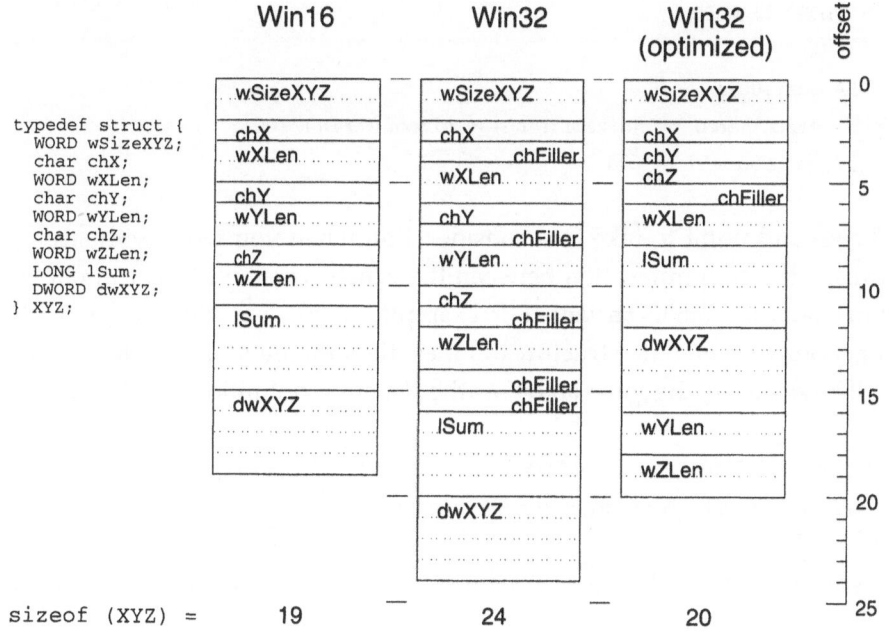

```
typedef struct {
  WORD wSizeXYZ;
  char chX;
  WORD wXLen;
  char chY;
  WORD wYLen;
  char chZ;
  WORD wZLen;
  LONG lSum;
  DWORD dwXYZ;
} XYZ;
```

sizeof (XYZ) =   19   24   20

Figure 3.6: The memory layout of structure XYZ under Win16 and Win32

The padding or alignment of structures can lead to a difference between the effective size of a struct and its theoretical* one. That's why you should *never* "manually" calculate the size of a structure and use it (possibly umpteen times) as a numerical constant in your source code! For that very purpose you should use sizeof()! This elementary rule is not only valid for structs, but also for all places where the size of variables or datatypes is needed (but often tends to be "forgotten" for standard types):

*won simply from adding the size of the members

```
typedef struct { UINT u1, u2; } REALLY;

...
```

169

```
hReally=GlobalAlloc(GMEM_FIXED,40); // Space for 10 REALLYs
// Really?!
```

If you want to find out the size of arrays of structs, you shouldn't trust implicit assumptions as well. A structure with a LONG and a WORD, 100 times squashed together, doesn't need 600, but 800 bytes under Win32! Or pressed into source code:

```
typedef struct {
  LONG l; WORD w;
} HA;
HA aha[100];
// sizeof(aha) == (sizeof(LONG) + sizeof(WORD))*100 ?
// No: 800      != 600
```

Communication between the Win16 and Win32 versions of your application

The second point to take into consideration when you work with structures is the communication between the Win16 version of your application and the Win32 variant. For example, if you use the normal I/O functions to save data structures in files, then the memory block written will have *exactly* the same layout as the structure definition.

```
_lwrite(hFile,&xyz,sizeof(XYZ));  // writes 19 bytes with
// the layout shown above (under Win16)
```

If you try to read the same structure under Win32, you won't get back anything sensible:

```
_lread(hFile,&xyz,sizeof(XYZ));  // reads 24 bytes with a
// completely different alignment under Win32
```

ASCII format for data exchange

Consequently, one of the applications must be able to communicate in the other format; I would probably prefer the Win16 part since it doesn't need to take any limits with structure definitions into consideration. Another solution could be to use a third uniform format by writing the individual components, for example with fprintf(), into an ASCII file. The other application will then be able to read the data with fscanf() without problems. However, this approach cannot be used if you exchange information between both programs via DDE, OLE, or a private clipboard format. Then, you'll have to create compatible struct defini-

And still an exception!

tions. Alas, most of the time, these considerations are just wasted time since thousands of users have already created their files in a certain format and simply expect that this format will be supported in the future. You'll find a prominent example in the file WINGDI.H: the structure BITMAPFILEHEADER defined there offends all rules concerning structure alignment. Nevertheless, it simply *had* to be defined like that in order to enable the reading of bitmap files in the "old" Win16 format. In such cases, either a conversion program should be supplied or the Win32 version works with non-properly aligned structures — at least when performing file I/O (in this special case it's possible to accept the resulting bus exceptions, since I/O operations are quite time consuming anyway).

3.6 Pointer Subtleties

"It is very easy to construct pointers that point anywhere." Brian W. Kernighan *and Dennis M. Ritchie*, Programming in C

There are mainly three things that will give some stomach aches to Windows developers: changes to the base types, incorrect use of casts, and — pointers, of course. If there are any doubtful or obscure places to discover in a C program, then a pointer is probably not far away. As the above quotation from K&R* shows pointers are to be used with caution anyway. Section 3.8 beginning on page 178 describes the diagnostic messages produced by the various compilers when they find something suspicious in the use of pointers and also shows possible work-arounds. Unfortunately, a Windows developer will need much more than just correct casts in order to use pointers in a platform-independent, portable, and safe way.

* who should know it best!

FAR? NEAR? Neither — nor: FLAT!

The first problem is that segmented environments such as x86 CPUs in real or 16-bit protected mode (in fact, the 32-bit mode also sports segments — after all, the CPU is from Intel — but they're not used in application programming) like to juggle around with two different pointer sizes: NEAR pointers, which just describe an offset into a certain segment (most often the data segment of the application), and FAR pointers,

Segment and offset?

which arbitrarily can address all of the available memory (at least in protected mode). Of course this wicked "duo infernale" cannot be ported easily to non-segmented architectures (e.g., UNIX machines). There the idea of a pointer comprised of two parts, namely a selector and the offset, appears rather bizarre. Instead those machines have just a linear and mostly rather large address space (something like 32 address bits, which corresponds to a 4 GB memory space). If one really insists, all addresses can be seen just as 32-bit offsets *without* a selector. So as far as conceptual issues are concerned, such a linear 32-bit pointer can be compared (if at all) to a Win16 NEAR pointer, albeit widened to 32 bit. This rather pleasant memory model is often called "flat memory" and therefore we can say a hearty "good-bye" to segments, FAR pointers, and real-mode addressing. (Honestly, I do feel a bit sorry about the latter: gone are the days when you could search through the whole memory in real mode and manipulate every single bit — protected mode and secure operating systems are all bad for hackers and patchers. Or maybe not?)

Linear address space means offset only!

The following advice seems appropriate for Win16 programs if you want to solve the NEAR/FAR pointer problem in the most portable way:

As much as possible, use a single memory model for all your Win16 projects and get familiar with the mechanisms of memory management and pointer arithmetics related to it. And if you don't have *really* good arguments for other models, then beginning with enhanced-mode Windows, you should *only* use the so-called "large model" (compiler switch -ml for Borland and /AL for MSC). I know that most textbooks related to Windows programming and nearly all authors of journal articles recommend the "small model" and, in the worst case, try not to get too dirty with the "medium model" (a notable exception is Matt Pietrek; see [Ref. 3]). But most of those books have been written by "Windows veterans" when Windows was only running in real mode (funny idea, isn't it?). At that time, certain restrictions were absolutely necessary or at least sensible. (After all, the memory manager had to perform efficient memory management with the help (?) of a relatively "simple-minded" processor. And due to the lack of hardware support, this required certain rules.) When Win16 finally turned away from real mode, many things that used to be "good manners" became plainly and simply superfluous (not to mention counter-productive). The simple reason: in protected mode the processor is taking over many aspects of the administrative tasks which the developer had to fight in the past (locking and unlocking of memory, managing movable memory, and the like). So, somebody who wrote* his

Just deal with one memory model!

And I mean one: namely the large model!

* *and hasn't turned away in disbelief and horror in the first place!*

first Windows program some eight or nine years ago has simply loads of old habits — as the saying goes: "Old habits die hard."

Of course, under Win16 if you want to allocate objects on the local heap, you'll still have to use NEAR pointers. And global allocations are made via FAR pointers, as always before. But *always* either use accordingly defined pointer types from the rich Windows stock (NPSTR, LPVOID, etc.) or, if you define your own data types, also invent the corresponding pointer types. For example:

Define your own pointer types.

```
typedef struct { ... } XYZ;
// Pointer to XYZ *not* like that:
XYZ NEAR* npXYZ;
// or this:
XYZ FAR* lpXYZ;
// Better create explicit type definitions:
typedef XYZ NEAR* NPXYZ;
typedef XYZ FAR*  LPXYZ;
...
NPXYZ npXYZ;
LPXYZ lpXYZ;
```

If necessary for Win32, these definitions of pointer types are very easy to adapt, whereas searching and modifying all those places where explicit NEAR or FAR attributed pointers are used (for example, as parameters of functions) and not defined in a portable way will cost considerably more effort. And one more hint: rather use the macros defined in WINDOWS.H* for these declarations instead of the "real" keywords __near and __far (again an additional level of indirection easing a later change!). This advice is also valid for all other compiler-specific non-ANSI C keywords such as __huge, __export, __pascal, etc. If necessary, you could define NEAR, FAR, etc., simply as empty macros (this is already partially done in the Win32 header files).

* for instance, "#define NEAR __near"

Segment and offset arithmetics: hands off!

Every now and then you'll find code written with the idea in mind that a NEAR pointer can only address 64 KB. The pointer is incremented above the magic number 65535 — and magically starts over with the offset 0.

Don't play arithmetic tricks with pointers.

That practice, like all arithmetic tricks with NEAR or FAR pointers, is not in the least portable. This broad field of misuse can be divided into two camps: computed accesses to arbitrary segments that are allowed in real mode are punished under the 3.x protected modes either with an "Unrecoverable Application Error" (the infamous UAEs) or, even more charming, with a system crash. But you have removed such bad practices from your programs already, haven't you? What's more, such artistic habits are not completely forbidden in protected mode: HUGE objects are made of several large memory areas with an individual maximum of 64 KB and corresponding LDT selectors (see figure 4.3 on page 210). And these have to be calculated according to some standardized method.... Consequence: certain selector manipulations often happen even in protected mode. Indeed, Microsoft offers a few macros and functions for this very purpose: MAKELP constructs a FAR pointer from a selector and an offset value; SELECTOROF and OFFSETOF take it to pieces again. And, not to be forgotten, there's the complete selector API. If you *really* have to deal with selectors and offsets, make sure you use these macros (or some of your own, adequately defined); therefore, later on, you'll find the points to change much easier. Because one thing is as clear as daylight: such code cannot be used with a linear memory model and hence is not portable at all!

Selector manipulations in protected mode

Another danger while using pointers is the fact that you have to convert them into integer types in Windows procedures (and vice versa). Traditionally, FAR pointers have been converted to LONGs or DWORDs, NEAR pointers to WORDs or ints. This practice is based on the implicit knowledge about the size of the pointer types. You shouldn't encounter many difficulties during the conversion of FAR pointers under Win32, but (there erroneous) NEAR conversions can easily provoke some perceptible complaints from your compiler. And worse: when implemented with particularly tricky code, even the compiler can't detect all the cases. Since NEAR pointers are all 32-bits wide under Win32 (i.e., there is effectively no size difference between so-called FAR and NEAR), a WORD cast will surely lead you into nirvana (no, luckily only your program). On the other hand, an int (or UINT) cast performs perfectly well since an int has also widened to 32 bit in the meantime. Result: if you have to convert NEAR pointers, then please cast with int or UINT only, but *never* with WORD!

Conversions: pointer to integer and vice versa.

If casting is really unavoidable, then please with int or UINT!

Last but not least, a final comment about actually harmless* pointer arithmetics, and especially the subtraction of pointers. In the segmented 16-bit world, it was sufficient to provide a 16-bit variable in order to store the result of a NEAR pointer substraction. As we have seen, this is generally not enough in the flat model: here, two (NEAR or FAR or whatever) pointers can be arbitrarily separated by a 32-bit wide chasm. So what is true elsewhere is also valid here: only an int (or UINT) is guaranteed to be wide enough under both operating systems, whereas a WORD (or a short) will almost never work under Win32!

*... because carried out with standard C mechanisms

Subtraction of pointers

3.7 Coding Practice

"Never change running code!" Old saying in programmers' circles

Now we are nearly through, after all: just a few words about the actual program code and then we're finished with this section. By the way, it is interesting that problems linked to code constructions are relatively infrequent compared to those coupled to type or data definitions. This is a clear sign that, when structuring our application, we should pay much more attention to data type creation. I think this difference is partly due to the fact that ANSI C clearly and strictly defines the language structures (*if, for, while*, etc.), while all simple scalar data types are almost fully dependent on the actual implementation.** A really portable language would cover this area by using various but strictly determined basic data types. Depending on your processor, this possibly could imply *minor* performance losses — and those accustomed to the community of C gurus is fully aware that this is *of course* totally unacceptable. Supporting some dubious or ancient processor architectures with a register size of 37 2/3 bits or with the fascinating feature sizeof(int *) != sizeof(int *()) often seems more important than having an appropriately written program that is easily portable with a minimum of effort between 99 percent of all modern (!) processors. Well, nothing and nobody are perfect...

Code problems are rare.

** ... and so unfortunately are platform specific!

Macros, prototypes, and libraries

The following points seem worth mention, in addition to the C compiler's warnings and error messages to be explained in section 3.8 which mostly take into account the various non-portable constructions.

Here too, a layer of macros
would prove to be helpful!

Actively use the possibility of packing compiler or system-specific extensions into an adjustable layer of macros (__loadds, __fastcall, etc.). Also check the use of #pragmas, which are almost always system or compiler specific. This is particularly important since ANSI C specifies that a compiler can simply *ignore* the pragmas it doesn't know without giving a warning or other message. This means you have to pay special attention *by yourself* to their adaptation!

#pragmas and other system-
specific features

Variable parameter lists

Functions with a variable number of parameters should, as all other functions, be declared with the correct prototype, for instance int Proc3(int i, …). Furthermore, to access the individual arguments, you should use the portable macros from STDARGS.H (called va_start, va_arg, and va_end) as much as possible.

Bit operations

There is a nice trap hidden at the bit operations. The setting or testing of bits is easily portable in most cases, but things become interesting when you want to clear a bit. Then code similar to the following is often used:

```
int iFlags;
... // iFlags somehow gets initialized
// And now you want to clear bit 0:
iFlags &= 0xFFFE;
```

Error through sign extension!

This solution works very well on 16-bit machines. But used on 32-bit CPUs, it can provoke rather unusual effects: when the expression 0xFFFE is considered as unsigned, the compiler will fill the upper 16 bits with 0s and not with 1s, as it should be. As a result, iFlags will probably receive a wrong bit pattern. An easy remedy is to refrain from using the explicit constant 0xFFFE but to favor the explicit inversion of the bit to be deleted:

```
// And now you want to clear bit 0:
iFlags &= ~1;
// ~1 is always correctly evaluated by the compiler!
```

Code with side effects

This actually should be self-evident: if code based on non-portable side effects runs bugfree under Win32, then it's *only* by accident. This, for example, is true for all calculations where the final result depends on the order of the analysis. Such code is indeed bad style but may slip in sometimes. Macros that evaluate their arguments several times also be-

Multiple evaluation of macro
arguments

long to this category. However, if the macro is equally defined on both systems, such effects shouldn't be of importance at all. On the other hand, when you use a macro on one platform and a real function on the other, you can quickly get some really puzzling bugs.

_asm blocks are also questionable when it comes to portability. First, things happening there are usually non-portable (such as playing around with segments, for example). But even if you mainly have performance reasons in mind to justify your excursion to the assembler world, you should realize that such code only runs on x86 processors (and even then has to be adapted to 32-bit mode). A conversion of such program parts to RISC CPUs implies either much work or a translation of the assembler part to C/C++.

Almost always troublesome: _asm blocks.

If you need to know the size of variables or data types, don't rely on your "learned" certain knowledge or, even worse, your instinct. Always use the sizeof operator — it definitely knows better than you do! I know that this has already been discussed several times, but I feel this hint is important enough to be said one more time. (Unfortunately, I still have to make corresponding corrections in nearly every one of my programs.)

Once again: sizeof()!

If you have to execute a certain job and search for a function to do it, look in the first place for a function in the Windows API (if at all possible, use a portable one). If you don't find anything there, then go on to the ANSI C standard library. If you still can't find a suitable function, you should try the extended run-time libraries supplied with your compiler — but be aware that almost all contain non-portable calls. Really *good* documentations will make detailed statements about the portability of non-standard functions. Minimize such usage and try as much as possible to put non-portable functions into a separate layer and to isolate this layer with as few functions as possible.

Correctly search the APIs.

Finally, refer to the documentation supplied with your compiler. First, it will (hopefully) describe the exact behavior required by an ANSI C compiler; second, and this is more important, you'll find (often hidden somewhere in one of the appendices) precise information on how the compiler manufacturer has implemented the various items left open in the ANSI C definition.

3.8 Compiler Warnings and Error Messages

"In questionable cases decide for the right thing." Karl Valentin, Maxims and Contradictions

Seems to be a very useful recipe! In order to facilitate your decision and to clarify the expression of "serious" warnings already mentioned (e.g., when discussing the STRICT option in section 2.5) I'll present in this section various fragments of a rather useless miniprogram having only one striking feature: it produces all kinds of interesting compiler warnings and error messages. In conjunction with compiling this little program, an important question, also of interest for the rest of the book, shows up: which compiler or development system shall I use to illustrate my code examples?

A "test" program for warnings and error messages

Included in the Win32 SDK prereleases and as a Visual C++ 2.0 component is Microsoft's C/C++ Compiler, which is similar to (but not fully compatible with) earlier versions yet of course generates 32-bit code. Since so many developers will be working with the SDK or VC 2, this system is obviously to be taken into account. On the other hand, many more software developers use Borland C++ than Microsoft likes to see. (Rumor has it that even in Redmond an astonishing number of BCC copies are in use. Why? Because Microsoft has acquired quite a few external products, e.g., some tools from Central Point. And at least some of these utilities were originally developed with Borland languages...). Moreover, Borland provides Win32 versions of its tools that are much more compatible to the DOS counterparts than Microsoft's 32-bit tools. So, to sum up, I'll take these two systems as examples to show the most important compiler diagnostics; if you're using another compiler, it should be quite easy to adapt the following remarks to your system.

Dealing with Microsoft and Borland C/C++

One warning: pay attention to the fact that at present some of these tools are only available as beta or early test versions. *Probably* no important changes will occur — but in detail the final versions may be a little bit different in some details (e.g., the exact wording of some messages, etc.). These should be insignificant changes, so just use your imagination to find out the meaning of such modifications (well, as already mentioned, I am also grateful for detailed feedback messages to take into consideration in future editions).

Attention: beta versions!

Warnings and errors in detail

If you have already studied the various compiler warnings and immediately after receiving them have made corresponding changes in your source code, you can skim over the following paragraphs and just look at messages that are new to you. But if you are a more magnanimous sort who thought until now that warnings are instead the sign of too sensitive a compiler, watch out! A great deal of non-fatal messages are definitely not to be ignored in Windows programming* — especially if you're working in STRICT mode and are hoping that your sources will perform under Win32 as they did with Windows 3.x!

in fact some of these warnings are serious error messages!

The following three dozen warnings and error messages are based, as said, on a stupid program that is shown fully in Appendix 4 and is also found on the accompanying disk. In the following the "culprit" line(s) are shown before the actual message text in order to save you the trouble of searching around. However, some of the error messages will only be fully comprehensible in the context of the whole program. (As a matter of fact, the appendix also contains a corrected and commented variant of the program which compiles in STRICT mode without any serious warnings.) The following paragraphs always show the Microsoft message first (provided there is one; they're easy to spot because of the warning numbers Cxxxx), and then, if applicable, the Borland text. The individual messages are separated by a single line.

Appendix 4: beginning on page 379.

Line 19

```
int Decr(LONG i);
...
Decr();

example.c(19) : error C2198: 'Decr' : too few actual parameters
Error example.c 19: Too few parameters in call to Decr in function
```

A function was called with at least one parameter less than what was defined in the declaration. Either an argument was forgotten in the actual call or the declaration is wrong.

Line 20

```
Decr(6,3);
```

179

```
example.c(20) : warning C4020: 'Decr' : too many actual parameters
Error example.c 20: Extra parameter in call to Decr in function
CallIncr
```

The same problem as above, just in the opposite direction: the function
was given more arguments than the declaration claimed. For Microsoft
this is interestingly enough just worth a warning (in this case), while
Borland (and I think justifiably) handles the problem with a corresponding error message. If you have to implement functions with a variable
number of parameters, then *always* use the ANSI C method for the prototypes (as well the standard access macros in STDARGS.H invented precisely to get at the actual values):

```
int IntLongDoubleVarParms(int i, LONG l,double d, ...);
```

Line 21

The next warning almost always points to an absent and/or faulty function prototype (or a misspelling of the function name) and as such
should be treated like an error message:

```
return Incr(6U);
```

```
example.c(21) : warning C4013: 'Incr' undefined; assuming extern re-
turning int
Warning example.c 21: Call to function 'Incr' with no prototype in
function CallIncr
```

In this case the following line would be necessary before the first call to
the function Incr() (just put into a suitable header file):

```
int Incr(DWORD j);
```

By the way, this declaration of the function leads to an interesting side
effect for 16-bit systems: the compiler can now perform the necessary
cast from unsigned int to DWORD automatically and delivers the four
bytes on the stack that Incr() expects to find there!

```
return Incr(6U);
```

```
example.c(21) : warning C4098: 'CallIncr' : 'void' function returning
a value
Warning example.c 21: Void functions may not return a value in func-
tion CallIncr
```

A simple problem: the function (in this case CallIncr()) was defined as returning nothing (VOID is a macro from WINDOWS.H which expands simply to void), but returns a value at least once in the body. Either one thing or the other! Any change to the return type (into LONG for example) must of course show up in the prototype as well! What's more: all places where the return value is used should be checked after changing the return type.

```
}
```

```
example.c(22) : warning C4101: 'z' : unreferenced local variable
Warning example.c 22: 'z' is declared but never used in function
CallIncr
```

The stated local variable (in this case z) is declared but is not used in the function body. This is often a consequence of optimizations in which the variable became superfluous. The statement can either be commented out or deleted altogether. Now and then one also finds typos or even logical errors...

```
int Incr(j)
DWORD j;
```

```
example.c(24) : warning C4131: 'Incr' : uses old-style declarator
```

This warning (which has no correspondence under Borland C) is given from the Microsoft compiler because the function was declared in the obsolete K&R style. The definition should be changed to ANSI C; if the function concerned will be called from more than one source module, the resulting prototype (see above) belongs in a header file.

Line 28

```
j+j;
```

```
Warning example.c 28: Code has no effect in function Incr
```

A gentle hint from the compiler (Borland only) that this statement has absolutely no effect and is therefore pointless. Either delete or correct as appropriate. Incidentally, Microsoft is silent about that fact (probably because no Microsoftie ever writes code with no effect...).

Line 29

```
if (j>=0) return ++j;
```

```
Warning example.c 29: Condition is always true in function Incr
```

Again Borland is better off and notifies you that the condition after the if clause makes no sense at all, simply because it will always return TRUE — since a DWORD (defined as *unsigned* LONG) in this world can't get negative. This warning is a serious one: presumably you've made a mistake that could prevent the whole statement from working properly.

Line 30

```
else if (j==-1) return --j;
```

```
example.c(30) : warning C4018: '==' : signed/unsigned mismatch
Warning example.c 30: Constant out of range in comparison in function
Incr
```

Comparing an unsigned variable (in this case a DWORD) with a negative value is almost never what the programmer had in mind. But if it is, he should compare with 0xFFFFU or 0xFFFFFFFFLU. Under no circumstances should he cast the variable j in order to silence the compiler. Much better and safer is the determination and use of the correct data type. This warning can also indicate a serious bug!

```
else return;
```

```
example.c(31) : warning C4033: 'Incr' must return a value
Warning example.c 31: Both return and return with a value used in
function Incr
```

Another return-a-value problem, similar to the second warning for line 21 above: a function with a return type other than void terminates without explicitly returning a value. In this case the actual return value is more or less random (namely the contents of the CPU register(s) used to carry the result).

```
}
```

```
Warning example.c 32: 'z' is assigned a value that is never Used in
function Incr
```

See the warning for line 22 given earlier. The small difference is that here the local variable z at least became initialized. Before simply removing the statement, check whether the initialization has a necessary secondary result (e.g., a function call with side effects) and therefore must be performed anyway.

```
return --i;
```

```
example.c(36) : warning C4135: conversion between different integral
types
Warning example.c 36: Conversion may lose significant digits in func-
tion Decr
```

The function Decr() receives a LONG (also shown in the prototype) but returns an int, however. The necessary conversion (at least for 16-bit systems) is indeed performed by the compiler, but not without some clearly audible grumbles. The Borland warning meets the heart of the matter somewhat better: with this conversion the upper 16 bits of the LONG are absolutely, positively lost. Always check whether the statement was intended that way; if yes, you should announce your intentions to the compiler through an explicit cast:

```
return (int)--j;
```

However, because now the warning is inhibited for the future, you should be 100 percent sure that chopping off the upper half is really desired!

Line 42

```
int PASCAL WinMain(HANDLE hInst,HANDLE hPrev,LPSTR lpszCmdLine,int
nCmdShow)
```

```
example.c(42) : warning C4028: formal parameter 1 different from dec-
laration
example.c(42) : warning C4028: formal parameter 2 different from dec-
laration
Error example.c 42: Type mismatch in redeclaration of 'WinMain'
```

A typical STRICT error! If until now you have defined WinMain() as above, then when using the STRICT option you must change your view. The first two arguments, as shown by the somewhat more detailed Microsoft messages, differ in the definition from the prototype in WINDOWS.H — a consequence of strict typing: an HINSTANCE (since this type is used in the prototype) is not a HANDLE anymore! Just change *Well, WinMain() may not be* both types into HINSTANCEs. Subsequently you may get warnings *the best example...* from those places where the now changed function is called,* since there the arguments provided may still be HANDLEs (or casted to a HANDLE).

Line 45

```
if (!ClientInit(hInst)) return 0;
```

```
example.c(45) : warning C4013: 'ClientInit' undefined; assuming extern
returning int
Warning example.c 45: Call to function 'ClientInit' with no prototype
in function WinMain
```

In this case as in the first warning for line 21 above the declaration of the prototype was simply forgotten. When performing the change due, also incorporate the correct (STRICT) data types (here HINSTANCE for hInst).

Line 55

```
}

example.c(55) : warning C4100: 'hPrev' : unreferenced formal parameter
example.c(55) : warning C4100: 'lpszCmdLine' : unreferenced formal pa-
rameter
Warning example.c 55: Parameter 'hPrev' is never used in function Win-
Main
Warning example.c 55: Parameter 'lpszCmdLine' is never used in func-
tion WinMain
```

Some friendly hints that certain function parameters are unused in the function's body. Principally these warnings fall into the same category as those for defined but unused local variables (see line 22).

Line 61

```
wc.lpfnWndProc=ClientWndProc;

example.c(61) : warning C4028: formal parameter 2 different from dec-
laration
example.c(61) : warning C4028: formal parameter 3 different from dec-
laration
Warning example.c 61: Suspicious pointer conversion in function Cli-
entInit
```

These warnings are a bit tricky, here Microsoft gives the more helpful information. The warnings result from the fact that the member lpfnWndProc (included in a WNDCLASS struct) receives the address of a window callback (here called ClientWndProc) which is not a true WNDPROC. Our prototype gives the data type WORD for the msg and wP parameters; WNDPROC, however, is defined with UINT and WPARAM, respectively. We mainly have to deal with the same problem as already showed up in line 42 (therefore the Microsoft messages are identical). Borland, on the other hand, realizes that the type of the mem-

ber lpfnWndProc does not exactly comply with the calling sequence for
the corresponding function, but reduces the whole problem to the simple
conversion of a pointer. The correct approach is, as already shown, the
exact declaration of ClientWndProc() such as in the definition for
WNDPROC (in WINDOWS.H) provided:

```
// WNDPROC in Windows.H :
typedef LRESULT (CALLBACK* WNDPROC) (HWND, UINT,
    WPARAM, LPARAM);


// the correct prototype is therefore:
LRESULT CALLBACK ClientWndProc(HWND HWND, UINT msg,
    WPARAM wP, LPARAM lP);
```

Both ignoring this warning or simply casting the address to whatever
type is required can have serious to fatal consequences, since all callback
functions defined as FAR Pascal are called directly from Windows! And
if the calling sequence is wrong, all sorts of exciting things can happen....

Line 74

```
LONG FAR Pascal ClientWndProc(HWND HWND, WORD msg,
    LONG wP, WORD lP)


example.c(74) : warning C4028: formal argument 3 different from decla-
ration
example.c(74) : warning C4028: formal argument 4 different from decla-
ration
error example.c 74: Model mismatch in redeclaration of 'ClientWndProc'
```

And once again the windows procedure! Here the error has to do with
the used types, too. The third and fourth parameters inadvertently became interchanged and don't correspond to the declaration in the prototype. The easy remedy is the re-exchange of both parameters. Generally a
warning like this shows that in the *definition* of the function some other
parameter types were used than the *declaration* of the prototype promised. By the way: if, after the warnings of line 61, you have made the
prototype of ClientWndProc() STRICT, the compiler will point out that
the types for msg and wP are still not correct (since a WORD is not the
same as a UINT or a WPARAM).

```
CallIncr();
```

```
Warning example.c 83: Call to function 'CallIncr' with no prototype in
function ClientWndProc
```

Hah! The Borland compiler is going wild, or? As one can easily discover, there *is* a prototype defined for the function CallIncr(), namely in line 11:

```
void CallIncr();
```

Well, this line indeed *looks* like a valid prototype (actually, for C++ it is one!). But in ANSI C this declaration tells the compiler only that nothing certain is known about the arguments of the function. If you declare a function with no arguments, then use (the pseudo-type) void or the macro VOID:

```
void CallIncr(void);
```

In order to show that the function actually has a variable parameter list (which, after all, must be possible; see wsprintf() for example), just write:

```
VOID CallIncr(int z,...);
```

See also the discussion for line 88 further on.

```
GetCursorPos(pt);
```

```
example.c(87) : error C2115: 'argument' : incompatible types
example.c(87) : warning C4024: 'GetCursorPos' : different types for
formal and actual argument 1
error example.c 87: Model mismatch in argument 1 in call to 'GetCur-
sorPos' in function ClientWndProc
```

Microsoft, as usual, has our interests at heart and graces us with a warning *and* an error message. The reason is simple: GetCursorPos()

expected the address of a POINT (&pt) as argument and not the POINT itself.

Line 88

```
CallIncr(&pt);
```

```
example.c(88) : warning C4087: 'CallIncr' : declared with 'void' pa-
rameter list
Warning example.c 88: Call to function 'CallIncr' with no prototype in
function ClientWndProc
```

In principle we have the same problem here as already mentioned in line 83. Admittedly the message of the Microsoft compiler is not fully correct, since CallIncr() wasn't declared with a "void parameter list," but without a parameter list at all. And according to ANSI C, these are two separate things. Probably the inaccuracy happened to the Microsoft developers because an empty list à la ( ) in fact means (void) for C++.

Line 89

```
HandleButton(pt);
```

```
example.c(89) : warning C4013: 'HandleButton' undefined; assuming ex-
ternal returning int
Warning example.c 89: Call to function 'HandleButton' with no proto-
type in function ClientWndProc
Warning example.c 89: Structure passed by value in function Cli-
entWndProc
```

First, the already familiar hint that no prototype was found for Handle-Button(). After this, still another hint from the Borland compiler that a function received a struct as value parameter. Normally, because it is much more efficient, the addresses are used as arguments. As a matter of fact, this message is only generated, because no prototype was defined for HandleButton(): in that case *both* compilers would have flagged an error message instead.

Line 90

```
CallIncr(2,3,4);
```

```
example.c(90) : warning C4087: 'CallIncr' : declared with 'void' pa-
rameter list
Warning example.c 90: Call to function 'CallIncr' with no prototype in
function ClientWndProc
```

See the notes for line 83, page 187, and line 88.

Line 94

```
OtherProblems(ps.hdc);
```

```
example.c(94) : warning C4049: 'argument' : indirection to different
types
Warning example.c 94: Suspicious pointer conversion in function Cli-
entWndProc
```

Another case where the STRICT option shows who's the boss. Indeed,
the function was declared in line 14 with the following prototype:

```
VOID OtherProblems(HWND hwnd);
```

Passing an HDC (ps.hdc) as parameter value seems pretty cheeky, and
the compilers acknowledge this with the corresponding messages. The
Microsoft compiler notices that both pointers refer to different types,
Borland complains about a "suspicious" pointer conversion. These two
warnings are serious (and not only in this circumstance!) and should be
removed through a corresponding source code change! An explicit cast is
only allowed if the effect is actually desired.

Line 97

```
return hfont;
```

```
example.c(97) : warning C4047: 'return' : different levels of indirec-
tion
```

```
error example.c 97: Nonportable pointer conversion in function Cli-
    entWndProc
```

And still more problems with the conversion of pointers: hfont being an HFONT is (STRICTly seen) a NEAR pointer, but the window callback function returns just a simple LRESULT (long). Here, as above, a cast can be carried out in order to achieve the desired effect without producing a warning. But be careful:

```
return (LRESULT)hfont;  // This cast is incorrect!
```

This simple approach can lead to madness, since it's not at all clear what the compiler shall do now: either the NEAR pointer is converted into a LRESULT and the upper 16 bits are filled with 0. Or the function shall return a valid FAR pointer, in which case the NEAR pointer must be converted so that the upper half of the LRESULT contains the correct data segment. Depending on the return value, the correct cast must be employed as follows:

```
return (LRESULT) (UINT)hfont;     // upper half = 0
return (LRESULT) (LPVOID)hfont;   // upper half = DS
```

In the first case the NEAR pointer is first transformed into an unsigned int, which is then converted to LRESULT (and thereby as requested filled up with 0). The second line, however, changes the NEAR pointer first into a FAR pointer (here the data segment is added), and the result is casted without information loss into an LRESULT. (Well, the necessity of such dubious constructions culminates in a simple discovery: instead of CPU design, Intel should have searched another playground for its segments — not completely off the mark would have been the design of steel segments for Russian oil pipelines).

In the 16-bit world all conversions of NEAR pointers into longs or DWORDs and vice versa are to be performed with utmost care! All warnings indicating problems in this area definitely have to be worked out. In doubtful cases, look at the assembly code for the related statement; only then you know for sure what really happens under the C facade.

```
return psz;
```

```
example.c(99) : warning C4047: 'return' : different levels of indirec-
tion
error example.c 99: Nonportable pointer conversion in function Cli-
entWndProc
```

The same problem as with the last warning, but this time with an explicit pointer type, namely PSTR. And while in the hfont example the correct cast was presumably (LRESULT)(UINT), here probably (LRESULT)(LPSTR) would be correct.

```
return DefWindowProc(hwnd,msg,wP,lP);
```

```
example.c(101) : warning C4135: conversion between different integral
types
Warning example.c 101: Conversion may lose significant digits in func-
tion ClientWndProc
```

This warning can be traced back to the fact that the types of the arguments wP and lP in the function declaration (see line 74) became interchanged. So wP is actually a LONG, so of course the compiler in the call to DefWindowProc() performs a conversion from LONG to WPARAM, and therefore this warning appears. It'll vanish if the type definitions are corrected.

```
VOID HandleButton(LPPOINT lppt,int z)
```

```
example.c(105) : error C2371: 'HandleButton' : redefinition; different
basic types
Error example.c 105: Type mismatch in redeclaration of 'HandleButton'
```

Two lovely messages mirroring the fact that no prototype exists for HandleButton() — however, the function was already called (in line 89).

If this happens, both compilers make certain assumptions based on the first call about the return and parameter types of the called function. If the actual function definition appears later on and those assumptions don't prove true, these error messages are due, which of course go away with the prototype declaration.

Line 106

```
LPRECT lprc=lppt;
```

```
example.c(106) : warning C4049: 'initializing' : indirection to dif-
ferent types
Warning example.c 106: Suspicious pointer conversion in function Han-
dleButton
```

An obvious problem: lppt is a FAR pointer to a POINT; lprc on the other hand points to a RECT. These pointer conversions are indeed carried out by both compilers, but not without a certain murmuring. Remedy: either correct or, if actually desired, use an explicit cast.

Line 107

```
LPVOID lp=z;
```

```
example.c(107) : warning C4047: 'initializing' : different levels of
indirection
Warning example.c 107: Nonportable pointer conversion in function Han-
dleButton
```

A similar case: the initialization of the FAR pointer is done with an int variable. The warning can of course be repaired with a cast. But watch out: for this special case (from int (16 bit) to FAR pointer (32 bit)) the remarks about the warnings for line 97 also apply!

Line 108

```
LPSTR lpsz=MAKEINTRESOURCE(ID_ICON);
```

```
example.c (108) : warning 4090: different 'const/volatile' qualifiers
Warning example.c 108: Suspicious pointer conversion in function Han-
dleButton
```

An interesting message tracked down to the fact that the macro
MAKEINTRESOURCE (which, by the way, is similar to its colleague
MAKEINTATOM) nowadays returns an LPCSTR (decoded: const char
FAR *). And this is something completely different than LPSTR, defined
as char FAR *. Either the type of the variable lpsz is changed to LPCTSR
or an explicit cast is used.

Line 110

```
lp++;
```

```
example.c(110) : error C2036: 'void __FAR *' : unknown size
error example.c 110: Size of the type is unknown or zero in function
HandleButton
```

The attempt to perform arithmetic exercises with an untyped pointer is
of course a bit naive. These warnings are more frequently obtained if the
return value of GlobalLock(), for instance, is correspondingly mistreated.
Earlier, this was of type LPSTR (so pointer arithmetic was easily possible); however, in a STRICT environment it is defined as LPVOID. Code
similar to the following has to be STRICTified:

```
*(GlobalLock(Hmem)+12)=c;
```

This will therefore change to (this is just an example, there are other
possibilities):

```
{ LPSTR lpChar=(LPSTR)GlobalLock(hMem);
*(lpChar+12)=c; }
```

However, the practice of directly manipulating function results seems
pretty dubious anyway.

Line 111

```
if (hwnd==1)
```

```
example.c(111) : warning C4047: '==' : different levels of indirection
Warning example.c 111: Nonportable pointer conversion in function Han-
dleButton
```

The warning is only given in STRICT mode, because only then an HWND is not an unsigned short, but a NEAR pointer. Check whether the statement is actually sensible. If yes, you should either cast or, if possible, use one of the predefined constants for window handles (such as HWND_DESKTOP, HWND_BROADCAST, etc.).

Line 112

```
*lp=CallIncr();
```

```
example.c(112) : error C2100: illegal indirection
example.c(112) : error C2120: 'void' illegal with all types
error example.c 112: Not an allowed type in function HandleButton
```

See the remarks about using untyped pointers accompanying the warnings for line 110.

Line 113

```
HWND=lp;
```

```
example.c(113) : warning C4059: segment lost in conversion
Warning example.c 113: Suspicious pointer conversion in function Han-
   dleButton
```

In most cases a serious problem is buried under this warning, since the direct assignment of a FAR address to a NEAR pointer easily produces undefined pointers (a general exception is FAR addresses pointing definitively into the program's data segment). If you really want to obtain this effect (which would astonish me), proceed as shown:

```
hwnd=(HWND)(UINT)(DWORD)lp;
```

Line 119

STRICTly seen, the next message is also based on a pointer conflict:

```
HBRUSH hbr=SendMessage(hwnd,WM_GETFONT,0,0);
```

```
example.c(119) : warning C4047: 'initializing' : different levels of
   indirection
```

```
error example.c 119: Nonportable pointer conversion in function Other-
Problems
```

SendMessage() delivers an LRESULT, while hbr is a NEAR pointer (if you follow the definition to the end). The statement above contains still another error: "logically" WM_GETFONT returns an *HFONT* and not at all a handle to a brush. The return value should therefore be casted accordingly, then such errors are a lot easier to spot. Apart from that the definition of hbr is replaced:

```
HFONT hfont=(HFONT)(UINT)SendMessage(hwnd,WM_GETFONT,0,0);
```

The discussion of the different error messages shows that the Microsoft compiler is somewhat more specific than Borland's product. On the other hand, the latter tracks down some fine points that the competitor won't catch. Hence, if at all possible, your source code should be hunted regularly through both compilers, in order to eliminate as many potential problems as possible.

Well, two just see more than one...

An especially ugly problem regularlay hides behind the various conversion warnings (pointer, integral types, etc.). The most obvious and simple approach, namely to introduce a cast, is sometimes* the correct one. But there are numerous cases in which the cast successfully buries the conflict — which later on, only when the program is used by your customers, brings itself back to attention under the most embarrassing circumstances. An example:

* but not as often as one believes!

```
int FAR Pascal DoSomethingWeirdWithText(void)
{
  TEXTMETRC tm;
  OUTLINETEXTMETRIC otm;
  LPOUTLINETEXTMETRC lpotm=&otm; // assignment is OK
  ... // Further code
  lpotm->otmLineGap=...; // Access also, since lpotm points
  // to a LPOUTLINETEXTMETRIC structure
  ... // Further code
  lpotm=&tm; // Tricky part, produces a warning
  ... // 30 Lines later...
  lpotm->otmLineGap=... // undefined access, since
```

```
// lpotm still points to a TEXTMETRIC
}
```

Removing the warning in the tricky part is child's play:

```
lpotm= (LPOUTLINETEXTMETRIC) &tm;
```

Unfortunately, the actual error happens but 30 lines later and is not at all prevented through inhibiting the warning with a cast. Sadly, C code often swarms of such pointer plays,* used either because of performance reasons or in order to save some memory (often, plain laziness may also be the reason). Admittedly, casts are frequently necessary in order to be able to compile a source file without warnings. But they also disable the compiler's possibilities to detect and point out serious programmers' errors. In the code fragment shown above, two local pointer variables could have been used. Each cast you can avoid based on a more defensive programming style is one invitation less for Mr. Murphy...** Cast operations used in excess can produce still other harm, as the following example illustrates:

```
// Compile for the small model!
#define STRICT
#include <windows.h>
#include <stdio.h>
int main()
{
  char c; PSTR p=&c;
  printf("Near: %x\n",P);
  printf("Far1: %lx\n", (LONG)p);
  printf("Far2: %lx\n", (LONG) (WORD)p);
  return 0;
}
```

The program produces this somewhat irritating output:

```
near: 0efa
Far1: 22850efa
Far2: 0efa
```

Evidently something went wrong with casting the NEAR pointer for Far2. Well, the compiler is fooled by the (WORD) cast and believes to be working with a non-pointer value. Therefore, the data segment won't be included in the final value (in contrast to Far1, where the (LONG) cast correctly adds the DS register). The (WORD) cast was certainly meant to help, but it can have very surprising outcomes, if the result is supposed to be a FAR pointer.

Much helps much?

All these examples and explanations lead to one statement: cast as little as possible. The three most important rules for all explicit type conversions are: first, check whether the cast is actually necessary; second, check *harder* whether the cast is actually necessary; and third, *scrutinize* whether the cast is actually necessary. And if the cast *really* is unavoidable, then make crystalclear why and what types you are planning to convert (a glance at the basic type definitions in WINDOWS.H as well as the table of data types in Appendix 1 can prove to be very helpful!).

Three simple rules about casting

As a matter of fact, most of the talk in this section is also true for Pascal and Modula-2 programmers (albeit in correspondingly translated form). After Wirth created them, when both languages were indeed in their original state, they were strongly typed and strictly standardized; however, an overexposure to Danish compiler writers* has in both cases led to a repeated "Fall of Man." Therefore, with most commercially available implementations today, it is possible to celebrate at least the same sacrileges as with C or C++....

* e.g., at Borland or JPI

3.9 And What about C++?

"Late you come — yet you come!" Friedrich Schiller, Wallenstein

Indeed: it took Microsoft quite long to release a C++ compiler. It's true, in this field other language specialists (first and foremost Zortech and Borland) have already been successfully romping; nevertheless in the PC marketplace a language seems to obtain the genuine consecration only if Microsoft also gets involved (perhaps this is one of the reasons why Modula-2 has never acquired real significance in the market). Anyhow: with the Borland and Microsoft systems, two useful and stable products are available that are also implemented in (more or less backward-compatible) versions for the 32-bit Windows platforms. And because C++ is pretty much downward compatible to ANSI C, there seem to exist

C++ — what's the hold-up?

no obstacles to the triumphant success of the language. Or are there some?

Actually, there *are* some reasons why C++ until now hasn't gained too much recognition and why this will be the case for quite a while to come. Without diving too deeply into the details, one can quickly discover the following problem areas:

Obstacles and difficulties

- *Downward compatible? It depends...* C++ indeed is designed to a large extent downwardly compatible to (ANSI) C, but there are some notable differences, which (at least partially) can require considerable changes to existing source codes. Besides basic differences (e.g., const vs. #define) the stricter type and consistency checking (compared to ANSI C) especially can lead to problems with older source code still K&R compatible (i.e., missing prototypes and the like).

- *Complex language definition* Furthermore, the language definition is, said with all respect due, a totally muddled collection of rules, exceptions to the rules, enhancements in order to partly consistently handle the exceptions and so on and so on. I strongly feel that less would have been more: after all, a language shall primarily be a useful tool and not a carved wooden altar in baroque style. (I know there are quite a lot of people who successfully work with C++ — but here I am talking about you and me, the man on the street.)

- *Unstable language definition* And to top it all, this monstrous language definition is still not at all stable: it is still being polished in every nook and cranny. While this certainly raises the "do-it-all-make-it-all" coefficient considerably and throws the C++ gurus from one frenzy of enthusiasm to the next, it hinders the general acceptance of the language.

- *Changing the development system is always troublesome.* Last but not least, the change to another language (or the used development system, respectively), as compatible as it claims to be, always involves for the developer very difficult estimations of the possible hazards and the resulting financial risks. After all, if you sell software, unstructured but running C code is always better than elegant but crashing C++ programs!

However, if you believe after this rather pessimistic opening that I condemn C++ to the deepest abysses of hell, you are mistaken. The Wallenstein quotation already lets you suspect that a conceptual enhancement of the ANSI C standards is required for better readability and maintainable programs. Indeed there are some points to criticize with C++, but someone who has fought his way successfully through the language definition and/or various C++ tutorials (the former [see Ref. 7] is something for those bean-counting types, who fluently talk EBNF; the latter are far and away better suited for us ordinary mortals, therefore see [Ref. 8]) can afterwards surely write better and, above all, more portable software than with ANSI C (and with smaller time requirements). *Can*, but not *must*. Since C++ allows the same extensive manipulations* of the underlying hardware as C, all remarks true for illegible or tricky C programs are absolutely valid and at any rate also possible with C++! However, if one sticks to some conventions, being more or less the "Knigge" of C++ programming (see [Ref. 9] for an example), one can enormously profit from the enhanced possibilities (an assertion rather impressively proved through [Ref. 10] or the ease of programming Windows with the Microsoft Foundation Classes or similar libraries).

EBNF — extended Backus Naur form

* Quite logical, else it couldn't be called downward compatible!

I see two other, deciding motives for Windows developers to work with C++ at least in the medium term. The short field trip about additional portable tool libraries in section 2.4, page 98 has already shown that with the aid of properly designed class libraries (e.g., MFC or OWL) it's relatively easy to put a nearly 100 percent portable C++ shell around the Win16/32 APIs. This shell hides to a much higher degree than C the actually boring, but yet necessary differences in detail between both APIs. The fact that MFC is designed and implemented especially for Windows gives the developer the possibility to deal with more essential design questions than with porting his application from Win16 to Win32; the bulk of the smaller (and bigger) differences between both systems are handled by the class library almost fully transparently, but without losing functionality "on the way." And similar remarks are certainly true for any other class library not too distant from the base APIs, so that Windows-specific qualities (e.g., DDE or OLE) can be supported.

Two more good reasons for C++

1. Portable class libraries

At long last the whole trend of development at Microsoft indicates that C as base SDK language has probably come to the end of its useful life. Just glance over the OLE 2 specs to see what I mean: both concepts and terminology could be quoted from a C++ book. In my opinion this is a clear hint that future SDKs will be even more under the influence of Visual C++ or comparable systems. Then at last our successors won't need to deal with the somewhat awkward WM_!@#&!Q#$@? messages but can juggle with methods, virtual classes and overloaded operators. (But whether their programs will indeed be better — well, let's wait and see...) In a certain sense the Windows API at present is only an

2. Trend to C++ in Windows programming and API definition

199

(admittedly rather) powerful device driver, which through additional layers sometime in the future will be hopefully as easy for programmers as it is right now as a user interface between endusers and applications.

Chapter 4

Portable Windows Programming

As we have already noticed, the Win32 API differs in some important basic properties from its 16-bit predecessor. Some of these changes (e.g., the use of memory areas greater than 64 KB, aka HUGE) can be handled often either completely transparently or needing only relatively small porting efforts (in this case simply removing the keyword HUGE or __huge). Unfortunately, many other dissimilarities are considerably less "cooperative" and force the developer to perform possibly far-reaching changes on the existing source codes. And the precise character of all these changes will occupy us in this chapter. In section 1.5, on page 44, I presented an overview of the six categories into which the most important differences and the resulting modifications can be divided. Some hints to DLL programming under Win32 were also given there. This chapter (alas, by far the most voluminous of the book) elaborates on this overview and shows in detail and with lots of practical examples the most important programming-related differences between the 16- and 32-bit Windows environments.

Porting issues: six categories plus DLL programming.

4.1 Some Signposts for Portable Windows Programs

"Look for the stars! But pay attention to the alleys!" Wilhelm Raabe, The People from the Wood

Roughly, we can distinguish two variants when it comes to the problems associated with porting to Win32: on the one hand, a lot of source code modifications will be necessary because syntactical elements have been modified (e.g., the naming of constants and data types or parameter types and/or order in function prototypes etc.). Such things provoke only limited changes: at most one or two lines of source code have to be modified, the procedure is usually straightforward and methodical. On the other hand, and this is the seamy side of the picture, such places are found rather frequently. For the indication of these issues and their ad-

Syntax versus semantics

Syntactical measures: numerous, but generally easy to apply.

aptation, Microsoft provides the SDK program PORTTOOL, which nevertheless is only partially able to handle this task (particularly its searching algorithms could be somewhat more intelligent). Anyway, one can find with this aid a lot of the corresponding problem areas. (As a matter of fact, on the accompanying disk you'll find an enhanced version of the text file that's loaded by PORTTOOL to do the job. More about this file and its use can be found in Appendix 2; the disk contents are explained in Appendix 7).

Semantic differences: often a lot of effort.

The second species, on the other hand, is of another breed: it deals less with simple syntactical changes and more with semantic differences, which often require considerable and not always uncomplicated changes to your sources. Fortunately, most of these issues have the pleasant characteristic of showing up and posing problems only a few times in the whole project. Alas, the prevailing part of these changes is only partially recognized by PORTTOOL (if at all). The reasons for this are found partly in the complex nature of the problem areas, which are often not bound to syntactical features (such as procedure names or messages) and partly from the somewhat simple-minded PORTTOOL implementation.

Syntax versus semantics: two perfect examples

Two authentic examples may help us clarify the differences between these two problem areas:

Syntax: change GWW_ID to GWL_ID.

- A typical syntactical problem (in fact a rather simple one) is the modification of the constant GWW_ID needed for calling [Get/Set]WindowWord() in order to read or write the id of a child window or a control. Under Win32 the id is no longer represented through a WORD but a LONG; consequently, the constant is renamed to GWL_ID, and therefore the functions to be called are [Get/Set]WindowLong(). A simple textual search in all source code modules (e.g., with an editor or via PORTTOOL) and the following substitution solve this problem. A whole list of similar small stumbling blocks has already been cleared up by Microsoft with the help of a header file (called WINDOWSX.H) including numerous portable macro definitions for Win16 and Win32. More about this file follows further down the road.

- An annoying semantical problem can arise from the fact that the second argument to a WinMain call, an instance handle usually called hPrevInstance, *always* equals 0 under Win32. As already mentioned in section 1.5 this is a consequence of the fully separated address spaces. So if a second instance of your program is loaded and has to exchange data with the first instance, you're unfortunately not done with a simple *syntactical* adaptation of the Win16 function GetInstanceData(): this API was simply dropped — instead you have to write quite a bit of additional program code (e.g., to implement a DDE communication* or memory mapped files). *All* important semantical differences between both APIs will be recorded in this chapter in the relevant sections and mostly illustrated through actual example programs (or at least code snippets).

Semantics: hPrevInstance is always == 0.

* DDE — dynamic data exchange

Windows portability: an overview

In most cases simple syntactical changes can be handled either through reasonably defined macros, small sections with conditional compilation, or, if things really get difficult, some short helper functions. And as said, Microsoft has already done some of this grunt work, probably not in the least because of its own purposes. Besides the use of correspondingly adapted and portable data types (which is explained in section 4.2) the header file WINDOWSX.H promises to be especially beneficial. This file was first made available with the Win3.1 SDK and is also delivered in appropriate form with the Win32 SDK. Both files contain a great deal of macro definitions, for the better part serving program portability, but also helping with source code clarity. You'll find more about that in sections 4.3 to 4.5. But an important consideration is already here: if at present you still work with the original Windows 3.1 SDK version of WINDOWSX.H, you should acquire the newest version, called WINDOWSX.H16, from the CompuServe MSWIN32 forum (see library #7, "Tools — Win32 SDK"). This file is also available with the Win32 SDK and found under X:\MSTOOLS\H\WINDOWSX.H16. Some macros for the decomposition of message parameters described in the following sections (e.g., WM_GET_COMMAND_ID) are only found in the newest version; moreover, some minor errors have been corrected.

The header file WINDOWSX.H

Macros in 16- and 32-bit versions

Considerations and adaptations relating to global changes in the three most important Windows modules are at the center of sections 4.6, 4.7 and 4.8. Here, all important semantical source code modifications necessary to support new or changed KERNEL, USER, and GDI functionality are described. Also some of the important syntactical changes are referenced; in order to keep the size and the explanations in this section manageable and reasonable, I have not treated all the minor details. Normally, when the compiler comes across syntactical problems, it gives a rather clear error message, which, together with the Win32 documentation (or the API WinHelp files), permits an easy and fast remedy to the issue at hand.

Changes in the most important Windows modules

The remaining four sections of this chapter in each case illuminate a clearly marked subarea of Win32 programming, which are not easily put into one of the so far described categories: all applicable changes when programming DLLs are discussed in section 4.9, while the following deals with Unicode functionality and explains this brand-new 16-bit character set. This section is meant to help you decide what character set(s) your programs should support. Section 4.11 gives important hints and advice to adjust your application to execute as a 16-bit program under Windows 3.x as before, but also to be fully operable as a binary compatible Win16 application under Win32 (either in Windows 95 or under NT's WOW). The chapter will be completed by a short study about porting MS-DOS based programs to the text-mode interface of Win32 (called "console functions"). Two main reasons have caused the inclusion of the latter section: first, especially bigger applications will often contain subprograms that can run conveniently in text mode under DOS (or even must; just think of the various system-related utilities like disk fragmenters that do not execute at all under Windows 3.1 so far). Their adaptation to the Win32 GUI is considerably more costly than just a simple port to Win32 text mode, so these functions are at the very least of medium-term interest. Second, after the GUI functions the console API is the next most important (and often much simpler) approach to implement user input and output under Win32; therefore, they should be mentioned for the sake of completeness in any case. After all, Windows NT and to a lesser extent also Win32c or Windows 95 *are* new operating systems and not only a GUI on top of the simple MS-DOS.

DLL programming

Unicode

16-bit programs under Windows 95 and WOW

Text mode programs

4.2 Using the Enlarged Win32 Data Types

"Who can just think of it and come to the assumption, who can exercise such superhuman caution to avoid such cussedness of the inanimate!" Friedrich Theodor von Vischer, Auch Einer

In Chapter 3, we dealt with the consequences of enlarged data types under Win32 in the light of portable C programming. Therefore, the following discussions are more concerned with the correct use of these data types in Win16 and Win32 programs, at the same time considering the specific conditions of both systems. The deciding change with the transition to Win32 is the widening of an int from 16 to 32 bit. From this growth it is possible to trace back directly or indirectly nearly all further type modifications. By the way, a detailed overview, including a table with the most important simple data types as well as their definition in both systems, is found in Appendix 1 on page 355.

32-bit CPU — 32-bit data types

Complete table of data types in appendix 1

WORD, the second...

Of very special interest for Win32 programmers is (still) the data type WORD, in Win16 responsible among other things for the second and third parameters of window procedures (and often called wMsg and wParam or wP). Under Win32 this data type won't grow (such as an int, for instance); it remains a plain unsigned short with just 16 bits. In plain language this means that quite a few places where a WORD variable or a (WORD) cast is used are not portable at all. The remedy in most cases is replacement with data type UINT, which has the pleasant feature of spanning either 2 or 4 bytes, depending on the operating system:

UINT instead of WORD

```
// Equal type definitions under Win16 and Win32!
// First for UINT:
typedef unsigned int    UINT;
// And for WORD:
typedef unsigned short  WORD;
// But: sizeof(int) == sizeof(short) under Win16
// against sizeof(int) == 2 * sizeof(short) under Win32!
```

Attention!

These definitions make sure that using UINT instead of WORD brings no alteration to the resulting program code under Win16 (since there sizeof(short) == sizeof(int)); on the other hand, the grown UINT fits the bill under Win32, too. Therefore the following advice: *hands off WORD!* Only if you're *absolutely* sure that an unsigned 16-bit variable should be used under Win16 *and* Win32 (which, as an example, might be necessary in frequently used structures due to memory space restrictions), you should employ WORDs. In all other cases, however, UINT is the proper selection! In times of doubt, glance at the function prototypes or use the WinHelp API reference files!

UINTs are used, for example, to transport message values to window procedures. They also carry the message parameter wParam (there indeed "disguised," since the explicit data type used is WPARAM, being a direct descendant of UINT). Explicit usage of WORDs is observed only very rarely in Win32 (and Win16 beginning with Windows 3.1).

UINT for wMsg — WPARAM for wParam

For existing sources the above-stated rule is of course valid as well: probably no way leads around the sad fact that both the definition of WORD parameter types or variables and also the use of WORD in type conversions and casts have to be checked *very* thoroughly. The extremely simple strategy to find and replace WORD with UINT with the help of a global search-and-replace works amazingly well. The (rare) places where you really want to keep a WORD also under Win32 are afterwards quite easy to figure out. But caution: if you use your editor for this job, pay attention to replace only the *type* WORD, but not the four-letter string WORD: to turn a DWORD into a DUINT certainly looks funny but is not exactly helpful. An editor offering regular expression search capabilities can prove to be very helpful (and not only in that case). Moreover, you should consistently replace PWORD and LPWORD, if applicable, with UINT NEAR * and UINT FAR *, respectively (or, even better, define and use corresponding typedefs for the pointer types).

An editor with "regular expression searches" helps.

Tightly connected with this WORD/UINT malaise are the two macros LOWORD and HIWORD: each and every use has to be checked for correctness under Win32! Frequently these macros are used to access the information hidden in the two message parameters for window procedures. And exactly this application is often not portable at all and must be changed accordingly for Win32 (see also section 4.4 on page 227). The reverse is valid, too: often under Win16 two words are packed into a LONG via MAKELONG (or with the help of MAKEL[PARAM-/RESULT] an LPARAM or LRESULT is constructed) and then used in a

Caution: LOWORD and HIWORD...

... as well as MAKELONG, MAKELPARAM, and MAKELRESULT.

SendMessage() call as the fourth argument. This non-portable practice is virtually impossible with Win32, since the so packed data (e.g., window handles) can't be easily squeezed into a single LPARAM. Therefore, pay close attention to the following sections 4.3 to 4.5 in which I address these problems.

Always (yes, already in your 3.1 source codes!) use the data type you really meant. Someone who, for instance, creates an atom should not store this in a variable of type WORD or UINT, because with that action implicit (and not always sane...) assumptions about the underlying types are linked. The only correct and portable way is to define a variable of type ATOM and to assign the value. The consistent use of the numerous typedef'd simple data types both in definitions of variables and function prototypes and also in cast operations is (besides the heavy usage of the macro processor) actually one of the most simple but also most effective means to portable Windows programming!

Always use the proper data type!

Where does the pointer point?

But the widening of data types is unpleasantly noticeable not only with WORDs: another minefield hides with NEAR pointers, which in Win32 double in size, too. The consequences on the portable formulation of C programs already became apparent to a large extent in the third chapter; here I just want to point you to some Windows specific issues. The first observation is that NEAR pointers until now *always* served as a (16-bit) offset into a certain segment. Probably this was the data segment of your application, and if you have programmed "after the cookbook" and used a NEAR pointer only in this way, you usually won't have to change too much code. Differently (namely, very gloomy) the issue looks if you have written code relying explicitly on the fact that a NEAR pointer points into a *specific* segment other than your program's DS. A popular exercise, for example, is accessing internal data in the KERNEL, USER, and GDI data segments. An HWND, for example, is nothing else than a NEAR pointer to an indeed undocumented but not unknown WND struct (see [Ref. 3]) located in a USER data segment.* That way some programs — being somewhat more generous when it comes to interpreting the textbook fashion of doing things — read internal values that either were not available with "legal" means or were very difficult to acquire (see figure 4.1). While often this action may be necessary in order

NEAR pointers

* whose value can be found relatively easily...

either to achieve very special effects or to fight some of the Windows design weaknesses, one must realize very clearly that such tricks can be ported only with great effort — or even not at all! The same observation is valid for a great many TOOLHELP functions that build on these internal data structures. (Indeed sometime in the future a portable Win32 version of TOOLHELP.DLL will be made available; but even then, the 16-bit specific APIs, such as SystemHeapInfo() for instance, are probably removed without replacement.)

Figure 4.1: Non-portable accesses to internal data structures in private Windows segments

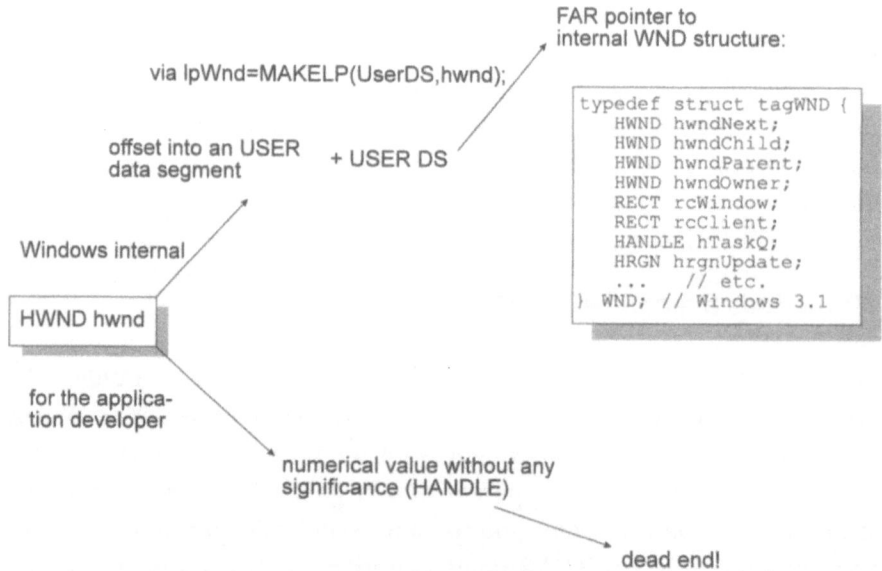

FAR pointers With FAR pointers (seemingly) nothing has changed; they were, are and remain 32-bits wide. Indeed this is true — but their internal interpretation is nevertheless totally different: the concept of a pointer built of a segment and an offset is null and void with the appearance of the flat memory model. Or put differently: a FAR pointer in the 16-bit world changes in a 32-bit environment to a simple NEAR pointer (but indeed *Sizeof(NEAR) ==* with a width of 32 bits). Both the difference in size and also the concep- *sizeof(FAR)!?* tual discrepancies between Win16 NEAR and FAR pointers simply vanish under 32 bit! (The thrilling consequences for local and especially global memory management are shown in detail in section 4.6.) In spite of the different sizes, a Win16 NEAR pointer has more in common with a

Win32 pointer than the (equally big) Win16 FAR pointer. Only a 48-bit pointer (with 16 bits for the selector plus the usual 32-bit offset) would theoretically correspond to the aged FAR pointer. However, the 32-bit Microsoft compiler doesn't know a built-in pointer type of this format; a 48-bit type is neither needed nor used in the Win32 API (some Win95 VxDs APIs require 48-bit addressing, but this is DDK stuff). The important segment registers (CS, DS, ES, SS) will be initialized only once* and after that keep their values throughout program execution. The separation of process memory spaces from each other isn't performed through LDT or segment switching, but exclusively through the paging carried out by the CPU (the CR3 register holding the page directory is simply switched on a per-process basis). Section 3.6 on page 171 is reserved to the subject of NEAR and FAR pointers, albeit more from the view of the language. The various pointer types in Windows are illustrated in figure 4.2.

* which means base == 0, limit == 0xFFFFFFFF

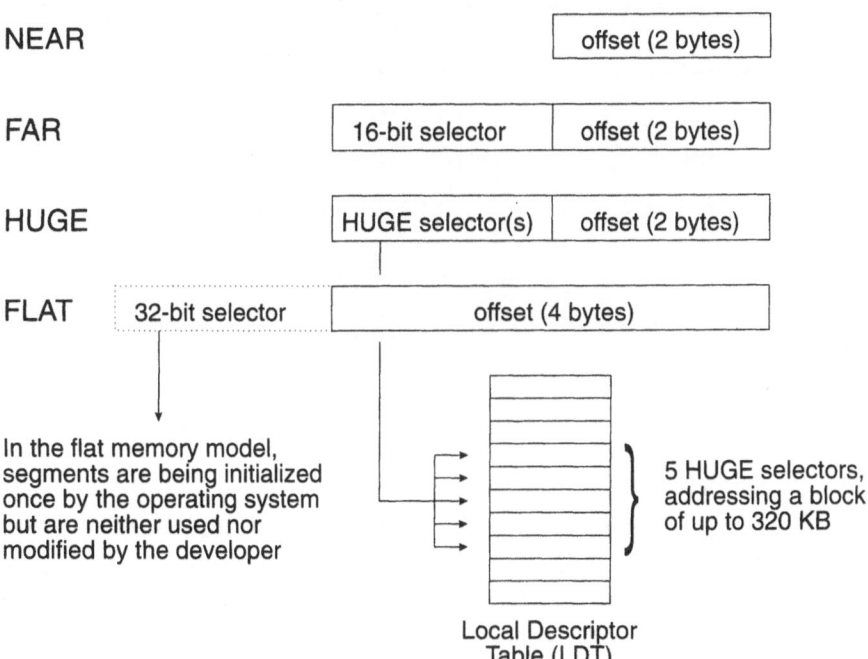

Figure 4.2: NEAR, FAR, HUGE, and flat: the pointer zoo of Windows.

The complete vanishing of segment values and the widening of offsets to 32 bits (if one insists on keeping this "old" terminology) of course render nearly all non-standardized** pointer manipulations non-portable: neither are the macros SELECTOROF and OFFSETOF to decompose a FAR

** i.e., not based on ANSI C mechanisms

pointer into the constituent parts usable under Win32, nor can a pointer be assembled (e.g., with the help of MAKELP). Ironically, the usage of HUGE pointers and memory areas must also be changed correspondingly; this should not be problematic in the normal case, since often only the keyword has to be removed. (If you have worked under Win16 with the macro HUGE, you are not even required to do this, as the macro is simply defined empty for Win32; this is a good example for the meaning of macro shells.)

*Figure 4.3: Addressing of
memory through HUGE
pointers*

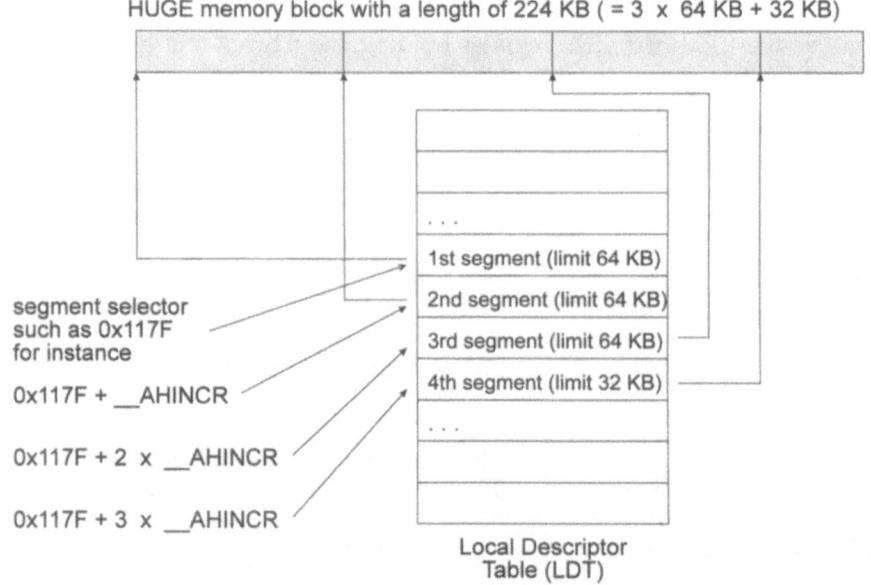

HUGE memory block with a length of 224 KB (= 3 x 64 KB + 32 KB)

segment selector
such as 0x117F
for instance

0x117F + __AHINCR

0x117F + 2 x __AHINCR

0x117F + 3 x __AHINCR

. . .

1st segment (limit 64 KB)

2nd segment (limit 64 KB)

3rd segment (limit 64 KB)

4th segment (limit 32 KB)

. . .

Local Descriptor
Table (LDT)

Self-addressed HUGE areas

This adaptation does not take place all that easily, however, if you have not left addressing of HUGE memory areas to the compiler but instead performed it yourself (e.g., because of efficiency reasons). In this case (and incidentally for all calculations with segment/selector values) you have to adapt your code to access the memory to flat memory model standards. A safe sign of such "homemade" memory management is the use of the two pseudo-variables __AHINCR (via KERNEL.113) and __AHSHIFT (KERNEL.114) (if this sounds like Chinese to you, you're probably not affected). These variables state the increment for a __huge segment, in order to reach the next valid selector for the huge array in the local descriptor table (LDT) (see figure 4.2, page 209 as well as figure

*Memory areas > 64 KB and
PASCAL or Modula-2*

4.3 on the preceding page). By the way: since neither PASCAL nor Modula-2 support an explicit HUGE model (or __huge pointers), programs working with memory areas > 64 KB will require significant modifications.

New polymorphic types: LPARAM and WPARAM

Next item: I have to make some comments about the two newly defined polymorphic data types for window procedures. The prototype of such a function up to Windows 3.0 was defined in the following way:

```
LONG FAR PASCAL xxxWndProc(HWND hwnd,WORD wMsg,
    WORD wParam,LONG lParam);
```

Window procedures up to 3.0

Basically nothing has changed for Windows 3.1, but some details introduced with that version and meant to better serve portability attract our attention:

```
LRESULT CALLBACK xxxWndProc(HWND hwnd,UINT wMsg,
    WPARAM wParam,LPARAM lParam);
```

Beginning with Windows 3.1

This prototype, in contrast to the first, can be adopted unchanged for Win32, simply because individual, portable typedefs for *all* used data types were introduced. Of course, when changing over existing software you can utilize the fact that both LRESULT and LPARAM can be traced back to a LONG under both systems — therefore changing LONG is not (yet) mandatory and does not need to be carried out immediately. Unfortunately, the story is different for the parameters wMsg and wParam: since both change size under Win32 (and hence base type), they have to be adapted as shown above while porting your program. The message value wMsg itself is represented by an UINT; the parameter type for wParam is cleverly called WPARAM. I would absolutely advise you to use these new, correct data types from the beginning, since the parameter types have to be changed for Win32 anyway. (At this occasion you should also modify the calling convention from FAR PASCAL to the newer CALLBACK macro; more on that topic is found in section 4.7 on page 262.)

Portable prototype through portable typedefs

4.3 WINDOWSX.H: A Way to Portable Programs

"It is medicine, not poison, what I'm offering you." Gotthold Ephraim Lessing,
Nathan the Wise

WINDOWSX.H — what for? Have you ever glanced at this interesting header file? Possibly not, since Microsoft unfortunately speaks only extremely laconically about the objective, let alone the usage of the macros in WINDOWSX.H in the commonly accessible reference materials for the 3.1 SDK. In a nutshell, this header file (about 70 KB long, with approximately 500 (!) macro definitions) pursues the following four aims:

Portable software
- to facilitate the creation of portable software through a set of macros for message handling, appropriately defined depending on the target system, but offering the user equivalent functionality (for details see section 4.4);

Easier communication with child windows
- to ease the communication with child windows as well as pseudo-APIs for using the predefined window classes (Edit, Button, Listbox, etc.). They also contribute to simplification and clearness of the sources and are discussed in section 4.5;

Simplification through pseudo-APIs
- to allow a certain simplification of Windows programming in general through simple and powerful pseudo-APIs;

Clearly laid out window procedures
- to make possible a cleaner design of complex window procedures and to prevent overly long switch statements (it would not at all be bad if these macros also could find their way into the source of DefWindowProc() — and the rest of the MS code — sometime in the future...). The latter two issues are detailed in the following.

Based on April 1995 beta as well as WINDOWSX.H16 from CompuServe As a matter of fact, the ensuing discussion refers to the latest version of WINDOWSX.H delivered with the Beta Win32 SDK from April 1995 as well as a newer version of this file for Win16 developers as mentioned above (found under the name of WINDOWSX.H16). In the form loaded from CompuServe's MSWIN32 forum or copied off the CD, this file is only suitable for the Microsoft compiler. For the Borland system some (insignificant) changes are necessary: especially the #pragmas in line 15 as well as line 1205 (may be slightly off in your version) must be modified as shown in the following lines (but beware: this is only valid for the 16-bit version of WINDOWS.H!):

```
// In line 15 instead of:
#pragma pack(1)          /* Assume byte packing throughout */
// for Borland use:
#pragma option -a-       /* Assume byte packing throughout */
// and in line 1205 instead of:
#pragma pack()           /* Revert to default packing */
// for Borland use:
#pragma option -a.       /* Revert to default packing */
```

Changes for Borland C

With the current Win32 SDK for Windows 95, another variant is available, which instead reads in two #include files for the very purpose of switching the byte packing. In this case just make the change in the relevant files.

The simple helper macros

Okay, first I'll address a small group of WINDOWSX.H macro definitions designed to ease memory management. Since Windows 3.1 supports only x86 protected modes, the continual locking as well as unlocking of dynamically allocated memory areas have considerably lost meaning (to say the least). Since in these modes move operations on segments can be performed through CPU hardware and the operating system and so are completely transparent for the application developer, the locking mechanism is explicitly needed only in the case of memory areas with the attributes "discardable" or "movable." In all other cases a single locking call after the initial allocation is sufficient; the memory can remain locked the whole time it is being used, and will only be unlocked directly before the deallocation. Therefore, the six macros in this group deliver some shortcuts, easing the handling of the global heap in the protected operation modes. They are relatively simple to derive from the basic Global...() functions (but pay attention to the use of the comma operator, e.g., in the macro GlobalFreePtr) and should be extended at any rate through one's own definitions — for example, for the local heap. The allocation and deallocation of global memory areas in a single step are performed with the aid of these macros as follows:

Macros for memory management

*Allocation and deallocation
of global memory in a single
step*

```
lpMem=GlobalAllocPtr(GMEM_WHATEVER,4096);
// lpMem is now either a valid pointer or null,
// an explicit lock is therefore superfluous.
...
if (fGetMore)
  lpMem=GlobalReallocPtr(lpMem,8192,GMEM_WHATSMORE);
// Ditto
...
// No explicit unlocking necessary before deallocating lpMem
GlobalFreePtr(lpMem);
```

GDI helper functions

Unfortunately, these and also the other API helper macros are *not* defined in upper case, so their use can be easily confused with an explicit function call. Modeled after a very similar pattern are the following 20 GDI helpers. Either they show existing functionality in a new attire including correct type casting (as, for example, in the group [Select-/Delete][Font/Pen/Brush/Bitmap]()) or they simplify the handling, for example, of regions, decomposing the function CombineRgn() into individual functions, depending on the fourth parameter. The definitions are rather simple and their use should be evident; therefore I probably don't need to discuss this group at any length.

*Macros for the mouse,
windows, and dialog boxes*

Mostly this is also valid for the following 25 definitions for the handling of windows, the mouse, and dialog boxes. Only the macro SetDlgMsgResult seems to be somewhat interesting: it permits composing the return value of the call for *all* messages in dialog box procedures instead of only the default messages (e.g., WM_CTLCOLOR). But since one thereby interferes with the "inner workings" of the DialogBox...() functions, one should first accurately know why a specific value is assigned; second, such activities possibly harm the portability, simply because it is nowhere unambiguously documented whether the corresponding Win32 function will permit the same manipulations. As a matter of fact, comparing the (partially rather different) macro definitions in both versions of WINDOWSX.H for 16- and 32-bit Windows is

Creation of portability macros

not at all a bad idea in order to gain some of the knowledge required for designing and writing portability macros yourself. First, you will develop some ideas where problems might lurk, and then you can get inspiration for your own creations.

To the fullest: message crackers

While all the thus far described macros (or groups, respectively) try to
simplify a certain aspect of Windows programming, they are to a large
extent independent from each other in their definition and usage. This is
not true for the next big cluster of macros (which means around 250
definitions and about half of all the definitions in WINDOWSX.H!). They
will indeed have a certain impact on your (possibly acquired over many
years) habit of writing callback window procedures. They are a kind of
"poor man's" version of object-oriented programming; unfortunately, not
much more is possible in this regard with a limited language like good
old ANSI C...

A puff of OOP...

So what is all that fuss about? In order to explain the objective and,
above all, the usage of these macros, we have to concern ourselves with
the case of the two message parameters (generally named wParam and
lParam) employed to transport necessary (or at least useful) information
to window procedures. Windows messages (such as WM_COMMAND)
consist of six parts, which also emerge in a C structure called MSG used
in the message loop of the program to pull messages off the application
queue and further dispatch them via DispatchMessage() to the appropriate window procedure:

*The making of a window
message*

```
typedef struct {
    HWND    hwnd;     // destination window
    UINT    message;  // message value (16 or 32 bit)
    WPARAM  wParam;   // 16 (or 32 bit) for further data
    LPARAM  lParam;   // 32 bit for further data
    DWORD   time;     // time stamp for the generation of the
                      // message
    POINT   pt;       // and corresponding mouse pointer
                      // location
} MSG;
```

*MSG: only the first four
members reach the window
procedure.*

Both the members time and pt aren't passed on to the windows procedure; if required, you can query them explicitly. However, the other four
components of MSG exactly build the four arguments of a windows procedure call and reach the corresponding window callback after a call to
DispatchMessage(). Arguments 1 and 2 are obvious: the first is the window handle describing the window for which the information is meant.

*wParam (no.3) and lParam
(no. 4) are used to deliver
further data.*

215

And wMsg is simply the numerical message value itself (WM_*, BM_*, CB_*, etc.), which is usually processed in a more or less gigantic switch orgy. Things get interesting with no. 3 (which is, as you should know by now, somewhat larger in Win32) and no. 4: *many* messages have to deliver further information (e.g.. about user input, window properties, etc.). The "needs" of the individual messages are at the same time rather different, as shown in the following small table (for Win16):

Table 4.1: Information sent with Windows messages

Message	wParam	lParam (lo, hi)
WM_COMMAND	idItem	hwndCtl, wNotifyCode
WM_KEYDOWN	wVKeyCode	wRepeat, bScan, fFlags
EM_SETTABSTOPS	wTabCount	lpTabStopArray
WM_SIZE	fSizeType	nWidth, nHeight
WM_MEASUREITEM	nIDCtl	lpMeasureItemStruct

As one easily realizes, there are counters, flags, ID values, pointers on arrays and structures, handles, etc., etc. heaved along — often lParam carries two or even more data items. The distribution of the various information bits on wParam and lParam in the case of WM_KEYDOWN is shown as an example in figure 4.4.

Microsoft decided over 12 (!) years ago to introduce these helper parameters (then admittedly an emergency solution): the first with a width of 16 bits, the second as a 32-bit value.* And the data to be delivered were crammed, just as it was suitable, into the six bytes of total available parameter space. The developer had to (has to!) pull off the parts he was interested in explicitly from the 48 bits of message data — this was a more or less tedious process. But this rather complicated and errorprone method seemed then the only feasible way to simulate polymorphic parameters in a language with so little object orientation like C (in C++ one could of course work with overloaded functions, or even better, with member functions). And so we have all unquestioningly written over and over again huge switch statements à la

* so that it was sufficient even for FAR pointers

Polymorphic arguments in C!?

```
switch(wMsg) {
    case WM_CREATE: ...;
    case WM_PAINT: ...;
    case WM_DESTROY: ...;
    case WM_WHATEVER: ...;
```

```
// etc. etc.
}
```

to process all the messages and at the same time always asked ourselves whether for WM_SIZE the width is found in the LOWORD and the height in the HIWORD,* or vice versa. All that misery has finally found its well-deserved end, thanks to Microsoft: namely, if you can make friends with the new macros found in WINDOWSX.H....

Well, at least a good crib!

Information for the WM_KEYDOWN message :

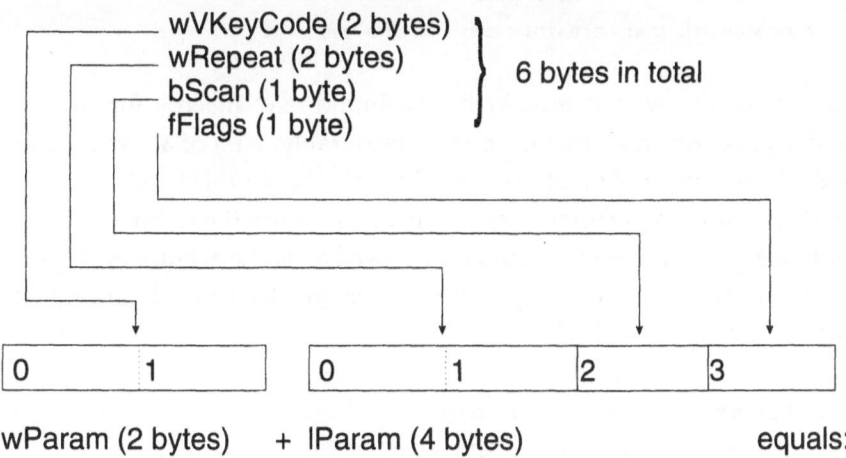

Figure 4.4: The distribution of data coming with WM_KEYDOWN

in total: 6 bytes of information in the message parameters

Examples: WM_COMMAND...

Actually these definitions *are* rather helpful, they've just the disadvantage of all new things: one doesn't know them and so can't** put them to use. So let's have a closer look at the whole stuff with the help of some messages (comments were intentionally *not* added to the following code!). The first object of our studies shall be WM_COMMAND:

** or doesn't want?

```
// Old and complex code:***
switch (wMsg) {
```

*** in a window procedure, where else?

```
...
  case WM_COMMAND:
    switch (wParam) {
      case ID_BUTTON_QUIT:
        if (HIWORD(lParam)==BN_DOUBLECLICKED)
          SendMessage(LOWORD(lParam),...);
        else if (HIWORD(lParam)==BN_CLICKED)
          EnableWindow(LOWORD(lParam),FALSE);
        break;
    }
    // How the code might look if another four
    // notifications for five further controls have to be
    // processed, you certainly can imagine yourself...
```

One message — one function!

Alas, that's the way it *was*. With the brand-new macros for message handling, however, all that changes considerably. First of all, you write a function dealing *solely* with the handling of WM_COMMAND messages for all windows of a certain class. This function has the following calling sequence (the naming of the function as well as of the arguments is yours to choose, but parameter types and order are determined through the macros in WINDOWSX.H):

int id == LOWORD(wParam)

HWND hwndCtl == LOWORD(lParam)

UINT codeNotify == HI-WORD(lParam)

```
// The new and much cleaner code:
void Input_WMCommandHandler(HWND hwnd,int id,HWND hwndCtl,
  UINT codeNotify)
// WM_COMMAND-Handler for all windows of class "Input"
{
  switch (id) {
    case ID_BUTTON_QUIT:
      if (codeNotify==BN_DOUBLECLICKED)
        SendMessage(hwndCtl,...);
      else if (codeNotify==BN_CLICKED)
        EnableWindow(hwndCtl,FALSE);
      break;
    ...
  }
```

More typing work?

The code is in fact cleaner, to a great extent self-documenting, and by being pulled from the often extensive switch statement of the window procedure, also much easier to identify and maintain. Objections that one has to write a whole function can actually be traced back only to two reasons: either the additional typing work or considerations for the efficiency of the program. For the first item I can just say that (according to my experience) most programmers spend considerably more time poking around in the giblets of their programs with a debugger than keeping their source codes to some extent fit and healthy. Perhaps it would be much more beneficial to the matter if we put some more effort and time into the *construction* of consistent, maintainable and clear source codes in the first place — the debugging sessions saved later on will certainly show that this was worth the trouble....

The second argument, too, is quite easy to invalidate: generally in the message handling there is so much juggling around with Windows API functions that the comparatively insignificant overhead of a simple function call shouldn't be of any significance. And with a lot of messages often a function for the additional handling is called anyway.* The overall effect of using these macros on the total performance therefore seems to be negligible. And those who still don't believe this should check with a profiler in which part of his program the most time dawdles away: at those places specific optimizations certainly have more reason (and effect) than the unspecific claim that the resulting code is inefficient and the subsequent renunciation of better code structuring. And here comes another argument: do you really know how many CPU cycles a call of the macros HIWORD or LOWORD costs? And now check all the places where these macros (in the above-mentioned style) are repeatedly called within the processing *of one individual message*! The single evaluation for the arguments of the handler function written by you might prove to be even *more* efficient!

And now we arrive at the main point: in which way and from which place are these nice functions for the message treatment finally called? This more than legitimate question is answered with the following just as short as impressive source code snippet:

```
switch (wMsg) {
...
    case WM_COMMAND:
        return HANDLE_WM_COMMAND(hwnd,wParam,lParam,
            Input_WMCommandHandler);
```

Or lower perfomance?

* But only after the arguments have been laboriously decoded!

So, who calls these nice functions?

*A macro named HAN-
DLE_WM_COMMAND*

And that's all there is to it! The macro HANDLE_WM_COMMAND (interestingly enough, the macro names in this group are completely written in upper case!?) distributes the data packed in the message parameters wParam and lParam as required to the last three arguments of the self-written function Input_WMCommandHandler() and automatically calls the function. This should also clarify why you *accurately* have to observe the predefined parameter types and order: otherwise the compiler acknowledges that with some warnings or even error messages. For the to-be-written function there are no explicit prototypes in WINDOWSX.H (that's not a big surprise, since you'll probably want to use your own function names). Instead the necessary calling sequence is always recorded in a comment line as a reference prototype just above

*Pseudo-prototypes or
"signatures"*

the macro definition: Microsoft calls these message-specific "fingerprints" also signatures; for example, the one for WM_COMMAND and the macro definition for Win32 looks as follows:

*These "prototypes" must be
observed.*

```
/* void Cls_OnCommand(HWND hwnd,int id,HWND hwndCtl,
    UINT codeNotify) */
#define HANDLE_WM_COMMAND(hwnd, wParam, lParam, fn) \
    ((fn)((hwnd), (int)(LOWORD(wParam)), (HWND)(lParam), \
    (UINT)HIWORD(wParam)), OL)
```

I have completely printed a copy of WINDOWSX.H, so I can easily find the signature of a certain message handler at any time (this would be even simpler if Microsoft would make up its mind to arrange the macros finally in an alphabetic fashion instead of the motley assortment we find in WINDOWSX.H). Therefore, in Appendix 3 on page 369 you'll find a

*Appendix 3: a sorted list of
all signatures.*

correspondingly sorted list of all message handler signatures.

And for the real type-o-lazy who are only to be convinced with much effort to write a handler function for these macro definitions (incidentally: also called message crackers), there is another, even simpler variant for the call:

```
switch (wMsg) {
...
    HANDLE_MSG(hwnd,WM_COMMAND,Input_WMCommandHandler);
```

*For the lazy ones: a still
shorter way!*

Here, several encapsulated macros are called. First HANDLE_MSG creates a line with "case WM_COMMAND:"; then in the second step the macro HANDLE_WM_COMMAND is expanded. (The whole matter is one of the trickier possibilities of C pre-processor usage and is absolutely a rewarding object for study — see also section 3.3 on page 142). Admittedly, using this fine macro implicitly requires that both message parameters are called exactly wParam and lParam, respectively. However, if this is made sure, the consistent use of the concept of handler functions and calling macros can lead to very short window procedures and very clear programs, indeed:

```
LRESULT CALLBACK InputWndProc(HWND hwnd,UINT wMsg,
  WPARAM wParam,LPARAM lParam)
{
  switch (wMsg) {
    HANDLE_MSG(hwnd,WM_CREATE,Input_WMCreateHandler);
    HANDLE_MSG(hwnd,WM_SIZE,Input_WMSizeHandler);
    HANDLE_MSG(hwnd,WM_CHAR,Input_WMCharHandler);
    HANDLE_MSG(hwnd,WM_COMMAND,Input_WMCommandHandler);
    HANDLE_MSG(hwnd,WM_CLOSE,Input_WMCloseHandler);
    // etc.
  }
}
```

The handler functions are defined further up or in another module.

(If you have named the messages parameters differently, e.g., wP and lP, a simple macro definition (i.e., #define wParam wp) might prove useful.)

... and WM_MOUSEMOVE

As a further example I want to show another frequently used message, namely WM_MOUSEMOVE. Both the following code snippets talk for themselves and probably don't need further comments:

```
Z z;   // local variable, will be used later on
...
switch (wMsg) {
...
  case WM_MOUSEMOVE:
    z.fMove=wParam&MK_CONTROL;
    z.fAdd=wParam&MK_SHIFT;
```

Still in a windows procedure

221

```
z.xNew=LOWORD(lParam);
z.yNew=HIWORD(lParam);
if (wParam&MK_LBUTTON) DoSomethingLeft(&z);
else if (wParam&MK_RBUTTON) DoSomethingRight(&z);
else MessageBeep(0);
return 0;
...
```

And here is the variant rewritten with the use of the WINDOWSX.H macros:

The function ...
```
void Input_WMMouseMoveHandler(HWND hwnd,int x,int y,
  UINT keyFlags)
{
  Z z; // Another small benefit: local variables can be
       // pulled off the windows procedure, if possible, and
       // put into the handler function. This can save some
       // stack space if the windows procedure is called
       // recursively.
  z.fMove=keyFlags&MK_CONTROL;
  z.fAdd=keyFlags&MK_SHIFT;
  z.xNew=x;
  z.yNew=y;
  if (keyFlags&MK_LBUTTON) {
    DoSomethingLeft(&z);
    // instead of the DoSomethingLeft() call you might
    // even include the corresponding code!
  }
  else if (keyFlags&MK_RBUTTON) {
    DoSomethingRight(&z);
    // ditto;
  }
  else MessageBeep(0);
}
...
```

... and your call.
```
// And the calling code in the windows procedure:
switch(wMsg) {
  ...
  case WM_MOUSEMOVE:
```

```
        return HANDLE_WM_MOUSEMOVE(hwnd,wParam,lParam,
          Input_WMMouseMoveHandler);
      // or HANDLE_MSG(...)
```

So far, so good. This fashion of distributing data from the two parameters to the handlers seems in fact to work pretty well and surely eases message processing. But what, so you could confront me with another perfectly legitimate question: what happens, if on the contrary, I have to reassemble the two message parameters from the individual data items? This can, for instance, be required for subclassing, and the direct dispatching of a message to another window would be another case. So Microsoft provided the necessary means for this too: each message for which a HANDLE_WM_... macro is defined also possesses a corresponding macro to rearrange the individual parameters back into wParam and lParam (see figure 4.5). The following piece of code extends the above shown procedure for the treatment of WM_MOUSEMOVE; in the last line instead of MessageBeep(0) the default window function DefWindowProc() is called via the macro FORWARD_WM_MOUSE-MOVE:

And vice versa?

FORWARD_WM_MOU-SEMOVE

```
Void Input_WMMouseMoveHandler(HWND hwnd,int x,int y,
  UINT keyFlags)
{
  // as shown above
  ...
  // but instead of MessageBeep(0):
  else FORWARD_WM_MOUSEMOVE(hwnd,x,y,keyFlags,DefWindowProc);
}
```

This dispatches the message to DefWindowProc().

In a very similar fashion other Windows API functions (or window procedures) can be called and supplied with the reassembled information:

```
FORWARD_WM_MOUSEMOVE(hwnd,x,y,keyFlags,SendMessage);
// or FORWARD_WM_MOUSEMOVE(...,PostMessage);
```

As mentioned, in WINDOWSX.H about 250 macros are defined in this style, covering all (documented) WM_*-messages (except, of course, WM_USER and WM_NULL). In the Win32 version even a few new macros have arrived, because some new messages were introduced there

All WM_* messages with the exception of WM_USER and WM_NULL

(respectively, as yet undocumented messages were finally documented in the Win32 API...). The enthusiasm of the Microsoft developers unfortunately didn't extend to exercising corresponding macros for the private messages of child controls (listboxes, buttons, and the like). Fortunately this limitation is easy to get around, because these are generally only of interest when sub- or superclassing the standard classes. Macros that on the other hand build and send certain messages to child windows (e.g., BM_SETSTYLE to a button window) are perfectly well provided; more about these in section 4.5 beginning on page 234.

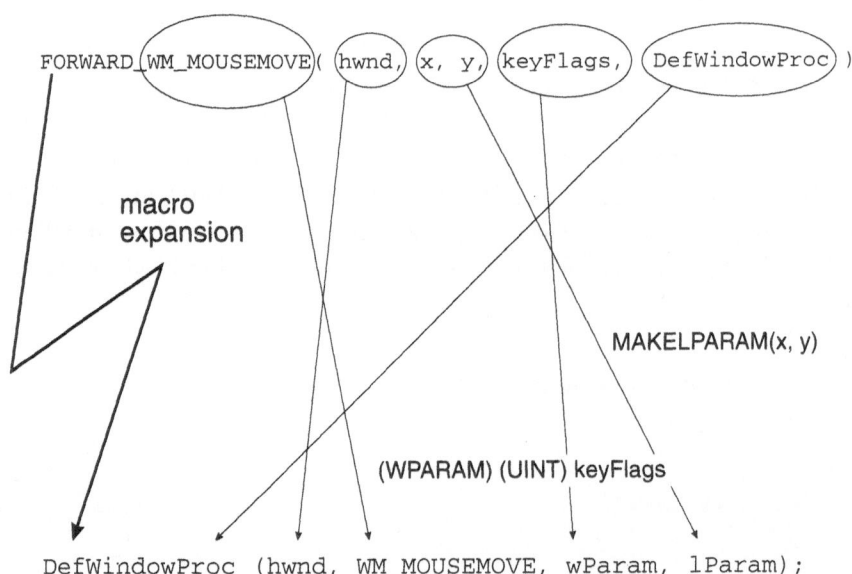

Figure 4.5: Macro expansion and recomposing the message parameters wParam and lParam

The most important benefit: portability

Ah yes, and now the most important reason for the as excessive as possible usage of message crackers occurs to me! Besides the already mentioned pluses, these macros show namely the (actually deciding) benefit

Portable message handling

that you can design the message handling in window procedures in an *absolutely* portable fashion (except on very few easily identifiable and seldom used messages). As the unpacking of the data items from the two message parameters (or vice versa: the reassembling) is carried out by the cracker macros, the developer can rest assured that his handler functions, once implemented correctly, will always be called with the desired parameters independently from the underlying Windows implementation. The macro HANDLE_WM_COMMAND for instance, called in the preceding example code, is defined as follows in both systems:

```
// In the 16-bit version:
#define HANDLE_WM_COMMAND(hwnd,wParam,lParam,fn) \
    ((fn)((hwnd),(int)(wParam),(HWND)LOWORD(lParam), \
    (UINT)HIWORD(lParam)), 0L)


// and in the 32-bit version:
#define HANDLE_WM_COMMAND(hwnd,wParam,lParam,fn) \
    ((fn)((hwnd),(int)(LOWORD(wParam)),(HWND)(lParam), \
    (UINT)HIWORD(wParam)), 0L)
```

Observe how simple an externally identical interface can be built through different accesses to wParam and lParam; this macro shell is portable programming at its best!

The few exceptions referred to especially concern the messages dealing with a string parameter: in the Win16 version the type LPSTR is used; under Win32, on the other hand, LPTSTR is employed. Indeed, this will have consequences probably only if your program works with the Unicode character set (see section 4.10, page 300). Some of the signatures in the 16-bit version use a UINT, whereas the 32-bit counterparts include an int; so the C compiler in some circumstances might react with a warning. Finally, a special case is the signatures for the message WM_ACTIVATEAPP, which exceptionally differ in the very last argument:

The (inevitable) exceptions

WM_ACTIVATEAPP

```
// 16 bit:
/*  void Cls_OnActivateApp(HWND hwnd, BOOL fActivate,
    HTASK htaskActDeact); */


// 32 bit:
/*  void Cls_OnActivateApp(HWND hwnd, BOOL fActivate,
    DWORD dwThreadId); */
```

But this is, as said, a genuine exception, otherwise the signatures are identical and therefore the functions you have to write can start with the same parameter lists under both systems. Yet, a warning is certainly in order: the extremely high degree of coincidence of parameter types doesn't guarantee an absolutely identical implementation of the corresponding handler function in all cases.* If the type of the parameter is the same, but not its meaning, you nevertheless have to distinguish between Win16 and Win32 semantics in the handler function and must provide in each case the proper code (e.g., through #ifdef branches). A good example here is the message WM_NCACTIVATE, which indeed has the same signature for Win16 and Win32, unfortunately the last two arguments are meaningful only under Win32! This is a beautiful example for the fact that even behind absolute syntactical congruence considerable porting work can be concealed!

After all, this is only a syntactical feature!

WM_NCACTIVATE

Using the message crackers

And a final comment concerning the usage of these macros in your programs: existing software can of course at any time be rewritten to include the message crackers; but the effort for the consistent conversion can be comparatively high. Therefore, check before beginning whether the "small brothers" described in the following section 4.4 are applicable for the adaptation of existing source code. With them you need to change the structure of your window procedures just at those places that are definitely not portable. Especially if you want to (or have to) provide quick results, this way seems to be much easier and appealing. In the medium term you should probably plan the changeover of your applications to the message cracker set (this, however, is not true if you think of recoding your program in C++ anyway, since there you have of course all the needed mechanisms for portable programming at full disposal).

Comparatively high effort for adapting existing software

Very good, however, for new projects

For new projects I would recommend not to make any compromises, but to start from the beginning with the consistent use of message crackers as well as handler functions. The additional typing work easily can be limited through some self-defined macros; on another occasion I have already pointed out that better and cleaner source codes will reduce the debugging effort more than proportionally anyway! And a last argument for the still unconvinced: if you plan to port your program to C++ and a nice class library sometime in the distant future, you have already done an all-important first step towards member functions and the use of methods with the distribution of individual messages to the corresponding handlers (see also section 3.9)!

4.4 Message Processing and Parameter Packing

"!@#$^&*^&*$#@%}"@!~#}}"{$]\!!!!!"* Non-printable curse from a slighty unwell Windows developer after first getting in touch with the parameter packing of the messages WM_KEYDOWN, WM_KEYUP and WM_CHAR

The last chapter already brought us quite deeply into the shoals of both Window message parameters and the information packed inside them according to the message value. Here, we will realize a solution similar to the message crackers on a smaller scale with a set of macros from WINDOWSX.H which are especially well suited for the adaptation or conversion of existing programs. In contrast to the approach described above, which assumes the writing of a handler function and changing the window procedure, the following variant manages with the latter.

The little brothers of the message crackers

We will continue with our favorite message WM_COMMAND, which has already been used above. Let's consider the following extract of a Win16 window procedure:

```
switch(wMsg) {
  ...
  case WM_COMMAND:
    switch (wParam) {
      case ID_BUTTON_QUIT:
      ...
```

This code is not portable, since under Win32 two pieces of information are packed into the wParam: in the lower 16 bits the id value of the sending control, and in the upper half the notification code. The switch(wParam) statement will be compiled unhesitatingly but will only be successful for WM_COMMAND messages that are sent from menus (because only then under Win32 HIWORD(wParam) == 0). For all other cases, the switch will only deliver garbage.* You may use the following solution:

* Well, garbage in, garbage out!

```
  case WM_COMMAND:
#ifdef WIN32 // now follows 32-bit code ...
    switch (LOWORD(lParam)) {
#else // 16 Bit
    switch (wParam) {
```

```
#endif
        case ID_BUTTON_QUIT:

        . . .
```

The solution: conditional compilation. Now, for both cases, the code is passed through conditional compilation depending on the constant WIN32, so that the code will be also compatible for Win32. Admittedly, this method is the simplest and the clearest for some rare differences occuring in the two APIs. But it seems very questionable whether a long window procedure with a large and mostly unclear message switch is exactly the right place for frequent #idefs. So, a coherent solution had to be found, which unsurprisingly is again based on cleverly defined macros — which, for their part, can be implemented in a system-specific manner thanks to conditional compilation.

The little brothers of the message crackers

Carefully study the following two groups of macro definitions (the first stems from the 16-bit version, the second from the 32-bit version of WINDOWSX.H):

Win16
```
#define GET_WM_COMMAND_ID(wp,lp)        (wp)
#define GET_WM_COMMAND_HWND(wp,lp)      (HWND)LOWORD(lp)
#define GET_WM_COMMAND_CMD(wp,lp)       HIWORD(lp)
```

Win32
```
#define GET_WM_COMMAND_ID(wp,lp)        LOWORD(wp)
#define GET_WM_COMMAND_HWND(wp,lp)      (HWND)(lp)
#define GET_WM_COMMAND_CMD(wp,lp)       HIWORD(wp)
```

The definitions are indeed different, but the results are the same! Hence, the excerpt shown above with conditional compilation becomes extremely simple but nevertheless remains completely portable:

```
case WM_COMMAND:
   switch (GET_WM_COMMAND_ID(wp,lp)) {
     case ID_BUTTON_QUIT:

     . . .
```

As already said, these macros enable you to directly change the corresponding non-portable code in a window procedure without modifying the program structure at all. That's why I like to speak about the "little brothers" of the message crackers, as they are particulary well suited for the rapid adaptation of existing programs.

The structure of the program doesn't need to be modified.

Which messages does by this modification concern? The following table lists both the messages and the distribution of the data in the two parameters. The abbreviations for the information contained in the message parameters are directly taken from the Microsoft reference guide.

Table 4.2: Messages affected by parameter modifications

System		Win16	Win32	
Message	**wParam**	**lParam (lo,hi)**	**wParam (lo,hi)**	**lParam)**
WM_ACTIVATE	state	fminimized, hwnd	state, fminimized	hwnd
WM_CHARTOITEM	char	pos, hwnd	char, pos	hwnd
WM_COMMAND	id	hwnd, cmd	id, cmd	hwnd
WM_CTLCOLOR	hdc	hwnd, type	see text, page 231	
WM_HSCROLL as well as WM_VSCROLL	code	pos, hwnd	code, pos	hwnd
WM_MDIACTIVATE	factivate	hwndact, hwnddeact	hwnddeact	hwndact
WM_MENUSELECT	cmd	flags, hmenu	cmd, flags	hmenu
WM_MENUCHAR	char	hmenu, fmenu	char, fmenu	hmenu
WM_PARENTNOTIFY	msg	id, hwndchild	msg, id	hwndchild
WM_VKEYTOITEM	code	hwnd, item	code, item	hwnd

The three edit control messages EM_LINESCROLL, EM_GETSEL, and EM_SETSEL are not listed in the table as they are out of place here (but see WINDOWSX.H for the actual definition). As can be seen, until now two data items were packed in an lParam: a window or menu handle and another information like an id value or a flag, for instance. The handle* is still to be found in the lParam, and the other information has moved to the wParam, where it slipped into the newly available upper half (see figure 4.6). The names of the access macros are very easy to build: you only add GET_ in front of the message name, followed by the message name itself, and finally the information that is to be retrieved (just use the designations shown in the table above but written fully in capital letters). When you call the resulting macro, don't forget that you always have to indicate wParam and lParam *together* — since the macro evaluation is defined differently according to the underlying system,

* grown to 32 bit

both values are required, even if *you* happen to know where the actual value is stored:

```
fMin=GET_WM_ACTIVATE_FMINIMIZED(wParam,lParam);
idSender=GET_WM_COMMAND_ID(wParam,lParam);
pos=GET_WM_HSCROLL_POS(wParam,lParam);
uMsg=GET_WM_PARENTNOTIFY_MSG(wParam,lParam);
// etc.
```

Figure 4.6: Data and their distribution on wParam and lParam

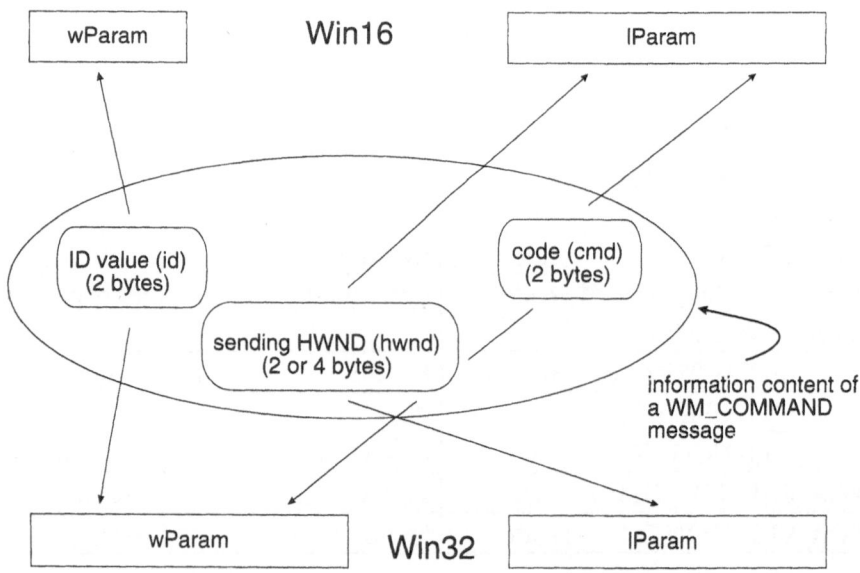

A note concerning WM_MDIACTIVATE

A remark concerning WM_MDIACTIVATE: the macros only cover the case when the receiver is an MDI child window having received the message from its parent MDI client window. Furthermore, in the Win32 version, there was no place anymore for the fActivate flag in the message parameters (since both handles already completely occupy the total space of 8 bytes). The accompanying macro GET_WM_MDIACTI-

Window handle plus wParam plus lParam

VATE_FACTIVATE is therefore an exception to the rule mentioned above always to use wParam and lParam in the unpacking macros: here, you first have to give the window handle, so that this flag can be "calculated" (through a simple comparison of hwnd == hwndact), afterwards, as usual, the two window parameters are given. A bit tricky, but portable!

```
// Win16:
#define GET_WM_MDIACTIVATE_FACTIVATE(hwnd,wp,lp)  (BOOL)(wp)


// Win32:
#define GET_WM_MDIACTIVATE_FACTIVATE(hwnd,wp,lp) \
  (lP==(LONG)hwnd)
```

The (Win16) message WM_CTLCOLOR, which delivers three packets of information, is another special case: in the wParam a handle to the device context of the child window is stored, and in the lParam the window handle and the window type (the seven constants CTLCOLOR_* are employed for that). Two handles — so the available space is already taken up under Win32. Hence, the type information has to be passed in another way. Nothing's easier than that: for Win32, Microsoft simply invented seven *completely* new type-specific messages, which replace the single WM_CTCOLOR of Win16:

WM_CTLCOLOR: seven out of one!

- WM_CTLCOLORMSGBOX   for message boxes
- WM_CTLCOLOREDIT   for edit controls
- WM_CTLCOLORLISTBOX   for listbox controls
- WM_CTLCOLORBTN   for button controls
- WM_CTLCOLORDLG   for dialog boxes
- WM_CTLCOLORSCROLLBAR   for scrollbar controls
- WM_CTLCOLORSTATIC   for static controls

In that case, wParam and lParam are unfortunately not sufficient to design a completely portable macro definition that could make conditional compilation superfluous. The following code fragment shows how you can obtain a maximum of clear formulation by using the macros from WINDOWSX.H:

Unfortunately, not completely portable

```
switch (wMsg) {
  ...
#ifdef Win32  // possibly not necessary, see later
  case WM_CTLCOLORMSGBOX:
  case WM_CTLCOLOREDIT:
```

```
      case WM_CTLCOLORLISTBOX:
      case WM_CTLCOLORBTN:
      case WM_CTLCOLORDLG:
      case WM_CTLCOLORSCROLLBAR:
      case WM_CTLCOLORSTATIC:
#else          // possibly not necessary, see later
      case WM_CTLCOLOR:
#endif         // possibly not necessary, see later
        hdcChild=GET_WM_CTLCOLOR_HDC(wParam,lParam,wMsg);
        hwndChild=GET_WM_CTLCOLOR_HWND(wParam,lParam,wMsg);
        wType=GET_WM_CTLCOLOR_TYPE(wParam,lParam,wMsg);
        ...
}
```

WM_CTLCOLOR: message value plus wParam and lParam.

Essentially, as far as the GET_WM_CTLCOLOR_* macros are concerned, you have to provide wParam, lParam, and also the message value (wMsg) itself. The macro definition GET_WM_CTLCOLOR_TYPE takes advantage of the fact that under Win32 each of the WM_CTLCOLOR... messages follows one another numerically, so that the type of the sending window can be easily calculated with a simple subtraction:

```
// Under Win32:
#define GET_WM_CTLCOLOR_TYPE(wp,lp,msg) \
   (WORD)(msg-WM_CTLCOLORMSGBOX)
// and Win16:
#define GET_WM_CTLCOLOR_TYPE(wp,lp,msg)   HIWORD(lp)
```

A simplification?

The program extract shown above could be written much simpler, provided that we could trust that Microsoft will not overlap the numerical values of the Win32 WM_CTLCOLOR... messages with other system messages in Win16 in the future. In that case, the conditional compilation can be completely omitted, since in both versions of WINDOWSX.H the missing message values from the other system have been correctly numerically defined afterwards. Unfortunately, with Microsoft's speed of creating new ideas, concepts, and APIs, this should be interpreted only as a *hint*. As usual, the documentation (rather meager anyway) remains persistently silent on that point.

Finally, some less significant macros have also been defined in WIN-
DOWSX.H: as for the already mentioned Edit control messages and
WM_CHANGECBCHAIN, which I don't need to treat in detail, a glance
at the header files will presumably say more than a thousand words....

Helper macros to reassemble the message parameters

Principally, the GET_WM_* macros correspond to the message crackers
(HANDLE_WM_*), but start one level lower. So it is not surprising that
simpler macro definitions also exist in order to assemble the message
parameters corresponding to the FORWARD_WM_... macros seen
above. These macros (two examples will just follow) take over the corresponding message-specific information and recreate wParam and lParam
out of them. To define the macro name, you just put a GET_ before the
message name and an _MPS behind (presumably an abbreviation for
Make ParameterS):

```
// The GET_..._MPS macros for WM_COMMAND
// Win16:
#define GET_WM_COMMAND_MPS(id,hwnd,cmd) \
    (WPARAM)(id),MAKELONG(hwnd,cmd)


// Win32:
#define GET_WM_COMMAND_MPS(id,hwnd,cmd) \
    (WPARAM)MAKELONG(id, cmd),(LONG)(hwnd)


// And a calling example:
   SendMessage(hwndParent,WM_COMMAND,
     GET_WM_COMMAND_MPS(ID_BUTTON,hwndButton,BN_CLICKED));


// ... and the definition for EM_SETSEL
// Win16:
#define GET_EM_SETSEL_MPS(iStart,iEnd) \
   0,MAKELONG(iStart,iEnd)


// Win32:
#define GET_EM_SETSEL_MPS(iStart,iEnd) \
    (WPARAM)(iStart),(LONG)*(iEnd)
```

233

```
// Again a calling example:
SendMessage(hwndEdit,EM_GETSEL,GET_EM_SETSEL_MPS(0,1));
```

Unfortunately, (not only) with the help of the second definition you can see pretty well that Microsoft often releases slipshod work: it is perfectly okay to use the (WPARAM) cast for Win32, but why the hell do they cast with (LONG) instead of (LPARAM) for the lParam? Of course, a LONG corresponds to an LPARAM, this is clear. But how will the data types *Win64?* LONG and LPARAM be defined in a *future* 64-bit version?* The same or differently? If LONG is used here, then Microsoft, please tell me why the data type LPARAM has been created in the first place?!? As already said, an unpleasant sloppiness that easily contaminates others, as I unfortunately experience myself....

Your own ideas and concepts A last remark on the subjects of message crackers and argument packing: you can (and definitely should) use the basic concepts and ideas for the portable handling of self-defined messages, for example, in self-written window classes. With the help of the Microsoft definitions, you should be able to reconstruct quite easily how to handle the different data types and messages (although a critical look or two will certainly do no harm — and as we have seen elsewhere, a wrongly defined macro can do much more damage than no macro at all!).

4.5 Portable Macros to Communicate with Child Windows

"Of what one can't speak, one should better keep silent about." Ludwig Wittgenstein, Tractatus Logico-Philosophicus

The last large group of macro definitions in WINDOWSX.H (about 125) hits out at all the messages that are usually sent to child windows in *Messages such as CB_DIR* order to get some work done (for example, CB_DIR) or to get back in- *or LB_GETCURSEL, for* formation (like LB_GETCURSEL). The names of the macros in this group *example* are formed with a prefix indicating the window class and a verb describing the action (for example, Edit_SetText); unfortunately, Microsoft here again chose not to write the names in capital letters (I really wonder who is responsible for all that chaos there). The definitions are divided into six subgroups according to the six predefined window classes:

- The prefix Static_ covers the messages for windows of class "Static" (just six macros, you can't do many useful things with static windows).

Static

- Button_* deals with the messages for push and radio buttons as well as checkboxes (nine macros).

Button

- The Edit_* macros are relevant for the single- and multi-line edit controls (32 macros).

Edit

- ScrollBar_* definitions pertain to horizontal and vertical scrollbars (six macros).

ScrollBar

- Macros with the prefix ListBox_* provide the interface for list boxes (39 macros).

ListBox

- And finally ComboBox_*, for the handling of combo boxes. Caution: edit fields or list boxes in combo boxes have to be addressed with these macros and *not* with the Edit_* or ListBox_* group (33 macros).

ComboBox

Some common definitions

The macro *_Enable is common to all six groups (see figure 4.7) and is used either to disable a window of the correspondig class or to revert a previous disable call; in fact, it is nothing more than a simple shell around EnableWindow():

The asterisk signals the six classes mentioned above.

```
Static_Enable(hwndStatic,TRUE);
ComboBox_Enable(hwndCB,FALSE);
```

Shell around EnableWindow()

The macros *_SetText, *_GetText, as well as *_GetTextLength are defined for all classes able to store or process a window text (hence scrollbars aren't concerned, because they don't manage a window text):

Further standard macros

```
Edit_SetText(hwndEdit,"News to edit!");
Button_SetText(hwndAction,fQuit?"Quit!":"OK!");
ComboBox_GetText(hwndCB,chBuf,BUFSIZE);
if (Static_GetTextLength(hwndStatic)>12) ...
```

For the four classes used in the example above, the macros are simply translated into the corresponding calls to [Get/Set]WindowText-[Length](). However, the ListBox_* macros play a special role in the ma-

ListBox specialties

nipulation of window texts. Since a list box normally does not have an explicit window text, the macro ListBox_GetText is interpreted as if the contents of a certain entry should be read (correspondingly, List-Box_GetTextLen delivers the length of the entry):

```
l=ListBox_GetTextLen(hwndList,iCurr); // Alas, ...Len
  // instead of ...Length!
ListBox_GetText(hwndList,iCurr,chBuf); // Buffer size?
```

I would have found it a much better idea to either use exactly the same names and the same calling sequence for both macros or, even better, to name them in such a way that they cannot be mixed up.

Figure 4.7: The six control classes and the _Enable macro

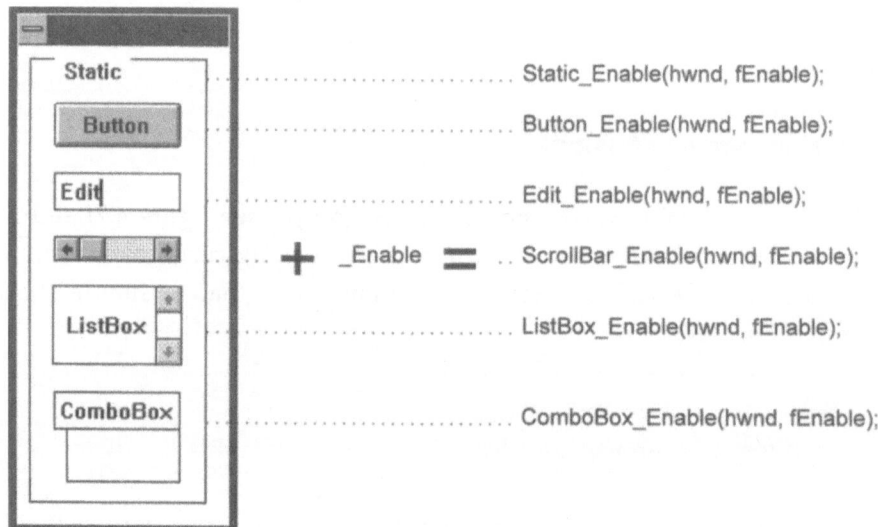

```
Static_Enable(hwnd, fEnable);
Button_Enable(hwnd, fEnable);
Edit_Enable(hwnd, fEnable);
ScrollBar_Enable(hwnd, fEnable);
ListBox_Enable(hwnd, fEnable);
ComboBox_Enable(hwnd, fEnable);
```

Class-specific macros

All the other macros in the six groups are class-specific and implemented in such a way that they use their parameters in order to build the

Build and send a message

wParam/lParam couple for the corresponding message you plan to send to the window concerned. Instead of listing and/or explaining all macros, I'd rather pick some of the more interesting macro definitions and describe them; you can always find the exact details of the other "functions" in the header file. Let's first have a look at the definition of the macro Static_SetIcon (which admittedly is identical for Win16 and Win32):

```
#define Static_SetIcon(hwndCtl,hIcon) \
    ((HICON)(UINT)(DWORD)SendMessage((hwndCtl),STM_SETICON, \
    (WPARAM)(HICON)(hIcon),0L))
```

Static_SetIcon

Besides the typing work saved by using the macros, the various cast operations that are performed within the macro expansion are particularly noticeable. For example, the return value gets casted from LRESULT to a DWORD, then to a UINT, and finally to an HICON. The reason for those multiple casts is the size difference between handles under Win16 and Win32, respectively. In the way the macro is formulated (see the following figure 4.8), a correct HICON will be returned in both cases (but is not necessarily to be used by the caller).

Multiple casts

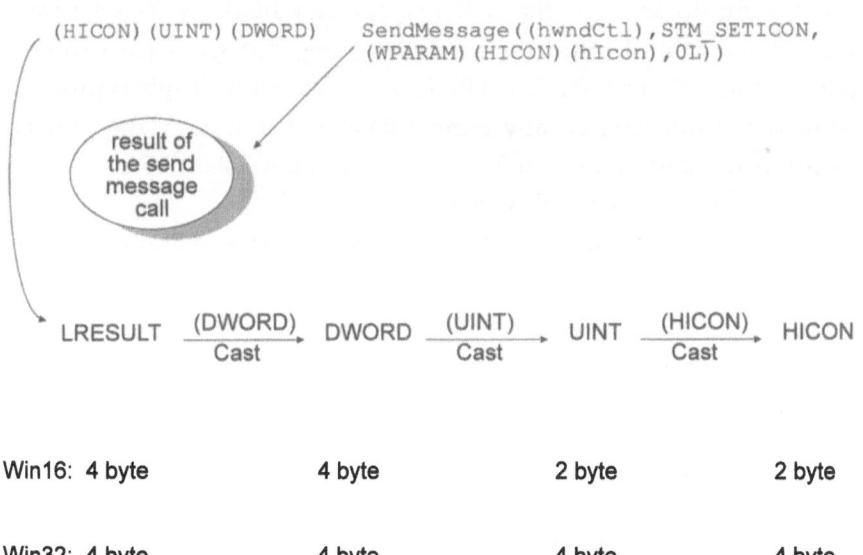

Figure 4.8: Investigation of casts: from LRESULT to HICON.

These "built-in" type transformations are one of the biggest advantages of these macros: the data type conversions and the resulting casts have to be designed bugfree only once and then can be written down explicitly at a single central place (but see my remarks farther down!). By using these macros later on in the source code, you can be sure that the necessary conversions will always be correctly performed independently of the target platfom.

Let's have a look at the transformation of the message BM_SETSTYLE of the "Button" class:

"Built-in" type transformations

Button_SetStyle

```
#define Button_SetStyle(hwndCtl,style,fRedraw) \
    ((void)SendMessage((hwndCtl),BM_SETSTYLE, \
    (WPARAM)LOWORD(style), \
    MAKELPARAM(((fRedraw)?TRUE:FALSE),0)))
```

Here, two things catch the eye: first, the "conversion" of the return value to the "type" void, which means that the return cannot be used anymore. Or put differently: practically Button_SetStyle has been implemented as a procedure call and the compiler can safeguard its correct use. Second, it is interesting to see that the BOOL parameter fRedraw is not simply given to the control (after the needed casting) but has been explicitly converted into either FALSE or TRUE. In that case, this magic is probably not necessary (doesn't do any harm either), but it stresses the problem already mentioned in section 3.4 concerning the constant TRUE and the usage of boolean expressions in general.

Implemented as a procedure call

Let's continue with a somewhat more extensive definition for the edit message EM_GETLINE:

Edit_GetLine

```
#define Edit_GetLine(hwndCtl,line,lpch,cchMax) \
    ((*((int *)(lpch))=(cchMax)), \
    ((int)(DWORD)SendMessage((hwndCtl),EM_GETLINE, \
    (WPARAM)(int)(line),(LPARAM)(LPSTR)(lpch))))
```

Quite a nice macro! First, lpch (the buffer address, probably of type LPSTR) is casted into a pointer to an int and the first two bytes (even four under Win32!) of the buffer are initialized* with its length. The other parameters are correctly converted, and the macro provides the return value of the SendMessage() call casted to an int (note the comma operator at the end of the second line). Pretty tricky, isn't it? You could say

* Well, in my opinion this is a rather questionable thing anyway.

238

whatever you want about this method of delivering the length of a buffer (I personally am skeptical), but using this macro definitely saves much work! And let's dwell on a further message of the class "Edit":

```
#define Edit_SetWordBreakProc(hwndCtl,lpfnWordBreak) \
    ((void)SendMessage((hwndCtl),EM_SETWORDBREAKPROC,0, \
    (LPARAM)(EDITWORDBREAKPROC)(lpfnWordBreak)))
```

Edit_SetWordBreakProc

Actually, this macro definition shows nothing special. But a trifle keeps bothering me — namely the fact that the given variable lpfnWordBreak is *explicitly* converted to an EDITWORDBREAKPROC *before* the (LPARAM) cast, something I think is completely unnecessary. In fact, the cast is not needed here and not only is superfluous but can also have quite negative consequences. The main reason for my concern is simply the following: *either* the variable lpfnWordBreak effectively contains the address of a function with the correct parameter types and calling sequence for an EDITWORDBREAKPROC, in which case the cast is just ineffective and unnecessary. *Or* this address points to a function with another, namely *incorrect* calling sequence (for example, because a parameter has been forgotten in the function declaration), then the compiler normally gives a warning* — unless an explicit cast occurs as shown above. This makes the compiler believe that the programmer really wanted to call the function with a wrong calling sequence! And this leads to the fact that eventually the function will be called by the system with a wrong number or type of parameters, which, when using the PASCAL calling sequences, will almost surely bring the program into the land of the reset buttons....

* Such as "formal argument 3 different from declaration" or "suspicious pointer conversion"

Admittedly, in this case the cast is not relevant, since the big egalitarian LPARAM strikes at the end anyway. But if a function with a parameter type of address of type EDITWORDBREAKPROC were called instead of SendMessage(), then the compiler could consult the function prototype to check the parameters. And such a cast prevents the compiler from checking whether lpfnWordBreak really points to a "suitable" function while passing on the parameters.** Or, in order to illustrate the same subject with a completely different callback type — as a test just try to compile both following statements (and, if still not convinced, to execute them...):

** Motto: cast succeeded — program crashed!

```
// Compile with the highest warning level!
EnumWindows(12345678L,0); // The compiler gets very angry...


EnumWindows((WNDENUMPROC)12345678L,0); // The compiler is
// indeed silent, but the program will most certainly crash!
```

As a matter of fact, the case shown above is not the only one within the WINDOWSX.H definitions; casts are unfortunately too often used where they shouldn't. And the use of superfluous casts* that prevent the compiler from performing any diagnosis can be such a cause of errors that I just couldn't suppress this consideration. The following definition seems quite strange too — the return value of a SendMessage() call (of type LRESULT) is first converted to DWORD and then again to LRESULT:

* You still remember the three rules for casting, don't you?

ComboBox_GetItemData

```
#define ComboBox_GetItemData(hwndCtl, index) \
    ((LRESULT)(DWORD)SendMessage((hwndCtl), CB_GETITEMDATA, \
    (WPARAM)(int)(index), 0L))
```

Either something very tricky happens here (I don't really understand what, so any clarification is welcome) or the Microsoft programmer responsible for these macros gets paid for the number of casts used per macro... Seriously, I think Microsoft should realize (and think about the implications) that their released source code *can and will* become a source of information and advice for third-party application programmers — whether MS likes it or not. So a little bit of caution and an exemplary programming style would prove to be prudent.

Nevertheless, these macro definitions can be extremely helpful. First, when used often, they save a lot of typing work, and second, they perform (almost) correctly most conversions from and to message parameters (and I think that the definitions I criticized will be revised and corrected in a future version). Of course, these "automatic" conversions as well as the message crackers particularly serve the portability of your sources. But the higher clarity and transparency of the macros (at least compared to the sometimes *very* cryptical SendMessage() calls) is another (and not to be neglected) advantage.

Helpful macros...

... instead of cryptical SendMessage() calls!

4.6 Changes in the Base Functionality

"... only in motion, as painful as it may be, is life." Jakob Burckhardt, Weltgeschichtliche Betrachtungen

This chapter deals with the most important changes in the Win32 base API area,* whose consequences can be caught neither through the already described macros nor with other simple syntactical replacements. Mainly, they fall into the category of semantical adaptations, as described at the beginning of this chapter with the example of hPrevInstance always being equal to 0.

* roughly the KERNEL module as well as the I/O system

The access to data of preceding instances

So, let's start with that issue "hPrevInstance == 0"! If you just want to discover whether a previous instance of your application is already loaded and therefore the newly started instance represents only the second (or third...), a simple FindWindow() call is enough:

hPrevInstance == 0

```
// Instead of:
if (hPrevInstance!=0) ... // Code for further instances
...
// Better code for Win32:
if (hwndPrev=FindWindow(szAppClass,"MyWindowTitle")) ...
// hwndPrev now initialized with the main window handle of
// the preceding instance or just 0.
```

The first argument is the window class, and the second the window text of the application's main window, so that FindWindow(), provided that a window with this caption exists, returns its handle. Observe that the shown call therefore only makes sense when the second instance has not yet created its *own* main window! Another, but somewhat costlier, possibility is passing a private message to the so found window. Indeed, this variant permits you (almost as compensation for the higher effort) to forward a maximum of eight bytes between the first and second (or more, respectively) instances. The following code excerpt shows the fundamental procedure:

FindWindow() or...

... message broadcasting

241

Global variable

In the main program

*Windows procedure for the
top level window*

```
#define WM_INSTCHECK  WM_USER  // private message
LRESULT lAppCount=1;
HWND hwndPrev;

...
// In WinMain *before* creation of the main window
if (hwndPrev=FindWindow(szAppClass,szAppTitle)) {
   lFromFirst=SendMessage(hwndPrev,WM_INSTCHECK,
     wToFirst,lToFirst);
   // 2. instance, lFromFirst may contain any data
   // from the 1. instance, [w/l]ToFirst can transport
   // an overall of 8 byte to the first instance.
else
   // Ah, nobody here, hence I am the 1. instance
...
// In the window procedure for the main window:
LRESULT CALLBACK MainWndProc(HWND hwnd,UINT wMsg,
   WPARAM wParam,LPARAM lParam)
{
...
   case WM_INSTCHECK:
      return hwndPrev?SendMessage(hwndPrev,WM_INSTCHECK,
        wPparam,lParam):++lAppCount;
...
}
```

*Beginning with the third
instance, which value has
hwndPrev?*

The source code shows two or three peculiarities: for the second instance the above code is still satisfactory, but for further instances we have to pay attention: FindWindow() when called with the same class name and window text returns not necessarily the window handle of the first instance's main window! Depending on the information to exchange between instances, for the different instances a unique window text must be created, if necessary. With posting the message you can supply eight bytes of data in the two message parameters to an already started instance. Vice versa, the latter can deliver up to four bytes in the return value. In the example above for each further instance a counter is incremented and its value is returned as the "starting point" of the new instance. The code is written in such a way that it is not important which of the already running instances receives the first SendMessage() call!

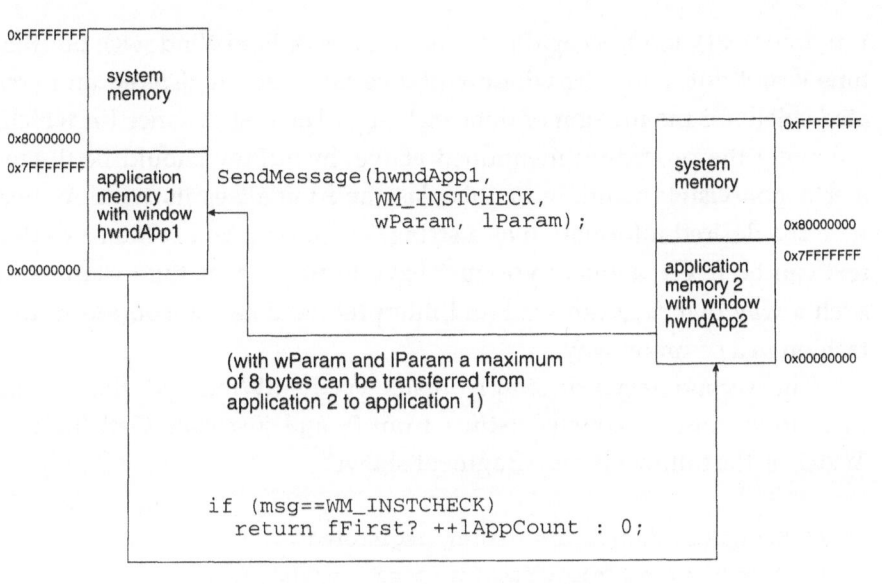

Now to the one *big* limitation: in both directions you can transport nei-ther pointers nor addresses since the individual instances of course have no access to the memory areas of other applications (or instances, re-spectively), as figure 4.9 illustrates.

Neither pointers, nor ad-dresses!

Therefore, the problem of exchanging data between instances gets somewhat more difficult if larger information blocks are to be trans-ferred: to achieve this feat under Win16, we enjoyed the function GetIn-stanceData(); this call, however, was removed from the Win32 API with-out replacement. Consequently you either have to fight with the risks and perils of a DDE conversation (which seems to be a good idea only if you already have DDE experience or if you have to work with DDE con-versations in your application anyway). Or you could use shared mem-ory accesses, e.g., through creating a memory mapped file; a complete code example for that approach is found in the following chapter at the discussion of DLLs (see section 5.3, page 339). If you can pack the infor-mation to be copied into a string, there is a third possibility; this one is somewhat unorthodox, but comparatively easy. It is absolutely possible to access the window text (e.g., the titlebar) of other windows under Win32, even of those belonging to separate processes. As usual, this is done with GetWindowText() (in fact, you can set the titlebar with Set-

GetInstanceData() is re-moved.

DDE?

Shared memory?

Or with the aid of [Set/Get]WindowText()?

WindowText(), too!). So again take advantage of FindWindow(), but this time search for a specific window of a certain class, registered and created solely for the mission of data exchange. The first instance (in which, following the procedure mentioned above, hwndPrev should be 0) creates a non-visible window of this class and initializes its window text with the desired information as a string. The format and contents of this text can be freely defined; you just have to implement the instances in such a way that they can read and interpret the data transported in this fashion in a common way.

An example for communication via window text

The second instance simply reads via FindWindow() the handle hwndPrev, now of course distinct from 0, and just calls GetWindowText(), as the following code fragment shows:

```
// The needed classes are already registered ...
if (hwndPrev=FindWindow("DataTransportClass",NULL)) {
    // hwndPrev!=0, therefore second (or further) instance
    char chBuf[SIZE_OF_DATA];
    GetWindowText(hwndPrev,chBuf,sizeof(chBuf));
    // now the needed information is found in chBuf:
    // chBuf == "data:123!456"
}
else // hwndPrev == 0, so we're first instance
    CreateWindow("DataTransportClass","data:123!456",...);
```

Second instance reads.

First instance writes.

Illustration 4.10 on the next page explains the teamwork of the two instances. As a matter of fact, there exist numerous different solutions to discover whether an application is the first or a later instance and of course also to send data between several instances or applications (e.g., the not yet mentioned new Win32 message WM_COPYDATA, which is explained with the description of memory management farther down). The basic approaches shown (and this is valid also for all further examples) are indeed fundamentally applicable to solve the particular task at hand, but they must be carefully selected and correspondingly implemented depending on the concrete application and the circumstances! Therefore, all those examples are meant rather as a stimulation, but certainly not as the best or only possible implementation.

Numerous basic approaches to program communication

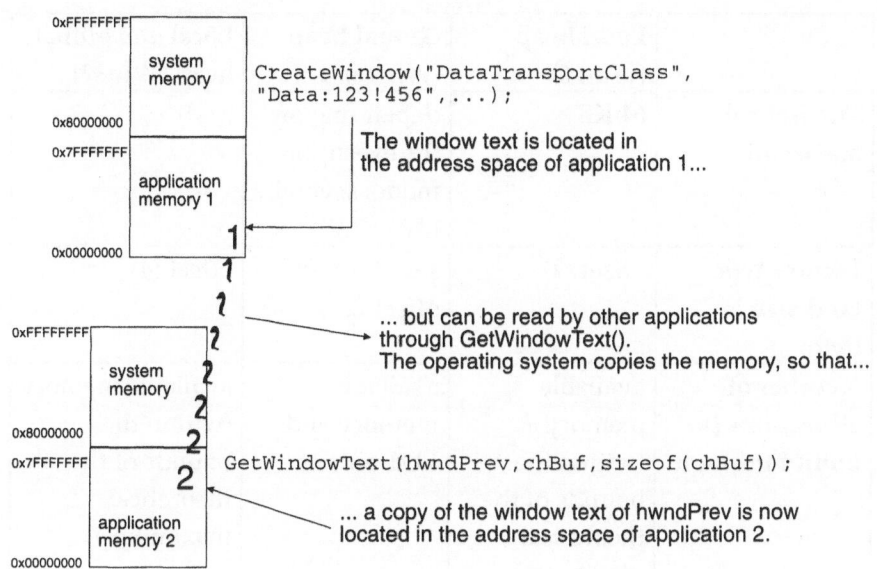

Figure 4.10: Simple data
transfer via window text

Memory management: the local and global heaps

Let's now address the area that has to take responsibility for the whole malaise and that is implemented completely differently under Win32 than with Win16: the dynamic memory management. Under Win16, as is generally known, two (to a large extent) independent mechanisms for dynamic allocation and administration of memory areas exist: the local *Local heap* heap, normally used rather for smaller objects (with a maximum size in the order of 100 to 200 bytes), and the global heap, mainly for the alloca- *Global heap* tion of bigger regions or for the exchange of data between applications. In the following I can't explain the particulars of both modes in gory detail, since here also the system mode in which Windows 3.x is currently executing plays an important role (but see [Ref. 11] and for internals see [Ref. 3]). Nevertheless, some similarities and basic observations valid for both the Win16 and the Win32 memory management can be captured in the following table:

Table 4.3: Differences and
similarities of Win16 and
Win32 memory management

	Local heap (Win16)	Global heap (Win16)	Local *and* global heap (Win32)
Theoretical maximum	64 KB	depending on the execution mode, several MB	2 GB
Pointer type (and size in byte)	offset (2)	selector and offset (2+2 = 4)	offset (4)
Number of allocations is bound through	available memory (within the bounds of the theoretical maximum)	available memory and LDT entries	available memory (within the bounds of the theoretical maximum)
Locking the handle	necessary for movable memory only	always necessary	necessary for movable memory only
Availability	application	systemwide	application

No significant differences between local and global heap

As you'll easily recognize, conceptually the Win32 management is found much nearer at the local heap than at the global heap of Windows 3.x. Apart from that it seems remarkable that I have not at all differentiated between local and global methods for Win32 in the list above. This is no wonder, because there are simply no significant differences between local and global memory allocations anymore! *Only* in order to ease the porting of existing Win16 source codes were this (finally obsolete) separation and the corresponding function groups included in the Win32 API. Independently from the type of allocation, the same predefined default heap is actually always used. Therefore, the Global/Local ...() calls under Win32 are nothing more than two nearly identical layers around the newly introduced Heap API (which on its part runs on top of the virtual memory management and makes available functions such as HeapAlloc() and HeapFree()). Figures 4.11 and 4.12 on the following pages picture the different levels of memory management under Win16 and Win32.

Local allocations: only very small changes.

Now, what consequences does this unification have for existing software? All the local allocations can be taken over without any change (provided that they were until now properly coded). The same is valid for the locking and unlocking of the so received memory handles. When working with pointers into the local heap (normally NEAR pointers), admittedly some minor changes may be necessary. The assignment of such a pointer to a 16-bit variable (e.g., of type WORD) will not behave as expected under Win32; for this job you should *always* employ a UINT. Also the sending of NEAR pointers in private messages can prove to be very problematic. It's true, the also widened WPARAM is even under Win32 big enough for a *single* pointer into the "local" heap, but the packing of two NEAR pointers into a single LONG (or LPARAM, respectively) is of course not possible anymore. LocalInit() and the corresponding calling logic (with data segment modifications and the like) can be removed under Win32. The concept of several local heaps is neither necessary nor implemented here (well, there is something similar, because you can easily create more heaps than the single default heap).

But caution: there are special cases.

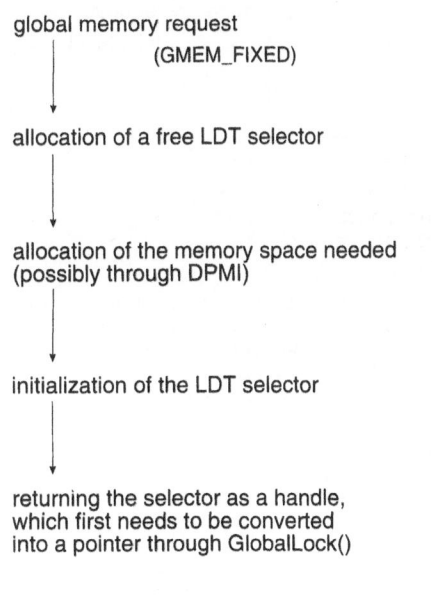

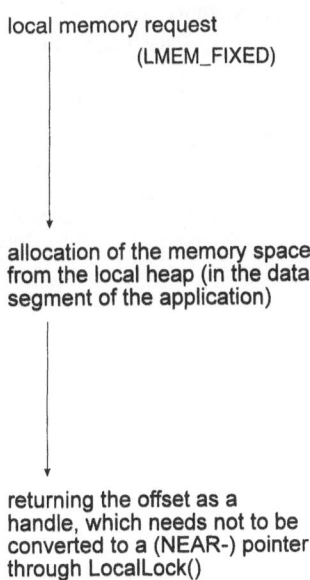

Figure 4.11: The mechanisms for memory management (Win16)

A local memory handle allocated with the LMEM_FIXED attribute until now could be used directly (meaning without an explicit call to Local-Lock()) as a NEAR pointer (offset) into the corresponding data segment; in contrast, globally allocated regions (even those with the attribute

To lock or not to lock?

GMEM_FIXED) independently of the actual allocations flags must be locked at least once, in order to obtain a valid address. The Win32 allocation routines resemble in this respect (also) the first method. It is even explicitly pointed out in the Win32 documentation that the return value of an allocation performed with [G/L]MEM_FIXED is not at all a memory handle, but directly the desired pointer. The GlobalLock() usually following a GlobalAlloc() call under Win16 is in this case nothing more than a no-op. But observe that this discussion is only valid for fixed

Handle or address?

memory! If you expressly allocate memory blocks with the attribute [G/L]MEM_MOVEABLE, you still have to perform a corresponding lock call in any case, since both ...Alloc() functions in this case return the actual handle and *not* the address based on the handle. Well, why one needs memory with the movable attribute in a system with a polished page-based, virtual 32-bit memory management certainly is another question....

Figure 4.12: Memory management under Win32

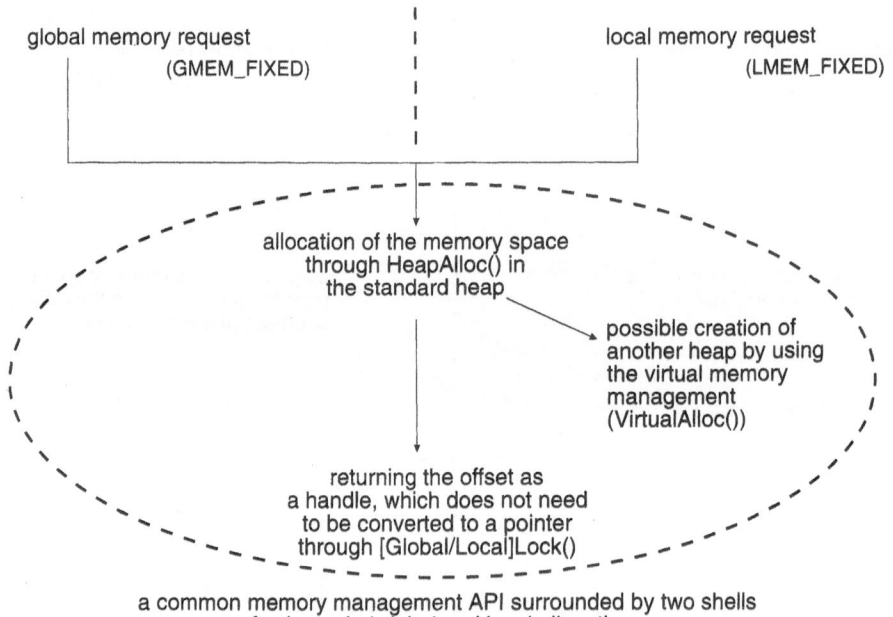

global memory request
(GMEM_FIXED)

local memory request
(LMEM_FIXED)

allocation of the memory space
through HeapAlloc() in
the standard heap

possible creation of
another heap by using
the virtual memory
management
(VirtualAlloc())

returning the offset as
a handle, which does not need
to be converted to a pointer
through [Global/Local]Lock()

a common memory management API surrounded by two shells
for (pseudo-)global and local allocations

Solved in a completely different way: shared memory

All global allocations that need memory for the purpose of data exchange with other programs (and therefore were allocated with the aid of the flags GMEM_(DDE)SHARE) have to be changed for Win32 because of the separated address spaces. For details see the examples shown above for copying data between several instances. By the way: the Win32 memory management can at any time generate the corresponding handle from a valid address via GlobalHandle() (as protected mode Win16 already could). (The macros discussed in section 4.3 for simplified memory management make use of this capability.) What's more, the functions malloc() and free(), somewhat discredited in developers' circles through the handle and locking based memory management, are finally gaining back reputation these days. Since the Win32 memory management builds on the paging of the processor the charming witchcraft we had to perform since the days of Windows 1.x in order to distribute the (at that time) scarce memory* (at least partially) acceptable on the running applications is now superfluous. (And a small side blow towards the advocates of this strange theory that software development *always* limps back *years* behind hardware design: when at the beginning of the 1980s the basic Windows APIs had to be designed, the 80286 CPU was just becoming available, but because of various design weaknesses and, above all, lack of public usage, was not exactly the CPU of choice. Thus the memory management of Windows was tailored and implemented for a processor, which *offered absolutely no useful support* for these objectives — namely the 8088. And after all, probably the failed introduction of OS/2 can be attributed to a greater part on the decision to use this processor and not its successor, the 80386, as the OS base. Only the improvements** introduced with this first real 32-bit Intel CPU changed the situation for system programmers dramatically: however, when the 386 finally appeared, the MS-DOS superiority was already so solid cemented that it was enormously difficult to establish something *not* 100 percent MS-DOS compatible in the market. If only the 386 had been available in 1982,*** it could have saved both the Windows developers at Microsoft and also numerous programmers around the world quite some headaches — or do you feel that the rather elegant [Make/Free]ProcInstance(), to mention just two of the dubious "supplemental" functions, is an absolutely necessary part of the Windows API?

Problems with global allocations and GMEM_(DDE)SHARE.

* which the 8088 CPU, to top it all, could not even administer properly!

** Keywords: 32-bit processing, V86 mode, demand paged memory.

*** Or if IBM had built a decent processor such as the 68000 into the first PCs...

But this child has already dropped into the well, so let's turn back to memory management: the casual to and fro of sending global memory handles or, even worse, FAR pointers between applications to perform data communication as fast as simple is decidedly *passé* under Win32.

Only DDE continues to work. Only those who bravely followed the standardized DDE protocol (or the DDE management library, respectively) will see a glimmer of hope: obviously with these messages the Win32 subsystem copies the handles (or the underlying memory areas, respectively) from one virtual address space into the other. And well understood: all this happens totally transparently under the hoods! Alas, all shared memory approaches based on exchanging global handles through private messages need a thorough renovation for Win32: either with the help of the newly introduced

New: WM_COPYDATA WM_COPYDATA messages or through the explicit creation of shared memory regions (via memory mapped files). For the latter you'll find a complete example in section 5.3; the first method will hopefully become somewhat brighter through the following small sample:

Copies a memory block with
WM_COPYDATA

```
#define BATCH_SIZE 2048
...
HGLOBAL hG=GlobalAlloc(GMEM_FIXED,BATCH_SIZE);
// The flags GMEM_(DDE)SHARE have no effect under Win32
 // anyway and are therefore neither used nor necessary!
COPYDATASTRUCT cds;
... // Memory area is initialized and then sent...
cds.dwData=12345678L; // 4 byte with any data
cds.cbData=BATCH_SIZE;
cds.lpData=(LPVOID)hG;  *
SendMessage(hwndOtherApp,WM_COPYDATA,(WPARAM)hwndSender,
   (LPARAM)&cds); // WM_COPYDATA *only* via SendMessage()!
```

* GlobalLock() is not necessary under Win32 because of GMEM_FIXED.

As the code shows, the sending application can either pack up to four bytes into the COPYDATASTRUCT (member dwData) or allocate a memory area and initialize it with the data to transport (or of course a combination of both methods: e.g., dwData might describe the kind of data in lpData). Win32 copies the area stated in cds.lpData (with a size of cds.cbData) within the SendMessage() call into the address space of the

The data area is not allowed to contain pointers to other memory areas! receiver, this happens completely transparently. Thereby you have to pay attention that the data area (cds.lpData) doesn't include further pointers into other memory areas, since these are *not* (and *cannot* be)

automatically copied into the address space of the receiving application by Win32. The latter can now either just read the data or alter the memory block. However, this works only on its private copy of the original data, therefore WM_COPYDATA does *not* realize genuine shared memory, but rather implements the simple exchange of data blocks. Actually, real *shared* memory between independent applications is only possible with memory mapped files.

Sorry, this is not genuine shared memory.

```
// In the window procedure of the receiver:
case WM_COPYDATA:
  pcds=(PCOPYDATASTRUCT)lParam;
  ...=pcds->dwData;
  memcpy(&myData,pcds->lpData,...);
  // Altering of myData is OK, changing *pcds->lpData is not
  // (says the Win32 doc!).
```

A certain disadvantage of the WM_COPYDATA message may lie in the fact that the receiver always has to initiate the exchange; this can be accomplished, for instance, by sending a message to the supplier. Anyway, with the aid of this mechanism you can implement relatively fast a simple private protocol for exchanging global memory (handles). Existing programs with a self-written protocol must indeed be adapted, but the efforts are quite limited. The fundamental activity in the Win32 subsystem when sending the WM_COPYDATA message is depicted in figure 4.13 on the next page.

Private protocols

A ticket to the I/O system and back, please!

Let's enter the next big problem area, namely the bindings to file systems and to the hardware. Windows NT and also Windows 95 (the latter not being MS-DOS based anymore) are quite lucky in this respect: here effectively no separation between the GUI components and the other parts of the operating system exists, hence almost automatically a consistent and portable use of all the machine's supported resources is possible. Unfortunately, the situation is not so bright with the current DOS versions, which have to teamwork with Windows 3.x. A lot of stuff has to be realized still "on foot": here a video BIOS call, there an INT 21H, elsewhere an access to the BIOS data segment, etc., etc.

Bindings to the I/O system and to the hardware

251

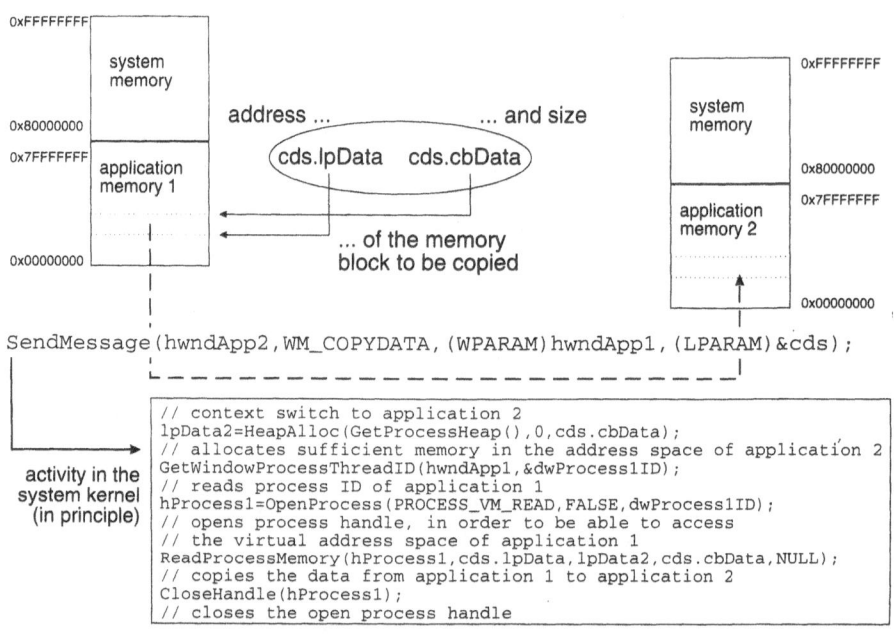

Figure 4.13: Copying memory areas with WM_COPYDATA

```
SendMessage(hwndApp2,WM_COPYDATA,(WPARAM)hwndApp1,(LPARAM)&cds);
```

activity in the
system kernel
(in principle)

```
// context switch to application 2
lpData2=HeapAlloc(GetProcessHeap(),0,cds.cbData);
// allocates sufficient memory in the address space of application 2
GetWindowProcessThreadID(hwndApp1,&dwProcess1ID);
// reads process ID of application 1
hProcess1=OpenProcess(PROCESS_VM_READ,FALSE,dwProcess1ID);
// opens process handle, in order to be able to access
// the virtual address space of application 1
ReadProcessMemory(hProcess1,cds.lpData,lpData2,cds.cbData,NULL);
// copies the data from application 1 to application 2
CloseHandle(hProcess1);
// closes the open process handle
```

Replaced: INT 21H calls, for instance, for directory management.

Removed: IBM PC and CPU specifics.

* e.g., the complete EMS interface

Two rather large areas are easily recognized: on the one hand, all those features for which the Win32 API introduces at least partially backward compatible functions. In this category we can find for instance nearly all the important INT 21H subfunctions for directory management, which were not supported through a named interface under Win16. The other group are simply all the calls and PC specialties for which the developers couldn't realize a meaningful (or portable) function under Win32. This might be caused by the fact that the functionality is CPU- or PC-specific and not at all (or only very difficult) portable to other CPU architectures (such as direct accesses to certain I/O ports); this would invalidate one of the main design targets of the Win32 API, namely extensive source code portability between *all* supported platforms. Then there are some calls that on principle are completely senseless under a 32-bit system.* You be confident that each and every direct hardware access is forbidden for applications running under Win32 (said more accurately: for software running in user mode); only the NT kernel and device drivers (or speaking more broadly: program parts running in kernel mode) will have the necessary authorization to do so (admittedly, Win95 is not as strict as NT; alas, the problem is that you never know on what platform an enduser will execute your application).

BIOS specialties too are normally not portable; every access to the BIOS data area starting at 0x0040:0x0000 (for which under Win16 even a separate selector named __0040H exists) will crash on a 32-bit system in the GP fault handler. Of course, the other selector values exported by the Win16 KERNEL module (such as __0000H, __A000H etc.) are also to be enjoyed with extreme caution. Windows 95 is also in this regard somewhat more "cooperative" than NT. Finally, Win95 is thought of as an *update* to Win16 and so it is just not possible to sell extensive changes.* Apart from that, Windows 95 will only run on Intel platforms, therefore some features that are extremely disgusting for NT will be at least tolerated there.

Quite literally!

While the last bell has definitely tolled for all access to the hardware outside of device drivers, Microsoft at last has made available all important MS-DOS calls in Win32 as more or less compatible functions (well, this is not really astonishing, since even Windows NT has to support the smallest common denominator: the good, old FAT file system). This trend was already recognizable with Windows 3.x, since already there some named INT 21H interfaces exist (e.g., _lopen(), _lread(), _lclose(), etc., or the somewhat lonely function OpenFile()). The big remainder had to be either called directly via an INT 21H or performed with the use of the fairly dubious DOS3Call(). The latter, as could be expected, was removed from the Win32 API (although the Win16 documentation — from Microsoft itself** — loudly and clearly praised the usage of this function — to increase portability…).

Hardware access only in device drivers

Win16: _lopen(), _lclose(), etc.

*** See Windows 3.1 Programmer's Reference, Vol. 1, page 396.*

Indeed, the Win32 documentation advises to discontinue the use of the above-mentioned named "old" Win16 functions for file I/O; nevertheless, they are still mapped to the new API and can be utilized until further notice. For the complete realm of file I/O, a completely new API is available, which probably will "find its way back" into future Win16 versions (provided that these are released at all…). There you can find such wonderful calls like CreateFile(), ReadFile(), WriteFile(), or CloseHandle(), etc., which shall fully replace the currently used functions (and even offer additional functionality — e.g., overlapping I/O operations). My advice, in order to be prepared for future API somersaults from Microsoft (which will come as sure as the Amen in church): you could write an interface layer for the existing I/O functions, which (another benefit) you can easily tailor to your special needs. Such a shell is relatively easy to design and implement and can, if well thought-out, even save quite some typing, thinking effort, and looking up API details. However, at

Win32: CreateFile(), CloseHandle(), etc.

Just write a simple I/O shell!

The handles "belong" to the corresponding API.

any rate work consistently with just *one* set of calls, since file handles can't be mixed between the old functions (so opening a file via _lopen()...) and the new Win32 functions (... and closing via CloseHandle() won't work)! This important observation is also valid for C runtime calls such as fread(), etc., which you should *not* directly supply with a Win32 file handle. For conversion between the two worlds, two C runtime functions named _get_osfhandle() and _open_osfhandle() exist.

* As a matter of fact, it builds upon a rather faulty list from the Win32 SDK documentation.

Let's now address all the MS-DOS functions that can be called through named functions under Win32. The following table covers the Win32 functions* known to me (in other words: if you find an INT 21H call used in your program here, just call the corresponding function; if, however, you find no entry, don't give up so easily, but you'd better glance over the API documentation). The sign in the last column gives my assessment of the compatibility of the new functions with the corresponding MS-DOS calls (+ means "good," 0 means "acceptable," and - means "needs some real work"):

Table 4.4: INT 21H calls and corresponding Win32 functions

INT 21H subfunction	Win32 function	Comp.
0EH, Select Disk	SetCurrentDirectory	+
19H, Get Current Disk	GetCurrentDirectory	0
2AH, Get Date	GetSystemTime, GetLocalTime	0
2bra, Set Date	SetSystemTime, SetLocalTime	0
2CH, Get Time	GetSystemTime, GetLocalTime	0
2DH, Set Time	SetSystemTime, SetLocalTime	0
36H, Get Disk Free Space	GetDiskFreeSpace	+
39H, Create Directory	CreateDirectory	+
3AH, Remove Directory	RemoveDirectory	+
3BH, Set Current Directory	SetCurrentDirectory	+
3CH, Create Handle	CreateFile	0
3DH, Open Handle	CreateFile	0
3EH, Close Handle	CloseHandle	+
3FH, Read Handle	ReadFile	+
40H, Write Handle	WriteFile	+
41H, Delete File	DeleteFile	+

INT 21H subfunction	Win32 function	Comp.
42H, Move File Pointer	SetFilePointer	+
43H, Get File Attributes	GetFileAttributes	-
43H, Set File Attributes	SetFileAttributes	-
47H, Get Current Directory	GetCurrentDirectory	+
4EH, Find First File	FindFirstFile	0
4FH, Find Next File	FindNextFile	0
56H, Change Directory Entry	MoveFile	+
57H, Get Date/Time of File	GetFileTime	0
57H, Set Date/Time of File	SetFileTime	0
59H, Get Extended Error	GetLastError	-
5AH, Create Unique File	GetTempFileName	0
5BH, Create New File	CreateFile	0
5CH, Lock	LockFile	+
5CH, Unlock	UnlockFile	+
67H, Set Handle Count	SetHandleCount	+

Strongly tied to the operating system traffic is another subject becoming current under Win32: the storing and handling of filenames. The 8.3 notation of MS-DOS (with which we're on intimate terms since 15 years) was already significantly enhanced with the high-performance file system (HPFS) of OS/2 1.x. And since Windows NT supports, as is generally known, HPFS partitions and makes available another, still more powerful, file system (NTFS), portable programs probably have to take long filenames into account for the future. But this proves to be not that laborious at all: some simple rules as well as the extensive use of explicit constants for the indication of buffer sizes allow to a large extent the portable treatment of this (long awaited) enhancement.

Storing and handling of filenames

Some rules and explicit constants may help.

Long or short: the treatment of filenames

Presumably the time when filenames could be stored in buffers with a length of just 12 or 13 bytes is gone forever: the introduction of hierarchically arranged directories with MS-DOS 2.0 and the subsequent enhancement of pathnames up to 80 bytes in length have already laid a certain base. The flexibility of programs when it comes to filename handling has improved considerably over the last few years. Neverthe-

à la "char chFilename[81]"

*These errors are often
hidden pretty well!*

Backslash as separator

Length of pathnames

less, in a lot of programs we still find this extraordinary 80-character limit *hard coded;** what's more, after isolating the filename from the path information, the code most often still assumes that the first conforms to the 8.3 format. These problems, however, don't lead necessarily to immediate program errors: only when a Win32 application has to work on a non-FAT file system and accesses a file with a "modern" filename longer than expected and/or violating the 8.3 rule, then you'll see some serious problems. Especially those parts of your application dealing with the handling of filenames should therefore be tested once again after a (supposedly successful) port with different path and filenames on the various file systems. The subsequent list explains some of the more important "manners" in conjunction with storing and handling filenames:

- All file systems supported by Win32 use the backslash (\ ) as a separator for individual path and filenames. Nevertheless, the definition and consistent use of character constants, as for the buffer sizes, is definitely recommended:

```
#define PATH_SEPARATOR  TEXT('\\')
// See chapter 4.10 about Unicode concerning the TEXT macro
#ifdef WIN32
  #define FILENAME_BUFFER_SIZE  260
#else
  #define FILENAME_BUFFER_SIZE  81
#endif
...
TCHAR chFileName[FILENAME_BUFFER_SIZE];
...
if (tcschr(chFileName,PATH_SEPARATOR)) ...
```

- Pathnames should always be treated as null-terminated strings. The maximum length of the pathnames supported in a specific file system can be queried easily with the function GetVolumeInformation(), which also delivers further important information about the available disk drives. According to the published data so far the existing limit of about 256 characters (already under HPFS) will indeed be effective for NTFS, too.

- Although NTFS stores filenames on disk exactly as given (so maintains case sensitivity), for the system software this is no actual means for the *distinction* of files. Basically your program text should therefore use and compare filenames in a case-independent fashion (e.g., through lstrcmpi()): winword.exe, WINWORD.EXE, and WinWord.eXe are all considered the same name in Win32 file systems). This observation is valid both for self-defined names and names supplied by the system software as the result of a system call!

  Pay attention to case sensi-tivity!

- Build your filenames in such a way that they don't contain invalid characters. Some characters are forbidden in all file systems anyway (e.g., < > : " \ / |); others could be classified through the particular file system as not allowed. Here, two strategies are possible: either you confine yourself to the common subset that is legal in all file systems or you have to find out for each pathname to which system it is finally bound and test with a corresponding list whether all characters in the name are legal. The first approach seems to be much simpler and more reasonable for the enduser — especially because with this method the copying of files between different file systems won't generate naming incompatibilities.

  Don't use invalid characters in path- and filenames.

- A single dot (.) either is the identification character for the current subdirectory or is used as a separator in a path- or filename. When decomposing pathnames, you have to pay extra attention to the possibility that components with more than one dot are acceptable under certain file systems: both the names "C:\SRC\PROJ. MARCH.11.1993\TEST.C" (with several dots in the second part of the path, obviously designating a date) and "D:\GARBAGE\ TODO.LIST.FOR.TODAY," where the filename itself contains three dots, are perfectly valid under NTFS! Because the dot in path- and filenames shall be used as a separator even with newer systems, pay attention to the fact that it is not allowed at the end of the name (in this case it will be simply suppressed from the system software). Indeed the repeated use of the dot within path- and filenames is no longer combined into a single dot (see also the following example).

  A single dot is a separator.

  More than one dot per name possible!

- Two successive dots as a separate element in the pathname (\..\ ) always designate the parent directory following the current directory and are, if used as such, only allowed in path components. But have care: with Win32 two (or more) dots can be embedded in

  Two dots: parent directory.

a filename (e.g., "My7Wives...DOC" would be a perfectly valid name for Windows 95)!

If used, adapt the character-by-character analysis of names.

- Basically all program parts analyzing path- or filenames character by character have to be checked and adapted, so that they also work properly with names that contain characters so far not valid. Under HPFS and NTFS it is possible for example to store multiple blanks or dots in the filenames, so both following system commands are completely correct (the quotation marks on the second filename serve only as delimiters):

```
copy  data94.txt  "my data from the last year as text"
copy  test.doc  JustForTesting...!
```

Conversion of long filenames to MS-DOS format

- Under Win32 even a "normal" MS-DOS or Win16 application can access the NTFS and HPFS partitions via 16-bit subsystem. The system software simply defines an algorithm for the necessary conversion from long filenames to shorter ones, with whose aid long filenames can be transformed into the MS-DOS compatible 8.3 format. Indeed this mapping is carried out entirely transparently for the MS-DOS application (well, this is to be expected); for the enduser, however, this transparency applies presumably only

MS-DOS alias

with some restrictions: the "symbolical" DOS name produced in this way is namely often rather cryptical. Therefore, when creating filenames a Win32 application (and the user) should, as far as justifiable, take the inevitable conversions for MS-DOS programs into consideration when it comes to choosing or generating a name. Unfortunately, Microsoft hasn't provided a means in the Win32 API in order to allow the Win32 application itself the explicit definition of the "MS-DOS alias."

INI files and registry

Initialization information

The next point on my list of differences also deals with files: we'll discuss the as famous as notorious INI files in which both Windows itself and many applications store initialization information or other program data needed between two calls of the program. The basic idea is of course very sound, but unfortunately the success of Windows 3.x led very fast

INI old: ASCII format.

to a complex and tangled mess of files in the \WINDOWS directory. (A great many programs have additionally put some stuff into WIN.INI to "eternalize" themselves; this didn't exactly help with the readability and maintainability of this crucial system file.) To worsen things, INI files are altogether available in standard ASCII format and therefore every enduser, even the most naive one, can freely manipulate them — this ability indeed comes in handy for the experienced user every now and then, but the inexperienced are often left with an unusable system after careless modifications.

Apart from that, modern possibilities such as OLE 2 make a better mutual check and communication of the installed software with each other and with the system necessary — and all the required data must of course be standardized and stored in a central pool. Therefore already for Windows 3.1 the mechanism of non-textual registration databases *INI new: registration data-* was created, in which applications could store, for example, the data *base.* necessary for OLE; second, this file (simply named REG.DAT) could also accumulate all kinds of initialization information (see also figure 4.14 on the following page). A rather powerful API (with calls like Reg-OpenKey(), RegQueryValue()) was made available, which probably should lead to the disuse of all functions for textual INI files (such as [Get/Write]ProfileString()) in the medium term.

Now, Win32 takes still a further step: the concept of registration databases was enhanced in such a way that it is possible to store the com- *Configuration plus private* plete hardware and software configuration of a certain machine includ- *settings plus further data* ing the private settings for all registered endusers as well as any further application-specific data (this extensive conglomerate of data is called *registry* under Win32). Thereby are not only textual entries possible, but arbitrarily formatted binary data can also be stored within the registry (such as figure 4.15 shows). The error-prone coexistence of two not always consistent levels of system information within Windows 3.1 (namely REG.DAT on the one hand; WIN.INI, SYSTEM.INI, etc., on the other hand) has finally found the well-deserved end, simply because Win32 completely goes without textual INI files (actually Windows 95 *Win32 registry* supports them for backward compatibility, but their use is strongly discouraged). For applications that have performed the accesses to INI files (also private ones) correctly with the API functions designed for that purpose, nothing important changes, as the system carries out the diversions from INI to registry under the hoods, invisible for the program.

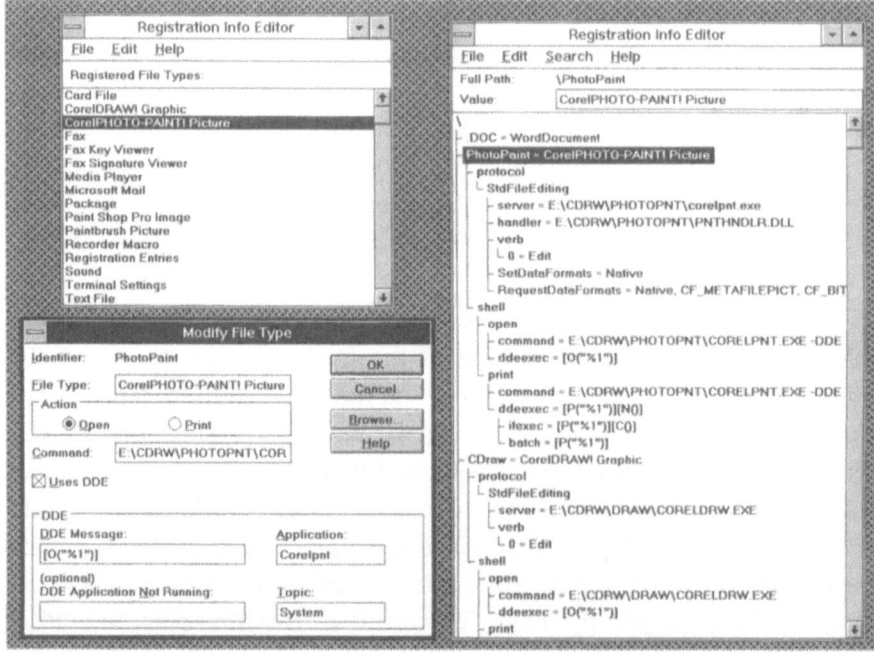

Alas, quite different things look, and now the reason for this whole ex-
emplification will get clearer, for software *directly* accessing INI files, e.g.,
through opening WIN.INI in the Windows system directory and reading
the required data straight into memory with self-defined I/O operations.
For the handling of extensive INI files, this way may even be necessary
under Win16, since it is considerably more efficient. This practice is not
possible anymore under future Windows versions! Put differently: either
you put private initialization information into the systemwide registry,
and then it's compulsory to access them *only* with the API designed for
that purpose. *Or* you write these data into an individual file (whose
name, format, etc. you can of course define yourself), then you don't
need the registry calls at all. But if you want to reach any system information, then definitely no way leads past the Reg...() functions!

*No textual INI files under
Win32...*

... therefore no direct access

Hierarchical multi-way tree

Since the Win32 registry is stored as a hierarchical multi-way tree,
access to the individual keywords takes place considerably faster than
with the rather unhurried (and unstructured) text files. So, the most important reason to manipulate INI information directly probably can be
neglected. And the second important excuse is also obsolete under
Win32: the registry can, as already mentioned, easily store binary data.
And because its size can increase up to a maximum of 32 MB, probably

even the most memory-hungry software should be delighted (well, provided that it actually stores only those information that must be saved
between two calls of the application, e.g., for initialization). And once
again to make it clear: as long as you access the systemwide and/or private INI files with the profile functions *designed for that very purpose*, the
conversion for the registry under Win32 is carried out transparently by
the system software. *Only* if you employ *non-standardized access methods,**
which are based on the direct access to the corresponding INI file, are
difficulties to be expected: these files simply don't exist anymore and
therefore can't be read in or changed at will.

* This means direct file I/O.

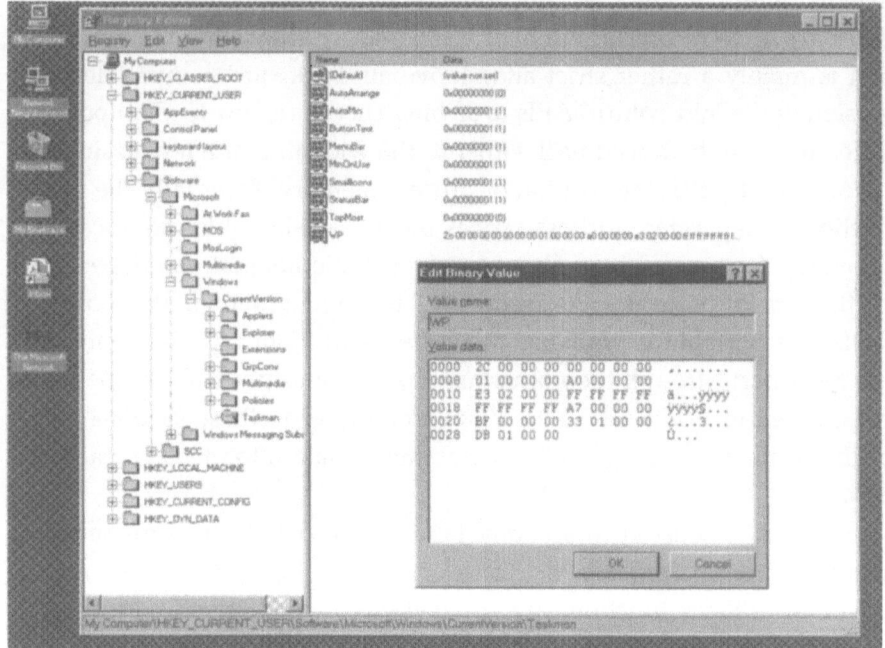

*Figure 4.15: The Win32
registry*

Numerous additional small differences and adaptations in the KERNEL
module are mostly of simple syntactical nature, and their treatment here
would just end up with a long-winded discussion. They are recorded
and discussed in the enlarged PORT.INI file (see Appendix 2, starting on
page 359). There you'll also find some hints to the necessary source code
changes, which mostly are quite easy to carry out. All differences described in this section are of course also taken into account.

*Further trifles: see Appendix
2, PORT.INI.*

4.7 Changes in the Window Management

"When programming for Windows, you're really engaged in a type of object-oriented programming. This is most evident in the object you'll be working with most in Windows — the object that gives Windows its name, the object that will soon seem to take on anthropomorphic characteristics; the object that may even show up in your dreams, the object known as the 'window'." Charles Petzold, Programming Windows 3.1

Conversion of the Win16 APIs to 32 bits

If windows play such an outstanding role in Windows, we should anticipate most changes and enhancements precisely in this area. In fact, together with the KERNEL functionality, here the most important differences are to be recorded. But at any rate the API for window manipulation is mainly a rather strict and, above all, backward compatible conversion of the "old" Win16 APIs to 32 bits. Therefore, nearly all important differences can be traced back either to the widening of a few basic data types or to the strict separation of process memory. Especially the introduction of separated address spaces makes considerable modifications necessary (or worse, partially even algorithmic adaptations depending on the type of program). As sections 4.2 to 4.5 have shown, it is possible to handle portability problems associated with data type widening for the most part through the numerous typedefs and particularly the macros defined in WINDOWSX.H. You should refer to these sections especially for the unpacking and reassembling of data into message parameters.

The parameters of window procedures

As was discussed in sections 4.2 to 4.5 in detail, the arguments of window procedures (in which category the DialogBox() family and all the other callback functions are also collected) were altered with Win32: until now an overall of 10 data bytes was given to these callbacks (2+2+2+4), but now they receive 16 bytes and are suitable even for cross-country work (4*4). Through explicit typedefs (partly defined just for window procedures) these modifications are however caught through some easy source code adaptations (invaluable is the aid of a powerful editor). And of course the message crackers (or GET_WM_* macros, respectively) make their little contribution to the creation of portable sources!

The calling sequence of window procedures

In the same category falls another, at first glance insignificant alteration: the Pascal calling sequence, until now practically hard coded via FAR PASCAL in the declarations and definitions of Windows callbacks, is now replaced by an all-new calling sequence, which is hidden behind a macro named CALLBACK defined just for the very purpose of declaring callback functions. Well, I'd call that a good idea; alas, Microsoft could have discovered (not only) this one a bit earlier.... Now in all existing programs a corresponding adaptation has to be performed — which could have easily been avoided if a corresponding macro had just been defined from the beginning for Win16 (however, it was unfortunately introduced first with 3.1 and until now is hardly used, not even in the Win16 SDK examples from Redmond). Anyway, the C/C++ programmer, apart from this finally uncomplicated change, has nothing else to do: the proper parameter passing and access as well as the work of cleaning up the stack are taken care of by the compiler. The (small) group of assembler programmers will probably feel somewhat less enthusiastic about the new calling convention: denoted as __stdcall, it forces the adaptation of all callback functions written in assembler and, even worse, of all Win16 system calls as well. The portable declaration of windows procedures in C or C++ looks as follows:

Instead of FAR PASCAL, now CALLBACK

A new calling sequence named __stdcall

```
// CALLBACK is defined as _FAR _PASCAL for 3.1,
// for Win32, on the other hand, as __stdcall
LRESULT CALLBACK XyzWndProc(HWND hwnd,UINT wMsg,
   WPARAM wParam,LPARAM lParam);
// In the dark ages before Windows 3.1:
// LONG FAR PASCAL XyzWndProc(HWND hwnd,WORD wMsg,
// WORD wParam,LONG lParam);
```

For the HLL* programmer the adaptation to the new calling mechanisms is settled** through the above declarations for Win16 and Win32. Therefore, consistently use the macros at last defined by Microsoft (e.g., CALLBACK for callback functions, WINAPI for globally known functions, etc.); first, this helps portability and second, it ensures that your callback and DLL functions are called correctly from the operating system.

* HLL — high-level language

** But don't forget the prototypes in the header files!

On the contrary, for assembly code *every* access to the function's arguments must be modified so that the proper register size is used (e.g., EAX
instead of AX, etc.); what's more, addressing and storing of arguments
on the stack has to be performed according to the __stdcall convention.
The detailed description of this calling sequence, probably important just
for assembler programmers and compiler writers, is discussed together
with some remarks about the current calling variants in Appendix 5
which also provides an example. There I describe the circumstances for
both ordinary procedures and functions with a variable parameter list —
however, the discussion can be transferred analogously to the callback
function types (windows, dialogs, hooks, enums, etc.). Of course, all
remarks to calling sequences are CPU-specific!

A further adaptation resulting in relatively simple textual replacements concerns WORD accesses to specific window or class information
as well as working with the so-called extra bytes aided by the function
groups [Get/Set]Class[Long/Word]() and [Get/Set]Window[Long/-
Word](), respectively. Under Win16 the various handles and other data
could be processed with the aid of constants such as GWW_HICON or
GCW_HCURSOR. The growth of handle types leads to storing these
data as LONGs in effect — and for that reason the names of the constants
were adjusted accordingly (e.g., GWL_HICON and GCL_HCURSOR),
and consequently the function pairs [Get/Set]WindowLong() and
[Get/Set]ClassLong() have to be used. Possibly the adaptation can be
somewhat puzzling, if you have stored further private data in the window's extra bytes. Check first whether the access functions have to take
into consideration the size proportions modified under Win32 (which
extends not only to handles: an int, UINT or NEAR pointer also doubles
in size). Second, you should make sure that sufficient space is allocated
with the class registration (see the two components cbClsExtra and
cbWndExtra in the WNDCLASS structure). If you don't work with
sizeof() — shame on you — presumably an adaptation is due. Otherwise
I refer you to the observations and macro definitions shown in section 3.3
on page 142.

DDE and colleagues

Let's now get to the subject of dynamic data exchange! Here we have to
view two strictly separate areas: first the DDE messages themselves,

which define the actual DDE protocol; and second the DDEML,* available since Windows 3.1, which implements a simple API (well, *simple* compared to the original definition...) in order to do the gory bulk of work when using DDE. All program parts relying on the latter must essentially pay attention only to the general porting measures for Win32 programs. Except for some very small differences, the DDEML API itself is totally portable between both systems. On the one hand, some DDEML data structures (CONVCONTEXT, etc.) were slightly enhanced, and on the other hand various functions (e.g., DdeImpersonateClient()) were added, in order to make sure that DDE conversations behave correctly in the context of NT security provisions. None of these changes should directly influence existing Win16 source codes, provided that these were written correctly in the first place.

DDE management library

The DDEML API is portable.

However, it comes as no big surprise that the format for the DDE message parameters used to transport DDE handles and data was significantly modified for Win32. Applications directly using the message protocol, instead of the DDEML, must be adapted. As before, the sender's window handle is stored in the wParam, which as a matter of fact grew as required, so that a single window handle still can be forwarded. Unfortunately, things look not so well for the lParam part of various DDE messages (but not all), which so far had to carry nearly without exception one global memory handle and further important data. But under Win32 there's just not sufficient room for both items. Microsoft devised a rather "tricky" scheme to escape that dilemma: before initiating a DDE message, once the Win32 function PackDDElParam() must be called. This API receives both the message value and the data items to be sent, and depending on the message either packages these so that the return value can be used as a regular LPARAM, or the function allocates an eight-byte memory area on the heap, stores both lParam information, and returns the handle** of the memory. A short snippet might serve as an example:

But changes to DDE messages

*** How pleasant: exactly 4 bytes long!*

```
// The following Win16 call is not Win32 compatible:
PostMessage(hwndDDEServer,WM_DDE_ADVISE,(WPARAM)hwndClient,
    MAKELPARAM(hOptions,aItem));


// Under Win32 both values for the lParam must first be
// packed through an explicit function call:
```

```
PostMessage(hwndDDEServer,WM_DDE_ADVISE,(WPARAM)hwndClient,
    PackDDElParam(WM_DDE_ADVISE,hOptions,aItem));
```

Packing...

... and unpacking!

Of course the recipient of a handle allocated in that way can't just access the information transported in the lParam, but obviously has first to call the function UnpackDDElParam(). This call (depending on the received message value) either unpacks the data in the lParam or pulls them off the area allocated by PackDDElParam(). By the way, this area became translated "on the fly" into the address space of the receiver by the system (necessary because of the address space separation!):

```
// This is Win16 compatible:
case WM_DDE_ADVISE:
  hOptions=LOWORD(lParam);
  aItem=HIWORD(lParam);

// Under Win32 the lParam must be unpacked first...
case WM_DDE_ADVISE:
  UnpackDDElParam(wMsg,lParam,(PUINT)&hOptions,
    (PUINT)&aItem); // If at all possible, not *that* way!
...
// ... and "freed" afterwards:
  FreeDDElParam(wMsg,lParam);
```

Actually, these changes are rather moderate and basically only necessary for those DDE messages that have to forward more than 4 bytes of data in the lParam under Win32. Unfortunately, the guy at Microsoft who has determined the design of these functions as well as the protoypes, was evidently in a big hurry:* first, the functions deliver (or accept, respectively) a LONG instead of an LPARAM (although LPARAM is even part of the name of these functions!). While this *is* sloppy, it is admittedly a rather formal problem; alas, with UnpackDDElParam() probably a genuine error has found its way into the API. According to the prototype, the function receives namely the addresses of two UINTs, which are to be initialized with the data items transported with the DDE message:

* Or somewhat less diplomatically: somebody has bungled it...

PUINT is the address of a UINT...

```
BOOL WINAPI UnpackDDElParam(UINT msg,LONG lParam,
    PUINT puiLo,PUINT puiHi);
```

Since so far (under Win16) hOptions and aItem were directly initialized
with LOWORD(lParam) and HIWORD(lParam), respectively, the typical
conversion of such a call will probably look like that shown above for the
message WM_DDE_ADVISE:

```
UnpackDDElParam(wMsg,lParam, (PUINT)&hOptions,
    (PUINT)&aItem); // A very careless implementation!
```

*... which has a size of 4
bytes under Win32!*

And exactly here an exquisite trap is camouflaged: an ATOM such as
aItem is (even under Win32!) only two bytes long, but UnpackDDEl-
Param() writes *four* bytes to the corresponding address! (And if you don't
believe this: just look at the assembly code of the function yourself). Under certain circumstances — if, for instance, aItem is not a local variable
on the stack — calling this innocent little function can easily destroy the
two bytes located *after* aItem in memory (which possibly have nothing at
all in common with aItem and DDE). And the whole story is even more
unfortunate, because this error renders impossible the creation of a single source for Win16 and Win32 even with the use of the portability macros (see ahead). The *only* correct way to call UnpacklDDElParam() looks
like this:

```
case WM_DDE_ADVISE:
  UnpackDDElParam(wMsg,lParam, (PUINT)&hOptions,
      (PUINT)&uintTemp);
  aItem=(ATOM)uintTemp;
// ... and "freed" afterwards:
  FreeDDElParam(wMsg,lParam);
```

I think all these problems finally come from the fact that an already un-
satisfactory design, namely the DDE protocol, had to be stirred up with
further dubious ingredients, in order to make it at least partly compatible
with modern Win32 concepts. Perhaps it would have been more prudent
to just grasp the opportunity with both hands and let DDE (not DDEML)
together with the Win16 protocol disappear from the scene into obliv-
ion.* At any rate, the serious developer is in the long run well advised to
use the DDEML instead.

* Exactly where it belongs!

As a matter of fact, the Win32 documentation tells us that Pack-
DDElParam() and colleagues should only be used with DDE messages
sent via PostMessage(); so not with WM_DDE_INITIATE (anyway, the

two atoms delivered with an initiate fit at two bytes each marvelously into an LPARAM). The following table shows all DDE messages and the proper way of generating the lParam:

DDE message	Is a PackDDElParam() call necessary?
WM_DDE_ACK	yes, if sent as acknowledgement for WM_DDE_EXECUTE
WM_DDE_ADVISE	always
WM_DDE_DATA	always
WM_DDE_EXECUTE	no, hCmd can be used directly
WM_DDE_INITIATE	never, since sent via SendMessage()
WM_DDE_POKE	always
WM_DDE_REQUEST	no, cfFormat and aItem can be used directly
WM_DDE_TERMINATE	no, since always LPARAM == 0
WM_DDE_UNADVISE	no, cfFormat and aItem can be used directly

Unfortunately, in current versions of the 3.1 SDK the new functions for the administration of DDE lParams are not (yet?) available. The simplest cure is to use the following helper macros under 16 bit (see also Appendix 7 and PORTUTIL.H on the accompanying disk):

```
// For 16-bit DDE only!
#define PackDDElParam(M,lo,hi)        MAKELPARAM(lo,hi)
#define FreeDDElParam(M,lP)           // just blank
#define ReuseDDElParam(lP,mi,mo,lo,hi) MAKELPARAM(lo,hi)
#define UnpackDDElParam(M,lP,plo,phi)  \
    * (LPWORD) (plo)=LOWORD(lP) ; * (LPWORD) (phi)=HIWORD(lP)
```

For the medium term I would indeed, as mentioned, advise each DDE programmer that instead of directly pottering around with the bulky DDE messages, it is better to employ the DDEML calls. First, this API, once you get it into your head, is much simpler to use than the naked DDE protocol; second, the portability is considerably improved. Last but not least, the DDEML will profit from further development and additional functionality dedicated to data communication and the integration of programs, which (hopefully!) won't be the case for the venerable DDE messages.

Cooperation with other programs

Generally, through the introduction of separate address spaces, but also through the ability to employ several threads in the same application, a lot of things coupled with the communication of applications among each other have been modified — a conglomerate we turn to in the following. Win16 puts a long list of functions for task manipulation at your disposal. Thereby a task is defined as the running instance of an application, DLLs, for example, are hence *not* tasks. Under Win32 the situation is somewhat more complicated: here we have to distinguish between processes and threads. The most important features of the first are the separate virtual address space as well as the possession of certain resources (such as open files and other system objects). Only through threads, however, does a process come to "life," since CPU time can be allocated only for a thread. The creation of a Win32 process is always coupled with the generation of (at least) one thread. Since a Win16 program ported without enhancements, however, must be single-threaded per definition, the difference is for the moment not so important.

Communication of applications

Win16: tasks

Win32: processes and threads.

Nevertheless, most Win16 task functions refer to threads and *not* to the underlying process under Win32. Both processes and threads are identified systemwide through unique DWORD values. With their aid (and assuming sufficient security clearance under NT) you can easily acquire a handle to the object (yes, threads and processes are to be seen as objects under Win32); with the latter you can operate on the process or thread. The Win16 data type HTASK has completely vanished, as well as a whole list of task-specific functions (IsTask(), GetCurrentTask(), etc.). Some others — such as GetWindowTask() — are mapped to their more or less compatible Win32 equivalents through corresponding macro definitions (in this case to the somewhat oblong GetWindowThread-ProcessId()). Moreover, the function PostAppMsg() was removed; however, through a mapper macro its Win32 counterpart PostThreadMessage() is called. Consequence: if you need a certain task-oriented function not directly supported under Win32, you will probably find it in the group of thread functions. Detailed information about all these changes are given in the enhanced PORT.INI file in Appendix 2.

Win16 task functions refer to threads under Win32.

A layer of macros reproduces the Win16 functions.

So in general we can record the fact that a Win16 task in most aspects corresponds to a thread under Win32. For example, each task so far had a message queue on its own; this resulted in one queue per application.

One thread, one queue This need not be the same for Win32: here *each and every* thread that creates a window receives a message queue that is created automatically by the system under the hoods. What's more: the queue size is dynamically adjusted through the window manager. In other words: a call to the function SetMessageQueue() can be removed without replacement. The relationships between processes, threads, queues and windows are explained by figures 4.16 (for Win16) and 4.17 (for Win32) on the following page.

Figure 4.16: Tasks, messages, and queues under Win16

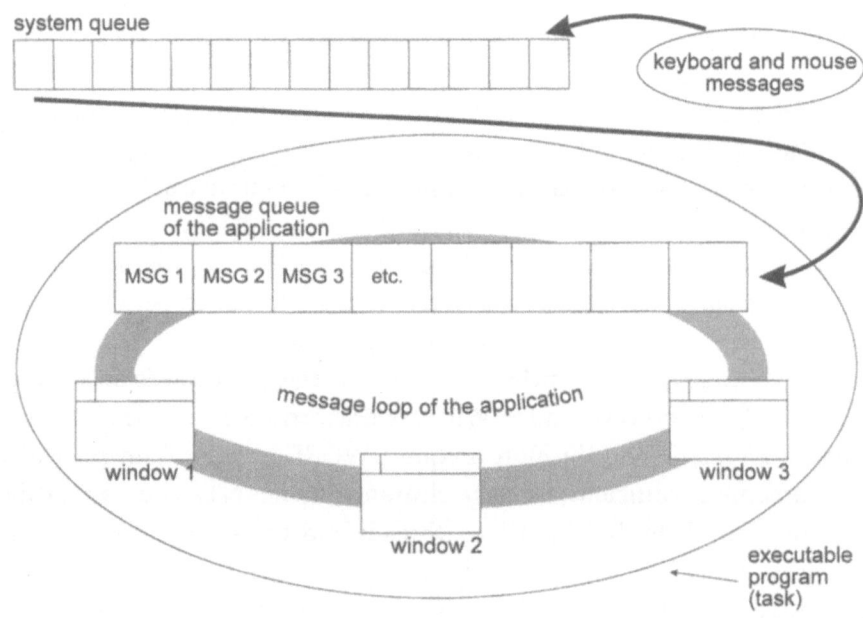

If you frequently manipulate windows belonging to other processes (applications) in your programs, these program parts will probably compile and link perfectly well under Win32 — but unfortunately they won't behave correctly. Indeed, nearly all functions that directly read or change (the latter possibly with some naughty intentions) the state of another process are only as an exception portable to Win32. Most often they require some significant changes to the program logic.

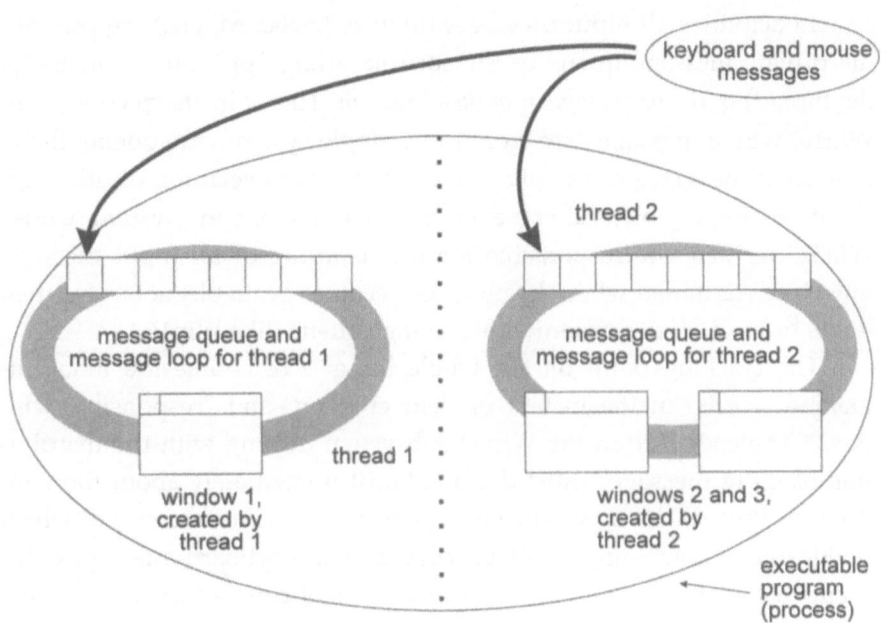

An example par excellence is found with the function DestroyWindow(), with whose aid you still can destroy windows in your own application — nevertheless, the attempt to destroy a window of another process (even a child process!) normally ends with the error code ER-ROR_ACCESS_DENIED. Therefore, such code must be removed or changed, for instance, to work through explicit interprocess communication: in trivial cases through the introduction of a simple self-defined message protocol (see, for example, WM_COPYDATA); in complex scenarios better with the help of already existing protocols (like DDEML) or advanced mechanisms such as memory mapped files or named pipes.* The latter will bring you into the neighborhood of client/server models (e.g., RPC), which possibly are also to be taken into account.

* Named pipes are efficient
one- or two-way communication channels

Mouse and keyboard: the local input model

The next big problem area is also linked with process communication and access to other processes or threads, respectively. I'm talking about the localization of user input, an interesting subject, treated already in

Input messages into a
private message queue

271

the overview in section 1.5. Put into a single sentence, through these system activities all input messages (mouse, keyboard, etc.) are put into the private message queue of the corresponding application (precisely: the thread) *in the very moment of their creation*. This is in sharp contrast to Win16, where messages are stored in a single systemwide queue; there, unfetched messages can easily render the further execution of other applications impossible and can even completely block the system. Under Win32 the window responsible for the handling of an input message must be determined when the message becomes available, not only when it will be read off the systemwide message queue (like Win16).

Distribution of input messages

The cracking point on the whole thing is of course the innocent-looking words "in the instant of their creation" and "responsible window." The code within the Win32 subsystem dealing with the distribution of input messages must decide almost immediately about the window (or thread) the input currently pending is directed to and to which queue the whole thing shall be copied. For keyboard messages this seems completely evident: the information is of course forwarded to the currently active application (or more accurate: to the child window of the active application with the input focus). However, the matter is not all

Complications

that easy: one of these entries might indeed lead to a focus change or, even worse, to switching the active application. And then all the following messages shouldn't have been placed in the first queue at all, but either in the queue for the now active application or simply deleted. Also the receiver of a mouse message isn't constrained to the window the mouse pointer is currently hopping over. First of all, a window might capture all mouse messages via SetCapture() between the instant the information is created and its later handling. Or the mouse pointer is moved to a location where a child window is created or shown, just before the corresponding information became processed. Now, which window shall receive the message?

No changes in handling the messages...

Luckily, Win32 itself takes care of most of these nagging questions and defines an appropriate and, above all, plausible administration of input messages. Therefore, neither the way these messages are administered internally nor their handling in your window procedures changes at all. Alas, the new, so-called local input model has some serious consequences when using functions that query or modify certain input state

... but with some functions

information (which is global under Win16). This especially concerns the administration of focus and active windows as well as the systemwide intercepting of mouse messages (i.e., mouse capture). We first address the problems bound to the focus handling.

Focus and active window

Each application (or under Win32 more precisely: each thread that has created a window) possesses, as discussed above, a message queue in which all messages directed for this thread (or its windows, respectively) are stored. Now, with this queue a further data structure is coupled, which solely describes the input state of the corresponding thread and is named "local input state." And here exactly the deciding difference between Win16 and Win32 is found: the first knows only a single, global input state on which all input functions and messages are based. Therefore under Win16 each application can locate *systemwide* the window with the input focus through calling GetFocus(). In general, GetFocus() delivers values other than 0 — most often a valid window handle is returned. Precisely the same statement is true for GetActiveWindow(), which under Win16 asks for the currently active application (or its top-level window, respectively). And, of course, similar observations apply to the corresponding Set...() functions, which also work on a systemwide basis.

Local input state

   Under Win32 this changes considerably: the introduction of local input states results in an application (or a thread) only being able to audit whether one of its *own* windows currently possesses the input focus (via GetFocus()). Then, and only then, this call delivers a valid window handle. If, on the other hand, a window has the focus that doesn't belong to the calling thread, GetFocus() just delivers the value 0 and *not* the wanted window handle. So, while it was always possible to query the handle of the focus window under Win16, under Win32 this only happens if this window was created ("is owned") by the calling thread. A similar observation is valid for the behavior of SetFocus(). Under Win16 any application could assign the focus to each and every window, provided that only its handle was known. Under Win32 this works only if the window was created by the calling thread. We notice that as long as [Get/Set]Focus() calls are exclusively used to manipulate *self-created* windows, Win32 behaves to a large extent as Win16 does. But as soon as windows created by other applications (or threads) are processed, both systems differ tremendously.

GetFocus()

SetFocus()

This observation of course is valid in analogous form for the pair [Get/Set]ActiveWindow(). With these functions each Win16 application could query the currently active window at any time or set any other top-level window active, respectively. However, GetActiveWindow() under Win32 delivers a valid handle only if the active window is part of the calling application. If a top-level window of another application is the active one, this function returns just 0. And SetActiveWindow() fails if a window not belonging to the calling application shall be activated. If until now you have switched to other applications or windows of other tasks with SetActiveWindow() and/or SetFocus() calls, you probably won't see the expected behavior under Win32, since these functions only operate on and change the local input state. Anyhow, for global measures, an all-new pair of functions was introduced, namely [Get/Set]ForegroundWindow(), with which the currently active window can be queried or modified systemwide. The usage of SetForegroundWindow() is mandatory to switch the focus or activation state between different windows or applications. As a matter of fact, GetForegroundWindow() doesn't necessarily deliver the focus window; it returns only the currently active top-level window (which is, nevertheless, directly or indirectly the parent of the windows having the focus at present). In one word: [Get/Set]ForegroundWindow() are simply the versions of [Get/Set]ActiveWindow() enhanced for global use.

If you call GetActiveWindow() or GetFocus() in your programs, then make sure that the treatment of the results is Win32 compatible. Especially the fact that both functions can return 0 at any time, even when a perfectly valid focus or active window exists in the system, must be taken into consideration. A SetFocus() call doesn't guarantee at all that a directly following GetFocus() will return a value distinct from 0! Pay close attention to all places where you operate on window handles of other applications!

[Get/Set]ActiveWindow()

SetActiveWindow() and SetFocus() don't activate other applications.

Instead use [Get/Set]Foreground-Window().

The mousetrap

However, not only the keyboard imposes difficulties, but the mouse handling also invites some changes. Normally the window on which the mouse pointer (precisely: the so-called "hot spot"*) is currently located receives the generated mouse messages. However, a window can easily circumvent this default behavior through a call to SetCapture(): now all

* A unique point defined when designing the mouse pointer shape

further mouse messages are diverted to the calling window (rather its window procedure) until the normal mode is switched back through a ReleaseCapture() call (or until another window on its own calls GetCapture() and grabs all mouse messages). Much like the focus, the mouse capture is a kind of pseudo-resource, and only a single window at a time can possess these strange beasts. For this reason the same rules apply for the function GetCapture() as for GetFocus(): only if a window that actually belongs to the calling thread has the mouse capture will a useful result be returned. In all other cases the return value is 0, although at the very moment of the call a capture window absolutely might exist (e.g., in another application).

The mouse capture is a pseudo-resource.

Easy: GetCapture().

Unfortunately, with SetCapture() the facts are somewhat more complicated. First of all, under Win32 *only* the window currently in the foreground (or one of its child windows, too) can receive the mouse capture at all! For all windows *not* in the foreground (non-active) even after a SetCapture() call only those mouse messages are supplied that are generated when the mouse pointer is actually moved across the window: effectively the call is pointless. But even if this first and most important condition is fulfilled, a window doesn't inevitably receive all further mouse messages after calling SetCapture() (in contrast to Win16). Believe it or not: when the mouse pointer is located on the window of another application, the mouse messages generated are only sent to the capture window *if at the very moment of the SetCapture() call a mouse button was pressed*! Overall, we have to distinguish three cases:

Involved: SetCapture().

- The mouse pointer is over the window that called SetCapture(): of course the messages will be sent to this window.
- The mouse pointer floats above a window pertaining to the same thread as the capture window: then all mouse messages are sent to the latter.
- Or, the third case, the window under the mouse belongs to another thread. Then the capture window receives the following mouse input *completely* only if one of the mouse buttons was pressed *in the very moment* of the SetCapture() call.

Three cases:

So applications that only grab the mouse capture if a button was pressed and release it when the button is released won't see many alterations through these changes. Solely the question whether another capture window exists can be answered only locally (based on the individual

Compatible when mouse button is pressed.

thread) and not systemwide. Code for acquiring and releasing the capture as well as all the actions in between can basically remain the same as under Win16; just take the modified GetCapture() function into consideration. (As a matter of fact, this compatible behavior is possible in spite of the local input model, because, unlike Win16, *all* mouse messages (in their "virgin" form of WM_NCHITTEST) generated after pressing a mouse button are sent to the corresponding window until the button is released! This is even true when this window hasn't (yet) called SetCapture() at all!)

Alas, changes when mouse button is not pressed.

Things look much different, however, if SetCapture() was called with no button pressed at that moment. Then you can forget about receiving all further mouse messages, since in this case, as explained above, messages are only sent to the capture window while the mouse is positioned over that window itself or a window pertaining to the same thread as the capture window. So an application that definitely needs all system wide mouse input — even if no mouse button was pressed at SetCapture() time — can't accomplish this with a simple SetCapture() call under Win32. The only meaningful capability (save a WH_MOUSE hook) that occurs to me for Win32 seems to be the creation of a transparent popup window exactly as large as the display (with the aid of the window style WS_EX_TRANSPARENT) put above all other windows. Then this window receives of course all mouse messages and the explicit capturing of the mouse is not at all necessary. (Actually, "under very bad conditions" the circumstances can be even more complicated than I've described above; in order to keep the discussion at least somewhat clear, I have included one or two simplifications. If you have to intercept and handle all mouse messages in a central place of your program and SetCapture() is (or could be) called without a pressed mouse button, I would recommend — besides the attentive reading of the WinHelp files concerning the capture API — to play around with a small test program for mouse and keyboard input. Hence on the disk for the book is a simple but illuminating program to experiment with mouse and keyboard input.)

Two approaches: mouse hooks or WS_EX_TRANS-PARENT.

This whole area is hardly unambiguous to describe, because even Microsoft doesn't deliver precise and easily interpretable statements. So with the rather complex region of local input states the fact that the functions [Get/Set]SysModalWindow() were simply removed from the API is also associated. On the one hand, this is surely a consequence of the modified input management; on the other hand the use of system

[Get/Set]SysModalWindow() are removed.

modal windows seems to be rather doubtful in an environment such as Windows NT (or 95) anyway. On the contrary: the new input model shall precisely, together with the preemptive multi-tasking and multiple threads, ensure the operability of all currently running applications. Of course, *application* modal windows (e.g., modal dialog boxes) are possible as before !

Last but not least: hooks

Several smaller items also have changed for hook workers. But fortunately, this field is a typical exponent of those Win32 API parts where Microsoft farsightedly (don't you laugh!) has already put (to some extent) upward compatible functions into the Windows 3.1 SDK. Hooks are probably not used that frequently, so I can keep this discussion short and refer you to Appendix 2 as well as to the Win32 documentation. Two hints shall be enough: first strive to build your software, as much as possible, on the new hook API available with Windows 3.1 (e.g. SetWindowsHookEx(), etc.) and modify your sources accordingly. These functions are namely "nearly" upward compatible. This recommendation is especially important if you need hooks for the *systemwide* analysis of messages. Admittedly, Win32 makes available (with the help of some macro definitions) also the older and somewhat simpler hook functions, but these can be used for message juggling *locally* only, that is, in the thread that called them! These macros definitely won't help with the installation of systemwide hooks. The second point concerns the last argument of the new functions: under Win16 a task handle (a HTASK) is necessary; however, Win32 needs a thread id (a DWORD). As already mentioned above, tasks on the one hand and threads on the other hand are just two sides of the same medal (said in a somewhat simplified manner). Therefore, small adaptations, mostly of syntactical quality, may be necessary.

Upward compatible functions are already available under Windows 3.1.

So change to the new hook API.

Task handles and thread ids

The changes in the coordinate spaces and problems associated with them, which absolutely can have repercussions to window management, are dealt with in the next section about GDI. Many less important Win16 functions were either completely removed or replaced with differently named counterparts, sometimes also with a somewhat different parameter list. Most often the necessary adaptations are relatively easy: a macro or a simple modification in the sources, possibly combined with condi-

Coordinate spaces: see GDI in the next section.

See Appendix 2, PORT.INI.

tional compilation, solves the problem. Some fortunately very rare places are indeed coupled with considerable efforts (such as, for example, the dynamic generation of dialog boxes via the structs DLGTEMPLATE and DLGITEMTEMPLATE). To list all these functions and the corresponding changes here in detail would significantly bloat the volume of this chapter (and possibly also be hard on your patience); therefore I refer you to Appendix 2 for the treatment of what's been discussed so far and all further differences known to me.

4.8 Changes and Improvements in the Graphics Device Interface (GDI)

"All art is at once surface and symbol." Oscar Wilde, The Picture of Dorian Gray

Comparatively few changes

Well, we'll have another rather wide field opening here: the graphics interface of Windows. But fortunately only relatively few piercing changes require your attention. Of course, there is, as in the other areas' statements, a bunch of small and infinitesimal syntactical differences, which are for the most part found in Appendix 2 (as far as they're known to me). But really, global semantic changes are the exception rather than the rule here. Anyhow: some important things have been nevertheless modified....

GDI: nowadays in C++

Graphics output only marginally modified

Example: drawing lines.

Perhaps the most interesting facet is the fact that nearly the complete GDI was recoded anew in C++. Indeed most functions have kept their calling sequences (apart from the usual widening of important data types to 32 bits), but in the course of the reimplementation some subtle changes have been introduced: some known errors and limitations that required some sophisticated around-programming were repaired (well, in all probability the sophisticated code won't run under Win32 as expected!); what's more, the new GDI contains on its part surely some new bugs, which are either removed in future versions or cultivated to features.... Therefore, don't pay attention just to your source code: not only should the GDI code of your application compile correctly, but the execution too should produce the expected results (especially for boundary

cases) — compare with the Win16 version (helpfully, the good old
ZOOMIN is also a component of the Win32 SDK). A warning especially
to the drawing of simple lines: the current Windows version uses a
slighty modified Bresenham algorithm. As a matter of fact, this algorithm is indeed fast and quite simple to implement, but it has a significant disadvantage: because of rounding errors, the actual graphical output can deviate slightly from the "theoretically correct" result. However,
with the high definition of modern graphics adapters, this effect is generally too small to be noticed, so it can be neglected. But there are (very
rare) cases, where this problem can indeed produce extremely negative
side effects: a line, drawn from point A to point B doesn't always contain
the same pixels as the same line just drawn vice versa from B to A. This
has consequences if lines are drawn in the foreground color and afterwards are "deleted" through XORing or drawing once again in the background color. Then, depending on your algorithm, here and there an
annoying pixel might stay on the display. Win32 fixes this problem
through the introduction of a corrected algorithm that produces consistent output. However, its usage can lead to very minor modifications in
the graphics output when compared to Win16. But as said, these effects
should be perceptible only in extreme cases.

Coordinates in wide-screen format

With these starting remarks out of the way, now it's time for the real
changes: first I'll discuss the most important GDI improvement, namely
the enlargement of GDI coordinates from 16 to 32 bits, here shown with
the struct POINT as an example:

*GDI coordinates grow from
16 to 32 bits.*

```
// Under Win16:
typedef struct tagPOINT {    /* pt */
    int x;
    int y;
} POINT;   // sizeof(POINT) == 2 * sizeof(int) == 4

// And under Win32:
typedef struct tagPOINT {    /* pt */
    LONG x;
```

```
        LONG y;
    } POINT;  // sizeof(POINT) == 2 * sizeof(LONG) == 8
```

That's valid for POINT,
RECT, SIZE, etc.

This widening also happened for all other structures dealing with coordinates and/or extent values (RECT, SIZE, etc.). What's more, the various window management functions using coordinate values, such as WindowFromPoint(), for instance, were accordingly adjusted. Hereby a small, but fine, portability trap opens: while all structure components describing coordinates are widened to 32 bits and therefore enable a consistent treatment of *GDI* coordinates, various *window* messages deliver positions or size values in a packed (and out of necessity Win16 compatible) format. This admirable format is constructed in such a way that a coordinate or dimensional information like x, y (or width, height, respectively) is packed and transported in the LPARAM message parameter; nice examples for this are the messages WM_MOUSEMOVE or WM_SIZE. So LOWORD(lParam) delivers the x component or the width, HIWORD(lParam) is dealing with the y value or the height. (An incidental remark: up to and including Windows 3.0, the function GetAspectRatioFilter() has even returned the two values reversed — an API design error which was repaired only with 3.1). A typical assignment of two packed values to a POINT looks like the following for Win16:

Caution, a trap: packed
coordinates in Win16 format.

```
case WM_MOUSEMOVE: {
    POINT pt;
    pt.x=LOWORD(lParam);
    pt.y=HIWORD(lParam);
    ...
    // Or use the MAKEPOINT macro instead...
}
```

* in this case pt.x

This code seems to do just the job. Well, indeed an int* receives a WORD as the result of LOWORD(lParam) (the same is valid for pt.y), but first the underlying types are of the same size; second, the mouse pointer coordinates delivered in the LPARAM are based on the client area of the corresponding windows, therefore only positive values are possible. Ergo: everything is as nice as a snowman on a bright winter day.

Unfortunately, not Win32
compatible

Unfortunately, under Win32 the snowman melts as fast as butter in the desert sun. Assumption one is no longer true: there pt.x is a plain LONG. And assumption two is not even valid under Win16! If namely a

WM_MOUSEMOVE happens in a window that currently has captured the mouse, the coordinates can absolutely get negative! The reason why the code snippet shown above works in this or similar form in innumerable programs so far without complaining is actually only traced back to the fact that sizeof(int) == sizeof(WORD) is true for Win16.

Therefore, all places where a transition from packed 16-bit coordinates to the new 32-bit format is carried out have to be studied with utmost attention and, if necessary, adjusted. The following code is 3.x *and* Win32 compatible through the explicit cast:

Transition from packed 16-bit coordinates to the new 32-bit format

```
case WM_MOUSEMOVE: {
  POINT pt;
  pt.x=(short)LOWORD(lParam); // explicit WORD to short,
  // then implicit to LONG (WIn32) or int (Win16 )
  pt.y=(short)HIWORD(lParam); // ditto
  ...
}
return 0;
```

Certainly not the worst idea is the creation of a few small helper functions that take over the conversion from packed LONGs to POINTs, and vice versa. Unfortunately, the macro MAKEPOINT defined under Win16 (which built a POINT from the corresponding LONG) is not available anymore for Win32. There a similar macro named MAKEPOINTS is defined, which converts a packed LONG to a Win32 POINTS structure, whose components are actually only 16-bits wide (i.e., similar to a POINT in Win16). And such a POINTS can be transformed with a second macro named POINTSTOPOINT to a POINT (or vice versa, see POINTTOPOINTS). Indeed, I don't see clearly why this structure and the macros were introduced in the first place: there are no further functions that require or at least work with POINTS. And since this struct is (so far) not defined for Win16, it can't even be used in a downward compatible fashion. Possibly the Microsofties had the following code in mind:

Helper functions for the conversion

MAKEPOINT was removed.

And who needs POINTS?

```
case WM_MOUSEMOVE: {
    POINTs pts; POINT pt;
    pts=MAKEPOINTS(lParam); // First make a POINTS,
    pt=POINTSTOPOINT(pts);  // then a POINT?
```

```
    ...
}
return 0;
```

Because the whole thing will surely again change anytime in the future, the approach to define helper functions appears to be the best. All transitions between 16-bit coordinates (which are mostly based on the screen display) and the new 32-bit values should be handled with self-written functions (which can easily be adapted). I would use the wider Win32 structures as much as possible, so call those functions as soon as you receive a packed value. An example for this approach can be found on the accompanying disk. A complete list of all relevant functions and messages follows farther down.*

* See table 4.7 on page 284.

Packed coordinates

Alas, the subject of packed x/y coordinates still has another facet: not only the window manager uses this appealing format, various Win16 GDI functions also deliver their results packed into a DWORD. Let's take as the simplest example the function MoveTo(), which might be used as follows under Win16:

With some GDI functions, too

```
dwXYOld=MoveTo(hdc,xNew,yNew);
// Now with LOWORD(dwXYOld) the x coordinate and with
// HIWORD(dwXYOld) the y coordinate of the current position
// could be read.
    ...
POINT ptOld;
ptOld=MAKEPOINT(MoveTo(hdc,xNew,yNew));
// ptOld now contains the current position
```

Sorry, MAKEPOINT is defined only under Win16.

A similar usage of the return value for a coordinate pair is of course *passé* under Win32, since the two 32-bit values can't be squeezed into a single DWORD. Microsoft has therefore done what would have been the best from the beginning: the coordinates are returned — wonders will never cease — in a POINT variable! And if you're *not* interested in the values at all, even NULL can be provided as the address! This API miracle named MoveToEx() looks "live" as follows:

Instead of DWORD a POINT variable as return type?

```
POINT ptOld;
MoveToEx(hdc,xNew,yNew,&ptOld);
// Now with ptOld.x the x coordinate and with
// ptOld.y the y coordinate of the current position
// can be read.
...
// And if the current position is not *that* interesting:
MoveToEx(hdc,xNew,yNew,NULL);
```

This change concerns all functions that return an x/y pair or an extent as their result, and they're listed in the following table:

Functions to set ...	or get the coordinates
MoveTo	GetCurrentPosition
OffsetViewportOrg	
OffsetWindowOrg	
ScaleViewportExt	
ScaleWindowExt	
SetBitmapDimension	GetBitmapDimension
SetBrushOrg	GetBrushOrg
GetTextExtent	
SetViewportExt	GetViewportExt
SetViewportOrg	GetViewportOrg
SetWindowExt	GetWindowExt
SetWindowOrg	GetWindowOrg
	GetAspectRatioFilter

Table 4.6: GDI functions returning coordinate pairs

The names of the "corrected" functions are easily formed: just attach the suffix ...Ex to the current names.* At the same time the parameter list is enlarged with the address of a POINT or SIZE variable. And since these wonderful functions are already available under Windows 3.1, their use is even downward compatible!

* Well, with Microsoft, no rule is without exception: GetTextExtent() changes to GetTextExtentPoint().

All these enlarged functions can also receive NULL as the last parameter (the address of a POINT or SIZE). In this case the particular information is simply *not* copied back. This can be important in connection with the buffering of GDI calls (LPC batching, see farther down) since a call that has to return coordinates can't be batched but must be processed immediately. Another comment in passing: the function SetBrushOrg(),

NULL as the address value

so far called when positional changes of a window occured to correct the brush output, can be removed in this context, because Win32 (hear! hear!) is finally able to perform the necessary adaptation itself.

Win32 functions with packed
16-bit format

A lot of functions and messages deliver coordinate or size values as before in the packed format also under Win32 (one can expect all sorts of wonderful things from Microsoft and may even get some of them after a while; an orthogonal and consistent API is even with the best will in the world just too much). The following list shows these exceptions as well as the category of the returned values (display or logical coordinates).

Table 4.7: Win32 messages
and functions returning
packed coordinates

Message or function	coordinate type
WM_SIZE	display
WM_MOVE	display
WM_NCHITTEST	display
WM_MOUSEMOVE	display
WM_[L/M/R]BUTTON[DOWN/UP/DBLCLK]	display
WM_NC[L/M/R]BUTTON[DOWN/UP/DBLCLK]	display
WM_SYSCOMMAND	display
GetDCOrg()	display
GetMessagePos()	display
GetTabbedTextExtent()	logical
TabbedTextOut()	logical

Display and ...

Well, that the first group returns the values in a packed format may be acceptable, since only display values are handled there anyway — and graphics adapters with more than 32,767 pixels are certainly a few months in the future... On the other hand, a true masterpiece of API design is the two last functions that (truly, no kidding!) return packed

... logical coordinates

logical size values! So if you attempt to calculate the width of a somewhat longer string with the help of GetTabbedTextExtent() in the mapping mode MM_HIMETRIC, some interesting numbers could be generated...

A final comment to Windows 95: although the API *accepts* 32-bit coordinate values, it only uses the lower 16-bit portions (remember: most of GDI's code is on the 16-bit side!). This means that "old" code is directly usable; alas, you can't use the advantages of 32-bit coordinates if your program might be run under Win95. Put differently: if you use the "32-bitness" of the new types, make sure your program either refuses to execute under Windows 95 or adjust your graphics calculations accordingly!

Brave, new-world transformation

As a matter of fact, the new 32-bit GDI uses not only the two coordinate transformations known from Win16, but above this makes available another level called world coordinate space. This additional transformation permits the simple implementation of rotations, shearings, and the like. The course of a coordinate value under Win32 is therefore as follows: the 32-bit wide GDI coordinate specifications are generally world coordinates, which are converted in a first transformation step to the so-called page coordinates (the latter correspond to the logical coordinates of Win16). Then, depending on the currently selected mapping mode, this level, similar to Win16, is changed to device coordinates. Ultimately, these undergo a last "transformation" to result in the final client area values. Worth mentioning seems the fact that the device coordinates are now available in a 32-bit format, which, however, is organized as a fixed-point integer with 28 bits for the integer part and 4 bits for the decimal places. Together with using the enlarged coordinates it should be possible to completely avoid truncation or rounding errors with a careful implementation (an annoying problem that always popped up under Win16 when drawing complex graphics and very quick led to lengthy and difficult to reproduce ad hoc solutions). Figure 4.18 on the next page shows the various transformation schemes for Win32.

Fortunately, under normal circumstances, these changes have no direct meaning for the portability, since the predefined default transformation matrix (of type XFORM) is simply the identity matrix and as such causes no alteration to the coordinates whatsoever when transforming from world to page (or logical) coordinates. And except for the coordinate widening to 32 bits, the following conversion from logical (page, respectively) to device coordinates is absolutely compatible to Win16.* Yet it is certainly advisable to keep the fact in the back of your head that under Win32 a further transformation level is introduced. Especially using another than the default XFORM transformation matrix (or alternatively switching via SetGraphicsMode() to the so-called GM_ADVANCED graphics mode) shows some unforeseeable specialties above the actual transformation: in this mode the lower right corner of a rectangle is interpreted as an inclusive value. This change has the consequence that a Win16 RECT "grows" a unit to the right and bottom (see figure 4.19).

Marginal notes:

Three levels of transformations:

1. World coordinates

2. Page coordinates

3. Device coordinates

Added benefit: no rounding errors.

* including the inexpressible tedious window and viewport calls

GM_ADVANCED graphics mode via SetGraphicsMode()

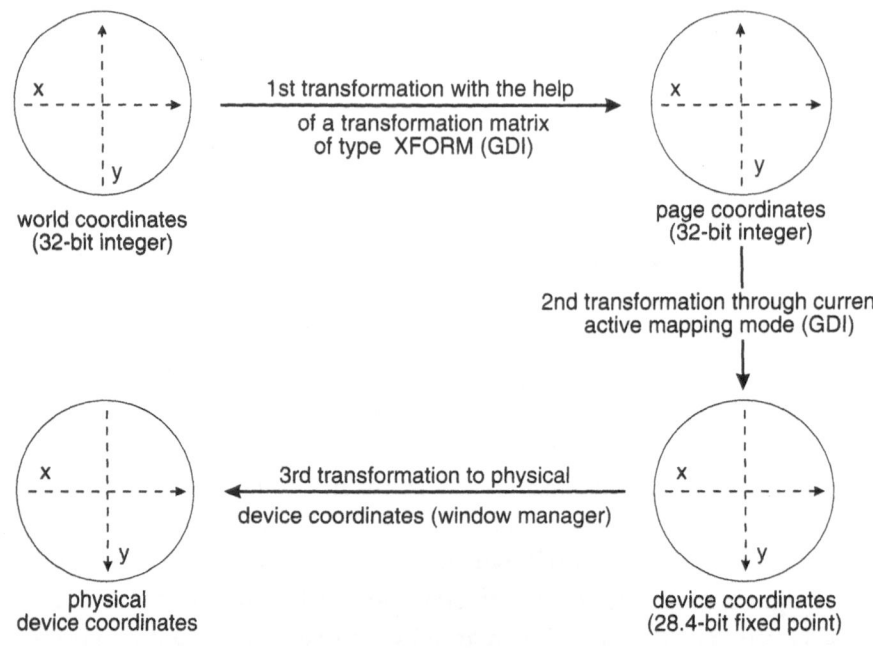

Figure 4.18: The GDI transformations of Win32

world coordinates
(32-bit integer)

1st transformation with the help
of a transformation matrix
of type XFORM (GDI)

page coordinates
(32-bit integer)

2nd transformation through currently
active mapping mode (GDI)

3rd transformation to physical
device coordinates (window manager)

physical
device coordinates

device coordinates
(28.4-bit fixed point)

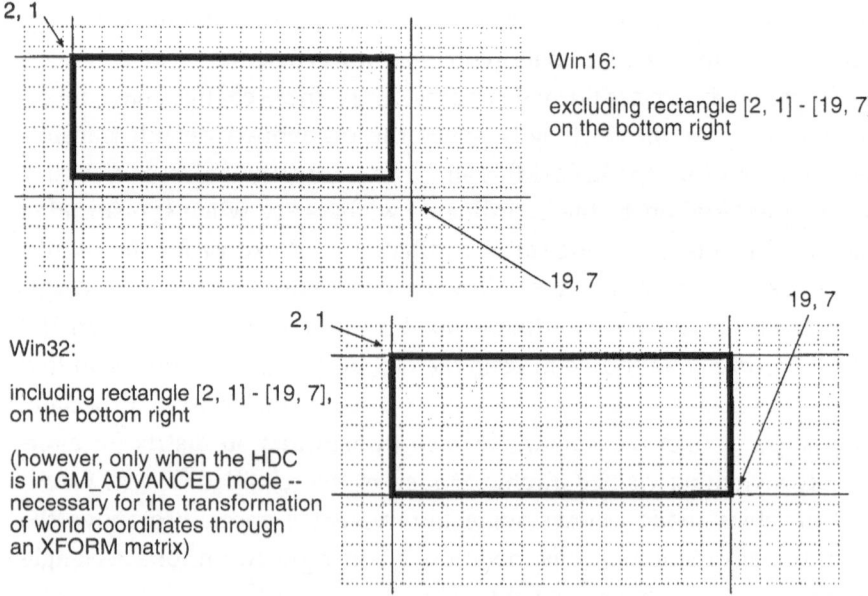

Figure 4.19: Two rectangles: Win16 exclusive and Win32 inclusive.

2, 1

Win16:

excluding rectangle [2, 1] - [19, 7],
on the bottom right

19, 7

2, 1

19, 7

Win32:

including rectangle [2, 1] - [19, 7],
on the bottom right

(however, only when the HDC
is in GM_ADVANCED mode --
necessary for the transformation
of world coordinates through
an XFORM matrix)

The reason for this seemingly superfluous change is simple: of course, a rectangle rotated by 180 degrees (or mirrored, respectively) should *not* differ from the unchanged original. However, exactly this happens if the bottom right corner — in contrast to the upper left edge — doesn't belong to the rectangle. The underlying dilemma can be put in other words: with a transformation scheme allowing full rotation, reflection, and mirroring, the concept of a corner in the bottom right or upper left loses any significance. On the included disk you'll find a small example program that illustrates this and some other interesting GDI effects.

Upper right — bottom left?

Handles: strictly private!

Graphical objects (pens, brushes, fonts, etc.) under Win32 are handled through handles — so HPEN, HBRUSH etc. have all survived well. Indeed these types, such as nearly all other handle types, have been widened to 32 bits. However, this modification should pose no special problems; of course all rules and notes that were given for window and memory handles are effective for the GDI handles too (incorrect cast operations, growth of structures, etc.). Yet, an additional specialty is remarkable for graphical objects only: as already mentioned, handles under Win16 are often nothing else than NEAR pointers into one of the various local heaps used by the Windows modules. That's also true for handles to GDI objects, which refer to a GDI data segment where the objects are actually stored. Under Win16 this segment, based on the maximum segment size of only 64 KB, was often somewhat "overcrowded," so some applications proceeded to share the used GDI handles, once created, jointly in different modules. This may have been desirable (or even necessary) because it was possible to start several instances of the same application; some really big software packages consisting of several separate programs have also keenly shared GDI handles between these. This worked simply because these handles define just offsets into a *global* GDI data segment. Under Win32, however, the GDI objects are stored either locally in the address space(s) of the corresponding process(es) or in the GDI server; both possibilities result in the sad fact that different applications (and for that reason, of course, also several instances of the same program) can no longer access these (now non-shared) handles. Of course, multiple threads of a *single* process don't know this limitation because they all execute in the *same* address space.

GDI handles in the GDI data segment

Impossible: common access to GDI objects.

But sending GDI handles to other applications and other miscellaneous methods of copying GDI objects around are therefore not portable (however, I have heard from several sources that Microsoft will define a protocol for Win32 for sharing and exchanging GDI objects; until now, however, still nothing really specific has come to my attention).

Exchanging bitmaps be-tween applications

At the very least, for the short term the utilization of device-dependent bitmaps (alias DDBs*) is not problematic. Indeed, the Win32 documentation predicts that these should be replaced with all possible haste with the "new" device-independent bitmaps (DIBs**) first introduced with Windows 3.0, because the former are available only to support "old" applications but could be removed anytime. Well, since the DDB functions already have found a very warm welcome in the Win32 API with quite good reasons (just think about the class style CS_SAVEBITS), they're probably not scheduled to leave us soon.... Finally, for a lot of applications DDBs are not only completely satisfactory, but considerably more efficient and simpler to operate. One field, however, where the use of DIBs is definitely desirable concerns exchanging bitmaps between different applications (or computers, respectively) with the clipboard, (Net)DDE, etc., and also via files. Using a DIB is the only way to ensure that the bitmap can be processed correctly by other programs on a different hardware. As a matter of fact, the usage of DIBs is one of the fields (as are hooks) where "old" code can be relatively easily changed to compile absolutely portably under Windows 3.1 *and* the Win32 platforms.

News also for metafiles

Modified format

Fundamentally we find a very similar situation for Windows metafiles (WMFs), which are also frequently employed for the exchange of graphics information between applications (albeit on another level). The format used for this under Win16 is of course supported under Win32; nevertheless, here also another, heavily improved variant is available, the so-called enhanced metafiles (EMFs). The advantages of this format in comparison to the "old" version are persuasive: it has considerably better device independence, all (!) GDI transformations are realized; there is complete support of the graphics API; informational queries to the metafile DC are now possible, and several more goodies also exist. Unfortunately, the format of and the API for enhanced metafiles are not

Enhanced metafiles (EMF)

backward compatible, so a ported application without further changes works with the Win16 format only (in other words: the old APIs are only used to process the old format; if you need or want to use the new format, you'll have to switch to another API). Luckily, the adaptation of the sources to the new functions is easy and there even exist procedures that can convert metafiles on the fly from Win16 format to Win32, and vice versa (e.g., [Set/Get]WinMetaFileBits()); however, hereby you lose the possibility to compile the source codes unchanged under both systems. The simplest approach seems to be the introduction of two separate program parts, which depending on the system are activated through conditional compilation (or a macro shell). What's more, for the Win32 version the implementation of corresponding conversion procedures should be considered. A small example:

```
void PlayMyMetafile(HWND hwnd,LPSTR lpszFile)
{
    HDC hdc=GetDC(hwnd);
#ifdef Win32                                               Win32
    // Use enhanced metafiles:
    HENHMETAFILE hemf=GetEnhMetaFile(lpszFile);
    RECT rc;
    GetClientRect(hwnd,&rc);
    PlayEnhMetaFile(hdc,hemf,&rc);
    DeleteEnhMetaFile(hemf);
#else // Win16                                             Win16
// Use normal metafiles:
    HMETAFILE hmf=GetMetaFile(lpszFile);
    PlayMetaFile(hdc,hmf);
    DeleteMetaFile(hmf);
#endif
    ReleaseDC(hwnd,hdc);
}
```

When exchanging metafiles, please observe that the file formats of "old" and "enhanced" metafiles differ significantly, so Win16 programs (at present) are not at all able to process the Win32 format! Here, as with other things, going from Win16 to Win32 is a true one-way street!

An alteration of the basic operating system concept, already shown in detail in section 1.3, page 22, is the division of Windows NT code in application-side DLLs on the one hand and the actual server applications* on the other hand. For reasons of efficiency, as many of the Win32 functions as possible without security losses are processed on the DLL side. Such calls, however (or the resulting LPCs, respectively), that simply *must* be processed through the corresponding subsystem are in certain cases first stored in the application-side DLL "belonging" to the subsystem and only later realized in a single batch, together with all other pending function calls ("LPC batching"). This mode enhances overall efficiency; however, under unfavorable circumstances it can lead to a somewhat bumpy screen display especially with graphical output. So far, I couldn't observe such effects in my graphics; possibly, though, on very slow processors (such as a 386 SX) and/or a correspondingly sluggish graphics adapter such a phenomenon might be noticeable. The example program mentioned above with the world transformations indeed illustrates that LPC batching can absolutely influence "clumsily implemented" programs negatively. In order to prevent unfavorable consequences, I'll point out the function GdiFlush(), which immediately sends all currently pending LPCs to the subsystem. Calling GdiSetBatchLimit() might also prove helpful: this sets an upper limit for the number of batched calls. And as already mentioned for the enhanced GDI functions (such as MoveToEx()), you should *only* deliver a valid address for the last argument (which returns coordinate values) if you *definitely* need the corresponding value. The reason is that these calls — if data are to be returned — in principle can't be stored but are sent immediately to the corresponding server (with other waiting LPCs). All in all, this area should hardly pose any problems; possibly you'll have to do some fine-polishing after the successful port and considerable testing.

the Win32 subsystems

LPC batching

And the consequences

*Remedy: GdiFlush() and
GdiSetBatchLimit().*

4.9 The Programming of DLLs

"From the safe port it's easy to advise, here is the boat and there the lake! Try for yourself!" Friedrich Schiller, William Tell

All that adventurous and audacious as Schiller's quotation seems to suppose, the generation of DLLs under Win32 is probably not (anymore?). Nevertheless, with Win16 there are quite a few tricks to pay attention to, and as you surely have realized already, under Win32 Microsoft has prepared some neat surprises. As a matter of fact, hereafter I deal just with programming issues and adaptations associated with self-written DLLs; all points dealing with the actual creation of the library (especially the substantially modified linking process) are treated in the next chapter (see section 5.3). There you'll also find two complete program examples with all the necessary options and definitions.

Programming issues

DLL building: see section 5.3, page 339.

DLLs and memory management

A Win32 DLL and also the underlying concepts of dynamic linking correspond for the main part to the situation under Win16. However, you should pay attention to the following fundamental differences to DLL programming in general and for porting:

A Win16 DLL is loaded just once into (global) memory and will be mapped systemwide afterwards — all the running processes can at any time access the DLL. DLLs possess separate code segments as well as a single data segment including a local heap (at least in the default case). Unfortunately, there exists no standard capability to create further data segments in an instance-specific way (e.g., one data segment per client). A DLL can perform global memory allocations either on behalf of the caller (the normal case) or via GMEM_SHARE "for the own account." In each case a globally visible memory area is created which principally can be read and — worse — written by all processes. Figure 4.20 shows the situation under Win16.

DLLs under Win16

Memory with GMEM_SHARE

The separation of process address spaces under Win32, however, leads to a state where *every* process must explicitly load the necessary DLL(s) (or their defined segments, respectively) and map them into its private address space once again. This procedure is called "DLL attaching." The code segments of a DLL are *not* concerned with this alteration, because they're only loaded once into physical memory anyway and mapped through the Win32 subsystem* to the address space of all concerned processes (here the paging logic of the CPU comes in handy). (A short sidestep: in a 32-bit flat memory space, segments in the 16-bit sense are neither necessary nor available. From pure habit I have just spoken of "segments"; in order not to complicate things unnecessarily, from now on I'll use for the code and data areas in a 32-bit DLL the designation "section," which is also used in the Microsoft documentation.)

DLLs under Win32

* or the virtual memory manager, respectively

Sections instead of segments

*Figure 4.20: DLL memory
management under Win16*

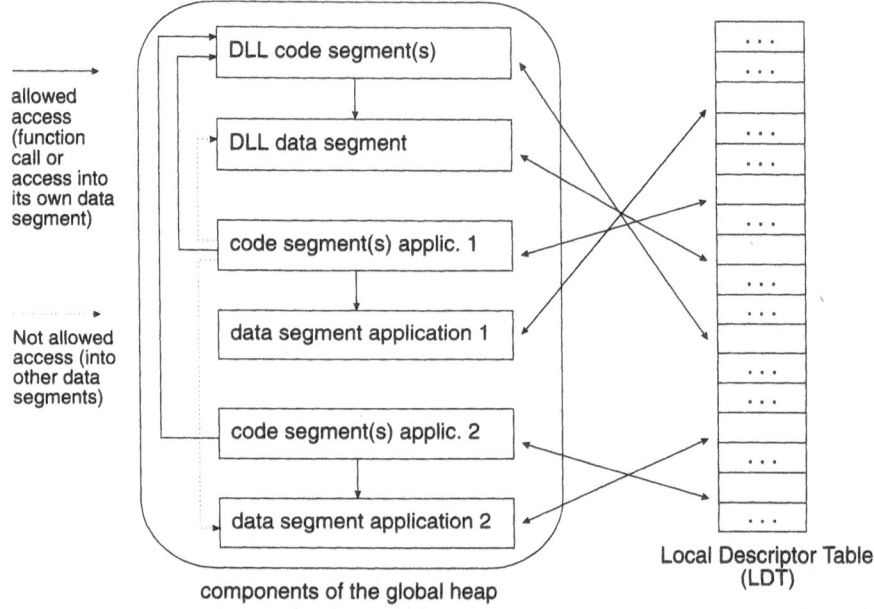

allowed
access
(function
call or
access into
its own data
segment)

Not allowed
access (into
other data
segments)

components of the global heap

Local Descriptor Table
(LDT)

*No shared DLL data under
Win32!*

The DLL data sections on the other hand (with all global and static variables) are normally created anew for every process attaching and are
mapped into the corresponding address spaces (we might call this access
model "private global"). This radical change results in each process
working practically with a "virgin" copy of the initialized DLL data. And
as long as the DLL only has to work with process-specific data, but not
with data items important to all processes (which we could call correspondingly "public global"), this approach is absolutely acceptable (or
even preferable: isolating applications from each other obviously makes
the system more stable). Let's remember: the second instance of an already running application will be loaded as a new, independent process,
with no implicit or explicit attachment to its predecessor — especially
with no access to the data sections of the first. And this consequent division of address spaces implies that a loaded DLL under Win32 is allocated for each process anew with a totally independent set of data sections, local for this one process. The following figure 4.21 demonstrates
the circumstances in this (standard) case. The Win16 model of a single
data segment per DLL — where it can rule as it pleases — is no longer
the default case under Win32!

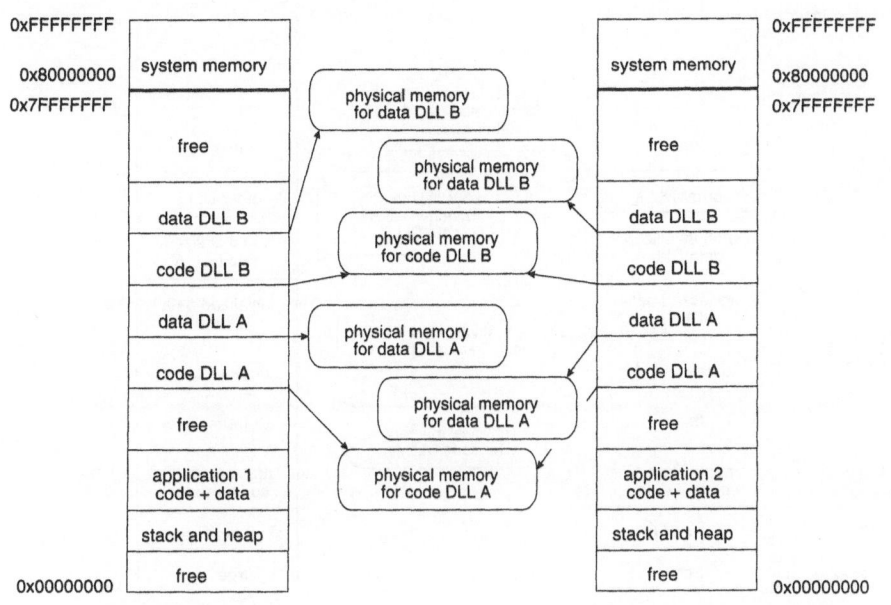

OxFFFFFFFF

0x80000000 system memory

0x7FFFFFFF

free

data DLL B

code DLL B

data DLL A

code DLL A

free

application 1
code + data

stack and heap

0x00000000 free

virtual address space application 1

physical memory
for data DLL B

physical memory
for data DLL B

physical memory
for code DLL B

physical memory
for data DLL A

physical memory
for data DLL A

physical memory
for code DLL A

OxFFFFFFFF

system memory 0x80000000

0x7FFFFFFF

free

data DLL B

code DLL B

data DLL A

code DLL A

free

application 2
code + data

stack and heap

free 0x00000000

virtual address space application 2

Figure 4.21: The normal case under Win32: one DLL data section per client.

Indeed, many DLLs are often used only to supply frequently needed functions in an efficient and centralized manner. However, lots of DLLs go beyond this simple utilization; they require additional data sections above the data areas needed just for administration of the individual process-specific private global data blocks. The allocation of public global areas, in order to satisfy this need, is performed actually only once (so for the DLL this apparently represents shared memory). In this case it must be accurately stated while linking the DLL which DLL data sections are mapped into the address space of the process every time anew when loading the DLL and which ranges are created exactly once, namely with the very first loading (so they are in fact public global). Only the *explicit* marking of a data section in the DEF file with the attribute "shared" leads to the creation of really shared sections. Only then the memory management makes available the concerned area for all applications that use the DLL. The necessary changes in the DEF files are shown in detail in section 5.3, page 339. Figure 4.22 shows the two cases schematically: the allocation of data sections in the event of a DLL with a shareable and all-normal, process-specific data section.

No shared memory?

Yes: through explicit section attributes.

293

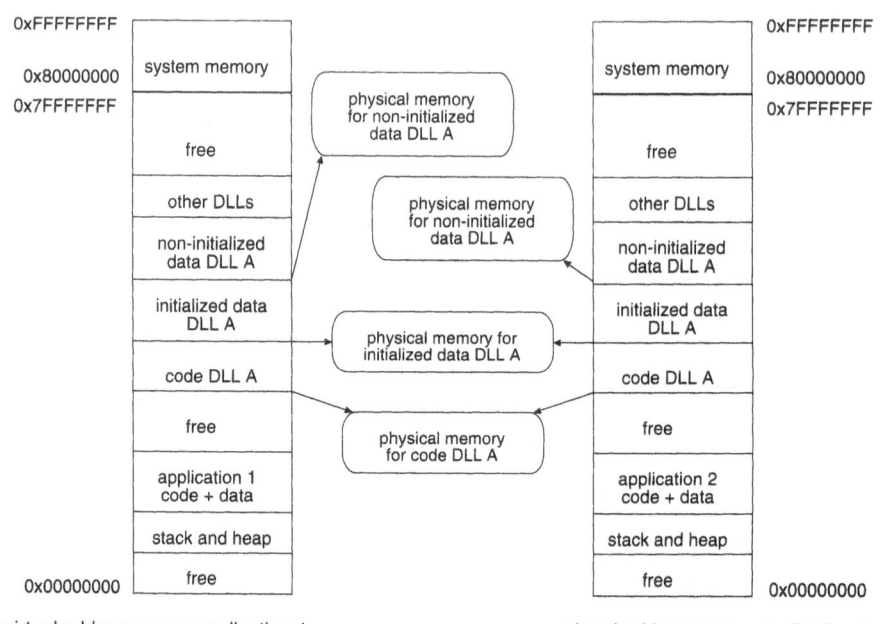

For the creation of DLLs it is therefore crucial that the developer has a clear picture about the usage of the global DLL variables: which variables are needed on a per-process basis and which are to be created only once. Correspondingly, the memory attributes in the DEF files should be defined: only for such data sections that appear in the DEF file explicitly as "shareable" with the second, third, etc., loading of the DLL, no further section in the address space of the concerned process is allocated. Instead, these are mapped (via CPU paging) onto the already existing original section, which became created when the DLL was loaded the first time.

Correctly define the attributes for data sections!

What's more, all dynamic memory requirements within a DLL are *in any case* executed in the address space of the calling process: they are absolutely, positively private (hereby don't forget the fact that under Win32 local and global allocations are intrinsically identical). In sharp contrast to this behavior, global allocations are performed under Win16: through DLL code globally allocated memory is principally available and accessible for *all* clients of the DLL. Admittedly, there the concerned memory areas, as usual, are automatically (!) deallocated if the program that indirectly caused the allocation is terminated. In order to prevent this from happening and to grant the DLL the capability to control the

Dynamic memory allocations

in a DLL

"life time" of global memory allocations itself, for Win16 allocations the flags GMEM_(DDE)SHARE could be used. Memory allocated this way within the DLL is only deallocated if the DLL itself is terminated and removed from memory (or, of course, explicitly through calling Global-Free()). Well, this mechanism isn't exactly portable: indeed both GMEM flags *exist* — but their usage has effectively *not the slightest influence* on the global memory management! The so allocated memory is *not at all* made available for all the running processes, but, as all other blocks, only in the context of the process, in which the allocation (directly or indirectly) actually happened.

GMEM_(DDE)SHARE is useless under Win32!

Moreover: since the Win32 memory management makes no genuine distinction betweeen local and global heaps, all local allocations are mapped into the address space of the corresponding process. The well-known Win16 capability to allow the DLL a separate local heap for small private memory needs doesn't exist under Win32 at all. Allocations in the local heap of a Win16 DLL definitely need a thorough renovation for Win32 if they especially serve the exchanging of information between several client programs. (The omission of local heaps (in the Win16 sense) in Win32 DLLs seems obvious, because these were always coupled to a data segment in Win16: either to that of a program or to that of the DLL. And since neither DLLs nor processes nowadays possess a separate data segment anymore, but live in an isolated address space, data sections are in the default case non-shareable.)

No local DLL heap!

Hence: use Win32 mechanisms for data communication such as memory mapped files.

In brief: apart from the capability to define certain data sections within the DEF file as "shareable," a DLL can create common memory areas only with the aid of the Win32 mechanisms provided for that very purpose, exactly like the process loading it. If you have to allocate public global information for the users of your DLL dynamically, you can't avoid the corresponding adaptations. Hence, the already mentioned example programs presented in the next chapter should be utilized for the investigation of the strange virtues of Win32 DLL memory management!

Initialization and termination

So far for DLLs an initialization function (named LibMain()) was necessary. And if required, another function (called WEP()) for cleaning up things could be thrown in, too. Thereby LibMain() was included in an

LibMain() and WEP()

assembler file (with the name LIBENTRY.ASM) and defined there as an
external function; the resulting OBJ file had to be included when linking
the DLL. Under Win32 for these purposes only a single (optional) function exists, which can even be arbitrarily named (what an unfamiliar
luxury!). This function has the following prototype:

```
BOOL WINAPI DLLInitAndExitProc(HINSTANCE hDLL,
    DWORD dwReason,LPVOID lpReserved);
```

The DLL instance handle The first argument gives the instance handle of the DLL, already known
from Win16 in similar form. (By the way: instance handles under Win32
are just simple offsets into the virtual address space of the process, which
state the memory area where the instance-specific data are administered.
Against it under Win16 the numerical value of the data segment of the
program or DLL was used instead. So instance handles under Win16
were unique, but they're normally *not* under Win32!) The second argument (called dwReason) gives the reason for calling the function.
WINNT.H predefines four constants for this:

Table 4.8: Constants for DLL initialization and termination

DLL_PROCESS_ATTACH	A process using the DLL was started (put differently: the DDL was at-tached to a process — hence the name).
DLL_PROCESS_DETACH	A process using the DLL was termi-nated (or the DLL was detached).
DLL_THREAD_ATTACH	A process using the DLL created an-other thread.
DLL_THREAD_DETACH	A process using the DLL terminated a thread.

Process and thread initiali-zation The first two cases cover the functionality so far available through the
two separate functions LibMain() and WEP(). New, but actually not very
astonishing, is the fact that single threads can also be (de)registered in all
DLLs attached to the corresponding process. Nevertheless, for porting
Win16 programs the two last cases are not important, because ported
applications are by definition still single-threaded. The last argument of
the initialization function, a pointer named lpReserved, is normally
NULL and finds at present no usage. (Actually it seems to be zero if the
DLL was explicitly loaded via LoadLibrary(), and nonzero if it was im-

plicitly loaded at program start). If you have to design DLLs in parallel
for Win16 and Win32, the following shell for the DLL initialization and
termination seems to be the most sensible approach under Win32:

```
#if defined(Win32)                                                    A simple shell for Win32
BOOL WINAPI LibMain32(HINSTANCE hDLL,DWORD dwReason,
  LPVOID lpReserved) // Name can be changed at will
{
  if (dwReason==DLL_PROCESS_ATTACH) { // Initialization
    ... // If necessary, here special Win32 initializations
    return (BOOL)LibMain(hDLL,0,0,NULL); // and here
        // all initializations common to Win16 and Win32
  }
  else if (dwReason==DLL_PROCESS_DETACH) { // Termination
    ... // If necessary, here special Win32 terminations
    return (BOOL)WEP(WEP_FREE_DLL); // and here
        // terminations common to Win16 and Win32
  }
  return TRUE;
}
#endif
```

Observe that the usual unlocking of the DLL data segment* should only   *through UnlockData()
be performed in the Win16 LibMain() function if the corresponding ar-
gument is != 0. Other than that, in the common LibMain() function to a
large extent the necessary initializations for both systems can be carried
out. By the way, the assembler file LIBENTRY.ASM unfortunately necessary under Win16 (or more precise: the generated OBJ file) was finally
removed under Win32: when linking the DLL you just have to inform
the linker with the option -ENTRY about the name of the initialization
function. More about this and the further minutiae of Win32 DLL creation follows in the next chapter.

Global windows classes

One of the typical initializations within LibMain() was the registration of   *Registration of global window
global window classes. As long as these classes were registered applica-   classes
tion global (through including the class flag CS_GLOBALCLASS) not

much changes: the until now used RegisterClass() call can be adopted unaltered. A small problem results possibly with loading the DLL: if the program doesn't directly call functions in the DLL, but only uses the global classes registered within the DLL via CreateWindow(), the DLL is not at all loaded into the memory (this was, by the way, already the case with Win16). Therefore, such DLLs must be loaded explicitly via Load-

Explicit loading through LoadLibrary()

Library(). Under Win16, this can be accomplished through a small loader, called once at system start-up, which loads the DLL and then stays in a message loop (e.g., Borland delivers such a simple loader for its BWCC.DLL). This neat trick of course doesn't work as expected with Win32. Here each and every process must explicitly load all needed DLLs itself (you remember: there are, apart from the system libraries, no globally known DLLs anymore!). Another possibility, mentioned in the

Mark as pseudo-system DLLs.

Win32 documentation indeed only in passing, is flagging the concerned DLL as a (pseudo-)system DLL. Unfortunately, such flagged DLLs will be mapped into the address space of *each* process loaded afterwards, regardless of whether the DLL is actually used. In order to achieve this, the following entry in the Win32-Registry must be modified via REGEDT32, the 32-bit equivalent of REGEDIT (attention: this is one logical line):

```
HKEY_LOCAL_MACHINE\Software\Microsoft\WindowsNT\
        CurrentVersion\Windows\AppInit_DLLs
```

Here the filename of the concerned DLL is either specified or simply

Better: explicitly load at program start-up.

added to the existing list. In my understanding, you should only use this method if it is definitely necessary. In the normal case it seems much better to explicitly load the needed DLLs at program start-up.

The circumstances are set differently for such classes that until now were registered application local in a DLL (i.e., without the

Modified: the registration of application local classes.

CS_GLOBALCLASS flag). Indeed, the registration itself takes place as expected, but the application cannot at all create a single window of the newly registered class! The reason for this strange behavior is the instance handle used for registering the class and the generation of the window, respectively. The two following code excerpts, the first from the initialization phase of the DLL, the second from the main program of the application, show the typical use of both functions:

```
// in the DLL, LibMain for registering the class
WNDCLASS WC;
wc.style=CS_HREDRAW|CS_VREDRAW; // application local!
... // Further WNDCLASS members are initialized
wc.hInstance=hInstDLL; // DLL instance handle!
... // Remaining WNDCLASS members are initialized
if (!RegisterClass(&wc)) ... // Registration succeeds

// And afterwards, in the main program:
hwndTestClass=CreateWindow(..., // various arguments
   hInstance, // next-to-last argument: the instance handle
            // of the application!
   NULL);
```

As you certainly have gathered with precision by now, the problem must *DLL instance contra application instance* have to do with the different usage of instance handles. For the registration the one of the DLL is used (something else the DLL has not at all available in its init routine), while the program of course employs its own HINSTANCE. And there you have it: with a "regular"* registered *so without CS_GLOBALCLASS* class Win32 makes sure that only those CreateWindow() calls lead to the generation of a window of the indicated class, when the "creation HINSTANCE" corresponds to the "registration HINSTANCE." Ergo: the above attempt of window creation fails. The approach to this question is fortunately relatively simple: just register the classes in a DLL actually defined only application local with the additional flag CS_GLOBAL-CLASS, et voilà! The only activity this flag causes under Win32 is namely the suppression of the check for equality of the two HINSTANCEs. Under *No global classes!* no circumstances are the so registered classes automatically known systemwide after this pseudo-global registration or available in other programs. As said: only those applications that load the concerned DLLs implicitly (through load-time linking) or explicitly (with the aid of run-time linking) can use the (global or local) classes registered in the DLL for window creation. (If you absolutely don't want to register certain classes with CS_GLOBALCLASS, instead of the HINSTANCE of the program you can use the HINSTANCE of the DLL in which the class was registered. This handle is easily obtained either as the return value of LoadLibrary() or through a call to GetModuleHandle().)

4.10 Unicode: Plus and Minus

"Be embraced, millions! This kiss to the whole world!" Friedrich Schiller, Ode to Joy

NT kernel and Win32 sub-system work with Unicode

Well, the trend towards internationalization, already recognizable with Windows 3.1, will perhaps achieve its breakthrough with Windows NT. After all, Windows NT is the first operating system available on a large scale which has been developed from the beginning with a comprehensive, worldwide character set in mind. Yes, you've read right: the NT kernel and also the Win32 subsystem don't work internally with ANSI, ASCII, ISO, OEM (or whatever other character sets may exist) anymore, but with an all-new standard called Unicode (that, I sincerely hope, has been defined in such a way that we're finally through with this eternal back and forth with the character sets). Alas, Windows 95 is not yet on the Unicode track (but in the long run I assume that almost all 32-bit systems will have support for it). For this reason the following discussion is of direct and practical importance only for NT developers.

No code pages anymore!

This character set theoretically includes 65,536 symbols and, besides all West-European characters such as umlauts, the common Greek, Cyrillic, Japanese, and Chinese (or whatever languages may exist) characters are also available. Thus, with appropriately implemented applications, the annoying switching to and fro of codepages finally becomes superfluous; nevertheless Win32 still supports (not the least because of compatibility) the corresponding conversions. As already said, internally Windows NT works *only* with Unicode; the mapping of ANSI or ASCII applications happens automatically. The fact that existing Win16 programs (which don't know anything at all about Unicode) have to run under Win32 without any modifications justifies the existence of a layer that absolutely transparently converts ANSI calls to the internally used Unicode. Figure 4.23 on the next page illustrates the binding of the various types of applications to the operating system. Unfortunately, I cannot describe the exact Unicode definition or the allocation of the various alphabets to the character range in detail; interested readers should consult [Ref. 12]. Instead, I'd like to examine the consequences this decisive change has for the Windows developer and how much an adaptation of your application is needed or is desirable.

The mapping of ANSI or ASCII applications happens automatically.

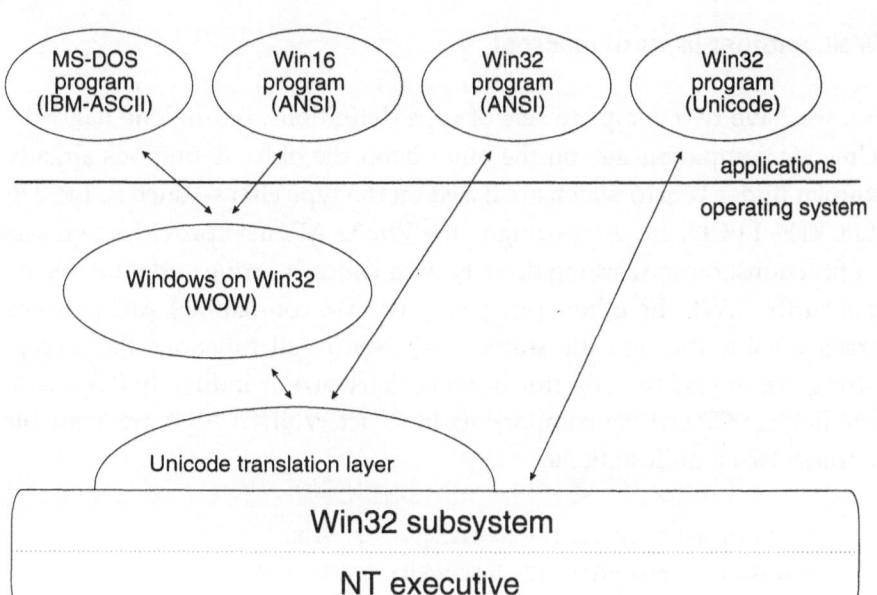

Exactly 16 bit == 2 bytes* are needed to represent 65,536 characters. Let's
put it another way: the equivalence between char (the C data type) and a
single character disappears with Unicode. That's why Win32 works with
a newly defined type called WCHAR (whose "Hungarian" type abbreviation is wc):

What a nice coincidence!

```
typedef unsigned short WCHAR; // wc, 16-bit UNICODE char
```

*Unicode character ==
WCHAR*

All other types that are based on char under Win16 (LPSTR and company) are also accordingly redefined:

```
typedef WCHAR *PWCHAR; // Pointer to a Unicode char
typedef CONST WCHAR *LPCWCH, *PCWCH; // Ditto, but constant
typedef WCHAR *LPWSTR, *PWSTR; // Pointer to a Unicode string
typedef CONST WCHAR *LPCWSTR, *PCWSTR; // Ditto, constant
..// etc.
```

Redefined string types

301

Well, another layer of macros!

Two groups of data types...

So, we have two complete sets of type definitions: on the one hand the Unicode compatible set; on the other hand the older definitions already known under Win16 which are based on the type char — such as LPSTR, LPCSTR, LPCH, etc. Accordingly, the Win32 API also provides two sets of functions: those working directly with Unicode strings (identifiable by the suffix ...W), the others processing (Win16 compatible) ANSI strings (recognizable through the suffix ...A). Nearly all functions that accept string arguments directly (for instance, lstrlen()) or indirectly (for example RegisterClass() via components in struct WNDCLASS) are available in these two manifestations:

... and two sets of functions

```
int WINAPI lstrlenA(LPCSTR lpString);   // ANSI
int WINAPI lstrlenW(LPCWSTR lpString);  // Unicode
...
ATOM WINAPI RegisterClassA(CONST WNDCLASSA *lpWndClass);
ATOM WINAPI RegisterClassW(CONST WNDCLASSW *lpWndClass);
... // etc.
```

The structures WNDCLASSA (or WNDCLASSW) again contain the ANSI (or Unicode, respectively) string data types. Presumably, the ...A versions don't do much more than converting all string parameters to Unicode and then calling the Unicode function (this means the corresponding ...W variant). Thus the function lstrlenA() could be implemented as follows (just to show the principle, the code for example ignores DBCS sequences):

Convert strings and call Unicode function

```
int WINAPI lstrlenA(LPCSTR lpString)
{
  // 1. Prologue:
  int cb=strlen(lpString);  // length of the ANSI-String
  // allocate buffer for Unicode string
  LPWSTR lpwstrBuf=malloc(sizeof(WCHAR)*(cb+1));
  // convert string to Unicode
  MultiByteToWideChar(CP_ACP,MP_PRECOMPOSED,lpString,
    1,lpwstrBuf,cb);
  // 2. Actual processing:
  cb=lstrlenW(lpwstrBuf); // and process with help of the
```

```
// correct Unicode function
// 3. Epilogue:
free(lpwstrBuf);
return cb;
} // I hope that Microsoft wrote the function a bit more
// efficiently, since in this (simple) case the buffer
// allocation and the following conversion are overkill.
```

But this whole Unicode story smells like much conversion work to me. That's what they also thought at Microsoft and that's why they quickly invented another #defined constant called UNICODE, which from now on determines in a transparent (and, above all, rather portable) way for which character set a program is to be compiled. This is done by freely using conditional compilation and by defining many, many macros.* First, various NT data types are defined dependent from this constant in such a way that they can be used equally in Unicode and ANSI programs, as is shown in the following extract from WINNT.H:

#define UNICODE

* What else!

```
// Neutral ANSI/UNICODE types and macros
#ifdef UNICODE    // Aha, UNICODE is your desire ...
    typedef WCHAR TCHAR, *PTCHAR;
    typedef LPWSTR LPTCH, PTCH;
    typedef LPWSTR PTSTR, LPTSTR;
    // etc.
#else    // No, the good old ANSI-character set
    typedef char TCHAR, *PTCHAR;
    typedef LPSTR LPTCH, PTCH;
    typedef LPSTR PTSTR, LPTSTR;
    // etc.
#endif
```

Unicode:
TCHAR == WCHAR,
so sizeof(TCHAR) == 2!

ANSI:
TCHAR == char,
so sizeof(TCHAR) == 1!

Second, of course all relevant functions and data types are provided with the suffix ...W, respectively ...A; but a further (macro) definition cares for the availability of a function name (or typedef, respectively) which is portable and suitable for the desired environment:

Plus a layer of macros for the functions

```
#ifdef UNICODE
    typedef WNDCLASSW WNDCLASS;
    #define RegisterClass RegisterClassW
```

```
#else
    typedef WNDCLASSA WNDCLASS;
    #define RegisterClass RegisterClassA
#endif
```

Result: backward compatible in spite of a new character set.

Tricky, tricky! The net result of all this tinkering around with the header files is that an existing program *not* #defining UNICODE can use neither the 16-bit character set nor the ...W types and function adaptations. This is good news for developers wanting to port their programs: although Windows NT is working internally with a totally different concept to manipulate character sets, existing programs can be taken over one to one (in this respect). And programs using Unicode can be written nearly just as easily through simply #defining UNICODE before #including the Windows header files.

The C compiler and Unicode strings

Then why all those long-winded explanations if essentially nothing changes on the surface? Good question, which I will answer in three parts. First and foremost, unfortunately, the switch to Unicode in existing programs cannot be carried out without modifications in a 100 percent transparent way in all cases; see the next paragraph for more information. Second, all string resources (not only the ones of type STRING but also character strings in dialog boxes, etc.) are stored without any

* means in memory as well as in the EXE file

exception* in Unicode format. This shouldn't be of any interest as long as you keep manipulating them with the Win32 functions for resource processing or with the SDK programs available for that. But if you plan to load (textual) resources into memory and have to perform some modifications of your own, you'll definitely have to take the Unicode format into account. The same is also valid for the dynamic generation of resources (such as, for instance, dialog boxes with the help of the structures DLGTEMPLATE and DLGITEMTEMPLATE). Finally, the consequences of defining a macro layer for the concerned functions is that you don't see the function's name you have used — e.g., in compiler messages or while debugging. And as you certainly like to know exactly what happens in your programs, the explanations above seem important to me, even if you're not that interested in using Unicode.

The possible modifications mentioned above, which have to be carried
out in spite of the portable type definitions and the macro layer, refer
mainly to the use of literal string constants in the program text. The 32-
bit C compiler doesn't work with Unicode characters as the default (since
#define UNICODE only changes the interpretation of the *header files* but
not the compiler!) but with just the normal char of one-byte length in the
(extended) ASCII character set:

```
#define UNICODE
...
// The following string will be stored, independently of the
// constant UNICODE, in the ANSI character set. Hence, it
// occupies 29 bytes (including the terminating 0). The
// resulting (UNICODE-) window text looks surely very
// interesting, but has nothing to do at all with the
// desired window title!
SetWindowText(hwnd,"Everything for your windows!");
// Through the macro layer, the Unicode function
// SetWindowTextW() is called. And this call expects
// a UNICODE string...
```

In spite of Unicode ...

*... the compiler produces an
ANSI-String.*

So far — so bad. But there *must* be a possibility to teach the compiler that
the following string has to be stored in Unicode format. And you'll find it
after exhaustively searching through various manuals. So the above
statement should be written like the following in order to compile correctly for Unicode:

```
SetWindowText(hwnd,L"Everything for your windows!");
```

A simple capital "L" in front of the string, that's it. Now the compiler
knows that it has to store the string in Unicode format (that is to say, as
16-bit character). However, this shouldn't yet satisfy us completely: what
happens with the string if the program line with #define UNICODE gets
deleted or commented out? Nothing! It still is stored as Unicode in the
memory and again ensures that the window text doesn't look the way
you'd expect. Dear macro, I can hear you mumbling.... In fact, you can
solve this problem with the following simple macro:

```
#ifdef UNICODE // also in WINNT.H
  #define TEXT(quote) L##quote
#else
  #define TEXT(quote) quote
#endif
```

Well, all good things come thrice, and thus, the third possibility to compose the window text is finally the wanted one:

```
SetWindowText(hwnd,TEXT("Everything for your windows!"));
```

So, before you compile your program in Unicode mode, check and, if need be, modify the use of string constants and of single characters (see page 256 for an example). The wording "check and, *if need be,* modify" gives ground for pondering that not all character strings are affected by *Strings that have to remain in* this modification: to make the confusion even bigger, some strings *in* *the ANSI format* *principle* must remain in ANSI format. This applies to calls to OpenFile(), _lopen(), _lcreate(), and some other functions. A look at the prototypes throws some light on the matter: if you have an LPSTR (or LPCSTR, respectively) there, the function will *only* accept ANSI strings. On the other hand, LPTSTR (or LPWSTR, of course) means Unicode support. There is another function that you *definitely* use as a Windows developer and that, independently from #define UNICODE, will get the string argument *only* *And WinMain()!* in ANSI format: WinMain()! The parameter lpCmdLine of type LPSTR always points to the ANSI version of the command line and *not* to the Unicode version. Thus, in case you ever write a Unicode compatible program and have to access the command line, you'll first have to convert it accordingly (for example, via MultiByteToWideChar()). Alternatively, you could also call the Win32 function GetCommandLine(), because this one is Unicode sensitive.

One character equals one byte?

You can expect further difficulties during your conversion to Unicode at all places where you *implicitly* assume in your program text that a char-*sizeof(TCHAR) == 1?* acter occupies exactly one byte — or put in another way: show me a single person using sizeof(char) to get the length of a character!? Code like the following is hence not Unicode compatible:

```
#define UNICODE
...
int cb=lstrlen(lpStr)+1; // lstrlen() becomes lstrlenW()
HGLOBAL hCopy=GlobalAlloc(GMEM_FIXED,cb); // Oh my God,
LPSTR lpCopyStr=GlobalLock(hCopy);
lstrcpy(lpCopyStr,LPSTR); // ... how dreadful!
```

I found hundreds of such or equivalent places in my programs. Consequently, I had to write some macros for this particular case in order to allocate and handle the strings and then adapted my sources accordingly. For example:

```
#define GlobalAllocStr(flags,cb) GlobalAlloc(flags,\
    cb*sizeof(TCHAR)); // sizeof(TCHAR) either 1 or 2!
```

So, while converting to Unicode, pay special attention to memory allocations for strings, to the use of the various functions that return the length of strings (also implicit ones like wsprintf(), for example, or messages like WM_GETTEXTLENGTH) as well as to the use of sizeof(char) or sizeof(CHAR). In order to ensure Unicode compatibility, you should use only sizeof(TCHAR)!

Check the memory allocations for strings.

Let's draw some interim conclusions: you can continue to use existing program text without changes as long as they're not compiled in Unicode mode (unless some Unicode resources have been manipulated in the memory as shown above). If you want to switch to Unicode, proceed step by step as follows:

- First, your program should run errorfree in the ANSI mode as a Win32 application (so port first, switch to UNICODE afterwards!).
- Where appropriate, you should proceed to the adaptations necessary for Unicode. This is quite simple:
- Adapt all string constants in the source codes and elsewhere that assume that sizeof(TCHAR) == 1.
- Define the constant UNICODE.
- Completely recompile your program.

Step-by-step action

Presumably, the resulting EXE file will not be errorfree straight off, but from my experience I can assure you that the remaining errors are rela-

Unicode support with little effort

tively quick to be found. The overall consequence is that you can add Unicode support to your program without too much effort.

Unicode: Yes or No?

Well, this brings us to the main issue of this section: should you support Unicode or not? After all, ANSI programs run perfectly transparently under Win32, have the advantage that they don't necessitate too much conversion effort, and furthermore can be used under Windows 95 (or Windows 3.1 via Win32s*). Particularly the last point doesn't apply to real Unicode programs: you can't operate them under Windows 95! At least in its first release there won't be any Unicode support — this means that NT Unicode applications won't run under Windows 95 at all.

* Provided that the other prevailing conditions for Win32s applications are considered...

That's why I think that in the medium term Unicode will only come into consideration for such applications that definitely run under Windows NT only *and* really need the extended character set. For this, the following three conditions must be true: first, the program's type must be of the sort to be used in markets with different languages. It may be exotic to have an Icelandic accounting program work with the Korean Unicode character set, but it doesn't make much sense. The other way around, you'll find it difficult to use text-processing software with only western characters in Russia or in Arab countries, although there is principally nothing to say against it. So, it depends primarily on the market you want to serve. An adaptation will make sense only if the market accepts *real* NT applications and requires (or awaits at least) simultaneous Unicode support.

Three requirements for Unicode

In case your program *is* qualified to be used in other parts of the world, the second requirement is that you (or a joint company working with you) have some adequate plans for its commercial exploitation there. The adaptation to other markets causes much effort and if it is not foreseeable that this work will pay off very soon, then you should postpone the Unicode enhancement for a while. This consideration applies rather to existing programs, since the conversion work for them is much higher than for programs where you have been working consistently with Unicode from the beginning.

The sort of program must be the right one.

The commercial exploitation must be clarified.

Let's come to the third condition: your Unicode modifications will only be sensible if you have also taken the other existing national premises (like data format, currency, etc.) into account while designing and implementing your program. The effort to make such a program Unicode compatible are relatively small, as shown above. But in general, you'll need quite some work to teach an until now NLS-*ignorant application how to support really efficiently all those national and cultural features; this effort is not to be compared to the simple conversion to Unicode. Put differently: NLS is much more than just Unicode! But Unicode without NLS doesn't make sense....

Other cultural peculiarities must be taken into account.

* NLS = National Language Support

Conclusion: Unicode indeed is a nice thing to have, but in most cases, its employment has some time to wait!

4.11 Some Guidelines for Binary Compatible Win16 Applications

"Quousque tandem...? (Still how long...?)" Cicero, Catilinariae Orationes

... will Windows 3.x keep its role as an important platform? Presumably a bit longer than we all would like! That's why it seems important to take a look at the modifications needed to make your Win16 applications binary compatible to Windows 95, respectively NT.** Don't misunderstand me: here we are speaking about completely normal Windows 3.x applications that know and use the Win16 API only. So, in the following, we'll deal exclusively with the things a Win16 application should consider in order to work properly under Windows 95 or NT's WOW layer (Windows on Win32). Fortunately, the list is not very long; furthermore, most of the following hints are important anyway for the future portability of the program.

** Well, both systems possess a layer supporting Win16 applications.

• If your program either runs in the Windows 3.0 real mode only or even is a 2.x fossil, the very first thing to do is to make sure that it will run without problems in the standard and enhanced modes of Windows 3.1. You must definitely perform the corresponding adaptations since Win32 (officially) doesn't support real mode programs anymore. Actually, most older programs will run more or less normally; however, I've never seen a 2.x program getting its bitmaps halfway reasonably to the NT screen. Thus, besides the

Executable in 3.1 standard and enhanced modes

fact that you (and the enduser!) will get quite a tormenting message box each time you'll start the program, indicating that you are working with an ancient version (see figure 4.24 on the following page), there are good reasons to make these adaptations.

If at all possible, don't use undocumented functions!

- Limit the use of undocumentated features to the absolute minimum necessary. Many unofficially documented internals are admittedly available in exactly the same fashion under WOW as under Win16, but there is unquestionably quite an important amount of unsupported "old" features. So, be particularly careful when testing all those program parts using undocumented Win16 functions under Win32!

Access to INI files

- The method already described in section 4.6 on page 258 to access INI files directly (that means without using Win16 profile functions but with self-defined file operations) should be avoided for binary compatible programs too. You may indeed continue to create and process *private* INI files, but at least the INI system files (WIN.INI, SYSTEM.INI etc.) won't be available in this form anymore and will be mapped silently to the Win32 register. Take a look at the section mentioned for more information.

Group files for the program manager

- The following hint presses home the argument: some Windows 3.1 programs copy a group file (XYZ.GRP) for use with the program manager during the installation. Win32 saves this information on a per-user basis, so you will surely fail when adding a new PM group in that way. Win32 compatible applications should rather use the documented PM DDE interface instead [Ref. 1, see volume 1, chapter 17].

Stack and heap sizes in the DEF file

- Under Windows 3.x, the stack and heap sizes of the application are given in the DEF file. If you plan to support your program under Win32, you shouldn't be too economical about the assigned memory in the case of stack size. Even if the program runs absolutely errorfree under Win16 because the stack is accidentally big enough (or because STACKSIZE has been optimized appropriately in the DEF file respectively), the same program could easily malfunction under Win32 because of a stack failure (since each single component of the WOW layer needs a bigger stack as the original Win16 DLLs do). To ensure WOW compatibility, you should increase your stack size by 2 KB compared to the actual minimum needed for Win16.

- Direct hardware manipulations will be detected under Windows NT, and the program concerned will be closed abruptly. For instance, this statement is valid for all I/O port access going beyond the commonly known standards (for example, 0x03F8 for COM1:). You'll have the same problem with programs (or DLLs) serving not only the standard equipment available (COMx, LPTx, etc.) but implementing the interfaces to additional devices. This especially means all non-default device drivers installed later and which, as far as I know, simply *can't* be written in a binary compatible way.

Hardware manipulations

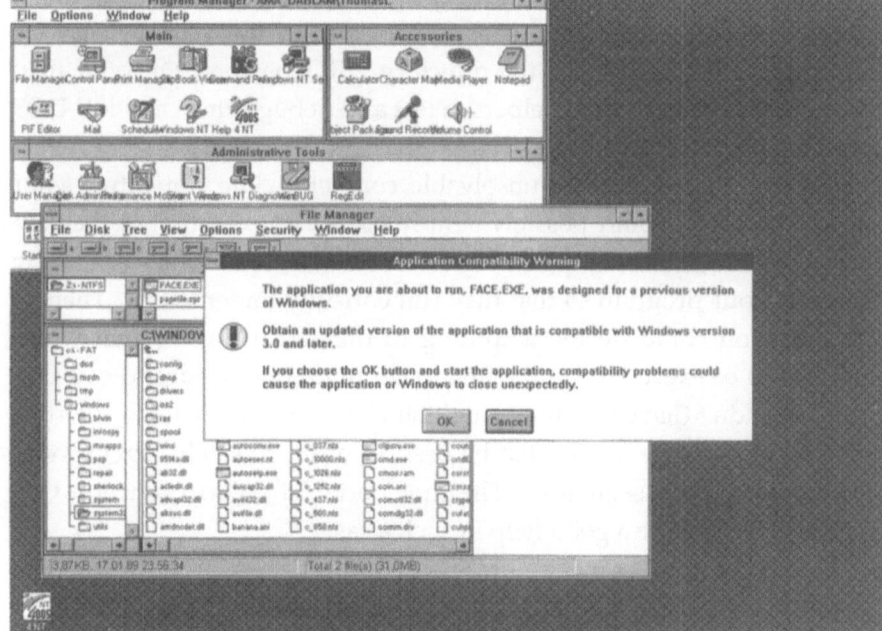

Figure 4.24: Too old: the Win32 message box for old 2.x programs.

- Even the access to standard PC hardware can become a problem: direct manipulations of the controllers, direct access to the screen, or to make it short, all modifications made to components important for the integrity of the whole system will have a similar effect: the program is simply halted. Admittedly, Windows 95 will be much less strict in this respect than Windows NT. However, are you sure that your program won't be run under NT? (In case you *know* that your program will misbehave under Windows NT, test the actual platform and refuse to run under NT. There is more on that later on.)

Neither manipulations at the disk controller nor direct accesses to the screen

Don't modify information that
is security relevant!

- The same is true for other security-relevant information such as the system date and time. Any modifications of such system wide data shouldn't be done through a Win16 program.

Taken all together, the work to render a Win16 application Win32 compatible is generally small; you should well be able to make the necessary modifications within a few days (well, as long as you don't have device drivers and the like waiting for you...). The be-all and end-all of the exercise is to ensure with the help of various test sessions that your program runs correctly under Win16 *and* all Win32 platforms you are planning to support. Here, I'd particularly like to refer you to the SCT tools* from Microsoft, which have been enclosed with the Win32 SDKs for more than a year now (see the directory \SCT on the CD). With that, Microsoft provides a set of helpers to test and debug Win16 and MS-DOS programs under Win32.

* SCT = Software Compatibility Test

In case you encounter unsolvable conflicts while converting your source code, you could possibly simply block the execution of the concerned parts of your application under Win32 or implement certain places in your program so that they run correctly under WOW. Then, at run-time you could decide according to the actual host system which code has to be executed. I'm the first to admit that in the ideal case a program shouldn't (have to) know anything about its host system; nevertheless this knowledge must often be used in order to safely "circumvent" incompatible code sequences. The (not portable!) Win16 function Get-WinFlags() might be a good help in such a case:

*Run-time check for the host
system*

```
#define WF_WIN32WOW 0x00004000  // (not yet) defined in the
                                // SDK header files!!!

...
#ifndef WIN32 // sic!
  if (GetWinFlags()&WF_WIN32WOW)
  // Ah, we are under Win32: here's the nice, new 32-bit
  // compatible Win16 code...
  else
  // Nope, good old Windows 3.X: terrible, ugly
  // Win16 code
#endif
```

If you have problems with the code fragment above, because there are two tests on Win32 (one for the conditional compilation to make sure that the code *doesn't* get compiled for Win32; the other in the code): consider that the same source code will have to run under (at least) three different platforms: as a Win16 program under Win16 (the conditional compilation will help here to avoid differences with Win32); second, as a Win16 program under Windows95 or WOW (as already shown, here only the *dynamic* mode identification can help); and finally as a real Win32 program, where differences from the Win16 API can be avoided by conditional compilation (and I haven't considered Win32s yet!). It may comfort you to know that I also needed quite some time to sort and unravel the knots in my brain.... Figure 4.25 shows the possible system variants (I can take *no* liability for a *complete* representation, since Microsoft is certainly hatching something new at this very moment).

Platform chaos or "Babylon à la Gates"

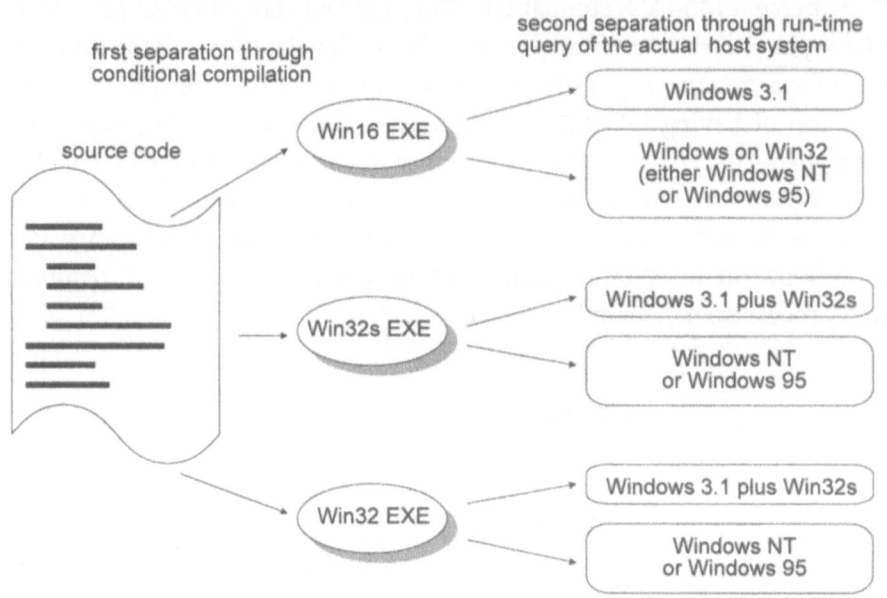

Figure 4.25: Lots of enemies, much honor: the Windows platforms.

4.12 A Study Trip: From MS-DOS to Win32

*"The operating system [of the IBM PC] was MS-DOS 1.0; primitive, compared
to today's MS-DOS standards..." Murray Sargent III and Richard L. Shoe-
maker*, The IBM PC from the Inside Out

* dated 1986
It seems that this quotation* manifests a rather effusive and optimistic
assessment concerning the qualities of the later MS-DOS versions. Compared to what can be expected from an operating system really deserv-
ing this classification, indeed *all* (existing) MS-DOS versions** have to be
called "primitive." Admittedly, one main reason for the continuous success of the simple DOS is the necessity of being downwards compatible.
A much better system (from a technical point of view) than MS-DOS had
already been implemented in 1986; but to be really successful, such a
product should have been, besides sporting enhanced features, at least
99.99 percent MS-DOS compatible. Well, the DOS box of OS/2 1.x was a
nice try, but certainly nothing more (which was not so much the fault of
the programmers responsible but much more due to the questionable
decision of having OS/2.1.x implemented on an 80286). Anyway, *only*
nine years later, we even have the agony of choosing: OS/2 Warp or the
Win32 platforms on the one hand have really functional MS-DOS support; on the other hand, both have all the enhancements necessary for
more performant 32-bit applications (especially in the areas of memory
and process management).

** including the "Special
Tools Editions no. 6.x"

Today: the agony of choosing.

DOS antiques under Win32

Even MS-DOS programs that have been implemented quite close to the
hardware can run under Windows NT in the MS-DOS subsystem. Admittedly, there *are* also some restrictions — you can use the preceding
paragraph concerning the Win16 binary compatibility as a rough guide;
of course you should consider MS-DOS internals instead of undocumented Windows features etc. More interesting for most DOS developers is the question of whether they can port their applications and the
corresponding efforts. Without losing too much time in the technical
details (after all, this is a book for Windows developers!), I'd like to make
some basic remarks concerning porting of DOS programs to Win32.

In the MS-DOS subsystem
museum

Porting DOS applications?

First of all, a Win32 program is by no means limited to the graphical user interface, so it can run not only as a GUI application. Unlike Win16, besides the windowing API the operating system provides another interface completely based on text mode and named "console functions." With appropriate calls, the output of characters, strings, and screen attributes as well as the input of keyboard and mouse actions are possible. This interface between system and application is not at all message based; instead, similar to DOS, the application has to query input explicitly. The "screen" can be displayed either in a full screen (text) mode or graphically as a completely standard pseudo-window. The latter capability and the distribution of input messages in a text-mode compatible way are carried out transparently by the MS-DOS and Win32 subsystems, so that programs using the console functions don't receive any notice from HWNDs, WM_PAINTs, and message loops.

Text mode and "console functions"

Text mode and Win32

The underlying model is obviously oriented towards the VIO functions of OS/2 — this is not very surprising when you remember that Windows NT was once called OS/2 3.0. A little program example that does nothing more than print a string on two places of the screen and wait for a keystroke will give you a first impression of the console functions:

Of course, any similarities with VIO functions of OS/2 are purely accidental....

```
// Either:
pos.X=10; pos.Y=20;
WriteConsoleOutputCharacter(hScreenOut,
   "Here we go!",11,pos,&dwProcessed);

// or:
pos.X=11; pos.Y=21;
SetConsoleCursorPosition(hScreenOut,pos);
WriteConsole(hScreenOut,"Here we go again!",
   11,&dwProcessed,NULL);
ReadConsole(hScreenIn,ch,1,&dwProcessed,NULL);
```

pos contains the cursor position.

It is relatively simple to adapt the various compiler run-time libraries and additional toolboxes, so we can quickly expect to obtain some speedy Win32 versions of all the important development systems that

DOS compiler run-time and additional tool libraries are easily adjusted.

315

will be at least of equal rank of their MS-DOS predecessors. The more you use such products, the more you'll be able to make the port easily and quickly. It is quite simple to write a layer around the console API which would correspond to your own needs and could also contribute to increasing portability. Let's get to the point: a DOS programmer using Turbo Pascal or Quick C who mastered his system and used the appropriate additional functions (such as GotoXY() or _kbhit()) shouldn't have any special problems when porting, except for the hardware-related issues (provided that he has the corresponding 32-bit compiler, of course!)

Under Win32 kernel and operating system functionality for text-mode programs

Besides, under Win32, a C program cannot use only the new text mode functions but the whole functionality of kernel and file management: so you can expect to see GlobalAlloc() or OpenFile() in a text-mode program! You can use multiple threads and processes, the memory-mapped file I/O or semaphores, clipboard and file I/O — in short and to the point, *everything* that is not *explicitly* related to window management or GDI. This also includes the possibility of using DLLs! And what's more: if cleverly done, a text application can even create windows or, to the contrary, a GUI program can send its text output to a console window!

* Well, compared to MS-DOS!

I am quite sure that the non-GUI interface of Win32, with its really phenomenal new possibilities,* will be followed by many new text-mode applications with some quite unfamiliar features. Even more: all programmers who could no longer manage with DOS and perhaps changed to text-mode OS/2 or UNIX in order to avoid the steep learning curve of a GUI will find here a really usable and expandable system. I would even maintain that Microsoft still underestimates this effect at the time being, paying too much attention to the GUI part and neglecting the use of Win32 as a simple but absolutely adequate text-mode vehicle for many (especially self-written) programs. Of course, the time when advanced word processing or DTP programs could run in text mode is over, but those who must heave matrices with, let's say, 1024 * 1024 elements (for example, in research departments) will not necessarily want to do that with a complicated graphical interface! All in all, I can only hope that the product managers responsible at Microsoft are not blind on the console eye....

Win32 is also a text mode system.

Sorry: no graphics!

Unfortunately, things look a bit more complicated for DOS-based graphic programs. If you don't want to (or can't) convert them to the windowing (or better GDI) interface, you must be prepared to encounter problems. First, it is still not yet clear how far Win32 will support the console functionality: whether it will be possible, for example, to switch to any graphics mode within a text program. Perhaps, similar to the console functions, a graphics library will be provided which could be able to run in its own session as well as under the Windows desktop (up to now, the C/C++ compiler is delivered without such support: no GRAPH-ICS.H!). Possibly, a split of the application into two programs might also be considered: the graphics elements would be handled in a small GUI application, which could communicate with the main program running in text mode (e.g., via DDEML or any other Win32 IPC mechanisms). The fact that Microsoft doesn't give any useful information (not to mention any *definitive* statements) speaks volumes and illustrates the above-mentioned point concerning the (too?) strong preference for the Windows API.

Graphics? GDI!

A small GUI application communicates with the main program in text mode.

Conclusion: after a certain warm-up period, we can certainly expect the same tools, utilities, and libraries for Win32 as were available under DOS in adapted, and above all, more powerful versions. I see more difficulties for the DOS developer who has to learn and digest laboriously all the concepts that over the years Windows developers had to master* (well, sooner or later the future catches up with everyone). And of course, there are so many new features that the poor programmers will be kept busy enough over the next years with studying, adapting, and debugging (this last observation is indeed also valid for Windows specialists).

* And with great efforts!

But, after all this theory, let's finally put the whole stuff into practice: programming under Windows 95 or NT with the help of the Win32 SDK as well as some other important utilities and tools. This is the theme of the final chapter.

Chapter 5

Win32 Development Tools and Their Use

This last chapter (whew!) is centered around the creation of Win32 applications: how to use the SDK tools; which points have been modified and what should you pay special attention to? Thereby the most important SDK components are covered; also the generation of both GUI and text mode programs is described. A detailed trip to the creation of DLLs and the use of shared data sections as well as the dynamic allocation of shared memory areas in DLLs shows you all the necessary changes in this domain. Afterwards I want to give a few remarks about the Win32 C/C++ tools from Borland and the new Visual C++ for Windows NT and 95. Last but not least, improvements for Win32 developers to be expected in the near future conclude the chapter.

Creation of GUI and console applications

DLLs and shared memory

The 32-bit tools from Borland

5.1 The Creation of Win32 GUI Applications

"Take advantage of your experience with Windows 3.x!" From a Microsoft brochure about the Win32 SDK

So, let's just do it: take advantage of our experience with Windows 3.x! Well, if this is as effortless as Microsoft seems to believe, why does the CompuServe forum MSWIN32 (invented especially for Win32 SDK developers) overflow with questions and problems related to the use of 32-bit SDK tools? As a matter of fact, there unfortunately *are* some serious changes in the process of programming for Windows NT (or 95, for that matter). (And apart from that, both the system software and the tools themselves are of course in beta stadium and correspondingly bug-endangered: without any doubt, my favorite here is the graphical debugger WINDBG, being rather buggy itself...)

CompuServe forum MSWIN32 for developers

The following remarks refer to the Win32 SDK for Windows NT from Microsoft if not explicitly stated otherwise. However, in sections 5.4 and 5.5 I also deal with the most important differences between this SDK and the 32-bit development tools from Borland and the current Visual

Base: The Win32 SDK for Windows NT.

C/C++ — so the information contained here can be used with all three systems. I am discussing only those features and options that are special (or necessary) to the creation of Win32 applications. Some useful features, which can get important for developer in certain situations (e.g., the use of precompiled headers), went by the board; in these cases the documentation of the respective manufacturer is probably the best place for further investigation. Another comment concerns the variety of APIs: at present, besides the full Win32 API, there's Win32c and Win32s. It is currently not always clear what features will finally be supported; both "subset" APIs are kind of moving targets.* The Win32 SDK for Windows 95 is heavily oriented towards the NT SDK, because Microsoft certainly won't deal with a third set of tools (Win16, Windows 95, and Win32 NT). Consequently the Chicago tools and the NT tools are very alike or even identical (it seems that they're even planning to release a single SDK for both systems). After all, Windows 95 accepts exactly the same EXE files as they execute under NT — therefore at least in theory the NT tools could be employed for Win95 programs and vice versa. Also, the tools for generation and manipulation of OBJ and EXE files can equally well be used under both systems.

So see the README on the accompanying disk.

But what is with Win32s?

Alas, I'll have to disappoint all of you who hoped that the Win32 tools would execute under Windows 3.1 (or MS-DOS, respectively) through the help of Win32s,. Unfortunately, the most important SDK tools such as the C compiler, the linker, etc., are ordinary Win32 text-mode (console) applications and as such won't run under Win32s (and not at all under MS-DOS**). A few GUI-based SDK tools (such as ZOOMIN.EXE) are indeed able to execute under Win32s, but sadly, *real* 32-bit program development under Win16 is just impossible (by the way, I consider this to be one of the bigger follies of Microsoft.) But as usual, if Microsoft leaves a gap, a tools developer jumps in at once to fill it — in this case the U.S. company Phar Lap, which gives away a utility package named QuickStart. With these tools a MS-DOS developer (owning at least a 386 machine and more than 8 MB RAM) can easily put the Win32 SDK tools under MS-DOS to use and can create an application for Win32s without any further investments. By the way, QuickStart itself is freeware and can be ordered until further notice from the manufacturer.

*** "This program cannot be run in DOS mode."*

The intentions of Phar Lap, however, go much farther: they've implemented a DOS extender that, among other things, makes available the complete Win32 kernel and I/O functionality (e.g., multiple threads) under MS-DOS and thus conveniently enables the execution of Win32 text-mode applications under MS-DOS (this product is cleverly named "TNT" and is *not* free of charge).

QuickStart replaces for the most important SDK tools* the barely helpful standard DOS stub (see above) with the call to a loader, which creates a 32-bit environment convenient for PE files, then reads this into memory and starts it (this is principally just a 386 extender emulating the necessary NT system DLLs). The so loaded software can now be used under MS-DOS just as under Windows NT (with a small limitation, see farther down). So, all remarks about the Microsoft tools are for that reason effective also for all those developers who create Win32s programs with the aid of QuickStart under MS-DOS. (The operation of the tools (i.e., the PE EXE part) is of course not at all changed by the QuickStart stub, so under Win32 they'll work exactly as before.)

e.g., CL.EXE, LINK.EXE, RC.EXE, MASM386.EXE, NMAKE.EXE

Since all switches and options behave exactly as under NT, one can easily compile the example programs contained in the SDK and even use the supplied MAKE files. Indeed, here a small trap opens (of course based on a DOS limitation — what else...): the Win32 NMAKE utility can easily build extremely long command lines (well, extremely long in this case means just more than 128 characters). These are smoothly processed under NT; however, things works out not so well with the aged DOS command processor COMMAND.COM.... The remedy is the temporary generation of a response file, which can be carried out even automatically by NMAKE itself (through the so-called inline files). A detailed example appears later (see page 333) with the discussion of the NMAKE utility and MAKE files.

NT command lines too long for MS-DOS!

Program creation at a glance

Fundamentally the generation of Win32 programs has not changed too much from the usual Win16 process. Illustration 1.14** shown already in the first chapter schematically shows the involved files, their handling, and the generation of the end result: just the executable file. For the most part the tools employed are known from the Win16 world; the differences I'm referring to deal less with completely new tools, but more with

** See section 1.6, page 60.

minutiae of their usage. The developer has to master the following SDK components in order to generate an executable Win32 program from his source codes:

- The C/C++ compiler (called just CL in the current SDK, but CL386 in former versions) in a version adapted to 32-bit circumstances serves for compiling the source code files. Here numerous differences for the compiler switches as well as #pragmas and the use of the non-standardized Microsoft extensions have to be observed. While the latter two can be hidden for the most part either through ingenious macro definitions in the Win32 header files or through small source code changes and conditional compilation (for more on that see sections 3.3, 4.2 and 4.6), the necessary adaptations for the most important switches are discussed in the next section. As usual, the compiler creates OBJ files, whose format has been significantly modified compared to the old Win16 and MS-DOS Intel-based format: they take advantage of a standard format named COFF,* which is well-known from the UNIX world.

- The usage of the resource compiler RC, which is available in a completely Unicode compatible 32-bit version, has hardly changed; both the source code (RC files) and also the switches for the compilation are nearly unaltered. Nevertheless, serious changes can be noted for the output format, the RES files. You have to convert these in a second, Win32-specific step into RBJ files with the aid of a new program called CVTRES (the extension RBJ is probably a mixture of RES and OBJ). Behind these RBJ files are concealed nothing other than all ordinary Win32 OBJ files, which contain the resources as initialized data sections. (In newer SDK versions this conversion is taken over by the linker.)

- Finally, the linker is used in the last step to construct the program from the various OBJs and RBJs as well as all kinds of LIB files. As under Win16, these LIBs can be either genuine code libraries, consisting of one or several OBJ files, or import libraries for separately linked dynamic link libraries. The generation of DLLs and the corresponding LIB files will be dealt with in section 5.3.

- Well, a certain familiarity with the Win32 debugger (see figure 5.1 on the next page) definitely can't do any harm. This product is even (what a giant move forward!) completely integrated into the graphical interface.** Strictly speaking, the debugger is not necessary for the creation of programs, therefore I'll only discuss its features in passing. The compiler and linker switches required for the generation and inclusion of debugging information will be detailed with the respective components.

- In a strict sense, the MAKE utility NMAKE is also not a necessary component for building Win32 programs. Nevertheless, it eases the handling even of small projects so greatly that a mention seems in order. NMAKE itself has experienced no important changes; however, to enable you to create a Win32 program with at least partly compatible MAKE files under both Intel- and RISC-based machines, I'll briefly discuss the default include file for NMAKE usage included in the Win32 SDK (called WIN32.MAK).

MAKE utility

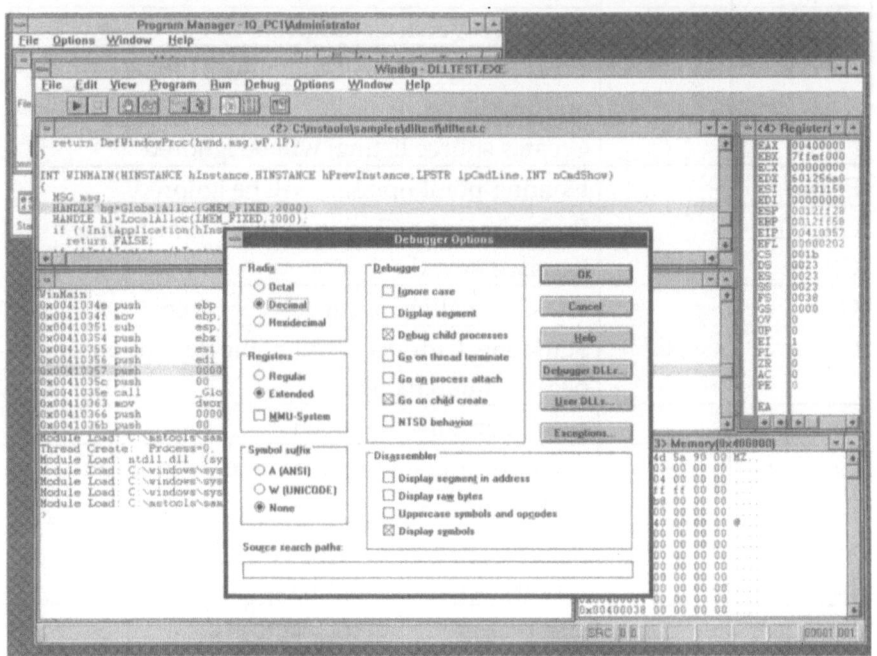

Figure 5.1: WINDBG, the graphical debugger of the Win32 SDK

The 32-Bit C/C++ compiler

Let's first address the C/C++ compiler. This program is started through typing CL (or CL386) on the command line and then, loaded with switches and filenames, goes to work. The command-line usage is almost identical under both systems; this also extends to using response files

Same call as under DOS

and the environment variable CL. The following table shows the essential compiler switches for Win16 programming and the usage with the 32-bit compiler as well as their meaning and, if necessary, differences (switches that have experienced no change at all and are used similarly under both systems (such as /C) are left out for the sake of brevity).

Table 5.1: MSC compiler switches compared

Win16	Win32	Meaning and differences
Ax	-	Memory model; removed
Axxx	-	Options to the memory model; removed
batch	BATCH	Batched call; must now be written in upper case
Bmxxx	-	Improves compiler capacity; removed
Fxxx	-	Stack size; will be ignored (but see linker option STACK)
F	-	Activates Quick C; removed
Fmxxx	-	Creates map file; will be ignored (but see linker option MAP)
Fsxxx	-	Creates source listing; will be ignored
FPxxx	-	Floating point options; will be ignored
GA, GD, GE	-	Prologue and epilogue code for Win16 functions; removed
Gc	-	PASCAL calling sequence; removed
Ge, Gs	Ge, Gs	Stack check (de-)activation; the default mode became interchanged
Gn, Gp	-	P-code options; removed
Gq, Gw, GW	-	Prologue and epilogue code for Win16 functions; removed
Gt, Gx	-	Allocation of data segments; removed
Ld, Lw	-	Library selection; removed
Lr	-	Use real-mode library; removed
MA	-	MASM options; removed
Mq	-	QuickWin support; removed
Of, Oo, Oq, Ov	-	Various P-code optimizations; removed
Oc, Oe, Oz, Or	-	Various optimizations; removed
qc	-	Activates Quick C; removed
Sxxx	-	Options for the source listing; removed

Win16	Win32	Meaning and differences
Taxxx	-	File contains assembly code; removed
Zc	-	Ignore case of identifiers; will be ignored
Zp	Zp	Packing of structures; default has been modified
Zr	-	Check for NULL pointers; removed

Fortunately, most of the concerned options in the table are just removals. Especially worth mentioning seems the omission of memory models,* the removal of the various switches for the Win16 prologue and epilogue sequences (after all, even at Microsoft presumably no human being was able to completely understand what all that stuff meant...) as well as the cancellation of the so far blessed FAR PASCAL calling sequence. Win32 programs, as already mentioned, instead make use of an all-new convention named __stdcall (for details see section 4.7, page 263, as well as appendix 5, page 387). Whether certain switches will be re-introduced with future versions of the compiler (especially with newer versions of the Visual C++ compiler) is currently difficult to estimate. Some options are surely and luckily gone forever (e.g., for the memory models and the entry/exit sequences); others, such as the P-code-support options, will probably be found again over time. In brief: just take the above table as it's meant: a list just valid for the current version of the SDK compiler. In case of doubt, simply check with the help of the documentation whether the options you're interested in have changed in the meantime. If uncertain, you should prefer the WinHelp files over the printed documentation, as the former are simply more complete and, as much as possible, also up-to-date.

With kind regards from the flat memory model!

The WinHelp files are more up-to-date than the printed documentation.

An additional comment seems in place for the options /ND, /NM, /NT, etc., used for the naming of segments: although finally segments as such don't play a significant role under Win32, the compiler supports as before the capability to create and name separate code and data areas (well, these are not called segments anymore, but sections). This can be used to load certain sections to predetermined addresses in the virtual address space. Second, and more important, this feature is employed for the creation of shareable DLL data areas. More about the latter is contained in section 5.3 on page 339.

Sections instead of segments

A serious modification compared to Win16 is the fact that you have to instruct the C compiler with some pre-#defined constants (normally

Important #defines

given on the command line) about the system environment and the target CPU. Two symbols *must* be defined in order to guarantee a successful compilation: -DWIN32 as well as (depending on the target processor) either -D_X86_=1 or -D_MIPS_=1 or -D_ALPHA_=1. The default include file for NMAKE described ahead in more detail takes care of these definitions by default; if, however, you write BAT or CMD files with C compiler calls, you definitely must take these command-line switches into consideration. A proper command for the compilation of file TEST.C on an x86 CPU might look as follows:

* Win32 API...

```
CL  -DWIN32*  -D_X86_=1**  -G3  -W4  -Zi  -Od  -c  test.c
```

** and x86 CPU

News from the Resource Compiler

Things look even more pleasant when it comes to changes to the resource compiler. Under Win16 this program takes two responsibilities: it first serves to convert textual RC files to RES files; this is the compiling component. And after linking it is used to fasten the compiled resources to the EXE file, a step conceptually more related to linking. Under Win32 a corresponding adaptation has been performed; actually RC.EXE is there just a resource compiler and as such can still create RES files (whose structure deviates considerably from the "old" 3.x RES format; a thorough description of the new Unicode compatible format is found in the SDK file X:\MSTOOLS\DOC\FILEFRMT\RESFMT.TXT). In older SDK versions the RES file is converted with the help of CVTRES into an RBJ file; this is read in afterwards by the linker and finally put into the EXE file. These RBJ files are ordinary Win32 object files that contain all RES information and can indeed be processed with the linker as any other OBJ file. In the current SDK version this step is performed by the linker. Those switches of the Win16 RC dealing solely with coalescing the EXE and RES files into one were consequently removed in the 32-bit version. On the other hand, the switches only dealing with the process of translating resources are still available in their full glory, as the following table shows.

RC.EXE is just a resource compiler, nothing more.

CVTRES: converts the RES file to RBJ format.

Switch	Meaning
R	Create RES file (actually superfluous, supported for compatibility reasons)
V	Gives messages about the progress of the compilation
dxxx	#defines a constant
foxxx	Gives the name of the output file (xxx.RES)
ixxx	Sets the path for #include files
X	Suppresses the use of environment variable INCLUDE

Table 5.2: The RC switches

Therefore, all calls of RC in which it acts as a pure compiler can remain unaltered. A typical command line looks exactly as it does under Win16:

RC calls remain unaltered.

```
RC -r xyz.rc
```

After successful compilation, the conversion of the RES file into the Win32 object format (this depends on the target CPU) has to be accomplished: for this you need to call CVTRES. However, thereby you don't #define a constant depending on the target system, but use the switch -i386, -mips, or -alpha to adjust the output (long lives inconsistency, else programming might possibly get too easy...):

CVTRES

```
CVTRES -mips xyz.res -o xyz.rbj // or -i386, -alpha
```

As a matter of fact, the next step due (under Win16) of binding the compiled resources to the linked executable can be completely removed, this function is taken over by the Win32 linker to which we'll turn in a moment. Please observe that CVTRES is not needed in the current version of the SDK, since that step is now moved to the linker. And as far as I see for the time being, VC++ 2 also integrates this step into the linking process (see section 5.5).

Binding of resources removed

LINK: one does it all

With this we finally approach the third in the bunch: the linker that produces from all the OBJ, RBJ and library files a PE, a portable executable. Unfortunately, I don't seem to have good news: the Win32 linker is a complete rewrite and has *nothing* in common with the segmented executable linker of Windows 3.x.* The switches are designed completely dif-

* Actually, this is a rather good sign...

ferently and the functionality was greatly enhanced. As a matter of fact, it has to offer so much more than the old linker that in the long run we will be better off with the new linker. Besides the already mentioned linking of resources, it replaces the library manager LIB as well as the IMPLIB and EXEHDR utilities. The following "master switches" are defined for LINK (formerly named LINK32) and choose one of the four modes:

LINK replaces LIB, IMPLIB and the EXEHDR utility.

Table 5.3: The four LINK modes

Switch	... serves to
LINK	Link EXE and DLL files (default mode)
LIB	Construction of LIB and EXP files (library manager)
DUMP	Display file contents (works among others with OBJ, RBJ, EXE, LIB, DLL and EXP files)
EDIT	Alter (!) sections in EXE files

(The EXP files shown with the -LIB option will be discussed later in conjunction with the generation of DLLs.) In order to call the "library manager," for instance, the following LINK command is necessary:

LINK -LIB activates the library manager.

```
LINK -LIB [further, lib-specific switches and statements]
```

For the plagued developer Microsoft even delivers a small program named LIB as a shell around LINK: this does nothing more than calling LINK with the switch -LIB and its own command line (for me it's totally incomprehensible why for this remarkable feat a 23 KB long program is needed: a small batch job or even a simple DOSKEY macro would have proved just as useful. Well, obviously the developers in Redmond have to fill hard disks with several gigabytes of available space, so it comes....)

Let's look at the individual linker options with more detail! In the following table the most important new LINK options are collected and explained.

Table 5.4: Important LINK switches

LINK switch	... and its meaning
DEBUG:xxx	Defines which level of debug information is placed in the EXE file
DEBUGTYPE:xxx	Defines the format of debug data
DLL	Creates a DLL (default is EXE)

LINK switch	... and its meaning
ENTRY:xxx	Gives the start address (entry point) for EXE and DLL files
heap:xxx	Defines the size of the default heap
machine:xxx	Identifies the target system (i386, MIPS, Alpha, etc.)
MAP:xxx	Creates a MAP file
OUT:xxx	Defines the names for the output file (EXE or DLL)
SECTION:xxx	Defines the attributes (read, write, shared, etc.) of sections
STACK:xxx	Defines the stack size
SUBSYSTEM:xxx	Indicates under which API subsystem the application will run

For someone switching from Win16 the options SUBSYSTEM, DEBUG, DEBUGTYPE, as well as HEAP and STACK are especially interesting. SUBSYSTEM gives the target system under which the resulting EXE will run. Here the following five options are available:

NATIVE	No specific system (in other words: an application relying only on NT kernel calls)
WINDOWS	Win32 subsystem, the EXE is a typical GUI program (the most frequent case when porting)
CONSOLE	Win32 subsystem, text-mode program using the console API, but no GUI calls
OS2	OS/2 1.x subsystem (currently only text mode)
POSIX	Posix subsystem (text mode only)

Table 5.5: Options for the selection of the API subsystem

On the one hand the switches for the debugging information define which amount of debug info is put into the executable; on the other hand (through the target debugger) they designate the format of the data (of course, the various NT debuggers don't work with the same debug formats — this would make things too easy...). In most cases applications will be debugged with the graphical debugger (WINDBG, which accepts the CodeView format (CV)); only command-line die-hards or device driver developers will make friends with NTSD (not to mention the still more spartanic kernel debugger). And the latter two debug aids wish to find their debugging information in the COFF format. Normally (for

WINDBG) the two switches are therefore initialized with the following settings:

```
LINK ... -DEBUG:full -DEBUGTYPE:CV ...
```

A *very* popular error Win32 newcomers make is to forget the statement -DEBUGTYPE:CV when linking; afterwards WINDBG has quite a problem doing anything useful with the EXE file to debug. (This happens because cleverly -DEBUGTYPE:COFF is the default of the NT linker — evidently the Microsoft developers are NTSD fans.)

A few words also about the HEAP and STACK options: while the Win16 developer had to write a DEF file for both executables and DLLs, this is *not* necessary anymore for Win32 applications. Yes, you have read

properly: there are no DEF files needed in order to link EXE files. Just for creating DLLs are these still required (but I assume that they will become completely obsolete in the future; see, for instance, the WinHelp entry for an interesting compiler feature named __declspec(dllexport)). All the information the linker as of now reads from the DEF file is under Win32 instead directly given on the linker command line as LINK switches. And here the STACK and HEAP options become important, because they define the sizes of the available memory blocks. The default size is a

whopping 1 MB (!) in both cases, but you can arbitrarily modify this when linking. (By the way: if now, in view of such monstrous stacks and heaps, you fear that two or three programs with their stacks and heaps combined already consume all of the physical memory — don't forget the demand paging the x86 and RISC CPUs can (and will!) perform.) From this huge pool actually allocated ("committed") and therefore consuming physical memory is only a much smaller area (which defaults as a matter of fact to just 4 or 8 KB, i.e., exactly one memory page). If in the course of the program execution more stack and/or heap space is needed (this means an access takes place to a reserved, but not yet committed

page), the VMM* immediately allocates another page (4 KB on x86 and MIPS CPUs and 8 KB on Alphas); for the mechanics see the following figure 5.2. Well understood: this happens under the hoods without any explicit activity of the program or the developer! This approach seems especially significant for the stack, because the minimal time needed that is required for allocating another page can surely be neglected. If, however, you know for sure that your program needs a minimum stack of

let's say 16 KB and a maximum of 24 KB, you can of course give these as
the defaults when linking (the same holds true for the HEAP switch):

```
LINK  ...  -STACK:24576,16384  ...
```

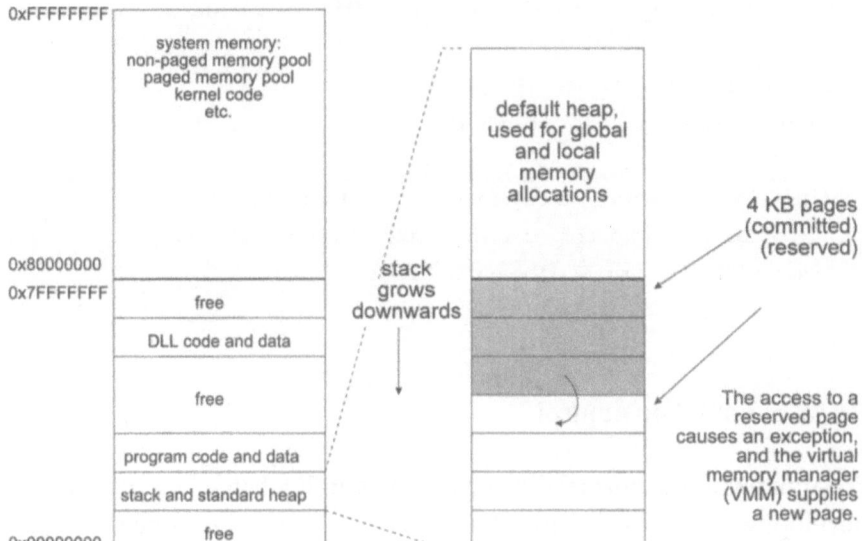

*Figure 5.2: Dynamic stack
growth with the aid of the
virtual memory manager*

Now the following interesting question pops up: if DEF files can be removed when linking applications, how do you tell the linker which
functions (e.g., window callbacks) in the program are to be exported?
The answer to this question is just as simple as surprising: not at all! Exporting callback functions is for the same reasons passé, as are calls to
[Make/Free]ProcInstance() for instance: this sinister witchcraft is only
necessary under Win16 so that upon entry to the windows procedure the
proper data segment can be loaded. And under Win32, where all software runs in the flat memory model with the same segment values, this
is absolutely irrelevant! Hence, the developer can finally forget the (well,
to be honest: absurd) effort for this entire complex. As already mentioned in Chapter 4: Windows NT (or OS/2 2.x) impressively shows
what is possible, if only the hardware (this means the processor) is adequate....

*And exporting callback
functions?*

Data segment? What's that?

As an example of a complete sequence for the generation of a Win32 application (on an Intel machine), the following batch job for compiling and linking is shown. It produces a simple Win32 GUI application, consisting of just a C module (GUI.C) and a resource file (GUI.RC):

```
cl  -DWIN32  -D_X86_=1  -G3  -W4  -Zi  -Od  -c  gui.c


rc  -r  gui.rc
cvtres  -i386  gui.res  -o  gui.rbj
```

The ⇒ signals that this command is a single "logical" line.

```
link  -debugtype:cv  -debug:full    subsystem: windows  ⇒
    -out:gui.exe  gui.obj  gui.rbj  libc.lib ntdll.lib  ⇒
    kernel32.lib  user32.lib  gdi32.lib
```

NMAKE: complete control

Presumably in the normal case you won't employ batch jobs for program development, but MAKE files for NMAKE. But if things don't work out at all with some of the numerous 32-bit NMAKE macro definitions or if you are a command-line fanatic, you can start with the example above. By the way: further switches are important for the creation of DLLs and more details about this can be found in the next section, dealing with DLL creation.

Now to NMAKE: the Win32 variant of this utility corresponds mostly to the DOS version; therefore fundamental changes to the logic and the structure of MAKE files are fortunately rarely required. Admittedly, Microsoft makes in the supplied MAKE files extensive use of an include file named WIN32.MAK (the NT SDK has a similar file named NTWIN32.MAK), residing in the same directory as the Win32 header files (namely X:\MSTOOLS\H). They've defined a whole bunch of global macros, which aid in the creation of Win32 programs and allow a compatible use of MAKE files also for RISC developers. Unfortunately, with this approach the Win16 programmer is somewhat left behind, since MAKE files written for WIN32.MAK aren't applicable without some further twiddling for Windows 3.x projects. Yet I'm sure we can get over this because the MAKE file for a project is probably written once

WIN32.MAK: global macros for NMAKE.

Non-Win16 compatible

and afterwards modified only rarely. The above-mentioned simple project would look like this as an NMAKE file:

```
!include <NTWIN32.MAK> # this includes WIN32.MAK

PROJ = GUI

all: $(PROJ).exe

$(PROJ).res: $(PROJ).rc $(PROJ).h                          Build RES file.
    rc -r -fo $(PROJ).res $(PROJ).rc
    cvtres $(CPU) $(PROJ).res -o $(PROJ).rbj

$(PROJ).obj: $(PROJ).c $(PROJ).h                           Compile C file.
    $(cc) $(cflags) $(cvars) $(cdebug) $(PROJ).c

$(PROJ).exe: $(PROJ).obj $(PROJ).res                       Link program.
    $(link) $(linkdebug) $(guiflags) $(PROJ).obj ⇒
    $(guilibs) $(PROJ).rbj -out:$(PROJ).exe
```

Of course this effort is hardly necessary for such a simple project, but if you work with two or three source code modules, the use of NMAKE already helps to save a great deal of time, simply because just the modified source code files are compiled. Apart from this, the macros for the compiler and linker switches* as well as the link libraries — e.g., $(guilibs) or $(conlibs) — considerably ease the proper generation of programs. A glance into WIN32.MAK and the MAKE files from Microsoft can prove invaluable for Win32 developers, since as described the use of the various tools has been modified (partially seriously). These files show almost at the "living object" what actually is happening.

i.e., $(cflags), $(cvars), $(linkdebug), $(guiflags), etc.

By the way: the MAKE file above will probably generate problems (as will nearly all SDK MAKE files) when used via Quickstart under MS-DOS. The reason is simply the restriction in the length of DOS command lines (MS-DOS 6? Don't make me laugh!). While the compiler most often operates as expected, the linker normally goes astray. In such a case just replace the entire link command (i.e., the last three lines in the file above) with the following statement:

```
$(PROJ).exe: $(PROJ).obj $(PROJ).res
    $(link) @<<link.cmd
    $(linkdebug) $(guiflags) $(PROJ).obj ⇒
      $(guilibs) $(PROJ).rbj -out:$(PROJ).exe
<<
```

Response files through inline files

This link command builds a response file named LINK.CMD (through inline files, created with the "<<" braces), which contains all linker switches, filenames, etc., and is read in by LINK. If you happen to find longer lines also when compiling C source files, you can proceed for the compiler command just as shown. As a matter of fact, LINK.CMD will contain the following text (or something very similar):

```
-debug:full -debugtype:cv subsystem:windows
-entry:WinMainCRTStartup gui.obj libc.lib
kernel32.lib ntdll.lib user32.lib gdi32.lib winspool.lib
comdlg32.lib gui.rbj -out:gui.exe
```

Two problem areas: the new linker...

According to my own experiences with the 32-bit SDK, two big problem areas exist with the creation of applications. First is the changeover to the new linker (and library manager, respectively), here probably only some patience, a closer study of the documentation, and, above all, using the supplied MAKE files will help. The second problem is that one often forgets to adjust the correct CPU type. More or less all tools have switches (-i386, -MIPS, etc.) or require a #define CPU ... before working properly. And if you forget this, you'll quickly be very baffled. That's another good reason to work with WIN32.MAK: then these flags are automatically taken into account!

... and the CPU switches.

The Win32 header files

WINDOWS.H: just a shell.

Several things have been changed in the header file WINDOWS.H. Until now it contained all the Windows-specific definitions and with its length of well over 100 KB already grew to a respectable size. Under Win32 it is of a rather modest size: approximately 3 KB. That's no wonder, since it is simply a shell for the numerous (all in all about 100) new header files, which comprise the C/C++ interface to the Win32 API. The disadvantage for developers is that one doesn't know at all in which file a certain

definition is found (luckily, in the SDK directory X:\MSTOOLS\LIB a
file named WIN32API.CSV can be found which contains information
about Win32 API elements, including the name of the header file with
the definition). Apart from that, some header files build upon others and
require certain declarations. Therefore, figure 5.3 shows the include file
tree for the 32-bit Windows header files.

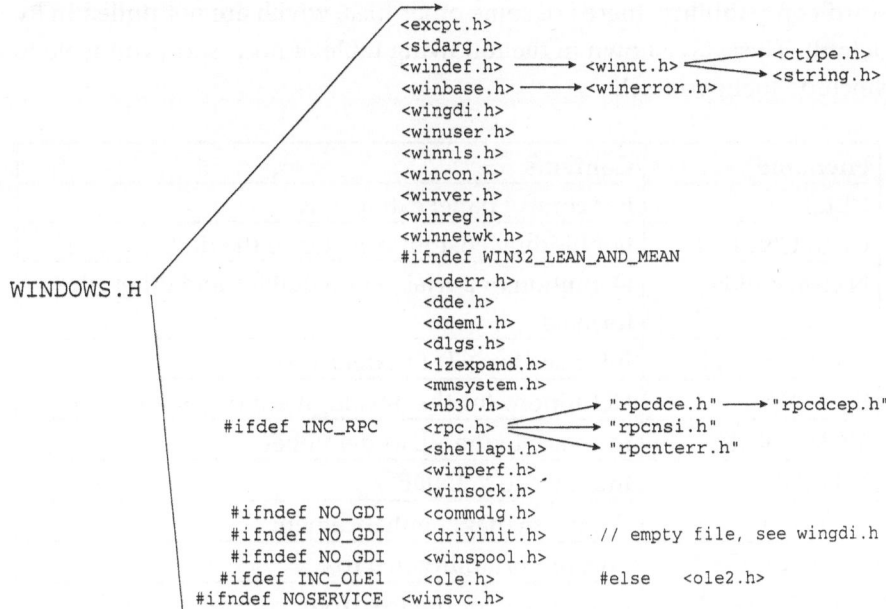

The following header files are especially important:

- \<windef.h\>   basic type definitions and macros
- \<winnt.h\>   NT-specific type definitions and macros
- \<winerror.h\>   error message codes
- \<winbase.h\>   base and I/O functionality
- \<winuser.h\>   window manager
- \<wingdi.h\>   GDI definitions
- \<wincon.h\>   console API and subsystem

As in the past through #defining certain constants the inclusion of the
corresponding definitions (or files, respectively) can be prevented:

```
#define NOWINMESSAGES  // no windows messages, etc.
#include <windows.h>
```

There is also a new constant called WIN32_MEAN_AND_LEAN, whose #definition includes just the most important stuff (files included with this constant set are marked with an asterisk in figure 5.3). Besides the files considered above (which are automatically included) to ensure backward compatibility, there are some other files, which are not pulled in by default. These are shown in the following table; if necessary, you have to #include them yourself.

Table 5.6: Header files not automatically included

Filename	Contents
CPL.H	For control panel extensions
CUSTCNTL.H	For binding custom controls to the dialog editor
NTIMAGE.H	Definition of portable executables and other file formats
NTSDEXTS.H	Interface for NTSD extensions
SCRNSAVE.H	Definitions for the development of screen savers
VDMDBG.H	Interface to the VDM debugger
WDBGEXTS.H	Interface to WINDBG
WFEXT.H	For file manager enhancements
WINDOWSX.H	Lots of portability macros
WINIOCTL.H	Definitions for device driver control (IOCTL)

Nearly essential: precompiled headers.

As a matter of fact, based on the gigantic volume of the Win32 header files (easily more than 3 MB), I would strongly recommend working with precompiled headers. A single precompilation can save an incredible amount of compile time — actually, the Microsoft compiler will get really quick!

5.2 Particularities for Text Mode Programs

"... I am better than my reputation." Friedrich Schiller, Mary Stuart

The console API

The small excursion to the console API in the fourth chapter already has shown that under Win32 not only Windows applications are possible and sensible. Indeed, with the text-mode interface a much simpler (but exactly for that reason for many programmers attractive) capability ex-

Porting of character-based UNIX and OS/2 programs

ists to finally free MS-DOS programs bursting at all seams from the infamous 640 KB limit. What's more, porting character-based UNIX and
OS/2 programs is considerably eased through this API variant (or often
enabled in the first place). In order to make this even simpler, Win32
makes available a POSIX compatible API, and ported versions of the
curses library and other UNIX goodies are already available from third-
party manufacturers. The OS/2 subsystem delivers nearly the complete
OS/2 1.x functionality, albeit without Presentation Manager support (as
of today). Reasons enough to briefly discuss the details of program creation with the character-based interfaces. I am concentrating (mostly for
practical reasons) on the creation of Win32 console applications; the details of programming for the other subsystems are still somewhat foggy.*
However, the remarks following are probably also valid for the generation of programs for OS/2 and POSIX subsystems — at the very least, if
you're using the Microsoft SDK products.

*VC++ 2.0 contains at least
the necessary POSIX header
files and libraries.*

Text mode: no big differences

The best discovery first: under Win32 (finally!) the compilation for certain modes finds its well-deserved end. Someone who fought bravely
through the jungle of DOS compiler switches discovered with great dis-
pleasure that an even more complex teamwork of compiler and linker
options was necessary for Windows programming. I think that certainly
a quarter of all problems with initally not-running programs have to do
with the improper selection and combination of the numerous switches
for compiling, linking, etc. As the table in the preceding section has already shown, most of these snares simply disappear under Win32.
What's more: the creation of text-mode programs demands no special
precautions or compiler switches whatsoever! So you can use *exactly* the
same command lines as you would for compiling GUI applications.**

Standardized programming

*** Well, UNIX programmers
will find that hardly surprising...*

Just the linking process shows some (insignificant) differences,
which relate to a modified switch and to the import libraries to be linked:
on the one hand, for the switch -SUBSYSTEM the value CONSOLE is
necessary to choose the proper target system; on the other hand, the
linker has to work with a somewhat different set of import libraries. The
first point means that another starting point is defined for the application: GUI programs are activated through calling WinMainCRTStartup(),
which itself calls WinMain() with the proper parameters. Console appli-

-SUBSYSTEM: CONSOLE

cations are started via mainCRTStartup(), which (as you'd expect) generates a call to the good, old main() function with the usual argc and argv values (by the way: the latter is even in Unicode programs supplied in ANSI format!).

The second change is also sensible: *of course* for linking character-based programs other libraries are required than for GUI applications. Wait a second, is that really true? Actually, it is not: under Win32 the separation between text and graphics programs is rather artificial. For linking text programs *other* libraries are neither used nor needed. Actually only a *restricted* set of LIB files is employed, simply because text applications normally don't call functions from USER32, GDI32, etc. The emphasis here is on the word "normally," since in principle a program using the console functions (or printf()) linked with -SUBSYSTEM: CONSOLE can call the Windows functions at any time (e.g., create a window, initialize a message loop, etc.). You just have to give the additional import libraries (e.g., USER32.LIB) on the linker command line (or use the macro $(guilibs) in the first place) so that all GUI calls can be correctly resolved (indeed, there are still one or two further trifles to pay attention to, but a Win32 text-mode program can easily work with windows — see some of the example programs on the disk). The reverse is of course also possible: a GUI application can at any time create text mode windows (aka console, see, e.g., AllocConsole()) and thereafter display or read things via printf() and scanf() or any other console API call!

Other import libraries for text-mode programs?

Conclusion: under Win32 only minor, formal differences between text-mode and GUI applications exist. Assuming a corresponding programming style, both types can access the other, the "hostile" API.

The separation between text and graphical programs is rather artificial under Win32.

Example: batch job and MAKE file

In order to follow these charming words with some genuine deeds, the following batch job shows the compile and link commands for a simple text-mode application:

```
cl  -DWIN32  -D_X86_=1  -G3  -W4  -Zi  -Od  -c  text.c

link  -debugtype:cv  -debug:full   subsystem: ⇒
  console  -out:text.exe  text.obj  libc.lib ⇒
  ntdll.lib  kernel32.lib
```

Compare these commands with the commands shown above for the GUI
application (see page 332): the compilation of the RC file* as well as the
following conversion of RES to RBJ was removed, and the command line
for the linker has been modified a little bit. And while we're at it — here
is the MAKE file for TEXT:

*Although text-mode pro-
grams absolutely can use
resources.*

```
!include <WIN32.MAK>

PROJ = text

all: $(PROJ).exe

$(PROJ).obj: $(PROJ).c $(PROJ).h
    $(cc) $(cflags) $(cvars) $(cdebug) $(PROJ).c

$(PROJ).exe: $(PROJ).obj $(PROJ).res
    $(link) $(linkdebug) $(conflags) $(PROJ).obj \
    $(conlibs) -out:$(PROJ).exe
```

Here too, the differences are due to the RC file being absent and the
slightly modified link instructions. Put together, the creation of applications (regardless of whether text or GUI) under Win32 has finally been
strongly unified,** which perhaps shows more clearly than any API extension that these are actually systems designed and written from scratch
(okay, for Windows 95 this is only partially true).

*** not to say simplified...*

5.3 DLLs: What Has Been Modified?

"It is more blessed to give than to receive." Bible New Testament, Acts 20, 35

If by now you suspect that the effort of building DLLs under Win32 has
been lowered considerably, you're right: the DLL creation has become
much simpler, even conceptually. Nevertheless, source code changes
(partially significant) will be necessary, particularly because of the
strictly separated address spaces of running processes. An overview was
given in section 4.9, and the following discussion will show two specific
examples of generating a standard DLL (in which the data sections are
process specific and each times created anew) and a DLL with a single

*Overall, the generation of
DLLs is simplified.*

shared section, identical for all processes (called a shared memory data section).

DLLs and data sections

The source remains the same. Amazingly, the source code itself remains the same in both cases; the distinction between private and global sections only happens when the linker comes into play: the access mode is determined through memory attributes in the DEF file. So first the (rather simple) source code (in TEST.C), with three functions to create and destroy a DLL thread as well as to query the value of a DLL variable:

```
#define STRICT
#include <windows.h>
#include <portutil.h> // Header with helper definitions,
                       // see also Appendix 7.
#include "test.h"      // contains just the prototypes


HINSTANCE hMod;    // global variable for the instance handle
HANDLE hThread;    // handle for the thread
BOOL fEnd;         // signal for thread termination
INT i=0, j=0;      // and two simple counters
BOOL WINAPI LibMain32(HINSTANCE hDLL,DWORD dwReason,
  LPVOID lpReserved)
{
  char chBuf[80];
  j++; // counts number of calls to LibMain32
  wsprintf(chBuf,"test.dll: j == %D",j);
  switch (dwReason) {
    case DLL_PROCESS_ATTACH: // new process
      hMod=hDLL;
      MessageBox(NULL,chBuf,"Process attaching",MB_OK);
      break;
    case DLL_PROCESS_DETACH: // process termination
      MessageBox(NULL,chBuf,"Process detaching",MB_OK);
```

Initialization: process

Termination: process

Returns the value of the thread counter break;

```
    case DLL_THREAD_ATTACH: // new thread                    Initialization: thread
      MessageBox(NULL,chBuf,"Thread attaching",MB_OK);
      break;
    case DLL_THREAD_DETACH: // thread termination            Termination: thread
      MessageBox(NULL,chBuf,"Thread detaching",MB_OK);
      break;
  }
  return TRUE;
}


DWORD WINAPI ThreadProc(LPVOID lpv);                         Implements the thread.
DWORD WINAPI ThreadProc(LPVOID lpv)
// A CPU bound job ...
{
  while (!fEnd) // for termination see EndThreadInDLL()
    if (++i%1000000==0) MessageBeep(0);
  return 0;
}
VOID StartThreadInDLL(VOID)                                  Creates a new thread
{                                                            executing ThreadProc().
  DWORD dwID;
  if (hT) return; // Nope, thread is already running.
  fEnd=FALSE;
  hT=CreateThread(NULL,0,ThreadProc,NULL,0,&dwID);
}


VOID EndThreadInDLL(VOID)                                    Terminates the thread.
{
  if (hT) { // Is thread running?
    fEnd=TRUE;
    hT=0;
  }
}


INT GetCounter(VOID)
{
  return i;
}
```

And here is the corresponding header file test.h for the protoypes of the three exported functions:

TEST.H

```
VOID WINAPI StartThreadInDLL(VOID);
VOID WINAPI EndThreadInDLL(VOID);
INT WINAPI GetCounter(VOID);
```

The program code for calling and testing those functions isn't shown, since each standard Windows program that calls the three exported functions and shows a message box with the results (e.g., in the treatment of the WM_CHAR message) can be used (an example is found on the accompanying disk). The MAKE file serving to generate the DLL seems to be *much* more interesting:

```
!include <WIN32.MAK>
```

Link the DLL.

```
test.dll: test.obj test.def test.rbj
    $(link) $(linkdebug)  -dll \
    -entry:LibMain32$(DLLENTRY)  -out:test.dll \
    test.exp  test.obj  $(guilibs)
```

Compile C (and RC) files.

```
test.obj: test.c
    $(cc) $(cdebug) $(cflags) $(cvars) test.c
```

Generate the import library.

```
test.lib: test.obj test.def
    $(implib)  -machine:$(CPU)  -def:test.def \
!IF "$(CPU)" == "i386"
    test.obj \
!endif
    -out:test.lib
```

Nothing special happens at the compilation of the C file; exactly the same switches as for the creation of EXE files are used. (This is a remarkable improvement over Win16, where depending on the destination file — DLL or EXE — *different* compiler switches had to be given!) The real differences, however, are found when the import library TEST.LIB and the DLL are generated. For both activities the linker is responsible — LIB is hidden behind the macro $(implib), which simply starts LINK with the master switch -LIB. On the one hand (last command), with the switch

Important differences for the generation of import libraries and linking

-DEF the DEF file TEST.DEF is processed and converted into a LIB and an EXP files; on the other hand (first control command), the DLL is linked from the individual components. Let's investigate these two activities a little bit further.

The linking of a DLL

In order to build TEST.LIB, LINK needs a DEF file besides the OBJ file, which, in the most simple case, looks as follows:

```
LIBRARY   Test
EXPORTS   StartThreadInDLL
          EndThreadInDLL
          GetCounter
```

The DEF file

Presumably these statements need no further comments; they correspond to those known from Win16. LINK interprets the DEF file and creates the import library, a LIB file that specifies the functions exported in the DLL. This LIB is used afterwards when linking client applications in order to resolve the dynamic links into the DLL.

Import library

What's more, and this is new, LINK creates another file, which plays an important role when linking the DLL itself. This additional file normally has the extension EXP, probably designating exports. I don't clearly see, why this file is needed at all, because the linker might as well read the DEF or LIB file when creating a DLL; anyhow, a meaningful reason *certainly* exists.... As said, the EXP file must be stated explicitly when linking the DLL itself. And if all that starts to look rather confusing — let's give the generation of a simple DLL once again, at lower speed and step for step (see also figure 5.4 on the following page):

EXP file

1. Compiling the C source code results in an OBJ file.
2. Compiling the resources (not shown here) leads to an RES file, which is, as usual, converted in a second step to an RBJ file. Both steps are exactly the same for EXEs and DLLs.

   Compile the C and RC files.

3. Processing the DEF file with LINK -LIB (here the linker acts as the library manager) generates two files: first the import library (a standard LIB file), which is *not* used with the DLL directly, but afterwards when linking other applications, which access the DLL

   Build the import library...

   and the EXP file.

functions. This file contains all necessary information about the functions exported from the DLL and is needed to resolve the dynamic links. Second LINK creates an EXP file, which also describes the exported functions, but *only* in a format palatable to the DLL.

Finally link the DLL.

4. In the last step everything with the exception of the LIB file is thrown into a pot: from OBJ, RBJ, and EXP files, the DLL is linked. Thereby of course the import libraries of other DLLs, which our DLL is accessing, must be given on the command line.

Figure 5.4: The steps to the generation of a Win32 DLL

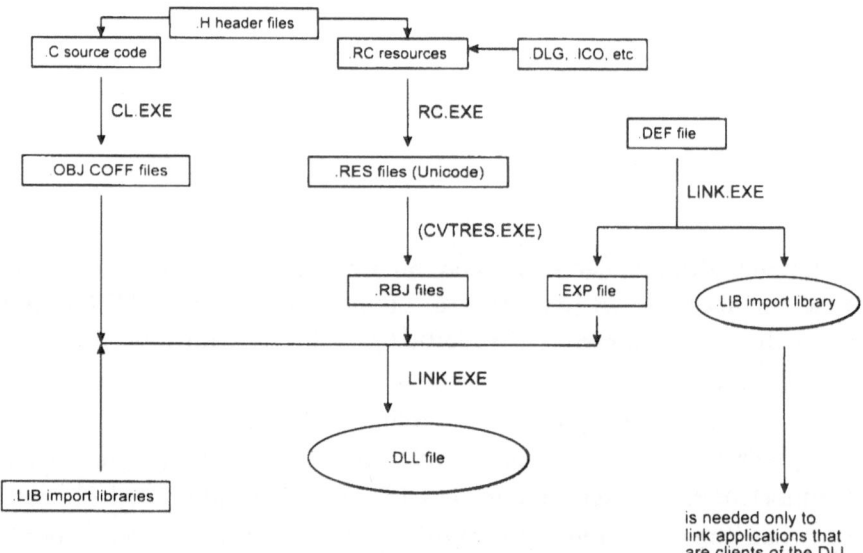

Working with DLLs under Win32 is simple and consistent.

Comfort yourself: once you have mastered these more mechanical chores, working with DLLs under Win32 is much simpler and more consistent than it was with Win16! It can even be fun! Just the fact that the data sections are always created anew, while Win16 DLLs could (respectively, had to!) use these as shared memory and the lack of dynamically allocated shared memory can still lead to some minor problems. So these are the next subjects to tackle!

Common data sections

Approach number 1 is very easy, since thereby just the DEF file must be modified in order to change the attributes of data sections:

Attributes of data sections

```
LIBRARY  Test
SECTION  .data read write shared
EXPORTS  StartThreadInDLL
         EndThreadInDLL
         GetCounter
```

Through the newly inserted line "SECTION .data read write shared" the data section .data (which contains all initialized data) will be created only once when the DLL is loaded the first time; afterwards, however, this section is mapped via CPU paging into the address spaces of all processes that further map this DLL. Each change to a global variable is therefore noticeable in all processes. The example above contains two explicitly initialized variables, namely the two INTs i and j, as well as a bunch of implicitly initialized data — the various strings serving the MessageBox() output in LibMain32(). The compiler puts these data into the section .data, which can be used as shared memory through the DEF statement shown (the Win32 linker has as a matter of fact a switch directly corresponding to the SECTION statement, not surprisingly named -SECTION).

Data section .data: initialized data.

On the other hand, the other non-initialized DLL variables (hMod, hThread, and fEnd) are created anew for each process using the DLL. Consequently a change in the line BOOL fEnd; to include an explicit assignment (e.g., BOOL fEnd=FALSE;) would bring fEnd from the non-initialized data section into section .data and therefore into the common data area. The following easy rule is applicable: non-initialized data can't be shared between several processes at all, and initialized data *only* with a SECTION statement in the DEF file or through the linker switch -SECTION with attribute shared. Both possibilities will indeed make available all data located in the respective section as shared memory. If this is not desired, you can easily define individual named sections via the compiler #pragma dataseg("..."). This gives you complete control over which variables are shared between the processes and which are not:

And non-initialized DLL variables?

#pragma dataseg("...") for individual named sections

```
// in the C file:
HINSTANCE hMod;               // global variable for the instance handle
HANDLE hThread;               // handle for the thread
BOOL fEnd=FALSE;              // signal for thread termination
#pragma data_seg("MySect")    // new data section
INT i=0,j=0;                  // and two simple counters
#pragma data_seg()            // and back to the default
...

// ... in the DEF file instead of:
// SECTION  .data read write shared
SECTION  MySect read write shared
...
```

A shared data section named MySect

Both INTs i and j will be allocated in a separate section named MySect, which is tagged in the DEF file as shared. The initialized BOOL fEnd is still located in the section .data and is therefore *not* put into the common area. Two warnings: until now the names for sections are not allowed to be longer than eight (yes, 8!) characters, a restriction that seems a bit bizarre in a 32-bit operating system. And second: supposedly* one can flag all data segments as shareable in a single step in the DEF file via the statement "DATA read write shared." This didn't work in previous releases, but was supposed to be repaired in the current version. Well, this hasn't happened; from what I've heard from a MS employee, eventually the DATA statement will be completely removed from the DEF file syntax. Since the SDK tools are still under development, such changes can't be excluded; hopefully this and many other small problems still open are clarified in the near future.

* according to the WinHelp files and the printed documentation

The problem of accessing shared data in DLLs of course has still another aspect, namely that of dynamic memory allocation for shared memory. If so far you have used calls like GlobalAlloc(GMEM_SHARE, ...) in your Win16 DLLs, you can expect to change that. As the discussion in sections 4.6 as well as 4.9 has shown, this call is indeed possible under Win32, but definitely creates *no* shared memory. Here you should employ one of the IPC mechanisms; presumably the use of memory-mapped files is the simplest. So, here we go!

Changes needed: a GlobalAlloc() with the flag GMEM_(DDE)SHARE.

And dynamic memory allocations?

The following source code illustrates the access of several processes to a
common memory area, which is allocated and administered by the DLL.
Please observe that the static data (especially the section holding the
pointer lpShared pointing to the common memory area) should *not* be
defined as shareable in the DEF file!

```
#define STRICT
#include <windows.h>
#include <portutil.h>
#include "shared.h"

#define SYSPAGINGFILE ((HANDLE)0xFFFFFFFF)

typedef struct {
  int iCountProcess;
  char chMoreInfo[64];
} SHARED, FAR* LPSHARED;

HINSTANCE hMod;     // global variable for instance handle
CHAR szMemName[] = "ShrMemName"; // name of the shared
                        // memory area
HANDLE hShared;     // handle of the shared memory area
LPSHARED lpShared; // pointer to the shared memory

BOOL WINAPI LibMain32(HINSTANCE hDLL,DWORD dwReason,
  LPVOID lpReserved)
{
  CHAR chBuf[80];
  switch (dwReason) {
    case DLL_PROCESS_ATTACH: // process attached
      hMod=hDLL;
      hShared=CreateFileMapping(SYSPAGINGFILE,NULL,
        PAGE_READWRITE,0,sizeof(SHARED),szMemFile);
      lpShared=(LPSHARED)MapViewOfFile(hShared,
        FILE_MAP_WRITE,0,0,sizeof(SHARED));
      if (lpShared->iCountProcess++==0) // only initialized
```

*Data structure for the shared
memory area*

*Global variable, for each
process created anew in its
address space*

Process attachment

347

```
                                       // with the first process
                                       SetMoreInfo("Test");
                                     break;
```

Process detachment

```
                              case DLL_PROCESS_DETACH: // process detached
                                 if (--lpShared->iCountProcess)
                                    wsprintf(chBuf,"Still %d process(es) attached",
                                       lpShared->iCountProcess);
                                 else
                                    strcpy(chBuf,"And I'm the last one...");
                                 MessageBox(NULL,chBuf,"Process detaching",MB_OK);
                                 UnmapViewOfFile(lpShared);
                                 CloseHandle(hShared);
                                 break;
                           }
                           return TRUE;
                        }
```

Read shared memory area...

```
                        VOID SetMoreInfo(LPSTR lpsz)
                        {
                           strncpy(lpShared->chMoreInfo,lpsz,
                              sizeof(lpShared->chMoreInfo)-1);
```

... and write.

```
                        }
                        VOID GetMoreInfo(LPSTR lpsz)
                        {
                           strcpy(lpsz,lpShared->chMoreInfo);
                        }
```

The header file, which contains only the prototypes for the two access functions (reading and writing the string), is not shown since it's trivial. All processes attached to the DLL can read and write the common memory area with the aid of these functions. (Actually, SetMoreInfo() ought to synchronize the access to the string, so that it is only written if no other process currently accesses the memory. Probably the simplest way

* The artificial name 'mutex' to accomplish this is a mutex object* (since critical sections can only be
stems from MUTual EXclu- used for the synchronization of threads within a single process, but not
sion. systemwide). For the sake of clarity I've not included the code for this but left that as an exercise for the reader...)

And the conclusion of all these discoveries: apart from the complications with common data areas (which are comparatively easy to solve), the implementation and generation of DLLs under Win32 has become much more consistent, simpler, and clearer. Cheers, Microsoft!

5.4 What Do the Borland Tools Offer?

"All Quiet on the Western Front." Title of a novel from Erich Maria Remarque

In fact, this quotation fits the 32-bit tools of Borland like a handmade glove. What has reached me from Scotts Valley as beta and final product* clearly shows that Borland, wherever possible, has left the Win32 tools just as we're used to from the 16-bit development system.

* Of course, also on CD-ROM

Nevertheless, this is an advantage and a drawback at the same time: on the one hand for the BCC developer going for Win32(s) the use of the tools has not changed very much, so he can therefore fully concentrate on the necessary source code modifications. Nearly all MAKE files, CFG and DEF files, etc., can be carried over to Win32 development either unaltered or with only insignificant modifications. On the other hand, the Borland developer pays for this advantage with a considerable departure from compatibility to the SDK products from Microsoft. What does that means in detail? As a striking example, as before, BCC32 creates the object files in the "old" Intel format (also called OMF). As long as you can remain in the Borland world, there are no objections against this. But in order to render the object files COFF compatible (or vice versa), you need a utility. And whether the actual conversions will be absolutely correct in both directions is a stimulating question. Another example: the new __stdcall-calling sequence will be slightly differently realized by the Borland compiler than Microsoft's. This could get you into deep trouble if, for instance, LIBs or OBJ files from different origins were to be combined. And an annoying difference especially for professional developers is the way in which Borland C performs DLL initialization and termination: as far as I can estimate, this is carried out as in Win16 — i.e., separate with LibMain() and WEP() — probably also because of backward compatibility to the 16-bit world. However, this leads to the unpleasant state that Borland DLLs don't always operate correctly with programs created with the Microsoft compiler (and vice versa).

Usage of the tools is hardly modified.

As a matter of fact, not Microsoft compatible

The list with such or similar changes could be nearly arbitrarily extended. All things considered, Borland seems to value backward compatibility much more than "cross compatibility" to its rivals. While in the

* Just think about the impossibility of creating standard object files.

** And that Microsoft dictates standards is a truth that Borland hardly can ignore (well, they tried hard, but the result is not pleasing...)

The Borland tools also work under MS-DOS.

C/C++ compiler: no important changes.

The linker still needs a DEF file.

first place this might look advantageous for the developer, in the long run we need to ask ourselves whether this way is really the better one. After all, Turbo PASCAL has never gained the reputation of being a truly professional development system. And why? Above all, because it is an indeed brilliant but somewhat isolated platform.* In this sense Borland must be careful that the C/C++ development tools don't move too far away from the Microsoft standards.** Possibly Borland will present an overhauled system with the launch of Windows 95, I don't know exactly which changes will be carried out until then. And filling pages now with discussions about (mis-)features possibly not anymore found in a future product is definitely not very helpful. But I certainly can draw some basic conclusions from the existing material.

With that in mind, let's have a glance at the individual Borland tools. An important statement valid for all command-line tools is that they can be used under MS-DOS. This is accomplished through a 32-bit loader (similar to Phar Lap's QuickStart) that grabs the PE-EXE and executes it in a convenient environment (of course assuming a 386 or better and sufficient RAM!). To be concise: the most important Borland tools (compiler, linker, etc.) directly execute under MS-DOS and therefore can be used for the creation of Win32s programs without Windows NT or 95. Well, a small hitch remains: the TD32 debugger does not run with Win32s (or Win16, respectively).

The compiler has not been modified in a significant way. It is, of course apart from the 32-bit code generation, nearly a 100 percent compatible copy of its 16-bit brother. Some switches have been removed which under a 32-bit system are not needed anymore: -mx for choosing the memory model; -Yx for the overlay management; -1 and -2 for 8086 and 286 code generation, and the like. The option -a (used for defining the packing of structs) was modified (for more about structure alignment see section 3.5, page 166). Now with a numerical argument (e.g., -a4 for a 4-byte alignment) a more flexible handling is possible. The various compiler extensions for Win32 introduced with Microsoft's compiler (e.g., the statements to structured exception handling or the __declspec() family of attributes) are mostly omitted in the current version; I very much hope that Borland supports these in a future version.

The linker is (excluding some minor minutiae) used just as known from MS-DOS. As already mentioned, it only accepts OMF files; from what I've heard from Borland employees, this won't be changed for the foreseeable future. As long as you only need to work with Borland tools (or compatible programs) and libraries, you can get by with that. Yet Borland should support the COFF format as soon as possible. And the Borland linker is loyal in still another way: as before for linking applications it needs a DEF file (or uses predefined default values). The obvious trend at Microsoft, however, is the complete elimination of these files; I don't know whether Borland is well advised to allow attribute definitions on EXE files and DLLs only with an old-fashioned DEF file.

All the other tools (TDUMP, IMPLIB, MAKE, Turbo Debugger, etc.) are working almost exactly as their 16-bit counterparts (partially they're even the "old" 16-bit programs, which are easily executable in the MS-DOS subsystem under NT). As said: someone who knows the 16-bit Borland tools well will relatively quickly find his way under Win32. And so the main audience of Borland seems to be defined: those Win16 developers who need rapidly and easily a 32-bit version of their software (e.g., for Win32s), without necessarily expecting to work with NT or Windows 95 in the near future.

And the rest?

Borland aims at Win32s developers.

Any plans Borland might have to offer the BCC product also for Win32 RISC platforms cannot be estimated currently. And whether the importance of Borland in the C/C++ compiler market is large enough so that the company can establish a second standard besides the Microsoft tools in the long run, is very, very unsure. Finally, many computer magazines, books and other products like additional tool libraries with source code will definitely adopt the Microsoft standards ("since then we're on the safe side...").

Does Borland take a RISC?

5.5 Latest News: Visual C++ 2 and Win32 Enhancements

"One would like to marry a tall slim, but gets a little thick — Ssälawih!" Kurt Tucholsky, Ideal and Reality

Like the (finally unified) Win32 SDK, Visual C++ 2 (VC 2) requires a CD-ROM drive. And the further requirements are also not too bad: of course Windows NT (or 95) must be installed (by the way, I prefer NT, the multi-tasking is just smoother and the system simply works faster), and some 80 MB on the hard disk and about 16 MB RAM are minimum (citing from Microsoft's leaflet: "... but 20 megabytes* is recommended for improved performance." Well, you certainly can imagine what *rec-*

* RAM, mind you! The time when a development system needed 20 MB on the hard disk is long gone...

351

ommended means in this context…). So what do you get for your money and hardware sacrifice?

In a nutshell, VC 2 is a Win32 version of VC with all the products and features also found in the Win16 version. There are of course some enhancements (more about that later on), but for me the most amazing thing was that the NT version actually contains everything in fully 32-bit adapted versions (AppStudio, the wizards, etc.) even for the other NT plaforms (e.g., MIPS, Alpha). This makes the transition from 16-bit Intel machines to whatever CPU very smooth and even pleasant. A single important feature is lacking: VC 2 doesn't support VBX controls. This is not without logic, because these are 16-bit DLLs anyway — so we'll have to wait until the corresponding 32-bit OCX controls (which are based on OLE 2 automation) will be available for Win32.

Figure 5.5: VC++ AppStudio under Windows NT

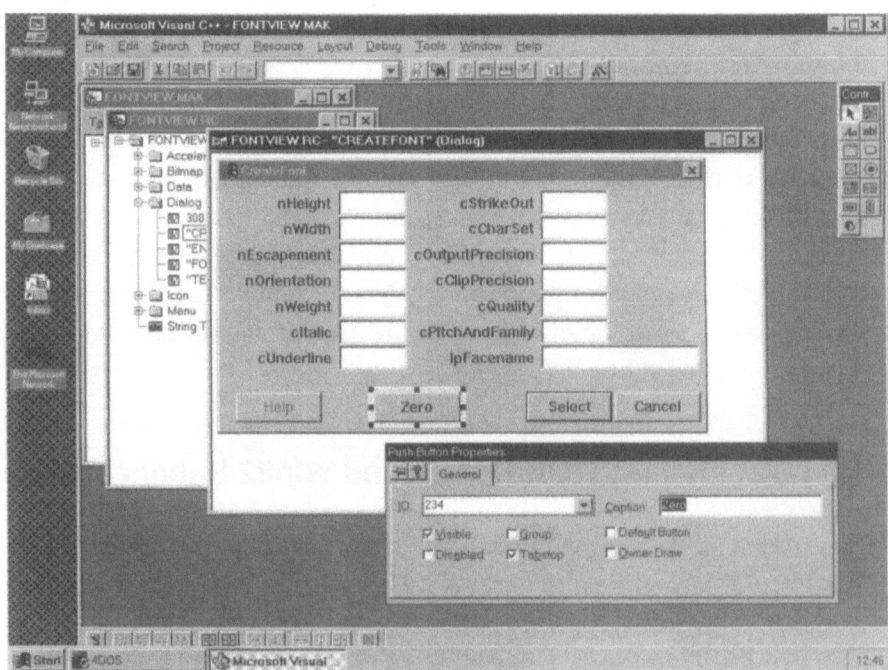

Otherwise I am very pleased: just as working with NT is much better (this means more productive) than working with Win16, using VC 2 too is considerably more agreeable than using the individual SDK components. And since nearly the total scope of delivery of the Win32 SDK is contained, there are almost no reasons ever to quit the IDE. Omitted compared to the SDK are only three toolkits: RPC, OLE 2.0, and setup.

Missing compared to the Win32 SDK: RPC, OLE 2.0, and setup.

Also important seems the consideration that Win32s (currently in version 1.25) is a component of VC 2.

CVTRES and CVTOMF aren't necessary with VC 2 because the VC linker can process all possible and impossible OBJ and RES formats; the conversions previously done with the help of these programs are with VC++ obsolete. The C compiler is practically the same as found in earlier versions of the Win32 SDK, so everything you've read so far remains valid. The only important change is the keywords for the exception handling: the macros try, except, finally, and leave (found in EXCPT.H) have been removed; therefore, the "original" keywords of the compiler have to be used (e.g., __try, __except, __finally and __leave. (Or just write some simple macro definitions* into a suitable header file...)

CVTRES and CVTOMF are superfluous.

* e.g., "#define try __try"

A very nice feature is the integrated profiler, which replaces both the API profiler and the working set tuner; the whole business of optimizing an application gets much easier (actually it's fun!). Another important new ingredient is the 3.1 version of the Microsoft Foundation Classes (MFC 3.1). First, this class library is *amazingly* downward compatible to the Win16 implementation (and so significantly helps with porting — if you used MFC in the first place!). As a matter of fact, nearly all my Win16 MFC programs could be used under NT VC++ with just a re-compilation. At some places, a bit of polishing for the 16-bit data types (especially WORD) was necessary, but the whole process was rather painless. Second, MFC is becoming more and more an indispensable shell for Windows programming altogether: trying to implement OLE 2 technology in raw C (or C++ without MFC) is more than brave; I'd rather call that ridiculous. All in all, this is the first time that I am actually working *with pleasure* on an integrated Microsoft development system....

The integrated profiler

And MFC 3.1

And what happens with Win32 itself? Windows NT is currently in 3.51 and the Cairo beta program (i.e., for NT 4.0) is about to start, so we should expect to see something "real" by the end of 1996 (but 1997 is as probable, just look at the ever-slipping schedule of Windows 95). Then we should for the first time have all the new nifty features of Chicago available in all Win32 systems; that will ease development for Win32 considerably. Also interesting is the availability of NT on various new platforms: the latest additions include PowerPC and the HP/PA architecture. This is a very remarkable development, and I won't be too surprised if finally slow-starting NT turns out to be the big winner...

NT 4.0, aka Cairo...

How about Windows 95++?

Windows 95 is expected at the latest by the end of 1995 (what mockery would be poured over King Gates and his API knights if Windows 95** had to be renamed Windows 96*...). The next version (code-named Memphis) is already under development; we'll see what this will bring (some guesses would include support for other file systems, more code moved from the 16-bit OS parts into 32-bit land, an enhanced GDI, and maybe stronger ties between the system and application suites like MS Office). In the long run I feel that Windows 95 will include more and more components from Windows NT until Windows 95 is just a somewhat slimmed-down version of NT for desktop machines.

And OLE 2?

What's ahead for OLE 2? This is possibly the most important question of all. The next major versions of Windows NT and 95 should include a much more integrated version of OLE, I'd even think that OLE concepts and a future version of the API could gain the role of the "native" system API in these environments. Currently OLE 2 is only in some clearly defined areas a serious competitor for the Win32 API (but there *is* definitely a competition between the two APIs), but this can easily change in the future: OLE 2 might develop into a full-fledged programmers' interface not only for object definition but for all aspects of the system. Even the window as we know it today (as an HWND) might then disappear... (well, actually for reasons of backward compatibility this won't happen, but you certainly get the general idea).

But this all is just speculation; let's face the realities and first put Win32 to work!

Important Data Types Compared

The following table shows the most important simple data types of Win16 and Win32 in direct comparison. The first column shows the type name, the second its definition and length (in bytes) under Win16, and the third the same under Win32. The last column (called Rem.) contains pointers to further remarks and explanations that are found in the margin. Please note that some portable and Unicode-compatible data types have been introduced with Win32 (TCHAR, and the like), which as of today have *no* equivalent in Win16. These have not been included in the table.

Data type	Win16 definition and size	Win32 definition and size	Rem.
int/INT	int (2)	int, INT (4)	[1]
char/CHAR	char (1)	char, CHAR (1)	
short/SHORT	short (2)	short, SHORT (2)	
BOOL	int (2)	int (4)	[1]
BYTE	unsigned char (1)	unsigned char (1)	
WORD	unsigned short (2)	unsigned short (2)	
DWORD	unsigned long (4)	unsigned long (4)	
UINT	unsigned int (2)	unsigned int (4)	[1]
LONG	signed long (4)	signed long (4)	
WPARAM	UINT (2)	UINT (4)	[1]
LPARAM	LONG (4)	LONG (4)	
LRESULT	LONG (4)	LONG (4)	
PSTR	char NEAR * (2)	char * (4)	[1]
NPSTR	char NEAR * (2)	char * (4)	[1]
LPSTR	char FAR * (4)	char * (4)	[2]
LPCSTR	const char FAR * (4)	const char * (4)	[2]
PBYTE	BYTE NEAR * (2)	BYTE * (4)	[1]
LPBYTE	BYTE FAR * (4)	BYTE * (4)	[2]

Table A1.1: The most important Windows data types in direct comparison

[1] The size of the type has changed.

[2] Win32 pointers are not built from segment and offset, but just contain a (widened) offset; therefore segment arithmetics are impossible. There's no distinction between NEAR and FAR pointers.

[1] The size of the type has
changed.

[2] Win32 pointers are not
built from segment and
offset, but just contain a
(widened) offset; therefore
segment arithmetics are
impossible. There's no
distinction between NEAR
and FAR pointers.

[3] ... similar to the other
handle types defined with
DECLARE_HANDLE (HDC,
HMENU, HGDIOBJ, etc.).

[4] One of those pointer
types that under Win16 were
dependent on the memory
model (small, medium, etc.).

[5] This is one of the rare
exceptions: a Win16 UINT
changes to a Win32 WORD
(i.e.,the size doesn't
change).

[6] One of the rare cases
where the two header files
are not consistent.

[7] Apart from the parameter
list also valid for other
CALLBACK functions (like
DLGPROC, etc.).

Data type	Win16 definition and size	Win32 definition and size	Rem.
PINT	int NEAR * (2)	INT * (4)	[1]
LPINT	int FAR * (4)	INT * (4)	[2]
PWORD	WORD NEAR * (2)	WORD * (4)	[1]
LPWORD	WORD FAR * (4)	WORD * (4)	[2]
PLONG	long NEAR * (2)	long * (4)	[1]
LPLONG	long FAR * (4)	long * (4)	[2]
PDWORD	DWORD NEAR * (2)	DWORD * (4)	[1]
LPDWORD	DWORD FAR * (4)	DWORD * (4)	[2]
LPVOID	void FAR * (4)	void * (4)	[2]
HANDLE (STRICT)	const void NEAR * (2)	void * (4)	[1]
HANDLE (normal)	UINT (2)	void * (4)	[1]
HWND (STRICT)	const struct HWND__ NEAR * (2)	const struct HWND__ * (4)	[1, 3]
HWND (normal)	UINT	HANDLE	[1, 3]
PHANDLE	HANDLE * (2)	HANDLE * (4)	[1, 4]
SPHANDLE	HANDLE NEAR * (2)	HANDLE * (4)	[1]
LPHANDLE	HANDLE FAR * (4)	HANDLE * (4)	[2]
ATOM	UINT (2)	WORD (2)	[5]
HFILE	int (2)	int (4)	[1]
FARPROC	void (CALLBACK *) (void) (4)	int (WINAPI *)() (4)	[2, 6]
WNDPROC	LRESULT (CALLBACK *) (HWND, UINT, WPARAM, LPARAM) (4)	LRESULT (CALLBACK *) (HWND, UINT, WPARAM, LPARAM) (4)	[2, 7]

Over and above these standard Windows data types, the Win32 API predefines a lot of other simple types, which for the better part stem from the time when Windows NT was still called OS/2 NT. Therefore it should not exactly be astonishing that these type definitions look quite familiar to OS/2 developers. The following small table shows the most important of those new, "old" types, which easily can be used in parallel to the well-known Windows types:

Win32 data type	Win32 definition	Win16 equivalent(s)
UCHAR	unsigned char	BYTE
USHORT	unsigned short	WORD, UINT
PVOID	void *	LPVOID
PUSHORT	USHORT *	LPWORD
ULONG	unsigned long	DWORD
PULONG	ULONG *	LPDWORD
PSZ	char *	LPSTR

Table A1.2: OS/2 compatible Win32 data types.

PORT.INI: Enhanced and Clarified

Appendix 2 shows an enhanced and clarified version of the PORTTOOL initialization file PORT.INI. Of course, a copy of the file is also found on the accompanying disk — possibly even in a somewhat more current version than is printed here (see the subdirectory \PORTTOOL). Using the file is simplicity itself: just rename the original PORT.INI found in X:\MSTOOLS\BIN (e.g., to PORT.OLD) and copy the enhanced version from the disk to X:\MSTOOLS\BIN. If you start PORTTOOL as usual, the program directly accesses the new file. (Another possibility would be to copy the file with another name, e.g., PORTENH.INI, and to use the PORTTOOL open command to read in an INI file.) The entries in PORT.INI are divided into seven classes: the section [APIS] is responsible for all Windows functions; [MESSAGES] deals with messages; [STRUCTURES] with struct definitions; [TYPES] handles the simple data types; I assume [CONSTANTS] and [MACROS] are self-explaining. Finally, [CUSTOM] is a dumping spot for all those items that are not easily assigned to one of the other categories. In a specific group the entries are sorted alphabetically, so the following listing can be used either as a reference or, if you have a specific question in mind, as an enhancement to the index. Of course, you can easily modify and enhance the file on your own (caution: *don't* use special characters above the standard 7-bit ASCII set, best regards of strtok()!). If you have to report an improvement or error, please inform me of the change or addition so that this information can be put into subsequent editions.

Divided in seven classes

The directory \PORTTOOL also sports a simple application called PORTVIEW.EXE (including source code). This program can be used for browsing and investigating PORT.INI (or any other file in the proper format). The program also allows you to search the whole file for a specific item and links to the API WinHelp files. The executable file is a standard portable executable (PE) and can be executed under Windows NT, Windows 95, and Windows 3.1 (with the help of Win32s, see subdirectory \WIN32S on the disk). Have fun!

PORTVIEW.EXE

```
[PORTTOOL]
; To get help for the various items from within PORTTOOL, specify the path
; where WinHelp can find the API help file. But be forewarned: PORTTOOL is
; (not only in this respect) somewhat "obstinate" (if not to say buggy)...
WinHelp=z:\hlp\api32wh.hlp

; Viewing 16-bit help is unfortunately not supported by PORTTOOL. This line
; is read and interpreted by my PORTVIEW program only; it should contain the
; location of the Win16 help files (if any).
WinHelp16=d:\bc\bin\tcwhelp.hlp


[APIS]
; The format for the follwing entries (which can be easily enhanced or changed)
; is defined as follows (alas, no special characters such as umlauts are allowed
; in the text):
;    SearchKey=Win32APIHelpTerm;Reason for the change;Proposed action;

; There are the following optional variants:
;    SearchKey=APIHelpTerm;Reason for the change; ;
;    SearchKey=APIHelpTerm; ;Proposed action;
;    SearchKey=APIHelpTerm; ; ;
;    SearchKey= ;Reason for the change;Proposed action;
;    SearchKey= ;Reason for the change; ;
;    SearchKey= ; ;Proposed action;
; Trailing semicolons are optional. By the way, more about the sections can
; be found in the book in appendix 2; there also a complete listing of this
; file is shown!


; The first line has to appear twice to be read once...
AccessResource=AccessResource;No 32-bit equivalent;Not required, just delete;
AccessResource=AccessResource;No 32-bit equivalent;Not required, just delete;
AddFontResource=AddFontResource;Only use file names (strings), no handles;;
AllocDSToCSAlias=AllocDSToCSAlias;No 32-bit equivalent;;
AllocResource=AllocResource;no direct 32-bit equivalent;Replace with Load/Find/LockResource;
AllocSelector=AllocSelector;No 32-bit equivalent;;
AnsiLower=AnsiLower;Macro around CharLower;;
AnsiLowerBuff=AnsiLowerBuff;Macro around CharLowerBuff;;
AnsiNext=AnsiNext;Macro around CharNext;;
AnsiPrev=AnsiPrev;Macro around CharPrev;;
AnsiToOem=AnsiToOem;Macro around CharToOem;;
AnsiToOemBuff=AnsiToOemBuff;Macro around CharToOemBuff;;
AnsiUpper=AnsiUpper;Macro around CharUpper;;
AnsiUpperBuff=AnsiUpperBuff;Macro around CharUpperBuff;;
Catch=Catch;No 32-bit equivalent;Replace with structured exception handling (SEH);
ChangeMenu=ChangeMenu;New functions available;Replace with portable functions;
ChangeSelector=ChangeSelector;No 32-bit equivalent;;
CloseComm=CloseComm;COMM functions mapped to file I/O;Replace with CloseHandle;
CloseSound=CloseSound;No 32-bit equivalent;Replace with multimedia sound support or PlaySo-
        und/Beep;
```

CountVoiceNotes=CountVoiceNotes;No 32-bit equivalent;Replace with multimedia sound support or PlaySound/Beep;

DefHookProc=DefHookProc;Old hook API, creates only thread-local hooks;Use new CallNextHookEx;

DefineHandleTable=DefineHandleTable;No 32-bit equivalent;Not required, just delete;

DeviceCapabilities=DeviceCapabilities;No 32-bit equivalent;Replace with portable DeviceCapabilitiesEx;

DeviceMode=DeviceMode;No 32-bit equivalent;Replace with portable DeviceModeEx;

DialogProc=DialogProc;Dialog procs should be defined portable;BOOL CALLBACK WndProc(HWND hWnd, UINT uMsg, WPARAM wParam, LPARAM lParam);

DirectedYield=DirectedYield;No 32-bit equivalent;;

DlgDirSelect=DlgDirSelect;No 32-bit equivalent;Replace with portable DlgDirSelectEx;

DlgDirSelectComboBox=DlgDirSelectComboBox;No 32-bit equivalent;Replace with portable DlgDirSelectComboBoxEx;

DlgProc=DialogProc;Dialog procs should be defined portable;BOOL CALLBACK WndProc(HWND hWnd, UINT uMsg, WPARAM wParam, LPARAM lParam);

DOS3Call=DOS3Call;No 32-bit equivalent;Replace with named portable Win32 API;

EnumTaskWindows=EnumTaskWindows;Macro around EnumThreadWindows;;

ExitWindows=ExitWindows;EW_* constants not supported anymore;See ExitWindowsEx;

ExitWindowsExec=ExitWindowsExec;No 32-bit equivalent;Possibly replace with ExitWindowsEx;

ExtDeviceMode=ExtDeviceMode;No 32-bit equivalent;Replace with portable ExtDeviceModeEx;

ffree=free;NEAR/FAR functions not defined anymore;Either use macros in WINDOWSX.H or free;

FlushComm=FlushComm;No 32-bit equivalent;Replace with PurgeComm;

fmalloc=malloc;NEAR/FAR functions not defined anymore;Either use macros in WINDOWSX.H or malloc;

fmemccpy=memccpy;NEAR/FAR functions not defined anymore;Either use macros in WINDOWSX.H or memccpy;

fmemchr=memchr;NEAR/FAR functions not defined anymore;Either use macros in WINDOWSX.H or memchr;

fmemcmp=memcmp;NEAR/FAR functions not defined anymore;Either use macros in WINDOWSX.H or memcmp;

fmemcpy=memcpy;NEAR/FAR functions not defined anymore;Either use macros in WINDOWSX.H or memcpy;

fmemicmp=memicmp;NEAR/FAR functions not defined anymore;Either use macros in WINDOWSX.H or memicmp;

fmemmove=memmove;NEAR/FAR functions not defined anymore;Either use macros in WINDOWSX.H or memmove;

fmemset=memset;NEAR/FAR functions not defined anymore;Either use macros in WINDOWSX.H or memset;

fmsize=_msize;NEAR/FAR functions not defined anymore;Either use macros in WINDOWSX.H or _msize;

frealloc=realloc;NEAR/FAR functions not defined anymore;Either use macros in WINDOWSX.H or realloc;

FreeModule=FreeModule;Macro around FreeLibrary;Replace with FreeLibrary;

FreeProcInstance=FreeProcInstance;Empty macro;Not required, just delete;

FreeResource=FreeResource;Not required under Win32;Just delete;

FreeSelector=FreeSelector;No 32-bit equivalent;;

fstrcat=strcat;NEAR/FAR functions not defined anymore;Either use macros in WINDOWSX.H or strcat;

fstrchr=strchr;NEAR/FAR functions not defined anymore;Either use macros in WINDOWSX.H or strchr;

```
fstrcmp=strcmp;NEAR/FAR functions not defined anymore;Either use macros in WINDOWSX.H or
        strcmp;
fstrcpy=strcpy;NEAR/FAR functions not defined anymore;Either use macros in WINDOWSX.H or
        strcpy;
fstrcspn=strcspn;NEAR/FAR functions not defined anymore;Either use macros in WINDOWSX.H or
        strcspn;
fstrdup=strdup;NEAR/FAR functions not defined anymore;Either use macros in WINDOWSX.H or
        strdup;
fstricmp=stricmp;NEAR/FAR functions not defined anymore;Either use macros in WINDOWSX.H or
        stricmp;
fstrlen=strlen;NEAR/FAR functions not defined anymore;Either use macros in WINDOWSX.H or
        strlen;
fstrlwr=strlwr;NEAR/FAR functions not defined anymore;Either use macros in WINDOWSX.H or
        strlwr;
fstrncat=strncat;NEAR/FAR functions not defined anymore;Either use macros in WINDOWSX.H or
        strncat;
fstrncmp=strncmp;NEAR/FAR functions not defined anymore;Either use macros in WINDOWSX.H or
        strncmp;
fstrncpy=strncpy;NEAR/FAR functions not defined anymore;Either use macros in WINDOWSX.H or
        strncpy;
fstrnicmp=strnicmp;NEAR/FAR functions not defined anymore;Either use macros in WINDOWSX.H or
        strnicmp;
fstrnset=strnset;NEAR/FAR functions not defined anymore;Either use macros in WINDOWSX.H or
        strnset;
fstrpbrk=strpbrk;NEAR/FAR functions not defined anymore;Either use macros in WINDOWSX.H or
        strpbrk;
fstrrchr=strrchr;NEAR/FAR functions not defined anymore;Either use macros in WINDOWSX.H or
        strrchr;
fstrrev=strrev;NEAR/FAR functions not defined anymore;Either use macros in WINDOWSX.H or
        strrev;
fstrset=strset;NEAR/FAR functions not defined anymore;Either use macros in WINDOWSX.H or
        strset;
fstrspn=strspn;NEAR/FAR functions not defined anymore;Either use macros in WINDOWSX.H or
        strspn;
fstrstr=strstr;NEAR/FAR functions not defined anymore;Either use macros in WINDOWSX.H or
        strstr;
fstrtok=strtok;NEAR/FAR functions not defined anymore;Either use macros in WINDOWSX.H or
        strtok;
fstrupr=strupr;NEAR/FAR functions not defined anymore;Either use macros in WINDOWSX.H or
        strupr;
GetActiveWindow=GetActiveWindow;Return value can be zero;Consider local input state;
GetAspectRatioFilter=GetAspectRatioFilter;No 32-bit equivalent;Replace with portable GetAs-
        pectRatioFilterEx;
GetAtomHandle=GetAtomHandle;No 32-bit equivalent;;
GetBitmapDimension=GetBitmapDimension;No 32-bit equivalent;Replace with portable GetBitmapDi-
        mensionEx;
GetBrushOrg=GetBrushOrg;No 32-bit equivalent;Replace with portable GetBrushOrgEx;
GetCapture=GetCapture;Return value can be zero;Consider local input state;
GetClassWord=GetClassWord;Consider widened data types;GetClassLong for values grown to 32
        bit;
```

GetCodeHandle=GetCodeHandle;No 32-bit equivalent;;
GetCodeInfo=GetCodeInfo;No 32-bit equivalent;;
GetCommError=GetCommError;No 32-bit equivalent;Replace with ClearCommError;
GetCurrentPDB=GetCurrentPDB;No 32-bit equivalent;Possibly use GetCommandLine;
GetCurrentPosition=GetCurrentPosition;No 32-bit equivalent;Replace with portable GetCurrent-
      PositionEx;
GetCurrentTask=GetCurrentTask;No 32-bit equivalent;Use GetCurrentThread/Process;
GetDOSEnvironment=GetDOSEnvironment;No 32-bit equivalent;Possibly use GetEnvironmentStrings;
GetEnvironment=GetEnvironment;No 32-bit equivalent;;
GetFileResource=GetFileResource;No 32-bit equivalent;;
GetFileResourceSize=GetFileResourceSize;No 32-bit equivalent;;
GetFocus=GetFocus;Return value can be zero;Consider local input state;
GetFreeSpace=GetFreeSpace;No 32-bit equivalent;Replace with GlobalMemoryStatus;
GetFreeSystemResources=GetFreeSystemResources;No 32-bit equivalent;;
GetInstanceData=GetInstanceData;No 32-bit equivalent;Replace with IPC mechanisms;
GetKBCodePage=GetKBCodePage;No 32-bit equivalent;;
GetMetaFileBits=GetMetaFileBits;No 32-bit equivalent;Replace with portable GetMetaFileBitsEx;
GetModuleUsage=GetModuleUsage;No 32-bit equivalent;;
GetNumTask=GetNumTask;No 32-bit equivalent;;
GetSelectorBase=GetSelectorBase;No 32-bit equivalent;;
GetSelectorLimit=GetSelectorLimit;No 32-bit equivalent;;
GetSysModalWindow=GetSysModalWindow;No 32-bit equivalent;;
GetTempDrive=GetTempDrive;No 32-bit equivalent;See GetTempPath;
GetTextExtent=GetTextExtent;No 32-bit equivalent;Replace with portable GetTextExtentPoint;
GetTextExtentEx=GetTextExtentEx;No 32-bit equivalent;Replace with portable GetTextExtentEx-
      Point;
GetThresholdEvent=GetThresholdEvent;No 32-bit equivalent;Replace with multimedia sound sup-
      port or PlaySound/Beep;
GetThresholdStatus=GetThresholdStatus;No 32-bit equivalent;Replace with multimedia sound
      support or PlaySound/Beep;
GetTimerResolution=GetTimerResolution;No 32-bit equivalent;;
GetViewportExt=GetViewportExt;No 32-bit equivalent;Replace with portable GetViewportExtEx;
GetViewportOrg=GetViewportOrg;No 32-bit equivalent;Replace with portable GetViewportOrgEx;
GetWindowExt=GetWindowExt;No 32-bit equivalent;Replace with portable GetWindowExtEx;
GetWindowOrg=GetWindowOrg;No 32-bit equivalent;Replace with portable GetWindowOrgEx;
GetWindowTask=GetWindowTask;Macro around GetWindowThreadProcessId;;
GetWindowWord=GetWindowWord;Consider widened data types;GetWindowLong for values grown to 32
      bit;
GetWinFlags=GetWinFlags;No 32-bit equivalent;Replace with GetSystemInfo;
GlobalCompact=GlobalCompact;Not required under Win32;Just delete;
GlobalDosAlloc=GlobalDosAlloc;No 32-bit equivalent;;
GlobalDosFree=GlobalDosFree;No 32-bit equivalent;;
GlobalFix=GlobalFix;Not required under Win32;Just delete;
GlobalLRUNewest=GlobalLRUNewest;Empty macro;Not required, just delete;
GlobalLRUOldest=GlobalLRUOldest;Empty macro;Not required, just delete;
GlobalNotify=GlobalNotify;No 32-bit equivalent;;
GlobalPageLock=GlobalPageLock;No 32-bit equivalent;Possibly use VirtualLock;
GlobalPageUnlock=GlobalPageUnlock;No 32-bit equivalent;Possibly use VirtualUnlock;
GlobalUnfix=GlobalUnfix;Not required under Win32;Just delete;
GlobalUnwire=GlobalUnwire;Not required under Win32;Just delete;

GlobalWire=GlobalWire;Not required under Win32;Just delete;
int86=int86;No 32-bit equivalent;Replace with named portable Win32 API;
intdos=intdos;No 32-bit equivalent;Replace with named portable Win32 API;
IsGDIObject=IsGDIObject;No 32-bit equivalent;;
IsTask=IsTask;No 32-bit equivalent;;
LibMain=DllEntryPoint;DLL initialization changed;Adjust to Win32;
LimitEmsPages=LimitEmsPages;No 32-bit equivalent;;
LocalCompact=LocalCompact;Not required under Win32;Just delete;
LocalInit=LocalInit;No 32-bit equivalent;;
LocalNotify=LocalNotify;No 32-bit equivalent;;
LocalShrink=LocalShrink;Not required under Win32;Just delete;
LockData=LockData;Not required under Win32;Just delete;
LockSegment=LockSegment;Not required under Win32;Just delete;
MakeProcInstance=MakeProcInstance;Empty macro;Not required, just delete;
MoveTo=MoveTo;No 32-bit equivalent;Replace with portable MoveToEx;
ncalloc=calloc;NEAR/FAR functions not defined anymore;Either use macros in WINDOWSX.H or
          calloc;
NetBIOSCall=NetBIOSCall;No 32-bit equivalent;Replace with named portable Win32 API;
nexpand=expand;NEAR/FAR functions not defined anymore;Either use macros in WINDOWSX.H or
          expand;
nfree=free;NEAR/FAR functions not defined anymore;Either use macros in WINDOWSX.H or free;
nmalloc=malloc;NEAR/FAR functions not defined anymore;Either use macros in WINDOWSX.H or
          malloc;
nmsize=msize;NEAR/FAR functions not defined anymore;Either use macros in WINDOWSX.H or msize;
nrealloc=realloc;NEAR/FAR functions not defined anymore;Either use macros in WINDOWSX.H or
          realloc;
nstrdup=strdup;NEAR/FAR functions not defined anymore;Either use macros in WINDOWSX.H or
          strdup;
OemToAnsi=OemToAnsi;Macro around OemToChar;;
OemToAnsiBuff=OemToAnsiBuff;Macro around OemToCharBuff;;
OffsetViewportOrg=OffsetViewportOrg;No 32-bit equivalent;Replace with portable OffsetVie-
          wportOrgEx;
OffsetWindowOrg=OffsetWindowOrg;No 32-bit equivalent;Replace with portable OffsetWindowOrgEx;
OpenComm=OpenComm;COMM functions mapped to file I/O;Replace with CreateFile;
OpenSound=OpenSound;No 32-bit equivalent;Replace with multimedia sound support or PlaySo-
          und/Beep;
PostAppMessage=PostAppMessage;Macro around PostThreadMessage;Replace with PostThreadMessage;
PrestoChangoSelector=PrestoChangoSelector;No 32-bit equivalent;;
ProfClear=ProfClear;Profiling API removed, see Tools documentation;;
ProfFinish=ProfFinish;Profiling API removed, see Tools documentation;;
ProfFlush=ProfFlush;Profiling API removed, see Tools documentation;;
ProfInsChk=ProfInsChk;Profiling API removed, see Tools documentation;;
ProfSampRate=ProfSampRate;Profiling API removed, see Tools documentation;;
ProfSetup=ProfSetup;Profiling API removed, see Tools documentation;;
ProfStart=ProfStart;Profiling API removed, see Tools documentation;;
ProfStop=ProfStop;Profiling API removed, see Tools documentation;;
QuerySendMessage=QuerySendMessage;No 32-bit equivalent;;
ReadComm=ReadComm;COMM functions mapped to file I/O;Replace with ReadFile;
RemoveFontResource=RemoveFontResource;Only use file names (strings), no handles;;

ScaleViewportExt=ScaleViewportExt;No 32-bit equivalent;Replace with portable ScaleViewportEx-
    tEx;
ScaleWindowExt=ScaleWindowExt;No 32-bit equivalent;Replace with portable ScaleWindowExtEx;
SetActiveWindow=SetActiveWindow;;Consider local input state;
SetBitmapDimension=SetBitmapDimension;No 32-bit equivalent;Replace with portable SetBitmapDi-
    mensionEx;
SetBrushOrg=SetBrushOrg;No 32-bit equivalent;Replace with portable SetBrushOrgEx;
SetCapture=SetCapture;;Consider local input state;
SetClassWord=SetClassWord;Consider widened data types;SetClassLong for values grown to 32
    bit;
SetCommEventMask=SetCommEventMask;No 32-bit equivalent;Replace with SetCommMask;
SetEnvironment=SetEnvironment;No 32-bit equivalent;;
SetFocus=SetFocus;;Consider local input state;
SetMessageQueue=SetMessageQueue;Not required under Win32;Just delete;
SetMetaFileBits=SetMetaFileBits;No 32-bit equivalent;Replace with portable SetMetaFileBitsEx;
SetResourceHandler=SetResourceHandler;No 32-bit equivalent;;
SetSelectorBase=SetSelectorBase;No 32-bit equivalent;;
SetSelectorLimit=SetSelectorLimit;No 32-bit equivalent;;
SetSoundNoise=SetSoundNoise;No 32-bit equivalent;Replace with multimedia sound support or
    PlaySound/Beep;
SetSwapAreaSize=SetSwapAreaSize;No 32-bit equivalent;;
SetSysModalWindow=SetSysModalWindow;No 32-bit equivalent;;
SetViewportExt=SetViewportExt;No 32-bit equivalent;Replace with portable SetViewportExtEx;
SetViewportOrg=SetViewportOrg;No 32-bit equivalent;Replace with portable SetViewportOrgEx;
SetVoiceAccent=SetVoiceAccent;No 32-bit equivalent;Replace with multimedia sound support or
    PlaySound/Beep;
SetVoiceEnvelope=SetVoiceEnvelope;No 32-bit equivalent;Replace with multimedia sound support
    or PlaySound/Beep;
SetVoiceNote=SetVoiceNote;No 32-bit equivalent;Replace with multimedia sound support or Play-
    Sound/Beep;
SetVoiceQueueSize=SetVoiceQueueSize;No 32-bit equivalent;Replace with multimedia sound sup-
    port or PlaySound/Beep;
SetVoiceSound=SetVoiceSound;No 32-bit equivalent;Replace with multimedia sound support or
    PlaySound/Beep;
SetVoiceThreshold=SetVoiceThreshold;No 32-bit equivalent;Replace with multimedia sound sup-
    port or PlaySound/Beep;
SetWindowExt=SetWindowExt;No 32-bit equivalent;Replace with portable SetWindowExtEx;
SetWindowOrg=SetWindowOrg;No 32-bit equivalent;Replace with portable SetWindowOrgEx;
SetWindowsHook=SetWindowsHook;Old hook API, creates only thread-local hooks;Use new SetWin-
    dowsHookEx;
SetWindowWord=SetWindowWord;Consider widened data types;SetWindowsLong for values grown to 32
    bit;
StartSound=StartSound;No 32-bit equivalent;Replace with multimedia sound support or PlaySo-
    und/Beep;
StopSound=StopSound;No 32-bit equivalent;Replace with multimedia sound support or PlaySo-
    und/Beep;
SwitchStackBack=SwitchStackBack;No 32-bit equivalent;;
SwitchStackTo=SwitchStackTo;No 32-bit equivalent;;
SyncAllVoices=SyncAllVoices;No 32-bit equivalent;Replace with multimedia sound support or
    PlaySound/Beep;

Throw=Throw;No Win32 equivalent;Replace with structured exception handling (SEH);
UngetCommChar=UngetCommChar;No 32-bit equivalent;;
UnhookWindowsHook=UnhookWindowsHook;Old hook API, creates only thread-local hooks;Use new
       UnhookWindowsHookEx;
UnlockData=UnlockData;Not required under Win32;Just delete;
UnlockResource=UnlockResource;Empty macro;Not required, just delete;
UnlockSegment=UnlockSegment;Not required under Win32;Just delete;
UnrealizeObject=UnrealizeObject;Not required under Win32;Just delete;
ValidateCodeSegments=ValidateCodeSegments;No 32-bit equivalent;;
ValidateFreeSpaces=ValidateFreeSpaces;No 32-bit equivalent;;
WaitSoundState=WaitSoundState;No 32-bit equivalent;Replace with multimedia sound support or
       PlaySound/Beep;
WEP=DllEntryPoint;DLL termination changed;Adjust to Win32;
WindowProc=WindowProc;Window procs should be defined portable;LRESULT CALLBACK WndProc(HWND
       hWnd, UINT uMsg, WPARAM wParam, LPARAM lParam);
WndProc=WindowProc;Window procs should be defined portable;LRESULT CALLBACK WndProc(HWND
       hWnd, UINT uMsg, WPARAM wParam, LPARAM lParam);
WriteComm=WriteComm;COMM functions mapped to file I/O;Replace with WriteFile;
Yield=Yield;No 32-bit equivalent;Replace with PeekMessage or Sleep;

[MESSAGES]
EM_GETSEL=EM_GETSEL;Information in wParam/lParam packed different;Use message cracker or
       alternate macro shell;
EM_LINESCROLL=EM_LINESCROLL;Information in wParam/lParam packed different;Use message cracker
       or alternate macro shell;
EM_SETSEL=EM_SETSEL;Information in wParam/lParam packed different;Use message cracker or
       alternate macro shell;
WM_ACTIVATE=WM_ACTIVATE;Information in wParam/lParam packed different;Use message cracker or
       alternate macro shell;
WM_CHANGECBCHAIN=WM_CHANGECBCHAIN;Information in wParam/lParam packed different;Use message
       cracker or alternate macro shell;
WM_CHARTOITEM=WM_CHARTOITEM;Information in wParam/lParam packed different;Use message cracker
       or alternate macro shell;
WM_COMMAND=WM_COMMAND;Information in wParam/lParam packed different;Use message cracker or
       alternate macro shell;
WM_COMMNOTIFY=WM_COMMNOTIFY;Message removed under Win32;See overlapping file I/O functions;
WM_CTLCOLOR=WM_CTLCOLOR;Replaced by 7 new messages, Information in wParam/lParam packed dif-
       ferent;message cracker or alternative Makroschale benutzen;
WM_DDE_ACK=WM_DDE_ACK;lParam for information not large enough;Use PackDDElParam etc.;
WM_DDE_ADVISE=WM_DDE_ADVISE;lParam for information not large enough;Use PackDDElParam etc.;
WM_DDE_DATA=WM_DDE_DATA;lParam for information not large enough;Use PackDDElParam etc.;
WM_DDE_EXECUTE=WM_DDE_EXECUTE;lParam for information not large enough;Use PackDDElParam etc.;
WM_DDE_POKE=WM_DDE_POKE;lParam for information not large enough;Use PackDDElParam etc.;
WM_DDE_REQUEST=WM_DDE_REQUEST;lParam for information not large enough;Use PackDDElParam etc.;
WM_DDE_TERMINATE=WM_DDE_TERMINATE;lParam for information not large enough;Use PackDDElParam
       etc.;
WM_DDE_UNADVISE=WM_DDE_UNADVISE;lParam for information not large enough;Use PackDDElParam
       etc.;
WM_HSCROLL=WM_HSCROLL;Information in wParam/lParam packed different;Use message cracker or
       alternate macro shell;

WM_MDIACTIVATE=WM_MDIACTIVATE;Information in wParam/lParam packed different;Use message crak-
ker or alternate macro shell;
WM_MDISETMENU=WM_MDISETMENU;Information in wParam/lParam packed different;Use message cracker
or alternate macro shell;
WM_MENUCHAR=WM_MENUCHAR;Information in wParam/lParam packed different;Use message cracker or
alternate macro shell;
WM_MENUSELECT=WM_MENUSELECT;Information in wParam/lParam packed different;Use message cracker
or alternate macro shell;
WM_PARENTNOTIFY=WM_PARENTNOTIFY;Information in wParam/lParam packed different;Use message
cracker or alternate macro shell;
WM_QUIT=WM_QUIT;If in a PostMessage call, malfunction possible under Win32;Replace with Post-
QuitMessage;
WM_VKEYTOITEM=WM_VKEYTOITEM;Information in wParam/lParam packed different;Use message cracker
or alternate macro shell;
WM_VSCROLL=WM_VSCROLL;Information in wParam/lParam packed different;Use message cracker or
alternate macro shell;

[STRUCTURES]
cbClsExtra=WNDCLASS;If != 0, consider widened data types;Possibly adjust size;
cbWndExtra=WNDCLASS;If != 0, consider widened data types;Possibly adjust size;
DCB=DCB;Bit fields changed, new members;;

[TYPES]
HTASK=HTASK;Data type removed;Replace with thread id (DWORD);
LONG=LONG;Check LONG variable or parameter;Possibly replace with LPARAM / LRESULT;
(short)=short;Check cast to 16- or 32-bit;Replace 16-bit data types with their 32-Bit equiva-
lents;
(WORD)=WORD;Check cast to 16- or 32-bit;Replace 16-bit data types with their 32-Bit equiva-
lents;
WORD=WORD;Check WORD variable or parameter;Possibly replace with WPARAM / UINT;

[CONSTANTS]
CS_GLOBALCLASS=RegisterClass;Windows classes are not global anymore;Explicit loading of cor-
respoding DLL;
GCW_ATOM=GetClassLong;No 32-bit equivalent;;
GCW_CBWNDEXTRA=GetClassLong;Data type widened;Replace with GCL_CBWNDEXTRA;
GCW_CBCLSEXTRA=GetClassLong;Data type widened;Replace with GCL_CBCLSEXTRA;
GCW_HCURSOR=GetClassLong;Data type widened;Replace with GCL_HCURSOR;
GCW_HBRBACKGROUND=GetClassLong;Data type widened;Replace with GCL_HBRBACKGROUND;
GCW_HICON=GetClassLong;Data type widened;Replace with GCL_HICON;
GCW_HMODULE=GetClassLong;Data type widened;Replace with GCL_HMODULE;
GCW_STYLE=GetClassLong;Data type widened;Replace with GCL_STYLE;
GMEM_DDESHARE=GMEM_DDESHARE;No effect under Win32;Replace with IPC mechanisms;
GMEM_SHARE=GMEM_SHARE;No effect under Win32;Replace with IPC mechanisms;
GWW_HINSTANCE=GetWindowLong;Data type widened;Replace with GWL_HINSTANCE;
GWW_HWNDPARENT=GetWindowLong;Data type widened;Replace with GWL_HWNDPARENT;
GWW_ID=GetWindowLong;Data type widened;Replace with GWL_ID;
GWW_USERDATA=GetWindowLong;Data type widened;Replace with GWL_USERDATA;

[MACROS]

HIWORD=HIWORD;HIWORD target 16 or 32 bit? If message parameter: changed packing?;Possibly use message cracker;

LOWORD=LOWORD;LOWORD target 16 or 32 bit? If message parameter: changed packing?;Possibly use message cracker;

MAKELONG=MAKELONG;If target is lParam: changed packing?;Possibly use message cracker;

MAKELP=MAKELP;No FAR pointer under Win32;Replace with flat memory model code;

MAKELPARAM=MAKELPARAM;Changed packing?;Possibly use message cracker;

MAKEPOINT=MAKEPOINT;sizeof(POINT) != sizeof(DWORD);Either replace with MAKEPOINTS und POINT-STOPOINT or conversion function;

OFFSETOF=OFFSETOF;No FAR pointer under Win32;Replace with flat memory model code;

SELECTOROF=SELECTOROF;No FAR pointer under Win32;Replace with flat memory model code;

[CUSTOM]

export=export;No export calling convention under Win32;Use CALLBACK or WINAPI;

far=far;Win32 API knows no segments, so FAR == NEAR == NOTHING!;;

FAR=far;Win32 API knows no segments, so FAR == NEAR == NOTHING!;;

huge=huge;huge areas not necessary;;

HUGE=huge;huge areas not necessary;;

near=near;Win32 API knows no segments, so FAR == NEAR == NOTHING!;;

NEAR=near;Win32 API knows no segments, so FAR == NEAR == NOTHING!;;

pascal=pascal;No pascal calling convention under Win32;Use CALLBACK or WINAPI;

PASCAL=pascal;No pascal calling convention under Win32;Use CALLBACK or WINAPI;

pragma=pragma;Check compiler pragma for compatibility;;

stress.h=STRESS.H;Stress functions not available;Replace with corresponding Win32 API or remove;

STRESS.H=STRESS.H;Stress functions not available;Replace with corresponding Win32 API or remove;

toolhelp.h=TOOLHELP.H;ToolHelp functions not available or changed;Replace with corresponding Win32 API or remove;

TOOLHELP.H=TOOLHELP.H;ToolHelp functions not available or changed;Replace with corresponding Win32 API or remove;

The Message Cracker Signatures

This appendix lists all signatures* for the message cracker functions defined in WINDOWSX.H. The following table shows in the left column the Windows messages (alphabetically sorted) and in the right column the parameter list and the return type of the corresponding message cracker function. Very few messages show differences in the signatures between Win32 and Win16; these cases are identified and both signatures are shown. Win32-specific messages either unknown under Win16 or undocumented are marked with a leading asterisk. As of today, for those messages no message crackers have been defined by Microsoft (but if at all required, you can easily supply a definition on your own).

Of course, the names of your message cracker functions and their parameters can be chosen at will. Nevertheless, a certain methodology — especially for the globally known functions — will definitely help you to keep your projects manageable (particularly larger ones).

Or a bit less pompous: the desired prototype.

Win32-specific messages

Table A3.1: The signatures of the message crackers

Message	Signature of the corresponding message cracker function
WM_ACTIVATE	void Cls_OnActivate(HWND hwnd, UINT state, HWND hwndActDeact, BOOL fMinimized);
WM_ACTIVATEAPP	**Win32**: void Cls_OnActivateApp(HWND hwnd, BOOL fActivate, DWORD dwThreadId); **Win16**: void Cls_OnActivateApp(HWND hwnd, BOOL fActivate, HTASK htaskActDeact);
WM_ASKCBFORMAT-NAME	void Cls_OnAskCBFormatName(HWND hwnd, int cchMax, LPTSTR rgchName);
WM_CANCELMODE	void Cls_OnCancelMode(HWND hwnd);
WM_CHANGECB-CHAIN	void Cls_OnChangeCBChain(HWND hwnd, HWND hwndRemove, HWND hwndNext);

Message	Signature of the corresponding message cracker function
WM_CHAR	**Win32**: void Cls_OnChar(HWND hwnd, TCHAR ch, int cRepeat); **Win16**: void Cls_OnChar(HWND hwnd, UINT ch, int cRepeat)
WM_CHARTOITEM	int Cls_OnCharToItem(HWND hwnd, UINT ch, HWND hwndListbox, int iCaret);
WM_CHILDACTIVATE	void Cls_OnChildActivate(HWND hwnd);
WM_CLEAR	void Cls_OnClear(HWND hwnd);
WM_CLOSE	void Cls_OnClose(HWND hwnd);
WM_COMMAND	void Cls_OnCommand(HWND hwnd, int id, HWND hwndCtl, UINT codeNotify);
WM_COMMNOTIFY	void Cls_OnCommNotify(HWND hwnd, int cid, UINT flags);
WM_COMPACTING	void Cls_OnCompacting(HWND hwnd, UINT cratio);
WM_COMPAREITEM	int Cls_OnCompareItem(HWND hwnd, const COMPARE-ITEMSTRUCT * lpCompareItem);
WM_COPY	void Cls_OnCopy(HWND hwnd);
* WM_COPYDATA	no message cracker defined
WM_CREATE	BOOL Cls_OnCreate(HWND hwnd, LPCREATESTRUCT lpCreateStruct);
WM_CTLCOLOR (Win16); for Win32 respectively: ...MSGBOX ...EDIT ...LISTBOX ...BTN ...DLG ...SCROLLBAR ...STATIC	HBRUSH Cls_OnCtlColor(HWND hwnd, HDC hdc, HWND hwndChild, int type);
WM_CUT	void Cls_OnCut(HWND hwnd);
WM_DEADCHAR	**Win32**: void Cls_OnDeadChar(HWND hwnd, TCHAR ch, int cRepeat); **Win16**: void Cls_OnDeadChar(HWND hwnd, UINT ch, int cRepeat);

Message	Signature of the corresponding message cracker function
WM_DELETEITEM	void Cls_OnDeleteItem(HWND hwnd, const DELETEITEM-STRUCT * lpDeleteItem);
WM_DESTROY	void Cls_OnDestroy(HWND hwnd);
WM_DESTROY-CLIPBOARD	void Cls_OnDestroyClipboard(HWND hwnd);
WM_DEVMODE-CHANGE	void Cls_OnDevModeChange(HWND hwnd, LPCTSTR lpszDeviceName);
WM_DRAWCLIPBOARD	void Cls_OnDrawClipboard(HWND hwnd);
WM_DRAWITEM	void Cls_OnDrawItem(HWND hwnd, const DRAWITEM-STRUCT * lpDrawItem);
WM_DROPFILES	void Cls_OnDropFiles(HWND hwnd, HDROP hdrop);
WM_ENABLE	void Cls_OnEnable(HWND hwnd, BOOL fEnable);
WM_ENDSESSION	void Cls_OnEndSession(HWND hwnd, BOOL fEnding);
WM_ENTERIDLE	void Cls_OnEnterIdle(HWND hwnd, UINT source, HWND hwndSource);
WM_ERASEBKGND	BOOL Cls_OnEraseBkgnd(HWND hwnd, HDC hdc);
WM_FONTCHANGE	void Cls_OnFontChange(HWND hwnd);
WM_GETDLGCODE	UINT Cls_OnGetDlgCode(HWND hwnd, LPMSG lpmsg);
WM_GETFONT	HFONT Cls_OnGetFont(HWND hwnd);
* WM_GETHOTKEY	no message cracker defined
WM_GETMINMAX-INFO	void Cls_OnGetMinMaxInfo(HWND hwnd, LPMINMAX-INFO lpMinMaxInfo);
WM_GETTEXT	int Cls_OnGetText(HWND hwnd, int cchTextMax, LPTSTR lpszText);
WM_GETTEXT-LENGTH	int Cls_OnGetTextLength(HWND hwnd);
* WM_HOTKEY	no message cracker defined
WM_HSCROLL	void Cls_OnHScroll(HWND hwnd, HWND hwndCtl, UINT code, int pos);
WM_HSCROLL-CLIPBOARD	void Cls_OnHScrollClipboard(HWND hwnd, HWND hwndCBViewer, UINT code, int pos);
WM_ICON-ERASEBKGND	BOOL Cls_OnIconEraseBkgnd(HWND hwnd, HDC hdc);

Message	Signature of the corresponding message cracker function
WM_INITDIALOG	BOOL Cls_OnInitDialog(HWND hwnd, HWND hwndFocus, LPARAM lParam);
WM_INITMENU	void Cls_OnInitMenu(HWND hwnd, HMENU hMenu);
WM_INITMENU-POPUP	**Win32**: void Cls_OnInitMenuPopup(HWND hwnd, HMENU hMenu, UINT item, BOOL fSystemMenu); **Win16**: void Cls_OnInitMenuPopup(HWND hwnd, HMENU hMenu, int item, BOOL fSystemMenu)
WM_KEYDOWN	void Cls_OnKey(HWND hwnd, UINT vk, BOOL fDown, int cRepeat, UINT flags);
WM_KEYUP	void Cls_OnKey(HWND hwnd, UINT vk, BOOL fDown, int cRepeat, UINT flags);
WM_KILLFOCUS	void Cls_OnKillFocus(HWND hwnd, HWND hwndNewFocus);
WM_LBUTTON-DBLCLK	void Cls_OnLButtonDown(HWND hwnd, BOOL fDoubleClick, int x, int y, UINT keyFlags);
WM_LBUTTONDOWN	void Cls_OnLButtonDown(HWND hwnd, BOOL fDoubleClick, int x, int y, UINT keyFlags);
WM_LBUTTONUP	void Cls_OnLButtonUp(HWND hwnd, int x, int y, UINT keyFlags);
WM_MBUTTON-DBLCLK	void Cls_OnMButtonDown(HWND hwnd, BOOL fDoubleClick, int x, int y, UINT keyFlags);
WM_MBUTTON-DOWN	void Cls_OnMButtonDown(HWND hwnd, BOOL fDoubleClick, int x, int y, UINT keyFlags);
WM_MBUTTONUP	void Cls_OnMButtonUp(HWND hwnd, int x, int y, UINT flags);
WM_MEASUREITEM	void Cls_OnMeasureItem(HWND hwnd, MEASUREITEMSTRUCT * lpMeasureItem);
WM_MENUCHAR	DWORD Cls_OnMenuChar(HWND hwnd, UINT ch, UINT flags, HMENU hmenu);
WM_MENUSELECT	void Cls_OnMenuSelect(HWND hwnd, HMENU hmenu, int item, HMENU hmenuPopup, UINT flags);
WM_MOUSE-ACTIVATE	int Cls_OnMouseActivate(HWND hwnd, HWND hwndTopLevel, UINT codeHitTest, UINT msg);

Message	Signature of the corresponding message cracker function
WM_MOUSEMOVE	void Cls_OnMouseMove(HWND hwnd, int x, int y, UINT keyFlags);
WM_MOVE	void Cls_OnMove(HWND hwnd, int x, int y);
WM_NCACTIVATE	BOOL Cls_OnNCActivate(HWND hwnd, BOOL fActive, HWND hwndActDeact, BOOL fMinimized);
WM_NCCALCSIZE	UINT Cls_OnNCCalcSize(HWND hwnd, BOOL fCalcValidRects, NCCALCSIZE_PARAMS * lpcsp);
WM_NCCREATE	BOOL Cls_OnNCCreate(HWND hwnd, LPCREATESTRUCT lpCreateStruct);
WM_NCDESTROY	void Cls_OnNCDestroy(HWND hwnd);
WM_NCHITTEST	UINT Cls_OnNCHitTest(HWND hwnd, int x, int y);
WM_NCLBUTTON-DBLCLK	void Cls_OnNCLButtonDown(HWND hwnd, BOOL fDoubleClick, int x, int y, UINT codeHitTest);
WM_NCLBUTTON-DOWN	void Cls_OnNCLButtonDown(HWND hwnd, BOOL fDoubleClick, int x, int y, UINT codeHitTest);
WM_NCLBUTTONUP	void Cls_OnNCLButtonUp(HWND hwnd, int x, int y, UINT codeHitTest);
WM_NCMBUTTON-DBLCLK	void Cls_OnNCMButtonDown(HWND hwnd, BOOL fDoubleClick, int x, int y, UINT codeHitTest);
WM_NCMBUTTON-DOWN	void Cls_OnNCMButtonDown(HWND hwnd, BOOL fDoubleClick, int x, int y, UINT codeHitTest);
WM_NCMBUTTONUP	void Cls_OnNCMButtonUp(HWND hwnd, int x, int y, UINT codeHitTest);
WM_NCMOUSEMOVE	void Cls_OnNCMouseMove(HWND hwnd, int x, int y, UINT codeHitTest);
WM_NCPAINT	void Cls_OnNCPaint(HWND hwnd, HRGN hrgn);
WM_NCRBUTTON-DBLCLK	void Cls_OnNCRButtonDown(HWND hwnd, BOOL fDoubleClick, int x, int y, UINT codeHitTest);
WM_NCRBUTTON-DOWN	void Cls_OnNCRButtonDown(HWND hwnd, BOOL fDoubleClick, int x, int y, UINT codeHitTest);
WM_NCRBUTTONUP	void Cls_OnNCRButtonUp(HWND hwnd, int x, int y, UINT codeHitTest);
WM_NEXTDLGCTL	HWND Cls_OnNextDlgCtl(HWND hwnd, HWND hwndSetFocus, BOOL fNext);

Message	Signature of the corresponding message cracker function
WM_NCRBUTTON-DOWN	void Cls_OnNCRButtonDown(HWND hwnd, BOOL fDoubleClick, int x, int y, UINT codeHitTest);
WM_NCRBUTTONUP	void Cls_OnNCRButtonUp(HWND hwnd, int x, int y, UINT codeHitTest);
WM_NEXTDLGCTL	HWND Cls_OnNextDlgCtl(HWND hwnd, HWND hwndSetFocus, BOOL fNext);
WM_PAINT	void Cls_OnPaint(HWND hwnd);
WM_PAINTCLIP-BOARD	void Cls_OnPaintClipboard(HWND hwnd, HWND hwndCBViewer, const LPPAINTSTRUCT lpPaintStruct);
* WM_PAINTICON	no message cracker defined
WM_PALETTE-CHANGED	void Cls_OnPaletteChanged(HWND hwnd, HWND hwndPaletteChange);
WM_PALETTE-ISCHANGING	void Cls_OnPaletteIsChanging(HWND hwnd, HWND hwndPaletteChange);
WM_PARENTNOTIFY	void Cls_OnParentNotify(HWND hwnd, UINT msg, HWND hwndChild, int idChild);
WM_PASTE	void Cls_OnPaste(HWND hwnd);
WM_POWER	void Cls_OnPower(HWND hwnd, int code);
WM_QUERYDRAG-ICON	HICON Cls_OnQueryDragIcon(HWND hwnd);
WM_QUERYEND-SESSION	BOOL Cls_OnQueryEndSession(HWND hwnd);
WM_QUERYNEW-PALETTE	BOOL Cls_OnQueryNewPalette(HWND hwnd);
WM_QUERYOPEN	BOOL Cls_OnQueryOpen(HWND hwnd);
WM_QUEUESYNC	void Cls_OnQueueSync(HWND hwnd);
WM_QUIT	void Cls_OnQuit(HWND hwnd, int exitCode);
WM_RBUTTON-DBLCLK	void Cls_OnRButtonDown(HWND hwnd, BOOL fDoubleClick, int x, int y, UINT keyFlags);
WM_RBUTTONDOWN	void Cls_OnRButtonDown(HWND hwnd, BOOL fDoubleClick, int x, int y, UINT keyFlags);
WM_RBUTTONUP	void Cls_OnRButtonUp(HWND hwnd, int x, int y, UINT flags);

Message	Signature of the corresponding message cracker function
WM_RENDERALL-FORMATS	void Cls_OnRenderAllFormats(HWND hwnd);
WM_RENDERFORMAT	HANDLE Cls_OnRenderFormat(HWND hwnd, UINT fmt);
WM_SETCURSOR	BOOL Cls_OnSetCursor(HWND hwnd, HWND hwndCursor, UINT codeHitTest, UINT msg);
WM_SETFOCUS	void Cls_OnSetFocus(HWND hwnd, HWND hwndOldFocus);
WM_SETFONT	void Cls_OnSetFont(HWND hwndCtl, HFONT hfont, BOOL fRedraw);
* WM_SETHOTKEY	no message cracker defined
WM_SETREDRAW	void Cls_OnSetRedraw(HWND hwnd, BOOL fRedraw);
WM_SETTEXT	void Cls_OnSetText(HWND hwnd, LPCTSTR lpszText);
WM_SHOWWINDOW	void Cls_OnShowWindow(HWND hwnd, BOOL fShow, UINT status);
WM_SIZE	void Cls_OnSize(HWND hwnd, UINT state, int cx, int cy);
WM_SIZECLIPBOARD	void Cls_OnSizeClipboard(HWND hwnd, HWND hwndCBViewer, const LPRECT lprc);
WM_SPOOLERSTATUS	void Cls_OnSpoolerStatus(HWND hwnd, UINT status, int cJobInQueue);
WM_SYSCHAR	**Win32**: void Cls_OnSysChar(HWND hwnd, TCHAR ch, int cRepeat); **Win16**: void Cls_OnSysChar(HWND hwnd, UINT ch, int cRepeat);
WM_SYSCOLOR-CHANGE	void Cls_OnSysColorChange(HWND hwnd);
WM_SYSCOMMAND	void Cls_OnSysCommand(HWND hwnd, UINT cmd, int x, int y);
WM_SYSDEADCHAR	**Win32**: void Cls_OnSysDeadChar(HWND hwnd, TCHAR ch, int cRepeat); **Win16**: void Cls_OnSysDeadChar(HWND hwnd, UINT ch, int cRepeat);
WM_SYSKEYDOWN	void Cls_OnSysKey(HWND hwnd, UINT vk, BOOL fDown, int cRepeat, UINT flags);
WM_SYSKEYUP	void Cls_OnSysKey(HWND hwnd, UINT vk, BOOL fDown, int cRepeat, UINT flags);

Message	Signature of the corresponding message cracker function
WM_SYSTEMERROR	void Cls_OnSystemError(HWND hwnd, int errCode);
WM_TIMECHANGE	void Cls_OnTimeChange(HWND hwnd);
WM_TIMER	void Cls_OnTimer(HWND hwnd, UINT id);
WM_UNDO	void Cls_OnUndo(HWND hwnd);
WM_VKEYTOITEM	int Cls_OnVkeyToItem(HWND hwnd, UINT vk, HWND hwndListbox, int iCaret);
WM_VSCROLL	void Cls_OnVScroll(HWND hwnd, HWND hwndCtl, UINT code, int pos);
WM_VSCROLL-CLIPBOARD	void Cls_OnVScrollClipboard(HWND hwnd, HWND hwndCBViewer, UINT code, int pos);
WM_WINDOWPOS-CHANGED	void Cls_OnWindowPosChanged(HWND hwnd, const LPWINDOWPOS lpwpos);
WM_WINDOWPOS-CHANGING	BOOL Cls_OnWindowPosChanging(HWND hwnd, LPWINDOWPOS lpwpos);
WM_WININICHANGE	void Cls_OnWinIniChange(HWND hwnd, LPCTSTR lpszSectionName);

For the sake of completeness, I'll give a very short summary for using the message cracker functions and macros, a much more thorough discussion can be found in section 4.3 starting on page 212.

Using the message cracker functions.
For each message found in the above table (with the exception of Win32-specific messages), two macros are defined: first HANDLE_WM_... to unpack the information in the two message parameters (i.e., wParam and lParam) and to deliver them to the handler function; second FORWARD_WM_... to recreate the original message parameters from the arguments of a handler function. As a specific example, I'll again show the use of the macros for WM_COMMAND (definitely for the last time, promised!):

```
VOID WINAPI MyCommandHandler(HWND hwnd, INT id, HWND hwndCtl,
    UINT codeNotify)
{
    ... // Your code for handling WM_COMMAND messages
}
```

```
// in the window procedure:
switch(msg){
// The following macro calls MyCommandHandler with the
// proper parameters, as shown in the table above:
case WM_COMMAND:
    HANDLE_WM_COMMAND(hwnd,wParam,lParam,MyCommandHandler);
...
// As an alternative you could use the generic macro
// HANDLE_MSG, which contains the "case WM_COMMAND:"
 // part *and* the function call:
HANDLE_MSG(hwnd,WM_COMMAND,MyCommandHandler);
// Please observe that this macro depends on the names
// "wParam" and "lParam" for the two message parameters!
...
// The following macro can be used in the handler function
// to recreate the message parameter and to forward them to
// another function.
FORWARD_WM_COMMAND(hwnd,id,hwndCtl,wNotify,DefWindowProc);
```

For the unpacking: Either HANDLE_WM_COMMAND

or HANDLE_MSG.

And the repacking: FORWARD_WM_-COMMAND.

The Example Program Used to Demonstrate Warnings and Error Messages

The following short program was used in section 3.8* to illustrate the most important compiler messages. For your convenience I have printed it with line numbers; with this aid you should easily find your way through the warnings discussed. After the original version, the program is shown in a modified form, which doesn't produce *serious* warnings (or errors) anymore (well, some hints to unused parameters and local variables are still given, which can be easily removed, if desired).

* See page 178.

```
1    #define STRICT
2    #include <windows.h>
3
4    #define ID_ICON   1
5    #define ID_MENU   1
6    #define IDM_ONE   1
7
8    char szClientClass[]="ClientClass";
9    char szAppName[]="Test App";
10
11   VOID CallIncr();
12   int Decr(LONG i);
13   LONG FAR PASCAL ClientWndProc(HWND hwnd,WORD msg,
        WORD wP,LONG lP);
14   VOID OtherProblems(HWND hwnd);
15
16   VOID CallIncr()
17   {
```

```
18    int z;
19    Decr();
20    Decr(6,3);
21    return Incr(6);
22    }
23
24    int Incr(j)
25    DWORD j;
26    {
27      int z=9;
28      j+j;
29      if (j>=0) return ++j;
30      else if (j==-1) return --j;
31      else return;
32    }
33
34    int Decr(LONG i)
35    {
36      return --i;
37    }
38
39    LONG FAR PASCAL ClientWndProc(HWND hwnd,WORD msg,
        WORD wP,LONG lP);
40
41    int PASCAL WinMain(HANDLE hInst,HANDLE hPrev,
        LPSTR lpszCmdLine,int nCmdShow)
42    {
43      MSG msg;
44      HWND hwnd;
45      if (!ClientInit(hInst)) return 0;
46      hwnd=CreateWindow(szClientClass,szAppName,
          WS_OVERLAPPEDWINDOW,
47        CW_USEDEFAULT,0,CW_USEDEFAULT,0,HWND_DESKTOP,
          0,hInst,NULL);
48      ShowWindow(hwnd,nCmdShow);
49      while (GetMessage(&msg,NULL,0,0)) {
50        TranslateMessage(&msg);
51        DispatchMessage(&msg);
52      }
```

```
53      DestroyWindow(hwnd);
54      return msg.wParam;
55    }
56
57    BOOL ClientInit(HANDLE hInst)
58    {
59      WNDCLASS wc;
60      wc.style=CS_VREDRAW|CS_HREDRAW;
61      wc.lpfnWndProc=ClientWndProc;
62      wc.cbClsExtra=0;
63      wc.cbWndExtra=0;
64      wc.hInstance=hInst;
65      wc.hIcon=LoadIcon(hInst,MAKEINTRESOURCE(ID_ICON));
66      wc.hCursor=LoadCursor(0,IDC_ARROW);
67      wc.hbrBackground=GetStockObject(WHITE_BRUSH);
68      wc.lpszMenuName=MAKEINTRESOURCE(ID_MENU);
69      wc.lpszClassName=szClientClass;
70      return RegisterClass(&wc);
71    }
72
73    LONG FAR PASCAL ClientWndProc(HWND hwnd,WORD msg,
      LONG wP,WORD lP)
74    {
75      HFONT hfont;
76      PSTR  psz;
77      POINT pt;
78      PAINTSTRUCT ps;
79      switch (msg) {
80        case WM_COMMAND:
81          switch (wP) {
82            case IDM_ONE:
83              CallIncr();
84              return 0;
85          }
86        case WM_LBUTTONDOWN:
87          GetCursorPos(pt);
88          CallIncr(&pt);
89          HandleButton(pt);
90          CallIncr(2,3,4);
```

```
91          return 0;
92      case WM_PAINT:
93          BeginPaint(hwnd,&ps);
94          OtherProblems(ps.hdc);
95          EndPaint(hwnd,&ps);
96      case WM_GETFONT:
97          return hfont;
98      case WM_USER:
99          return psz;
100     }
101     return DefWindowProc(hwnd,msg,wP,lP);
102 }
103
104 VOID HandleButton(LPPOINT lppt,int z)
105 {
106     LPRECT lprc=lppt;
107     LPVOID lp=z;
108     LPSTR  lpsz=MAKEINTRESOURCE(ID_ICON);
109     HWND   hwnd;
110     lp++;
111     if (hwnd==1)
112        *lp=CallIncr();
113     hwnd=lp;
114     hwnd=(HWND)lp;
115 }
116
117 VOID OtherProblems(HWND hwnd)
118 {
119     HBRUSH hbr=SendMessage(hwnd,WM_GETFONT,0,0);
120 }
```

And now the corrected version, albeit without line numbers — since through the necessary modifications the number of lines has changed; the numbering wouldn't exactly be helpful anyway. Instead, I have marked all the places where modifications were necessary and have explained the changes with a short comment. Together with the discussion in section 3.8, you should be able to get a clear picture of the various problems and their solution:

```
#define STRICT
#include <windows.h>

#define ID_ICON  1
#define ID_MENU  1
#define IDM_ONE  1

char szClientClass[]="ClientClass";
char szAppName[]="Test App";

VOID CallIncr(VOID); // prototype corrected
int Incr(DWORD j);    // prototype defined
int Decr(LONG i);
LRESULT CALLBACK ClientWndProc(HWND hwnd,UINT msg,WPARAM
   wP,LPARAM lP);   // STRICT compatible prototype
VOID OtherProblems(HWND hwnd);

VOID CallIncr()
{
// int z;     // z is not needed and therefore commented out
  Decr(6);     // missing parameter inserted
  Decr(6);     // parameter removed
  return;      // Incr(6) as result is pointless, because
  // of return value VOID
}


int Incr(DWORD j)
{
// int z=9;  // z is not needed and therefore commented out
// j+j;         // statement without effect, commented out
  if (j>=1) return (int)++j; // comparison with 0 is wrong,
  // int cast introduced
  else if (j==0xFFFFFFFFL) return (int)--j;  // comparison with -1
  // is wrong, int cast introduced
  else return 0; // return changed
}


int Decr(LONG i)
{
```

```
    return (int)--i;  // int cast introduced
}


BOOL ClientInit(HINSTANCE hInst); // prototype introduced

int PASCAL WinMain(HINSTANCE hInst,HINSTANCE hPrev,LPSTR
lpszCmdLine,int nCmdShow)
{
  MSG msg;
  HWND hwnd;
  if (!ClientInit(hInst)) return 0;
  hwnd=CreateWindow(szClientClass,szAppName,
    WS_OVERLAPPEDWINDOW,CW_USEDEFAULT,0,CW_USEDEFAULT,
    0,HWND_DESKTOP,0,hInst,NULL);
  ShowWindow(hwnd,nCmdShow);
  while (GetMessage(&msg,NULL,0,0)) {
    TranslateMessage(&msg);
    DispatchMessage(&msg);
  }
  DestroyWindow(hwnd);
  return msg.wParam;
}


BOOL ClientInit(HINSTANCE hInst) // HANDLE changed to HINSTANCE
{
  WNDCLASS wc;
  wc.style=CS_VREDRAW|CS_HREDRAW;
  wc.lpfnWndProc=ClientWndProc;
  wc.cbClsExtra=0;
  wc.cbWndExtra=0;
  wc.hInstance=hInst;
  wc.hIcon=LoadIcon(hInst,MAKEINTRESOURCE(ID_ICON));
  wc.hCursor=LoadCursor(0,IDC_ARROW);
  wc.hbrBackground=GetStockObject(WHITE_BRUSH);
  wc.lpszMenuName=MAKEINTRESOURCE(ID_MENU);
  wc.lpszClassName=szClientClass;
  return RegisterClass(&wc);
}
```

```
VOID HandleButton(LPPOINT lppt,int z); // prototype introduced

LRESULT CALLBACK ClientWndProc(HWND hwnd,UINT msg,
  WPARAM wP,LPARAM lP) // angepaßt an Prototyp
{
  HFONT hfont;
  PSTR  psz;
  POINT pt;
  PAINTSTRUCT ps;
  switch (msg) {
    case WM_COMMAND:
      switch (wP) {
        case IDM_ONE:
          CallIncr();
          return 0;
      }
    case WM_LBUTTONDOWN:
      GetCursorPos(&pt); // address-of (&) included
      CallIncr(); // parameter removed
      HandleButton(&pt,1); // address-of (&) and another
      // parameter included
      CallIncr(); // three parameters removed
      return 0;
    case WM_PAINT:
      BeginPaint(hwnd,&ps);
      OtherProblems(hwnd); // ps.hdc replaced with hwnd
      EndPaint(hwnd,&ps);
    case WM_GETFONT:
      hfont=GetStockObject(ANSI_VAR_FONT); // initialize hfont first
      return (LRESULT)hfont;
    case WM_USER:
      psz=NULL; // please initialize psz first
      return (LRESULT)(LPSTR)psz;
  }
  return DefWindowProc(hwnd,msg,wP,lP);
}

VOID HandleButton(LPPOINT lppt,int z)
{
```

```
      LPRECT lprc=(LPRECT)lppt; // cast introduced
      LPVOID lp; // =z; commented out, since pointless
      LPCSTR  lpsz=MAKEINTRESOURCE(ID_ICON); // LPCSTR instead of LPSTR
      HWND    hwnd;
//    lp++; // commented out, since pointless
      hwnd=GetDesktopWindow(); // please initialize hwnd first
      if (hwnd==(HWND)1) // cast introduced
        CallIncr();  // assignment to *lp removed, since
        // CallIncr() doesn't return anything
//    hwnd=lp; // auskommentiert, da sinnlos
      lp=NULL; // please initialize lp first
      hwnd=(HWND)(UINT)(DWORD)lp;
}

VOID OtherProblems(HWND hwnd)
{
    HFONT hfont=(HFONT)(UINT)SendMessage(hwnd,WM_GETFONT,0,0);
    // cast introduced and HBRUSH replaced with HFONT
}
```

The New __stdcall Calling Sequence

As already explained in section 4.7, the 32-bit compiler from Microsoft employs an all new and improved calling convention named __stdcall. For high-level language programmers this fact is only of interest when creating function prototypes; if you properly use the predefined macros for that purpose (CALLBACK, WINAPI, etc.), you need not even care about that.

Predefined macros CALL-BACK and WINAPI

Assembler programmers will embrace the new standard somewhat less enthusiastically: the __stdcall convention necessitates some significant adjustments. The same holds true for developers who performed non-portable manipulations (this means without the access macros defined in STDARGS.H) with stack-based variables or addresses for whatever reason. Fortunately, the required changes are in most cases limited, since the new convention is a rather clever mixture of the two important 16-bit variants now in use. For that reason I'll shortly discuss these; most of this information can be carried over to Win32.

__stdcall and assembler programmers

The two most important »old« calling conventions are _cdecl (or disguised as macro CDECL) and _PASCAL (as macro PASCAL and most often used together with _far or just FAR). _cdecl is the standard C calling sequence and as such permits variable parameter lists. _pascal is a more rigid convention that most Pascal and Modula-2 compilers employ, it doesn't permit variable parameter lists (well, in those languages this feature is seen as devil-made anyway). The following table shows the most important differences for a function call for both calling sequences:

Until now: _cdecl and _pascal.

_cdecl	_pascal
Parameters are put on the stack from right to left.	Parameters are pushed in the opposite direction, from left to right.
The function is called, thereby the return address is stored automatically on the stack.	Ditto.

Table A5.1: _cdecl and _pascal calling sequence

_cdecl	_pascal
After performing their job, the called function simply returns to the caller.	Just before returning, the called function adjusts the stack pointer, so that the parameters pushed from the caller simply disappear.
The caller has to correct the stack pointer, so that the parameters are gone.	The caller has nothing more to do.
The function name is prefixed with an _ (underscore); case is preserved.	The function name is completely transfomed to uppercase letters.

To make these dry explanations a little more lively, let's look at a specific example:

A specific example

```
void CDECL FAR cFunc(int i,char *pch,long l);
void PASCAL FAR pascalFunc(int i,char *pch,long l);


// Now, calling cFunc:
cFunc(42,&chBuf,34L);
/* generates the following (pseudo-) assembly code:
   PUSH  34
   PUSH  &chBuf
   PUSH  42
   CALL  _cFunc
   ADD   ESP,12
The latter is based on the assumption that sizeof(int) == sizeof(char
*) == sizeof(long) == 4); this happens to be true in 32-bit mode. A
16-bit compiler would instead generate ADD SP,10.
*/
// And calling pascalFunc:
pascalFunc(42,&chBuf,34L);
/* generates the following (pseudo-) assembly code:
   PUSH  42
   PUSH  &chBuf
   PUSH  34
   CALL  PASCALFUNC
The called function has cleared up the stack via RET 12 (or RET 10 for
```

```
a 16-bit CPU).
*/
```

In the called function the parameters (and local variables) are usually accessed via EBP plus offset (remember: 32-bit mode!) as shown in the following pseudo-code:

Access to the parameters

```
_cFunc:
SAVE_AND_SET  EBP        ; save EBP and set up a new stack frame
MOV  EAX,[EBP+8]         ; int i
MOV  EBX,[EBP+12]        ; char *pch
MOV  ECX,[EBP+16]        ; long l
...
GET  EBP                 ; restore old EBP
RET                      ; and jump back


PASCALFUNC:
SAVE_AND_SET  EBP        ; save EBP and set up new stack frame
MOV  EAX,[EBP+16]        ; int i
MOV  EBX,[EBP+12]        ; char *pch
MOV  ECX,[EBP+8]         ; long l
...
GET  EBP                 ; restore old EBP
RET  12                  ; and jump back
```

By the way, since the _pascal sequence was completely removed from the 32-bit C/C++ compiler, the example shown above wouldn't even compile there! Nevertheless, for Windows programmers it was the most important convention until now (and will continue for Win16), therefore it deserved a short mention. This brings us to the question of why _pascal became so important in the first place, when with _cdecl an accepted and reliable standard was available? The main reason is simply efficiency: _pascal is namely more memory friendly (especially if the function is called very often), because the stack is *not* cleaned up explicitly after each call through an ADD SP, sizeof(parameter list) — per call on a 386 machine, this generates 3 bytes after all. In addition, with _pascal the call is slightly more efficient than with _cdecl. The latter is used in Win16 only if a variable parameter list is definitely required (the corresponding functions are wsprintf() und DebugOutput()). Obviously,

32-bit compiler: _pascal sequence simply removed.

Why _pascal?

a new calling sequence must somehow bring the advantages of _pascal and _cdecl under one hat, otherwise it would be rather useless. (Well, admittedly *this* argument has never stopped Microsoft from inventing and spreading useless innovations — just think about the Win16 functions DOS3Call() or NetBIOSCall(), which (apart from some modification effort) haven't yielded any profit.) So armed with a healthy portion of skepticism, let's investigate the new convention: what is hidden behind __stdcall?

The single most important feature of __stdcall is the (well, after all that introductory speech, barely astonishing) fact that both functions *with* a variable parameter list and those *without* one (in other words, with fixed arguments) are perfectly well supported. As a matter of fact, with __stdcall not only _pascal but also _cdecl are absolutely superfluous. (Well, the latter has at least found a refuge in the C run-time library under 32 bit — either out of reverence or perhaps simply because existing assembler source codes would require fundamental adapations for all the accesses to the parameters on the stack.)

__stdcall: optimum support for variable and fixed parameter lists.

The proceedings in detail:

The proceedings of _stdcall are the following: through a simple analysis of the function prototype (if available!) the compiler checks whether the function is defined with a variable parameter list. If yes, and that is the good news, exactly the same convention as for _cdecl is employed. This affects both pushing the parameters (and stack clean-up) and the external name of the function: for a variable parameter list __stdcall corresponds *to the finishing touch* with the good old _cdecl convention. In this case adaptions or changes are not necessary at all.

Variable

Fixed parameter list

Now for the bad news: with a fixed parameter list (according to Murphy by far the most frequent case, needless to say) __stdcall doesn't work exactly like _pascal, but similarly: first the parameters are pushed to the stack; yet, this happens from right to left (as with _cdecl). Then the function is called, which on its part cleans up the stack just before jumping back (as did _pascal). For assembler programmers the first observation is especially important: they have to adapt all accesses to parameters on the stack (e.g., via [EBP + offset]) to the reversed sequence (when compared to _pascal). And still another question pops up: what happens with _stdcall and fixed parameter list with the name of the function? Here Microsoft has devised a really tricky scheme: first the name is prefixed with an underscore, then the at sign (@) is appended, and, as if this were not enough, the total size of all parameters is attached. A few examples in order to throw light on the matter:

The function name

```
// Prototype:
void __stdcall TestProc1(int i,char *pch,long l);
// resulting name: _TestProc1@12, because 3*4 == 12


// Prototype:
void __stdcall TestProc2(char ch1, char ch2);
// Name: _TestProc2@8, since the compiler always pushes
// (32 bit wide) ints on the stack. And 2*4 == 8!


// Prototype:
void __stdcall TestProc3(void);
// Name: _TestProc3@0, since void means empty
// parameter list...



// Prototype:
void __stdcall TestProc4(int i,...);
// Name: _TestProc4, because the three dots signalize a
// variable parameter list, therefore the _cdecl name
// is used.
```

The decisive advantage of this naming scheme is that all functions declared with __stdcall (especially those exported from a DLL) are either
not at all called or always called with the proper parameter count (more
accurate: the proper number of bytes on the stack). If too many or not
enough parameters are supplied (e.g., because the header file with the
prototype is wrong), the name generated for that call will be wrong too;
at the latest this is noticed when the program is linked. A final question
remains: what happens, if the compiler can't find a prototype in the first
place? First it prints a warning (nice!) and second it assumes that the
corresponding function will be defined with _cdecl (this behavior is K&R
C compatible). As long as the function is found in the same module, but
is defined with __stdcall, the compiler will already have generated a
corresponding error message. If on the other hand, the function is located in another source code file, only the linker will draw your attention
to the problem with a message like "unresolved externals found" or
something similar.

Well, if now you need (or just want) to know even more about the
really gory details of old and new calling conventions, I recommend the

And where is the advantage?

free and easy use of the compiler switches /Fa (Microsoft) and -S (Borland) and the close investigation of the generated assembler listings.

Some Hints for Pascal and Modula-2

This appendix is provided for Windows developers who don't work with C/C++, but with Pascal or Modula-2 instead. Indeed, currently no 32-bit implementations for these two languages are available, so porting your programs to Win32 is yet impossible — but this will certainly change in the near future. Apart from that, the wish to create program code in an already portable fashion today is of course completely understandable. Therefore I'll give some basic remarks valid for both language variants and aimed at helping you to put the information in the main part of the book to good use:

- As far as possible (or reasonable), try to understand C at least well enough so that you can comprehend the examples, code excerpts and explanations in the rest of the book. Don't waste your time with learning older C versions (called Classic or K&R C), but concentrate from the beginning on ANSI C. A certain knowledge of the language is advantageous anyway, because the Win32 reference material from Microsoft is strongly oriented towards C/C++ as the developer's language (as was the documentation for Win16, see [Ref. 1]). For instance, all SDK example programs are written in C, some even in C++. Samples and suggestions from computer magazines and books can also be converted much easier if you understand C (you need not work with the language, just having a working knowledge of its principles is required. Two useful books for learners are [Ref. 6] and above all [Ref. 13].

  Do you understand C?

  Only ANSI C!

- Make very clear which and how special C mechanisms can be mapped as similarly as possible to the corresponding Pascal or Modula-2 constructions. In this category probably you'll find working with pointers and arrays, the possibilities for code modularization (see the keywords *static* and *external*), the casting of variables, as well as the use of the C pre-processor. Possibly you should also glance at the *switch*, *break*, and *continue* statements. Es-

  Special C mechanisms

pecially tricky for Pascal developers are most likely the comma operator and the capability for repeated assignment.

Conditional compilation

- Particularly the pre-processor is definitely indispensable for portable programming; therefore try as much as possible to work with a Pascal or Modula-2 implementation, which at the very least allows conditional compilation (well, not to talk about macro definitions with parameters...).

Self-written portability modules

- To compensate for this deficiency, implement a few portability modules that can be compiled depending on the target system and that contain the necessary primitives for the portable formulation of your sources. A (trivial) example for Borland Pascal follows later on.

OOP shell for GUI programming

- If you can use or obtain object-oriented extensions and/or libraries for GUI programming, *absolutely use them!* Reasonably structured OOP shells extraordinarily simplify the creation of portable source codes.

DLLs: independent units

- The DLL model very nicely supports the separation of a single, large project into smaller, mostly independent units. Possibly you can translate certain parts of your project without too much effort to C (and so profit from its features), while other, still too complex fragments can very well be kept in Pascal.

And the C pre-processor?

- Last but not least, a somewhat unusual but certainly practicable proposal for special applications: most C compilers offer the capability to skip the actual compilation phase and to send the source code just through the pre-processor. In this case everything over and above the statements for the C pre-processor (which all begin with #...) is not examined further, but is written either to a text file or to the standard output. And whether these output texts are C/C++ or Pascal/Modula-2 source codes is absolute insignificant for the pre-processor! Or put differently: it can be used with all its possibilities also for Pascal/Modula-2 or any other programming language! Well, the advantages are evident, but unfortunately so are the disadvantages: prior to the actual compilation, the source codes must be chased through the C pre-processor; this can obviously slow down the programmer's job with today's interactive IDEs. Yet, for developers who can easily include further tools in their working environment or who work with another editor and an external MAKE utility anyway, this way can be very attractive, depending on the circumstances. This is particularly valid if the module under discussion is a portability layer, which after inital correct implementation is only very seldom changed and recompiled. For this proceeding you'll find a small example later, too.

I am working on the assumption that comparatively few developers work with a Modula-2 system under Windows. The language has been established (at least in the professional area) only in marginal areas. To make things even worse, at present at least three or four useful implementations are available, which unfortunately all differ in a lot of minutiae as well as some actually important spots. Therefore, I can't give you detailed hints for specific versions. Anyhow, nearly all commercially available PC implementations offer the capability to build program code with conditional compilation; in all other respects orient yourself on the following discussion for Turbo PASCAL — a glance into the following section might prove useful even for Modula-2 disciples.

Modula-2 systems are similar to Turbo Pascal.

And some remarks specifically for Pascal

The generic name "Pascal" refers for the rest of this section to Turbo or Borland Pascal, since on the PC level no other product has won measurable importance. Alas, I know exactly as much about the future 32-bit versions as about the next tax hike: it'll come *definitely*, but when? Unfortunately, I am largely dependent on speculations.

Turbo or Borland Pascal

On principle, you as a Pascal programmer should expect to face similar problems as do C developers. Let's face it: TP 7.0 has nowadays so much less in common with the original definition from Jensen/Wirth that in Zurich it is either not touched at all or only with fireproof asbestos gloves. Or said provocatively: almost all the "mean tricks" for which C became famous (or *in*famous?) are possible with at least the same elegance in TP. To this extent you can stir Chapters 3 and 4 with a pinch of Pascal, then shake a bit and enjoy…. Especially if you can read C programs halfway fluently, you should expect no real difficulties. The only genuine drawback is the missing macro definitions. I suppose that Borland will make available a compatibility unit (fundamentally the Pascal equivalent of WINDOWSX.H) that implements the corresponding functions (for the better part probably as inline). With such a unit a lot of problems can be caught; for the rest you should take it as a guide and

Drawback: the missing macro definitions.

write portable units yourself. The implementation of portability units is namely the most promising alternative (if not the only) to C's macro definitions. While there you can hide certain non-portable constructions behind macros that afterwards can be used umpteen times, the Pascal developer has to pack his portability functions into separate units. A certainly trivial example (see for a comparison the macros in section 3.3 on page 146) is shown in the following listing:

```
UNIT PortUtils;

INTERFACE USES WinTypes, WinProcs;

FUNCTION DLGBOX(hInst: HInstance;lpszTemplate: PChar;
    hwndParent: HWnd;DialogFunc: TFarProc): Integer;

IMPLEMENTATION

FUNCTION DLGBOX(hInst: HInstance;lpszTemplate: PChar;
    hwndParent: HWnd; DialogFunc: TFarProc): Integer;
{$IFDEF WIN32}
BEGIN
  DialogBox(hInst,lpszTemplate,hwndParent,DialogFunc);
{$ELSE}
VAR dlgproc: TFarProc;
BEGIN
  dlgproc:=MakeProcInstance(DialogFunc,hInst);
  DialogBox(hInst,lpszTemplate,hwndParent,dlgproc);
  FreeProcInstance(dlgproc);
{$ENDIF}
END;

BEGIN
END.
```

Memory models   An area where Pascal programmers clearly have caught the better part is the malaise with the memory models. Indeed, TP knows some keywords that can be used to change the attributes of functions (e.g., FAR); nevertheless, the basic memory model fundamentally corresponds to the FAR model of C. Particularly all pointers or addresses are 32-bits wide, so you can save yourself quite a bit of confusion when it comes to pointers. Unfortunately, this has also some drawbacks, since pointers in Pascal so far were always segment/offset values and were of course manipulated as such. So, Pascalists should study all discussions and hints concerning this subject (see sections 3.6 and 4.2) with great attention. And pointer addressing has still another facet: in TP there are no huge pointers or segments (this means, segments > 64 KB must be implemented "on foot" by the developer). If you have these in your programs, probably some corresponding adaptations are due. When implemented properly, you should indeed have no difficulties to identify these places, since in order to perform the addressing of multi-segment memory areas in a proper way, the necessary arithmetic operations under Win16 generally need to import __AHINCR or __AHSHIFT (see also section 4.2, page 205). The corresponding definitions should be similar to the following:

Confusing: pointer manipulations.

And of course areas larger than 64 KB!

```
function __AHINCR;    external 'KERNEL' index 113;
function __AHSHIFT;   external 'KERNEL' index 114;
```

Well, all places where these pseudo-variables are used should be easy to find; they definitely need a thorough renovation.

I promised an example explaining the subject "C pre-processor and Pascal": here it comes. The following program code looks like a strange mixture of C and Pascal, but can be perfectly well processed from an ANSI C pre-processor and creates, depending on the #defines, either 16-bit or 32-bit source code that can be fed directly to the Pascal compiler. Of course, this detour makes sense only if you can exploit the possibilities of the pre-processor for macro definitions with parameters to a considerable extent: TP is just as good on conditional compilation as C! In the example shown, two layers of macros are defined, the first for DialogBox() (see above), the other, inspired by the macro definitions in WINDOWSX.H, for the portable treatment of WM_COMMAND:

C pre-processor and Pascal

```
{$X+}
UNIT PortUtils;

INTERFACE USES WinTypes, WinProcs;

#ifdef WIN32
#define HANDLE     LONGINT
```

```
#define INT        LONGINT
#define UINT       LONGINT
#else
#define HANDLE     WORD
#define INT        INTEGER
#define UINT       WORD
#endif


TYPE HWNDX= HANDLE;   (* These TYPEs are just for
     BOOL= INT;           demonstration puposes! *)
     WPARAM= UINT;
     LPARAM= LONGINT;
     LRESULT= LONGINT;


FUNCTION MyPortableDlgBox(hinst: THandle;lpszTempl: PChar;
  hwndOwn: HWND;lpProc: TFarProc): INTEGER;


IMPLEMENTATION


#define WNDPROC_BEGIN(name)   FUNCTION name(hwnd: HWNDX; \
  msg: UINT;wP: WPARAM;lP: LPARAM): LRESULT; \
  VAR lR: LRESULT; BEGIN CASE msg OF


#define WNDPROC_END(name)   ELSE \
  lR:=DefWindowProc(hwnd,msg,wP,lP); \
  END; name:=lR; END;


#ifdef WIN32


#define DLGBOX(hinst,lpszTempl,hwndOwn,lpProc)   nRes:= \
  DialogBox(hinst,lpszTempl,hwndOwn,@lpProc)
#define HANDLE_WM_COMMAND(fn)   WM_COMMAND: \
  lR:=fn(hwnd,LoWord(wP),HWNDX(lP),UINT(HiWord(wP)))


#else


#define DLGBOX(hinst,lpszTempl,hwndOwn,lpProc)   DlgProc:= \
  MakeProcInstance(@lpProc,hinst); \
  nRes:=DialogBox(hinst,lpszTempl,hwndOwn,DlgProc); \
```

```
    FreeProcInstance(DlgProc)
#define HANDLE_WM_COMMAND(fn)   WM_COMMAND: \
  lR:=fn(hwnd,wP,HWNDX(LoWord(lP)),UINT(HiWord(lP)))


#endif


FUNCTION MyDlg(hdlg: HWND;msg: UINT;wP: WPARAM;
  lP: LPARAM): LRESULT;
BEGIN
  (*...*)
END;


FUNCTION MyPortableDlgBox(hinst: THandle;lpszTempl: PChar;
  hwndOwn: HWND;lpProc: TFarProc): INTEGER;
VAR  DlgProc : TFarProc;
     nRes    : INTEGER;
BEGIN
  DLGBOX(hinst,lpszTempl,hwndOwn,MyDlg);
  MyPortableDlgBox:=nRes;
END;


FUNCTION WM_CommandHandler(hwnd: HWNDX;id: UINT;
  hwndCtrl: HWNDX;notify: UINT): LRESULT;
BEGIN
  (*...*)
END;


(* The revenge of the C macros ... *)


WNDPROC_BEGIN(MyOwnWndProc)
  HANDLE_WM_COMMAND(WM_CommandHandler);
WNDPROC_END(MyOwnWndProc)


BEGIN
END.
```

As already pointed out, using the C pre-processor is just a crutch for special cases; however, depending on the circumstances it can prove to be rather useful (as all crutches). The source above is first chased through

First through the pre-processor, then through the compiler!

399

the pre-processor, thereby a compilable Pascal program either for Win16 (no #define) or for Win32 (#define WIN32 or compiler switch /DWIN32) results. The following command lines are used to convert the file TEST. PPP (as in Pascal Pre-Processor):

```
// first Microsoft, for Win16
cl  /EP  test.ppp  >test.pas
// then Microsoft, for Win327
cl  /EP  /DWIN32  test.ppp  >test.pas


// Borland delivers the pre-processor as a separate program
// for Win16:
cpp  -P-  -o test.pas test.ppp
// and for Win32:
cpp  -P-  -o test.pas  -DWIN32  test.ppp
```

The resulting file TEST.PAS can be treated with the corresponding Pascal compiler (32 bit: as far as available). If you happen to find syntactical errors in the generated Pascal source: the PPP file, *not* the PAS file, has to be changed accordingly! (Although it can prove to be advantageous to first create two separate, working prototypes with the Pascal system and to put these into a PPP file only if they are thoroughly tested and de-bugged and if only insignificant changes are required.)

The Contents of the Enclosed Disk

The accompanying disk contains three categories of files: first a rather long list of example programs, which all can be executed under Windows NT and Windows 95 and partly also under Win16 plus Win32s. All programs were compiled with the current Win32 SDK (from March of 1995); there they translate as expected. I tested them with Windows NT 3.5 (no problems whatsoever) and the final beta of Windows 95 (there some minor glitches are seen; you'll find more in the corresponding README.ME). If you experience any other problems when compiling, linking, or executing, please carefully check your compiler, linker and make options and switches. The programs were partially produced with the help of QuickStart (see section 5.1, page 319) under MS-DOS — I didn't observe any problems, not counting the misery with command lines, of course. All program examples including the MAKE files are found in separate directories below \SAMPLES.

Directory \SAMPLES

Here (subdirectory \SAMPLES) you'll also find the header file PORTUTIL.H, which contains most of the macros mentioned in the text, useful data types, etc., and some other helpful definitions. These are (with the help of conditional compilation) adjusted to the environment they're compiled for — of course the example programs make thorough use of the definitions.

File PORTUTIL.H

Next, in the directory \PORTTOOL, you'll find a greatly enhanced version of PORT.INI, which is directly designed for usage with PORT-TOOL.EXE. More advice and hints about this file and a listing for all cases are in Appendix 2. A small helper program (named PORTVIEW.C) for browsing and searching the PORT.INI entries is also contained in this directory (in source code form with a MAKE file; just compile to get an executable. This is also executable under Windows 3.1 or higher with the help of Win32s — see later on). The READ.ME file in the subdirectory explains the usage of the program.

Directory \PORTTOOL

Third, in the directory \BOOK you'll discover (if and when available) by chapter all the issues, news, and other information that simply

Subdirectory \BOOK

did not make it into the book. As discussed in the book, I'll make available text files with information about errors, enhancements and the like (the contents and frequency of these "updates" largely depends on your feedback!). These files will be available in at least three places: first in the MSWIN32 forum on CompuServe (see Library #1, New Uploads); second on the ftp server of Springer NewYork:

```
ftp.springer-ny.com/pub/supplements/tlauer/
```

The third place is on the Springer Web site:

```
http://www.springer-ny.com/supplements/lauerw32.html
```

The files will be named PRT32_1.ZIP, PRT32_2.ZIP and so on. The READ.ME file on disk will inform you about other online services where these files will be placed in the future (the MS Network would be an obvious candidate).

Subdirectory \WIN32S

Fourth, all files required for executing the 32-bit helper program PORTVIEW.C (see \PORTTOOL) under Windows 3.1(1) are located in the directory \WIN32S. Here you'll find Win32s distributed to two self-extracting ZIP files (W32SDSK1.EXE and W32SDSK2.EXE), which include all necessary files. Read the READ.ME and then just start the installation batch file (called W32SINST.BAT) to perform the installation. And here are two *extremely important* remarks from the "Law and Order" department: first Win32s is Copyright © 1992, 1995 by Microsoft Corporation, all rights reserved. And second you as an end user (namely of PORTVIEW.EXE) are *not* allowed to distribute the Win32s file *under any circumstances* (says Microsoft). So, please, no villainous deeds, if you don't mind! Well, if you're in possession of the Win32 SDK or a member of MSDN Level II — Appendix E of the Release Notes specifies the detailed licensing conditions for Win32s — according to this text you can of course distribute the version found on *your* CD with *your* 32-bit programs to *your* endusers....

File READ.ME!

Last but not least, in the root directory you'll find the inevitable READ.ME file with further information and details. A detailed description of all files found on the disk is also given there. Be sure to read this file before installing the software!

Annotated Bibliography

The following compilation lists and describes all the books and articles mentioned in the text and gives my personal view about content, style, and the like. The single most important work for Win32 programmers is not shown here: getting acquainted with the Win32 API without having access to the corresponding reference materials[*] definitely requires an ample portion of optimism. It's true and an important consideration that the printed docs are in some respects incomplete and sometimes even wrong or misleading. So here is a vital hint: there exist several WinHelp files describing the Win32 API (e.g. on the Visual C++ CD or on the Win32 SDK CDs — there in X:\MSTOOLS\HELP\API32WH.HLP). This subdirectory also contains some WinHelp files describing all the new SDK tools, about program development and various articles from the MS Knowledge Base[**] dealing with miscellaneous Win32 issues. Okay, let's now discuss the rest of the important stuff:

[*] Microsoft: Win32-SDK Programmer's Reference, 5 Volumes, Microsoft Press, Redmond, WA, 1994.

[**] The MS Knowledge Base is accesible via CompuServe or Internet. Here Microsoft publishes know-how articles on a regular basis.

[1] *Microsoft: Programmer's Reference for Windows 3.1, Guide to Programming and 4 additional volumes, Microsoft Press, Redmond, WA, 1992*

For starters, there is another Microsoft product: this one is definitely *the* bible for Windows programmers. Well, even the current 3.1 SDK documentation is still not really complete and often does not fully deal with the circumstances under Window 3.1(1) — nevertheless these books are a *definite* must for any serious development. And since the Win32 API is often directly building upon its 16-bit predecessors in his models and concepts, each minute you have (or will) invested here will sooner or later bear fruit.

[2] *Helen Custer: Inside Windows NT, Microsoft Press, Redmond, WA, 1993*

Well, after the first reading I was somewhat disappointed by this book, since it didn't discuss the Win32 subsystem in the necessary depth (in my opinion). I needed another two or three weeks and a thorough re-reading until I finally understood that Windows NT is much, much more than just the functionality found in the windowing system (after all, this is by and large the widened Win16 API plus threads, flat memory, and some other ingredients). After a few months with the book and especially with NT itself I realized that Helen Custer indeed has somewhat neglected the (very well-known anyway) windowing component, but that this is more than compensated by the complete and detailed descriptions of the system architecture and the internal services. For all developers who not only seek information about the Win32 programming interfaces but Windows NT as a whole (and its internals), this book is for the time being without competition.*

But Andrew (see [3] and [4]) doesn't sleep...

[3] *Andrew Schulman, Dave Maxey, and Matt Pietrek: Undocumented Windows, Addison-Wesley, Reading, MA, 1992*

[4] *Andrew Schulman et al.: Undocumented DOS, Addison-Wesley, Reading, MA, 1992*

These two works definitely belong in the category "books Bill Gates would have *never, ever* have published." Luckily, that doesn't really matter, since for this purpose we have Andrew Schulman and his gang of bit twiddlers. Both books are written in a casual style and deliver lots of background information and valuable details about poorly or not at all documented MS-DOS and Windows features. Partly these are more of an odd nature; however, many hints and advice are not only interesting, but can prove really important for everyday work. Fortunately, the authors also discuss the problems and issues tied to the usage of undocumented properties. To cite them: »In other words, using undocumented Windows is okay, but only if you have *no choice*: if you have really been responsible, looked for alternatives [in the documented API], and found that there really were none.« Well, that marks the point!

[5] *P.J. Plauger, Jim Brodie: Standard C, Microsoft Press, Redmond, WA, 1989*

One of the somewhat boring books about standards. Nevertheless it *is* usable: first it's relatively thin and handy, so you can quickly locate the heart of the matter; second it's comprehensive: besides the ANSI C language description (including syntax diagrams) it gives detailed information on the C standard library and all run-time functions. Two appendices dealing with portability questions and a cross reference of all names and identifiers defined in ANSI C complete the book.

[6] *Ken Arnold and John Peyton: C User's Guide to ANSI C, Addison-Wesley, Reading, MA, 1992*

A tiny volume that presents a very usable introduction to the new ANSI C features — new in the sense of going beyond K&R C. The authors don't deal with all the basic language features of C, but concentrate more on showing the characteristics and advantages of ANSI C for the C proficient.* The first part deals with the language definition as such and shows in a friendly manner the usage of all the modern features. Now and again you'll hear a word of criticism — after all, even ANSI C is by far not a perfect definition. The second part describes in great detail the most important enhancements and changes in the standard library compared to classic C.

* You won't learn C programming here!

[7] *Margaret Ellis and Bjarne Stroustrup: The Annotated C++ Reference Manual, Addison-Wesley, Reading, MA, 1990*

Well, while the above-cited standard book about ANSI C [Ref. 5] is only *sometimes* a bit tedious, this book definitely belongs in the category of "completely unreadable." This somewhat harsh observation is not due so much to the style of the two authors, but because of the complex language definition of C++, which (in my opinion) got a bit out of control. Admittedly, the book has to be precise, since its purpose is to define the standard. But a better structure and more concentration on the essential language parts important in everyday practice would certainly have done no harm.

[8] *Bruce Willis: Using C++, Osborne McGraw-Hill, Berkeley, CA, 1989*

The book from Willis is much better suited for learning C++. He takes a reasonable pace and proceeds in compehensible steps; introducing the reader to the most important language features one after the other. The entire presentation is garnished with lots and lots of example code. The structure of the book and the division into single chapters are done in a logical manner, and Willis just assumes a moderate understanding of C. After reading and thorough study of the examples, you definitely don't know *all* about C++,* but at least you have a pretty good idea that (and why) today C++ is the better language. And, moreover since the important language features are explained very clearly, you can even start to code in C++ almost immediately.

[9] Ira Pohl: Object Oriented Programming Using C++, Benjamin/Cummings, New York, 1993

This one is a combination of an OOP textbook and a C++ style guide. On the one hand all the characteristics of C++ in the light of OOP are illuminated and practically applied with the help of some concrete programmimg projects. On the other hand, the author achieves (aided by a relatively strict and consistently applied methodology and nomenclature) very clear and comprehensible source codes. He also gives a lot of useful hints and advice which promote a homogeneous and readable C/C++ programming style.

[10] Paul di Lascia: Windows++, Addison-Wesley, Reading, MA, 1992

A guide to the implementation of an OOP shell (of course written in C++) around the Windows API. The book is didactically very well conceived but unfortunately the subject is so complex that you'll have to invest certainly more than just a few days to fully comprehend the concepts and their realization. But if you do, all the stuff you've read and thought of really begins to bear fruit: first, even when using a commercially available class library, you'll understand many issues that normally remain in the dark in the respective library. Second, the book shows really impressively how to implement (in an acceptable time frame) a class library of your own.* C++ knowledge is desired, but not absolutely necessary: the author gives in the first two chapters enough basic hints for C programmers, who will just have to invest a little bit more of their time...

[11] James L. Conger: Windows API Bible, The Waite Groupe, Mill Valley, CA, 1992

As a reference work for the Win16 API, this book is a good source for Win16 programming. It is filled with lots of small, but useful examples. Strong points include that the API is almost fully presented and that

* Is there — with the possible exception of Stroustrup — anybody who knows all about C++?

* Motto: "If I need four weeks to comprehend the class library of manufacturer X, I could just as well write it myself."

Conger explains things (concisely, but adequately) and tries to distill matching concepts into one or two chapters. The 30 chapters (over some 1000 pages with rather small print — there really *is* a lot of information) also discuss issues that are often neglected, such as building WinHelp files or execution profiling. There's another book from Conger in that series, called *Windows New Testament*, which complements this work and discusses some Windows 3.1x features not covered here. In that book Conger also includes some basic hints for MFC programming.

[12] Unicode Consortium: The Unicode Standard, Addison-Wesley, Reading, MA, 1991

More details about the Unicode standard which by far exceed the basic introduction found in the Win32 documentation are best taken from this two-volume work. Both books literally define the standard and contain, besides detailed information about the division of the character space, general hints for the implementation of Unicode-based applications. In addition, one can discover some quite interesting facts about alphabets and special characters used in other parts of the world (and also about the problems they can create in data processing).

[13] Ira Pohl: C for Pascal Programmers, Benjamin/Cummings Publishing, New York, 1993

Pohl gives a rather complete description of (ANSI) C for programmers coming from a Pascal-like language.* He builds on your Pascal experience to explain the C features and especially discusses all those areas that might look strange (or frightening) to a Pascalist. A certain criticism is that he's too concerned about standard Pascal (in my opinion) and doesn't always include the proper way of doing things for a rather "developed" language like Borland Pascal (which by far has the greatest worldwide significance). Neverthless, if you're good in Pascal and need a quick method to comprehend C, this is the way to go. Pohl has also written a book called C++ *for Pascal Programmers*, which is oriented more towards object oriented concepts and features; it might prove useful only if you definitely intend to switch your development language from Pascal to C++.

* So the book is also suitable for people with a Modula-2 background.

[14] *Guillaume H. Tore-Trois: How Bill Cracked Big Blue, Traded in a Bit of GUI for Lots of Money (and in Passing Drove Numerous Hackers to API Madness), Les Presses de Microzophe, Rougemonde, XB, 2001*

This is a rather nice book, which the publishers are unfortunately still a bit reluctant to print (certainly it'll be announced sometime in the next years). Detailed, with intimate knowledge and deep insight Mr. Tore-Trois (possibly French?) describes much in the style of an autobiography (one could almost believe he *actually* was in the plot) the religious wars with the once almighty mainframe church. Then he examines the long-winded controversies with MS-believing endusers all over the world, who, after having donated *ridiculously* low license fees to the great leader *truly* had the indignity to demand halfway working and bugfree applications. (Self-?)Ironically he also discusses the attempts of that time to flood (and bewilder) the world with so many APIs that the MS "technical evangelists" with a so-called NT (New Testament? Nice try?) in the bag appeared to many to be the heralds of the one and only true belief. Definitely recommended!

Glossary

This glossary explains a lot of technical terms specific to Win16 and/or Win32. On the one hand, I've included quite a few definitions that are used in the text to describe new Win32 API features.* On the other hand, I have also explained numerous definitions from the Win16 world in order to give readers that are not so strong on the minutiae of Win16 programming (e.g., project leads) the possibility of comprehending the corresponding sections (for example, "window subclassing"; not, however, standard terms such as window handle or message). Finally, you'll find some important concepts and explanations from general operating system technology (such as "virtual memory").

* Example: memory mapped files.

broadcasting a message: is the posting of a message to all top-level windows (works systemwide).

C calling convention: is the standard calling convention used by most C compilers and required for variable parameter lists.

⇒ *"calling convention"*

callback function: is a programmer-defined function in an application which is called by Windows when necessary. They are almost never called from the application itself. Examples: window/dialog procedures, enum, or DDEML callbacks.

calling convention: defines the mechanisms of parameter passing and returning values for function calls.

capture (mouse): a window has the capture if all further mouse messages, independently from the position of the mouse, are sent to its window procedure.

code segment: is an area in which executable code is loaded. In a code segment normally no writing access is allowed.

committed memory page: is a memory page in the address space of an application for which actual physical memory or at least an area in the

⇒ *"reserved memory page"*

system paging file is allocated. The contrary is a ⇒ "reserved memory page."

compact memory model: is one of the memory models of 16-bit compilers. It supports a code segment with no more than 64 KB as well as several data segments (NEAR code, FAR data). Further models are: ⇒ "small"; ⇒ "medium"; ⇒ "large"; ⇒ "huge"; also ⇒ "mixed memory model programming."

console functions (API): are text-mode functions in the Win32 API and support the "conventional" way of programming (i.e., no messages and window handles, etc.).

control notifications: are sent to the corresponding parent window by controls (e.g., a listbox), in order to inform the parent of changes to or actions on the control (e.g., LBN_DBLCLK for a mouse double click.)

⇒ *"preemptive multi-tasking"* **cooperative multi-tasking**: means that several running programs (should) give up control to their respective successors *voluntarily* in a clearly defined fashion. The opposite is called ⇒"preemptive multi-tasking."

critical section: describes a (hopefully) small code area that can be executed only by a single program part (or thread) at a time. Critical sections serve among other things to synchronize the access to shared resources.

custom control: is a new window class designed to enhance the default controls of Windows (static, button, edit, etc.). Most often custom controls can be integrated into the various dialog editors.

data segment: is a memory area sufficiently large for the initialized and non-initialized data (variables, etc.) of a program. The initialized data are loaded from the EXE file into the data segment.

DDE: is the abbreviation for ⇒ "dynamic data exchange."

⇒ *"virtual memory"* **demand paging**: is an approach to virtual memory management. A physical memory page is not necessarily allocated with the actual allocation call, but only if the program (e.g., through a memory access) definitely needs the memory (⇒ "committed memory page" and ⇒ "reserved memory page").

discardable memory: is a memory area that can be freed when memory is low, since the contained information can at any time be reloaded (e.g., unneeded code segments can be read from the EXE file) or recreated.

disk mirroring: is the mapping of a single disk partition to one or more other hard disks.

disk striping: permits access to several physical partitions on different hard disks as one large logical drive.

DLL: is the abbreviation for ⇒ "dynamic link library."

dynamic data exchange: is a theoretically simple but rather confusingly defined protocol for the exchange of global memory handles (and therefore data blocks) between different applications. It also permits the passing of macros or commands to other software.

dynamic link library: contains further code and data sections, which can be loaded through dynamic linking to the actual program code.

dynamic linking: permits the binding of additional code either while loading a program (⇒ "load-time dynamic linking") or while executing (⇒ "run-time dynamic linking") the application. The opposite is "static linking," where the linker lumps all required code segments from other object files or libraries into the executable program.

⇒ *"load-time dynamic linking"*

environment subsystem: ⇒ "protected subsystems."

far address (pointer): is a 4-byte pointer built from a ⇒ "segment selector" and an offset value. It allows 80(2)86 processors to access more than 64 KB (alas, only with the help of segment arithmetic or manipulation, respectively).

flat memory model: is a linear memory model and allows with the aid of a single large offset (most often 32-bit) access to all of a process' memory. Segment arithmetic is omitted.

⇒ *"local heap"*   **global heap**: is Win16 memory that can be accessed by all applications via calls to GlobalAlloc() and GlobalLock(). A corresponding mechanism is *not* directly available under Win32.

HAL: is the abbreviation for ⇒ "hardware abstraction layer."

hardware abstraction layer: is a small code shell accessing the hardware on behalf of the NT kernel. It defines an abstract hardware interface and facilitates the portable implementation of NT.

huge memory model: is one of the memory models of 16-bit compilers. It supports several code segments and several data segments; the latter are used to store objects > 64 KB (FAR code, HUGE data). Further models: ⇒ "small"; ⇒ "medium"; ⇒ "compact"; ⇒ "large"; also ⇒ "mixed memory model programming".

integral subsystem: ⇒ "protected subsystems."

interprocess communication: is a collective term for all mechanisms that allow communication between applications. Examples are ⇒ DDE, ⇒ "named pipes," and ⇒ RPC.

IPC: is the abbreviation for ⇒ "interprocess communication."

large memory model: is one of the memory models of 16-bit compilers. It supports several code segments and several data segments (FAR code, FAR data). Further models: ⇒ "small"; ⇒ "medium"; ⇒ "compact"; ⇒ "HUGE"; also ⇒ "mixed memory model programming".

LDT: is the abbreviation for ⇒ "local descriptor table."

linear memory: ⇒ "flat memory model."

⇒ *"dynamic linking"*   **load-time dynamic linking**: is a variant of ⇒ "dynamic linking." In load-time dynamic linking, *while* loading the application itself other required

DLLs are also loaded in order to make available the contained functions and data for the application. The loading process is checked by the system, and a non-loading (or not found) DLL cancels the whole operation.

local descriptor table: is one of two central x86-CPU tables for the administration of segment information. The LDT has a maximum of 8192 segment entries, in which the start addresses, lengths (limits), and further attributes of the currently allocated segments are recorded.   ⇒ *"segment selector"*

local heap: is an area within the data segment of a program (or DLL) for small dynamic memory allocations. It roughly corresponds to the dynamic memory management of Win32 (apart from the smaller 16-bit offset used in Win16).   ⇒ *"global heap"*

local input state: this stores the input state of the concerned thread only, but contains no systemwide information about these items (⇒ "capture," input focus etc.).

local procedure calls: a variant of ⇒ "remote procedure calls" optimized for local access (both partners are running on the same machine).

locked memory: is a dynamically allocated area that is explicitly guarded from being displaced through the Windows kernel. Because all that circus was necessary *only* for the 8086/8 CPU (or the real mode, respectively) — really usable CPUs implement issues of this kind transparently for the application programmer — corresponding calls under Windows 3.1 (and even more under Win32) can be omitted (⇒ "unlocked memory").

mapping modes: is the collective term for the eight GDI modes that perform the conversion from logical coordinates to device coordinates (see the function SetMapMode()).

medium memory model: is one of the memory models of 16-bit compilers. It supports several code segments and one data segment with a maximum size of 64 KB (FAR code, NEAR data). Further models: ⇒ "small"; ⇒ "compact"; ⇒ "large"; ⇒ "HUGE"; also ⇒ "mixed memory model programming".

⇒ "shared memory"

memory-mapped file: is a Win32 mechanism for data communication between different applications and for ⇒ "shared memory." Thereby a file is loaded into memory and this area is mapped into the virtual address spaces of all concerned applications. Alternatively, instead of a real file the system paging file can also be used.

message broadcasting: ⇒ "broadcasting a message."

* See page 212 and 227.

message cracker: is a set of macros explicitly defined by Microsoft for portable access to the message parameters wParam and lParam. See the sections 4.3* and 4.4 as well as the header file WINDOWSX.H.

message loop: is the central message dispatcher of a program. Here messages are pulled off the application or system queue and sent to the concerned window (procedures).

mixed memory model programming: is a strange technique developed to deal with the disadvantages of specific memory models. It permits such wonderful things as the usage of FAR data in programs written for the ⇒ "small memory model." Source code making explicit use of these possibilities is often somewhat difficult to port (well, this is a polite understatement).

mouse capture: see ⇒ "capture."

movable memory: is one of the standard attributes for Win16 memory. All memory allocated in this way can be moved around by the Windows kernel at any time if not explicitly locked (⇒ "locked memory").

multi-threading: is the capability to create and execute several independent execution paths in a single application. On the user level threads appear to run in parallel (actually they will on an NT-based multiprocessor machine!).

⇒ "typesafe linking"

name mangling: is a method to include in the compiler-generated names of functions the data types of the parameters and the return value. It is used by C++ compilers for the implementation of ⇒ "typesafe linking".

named pipes: are a method for interprocess communication (⇒ IPC). A named pipe is a one- or two-way channel and can be used to exchange data between programs (also networkwide).

near address (pointer): is a 2-byte pointer consisting only of an offset value. It permits 80(2)86 processors to access a single segment with a maximum size of 64 KB.

PASCAL calling convention: is the calling convention used by most Pascal and Modula-2 compilers. It *of course* permits no variable parameter lists and is therefore in the normal case somewhat more efficient.

⇒ *"calling convention"*

portable executable: is the expression used for Win32 executable files. A PE contains several linear memory sections, which contain all the needed program information (code, data, resources, etc.). The format has practically nothing in common with the so-called ⇒ "segmented executables."

precompiled header: are standard C header files once compiled into an auxiliary file, so they don't need a time-consuming analysis in further compilations anymore. In a system with header files summing up to more than 3 MB, their use is no luxury, but pure necessity.

preemptive multi-tasking: is the multi-tasking variant where the system software can at any time preempt the currently running process (respectively, thread) *without* its explicit accord ("kernel preempts thread"). It is an important requirement for safe and effective work with several programs executing in parallel.

⇒ *"cooperative multi-tasking"*

protected subsystem: is a Windows NT program that builds upon NT kernel calls and makes available a certain OS API (Win32, OS/2, POSIX) or other useful system services. The former variant is called also "environment subsystems"; the latter are known as "integral subsystems" (the security subsystem is an example). A protected subsystem can be seen as a server that exports certain services to its clients (other executable programs). The communication between a protected subsystem and the clients normally happens via ⇒ "local procedure calls."

⇒ *"environment subsystems"*

quota: is on the one hand the limit on system resources (memory, handles, etc.) that a process is allowed to consume. When reaching its quota no further resources can be allocated (unless the process first frees some of the already allocated resources). On the other hand, each NT object type has a quota that defines how much the allocating process is charged for using that specific object.

Abbreviated RPC   **remote procedure calls**: are procedure calls over a network. A procedure identification and all the arguments are packed in the client machine; the whole package is then sent to the server machine. There the RPC server unpacks the data, calls the procedure, packs, and delivers the result back. RPC is one of the founding pillars of distributed processing (the distributed execution of programs on several machines).

reserved memory: is the part of a Win32 memory allocation that is indeed reserved, but for which no physical memory (or space in the system paging file) was made available. Only with the first access to a reserved page is a page actually allocated through the virtual memory manager (⇒ "committed memory").

RPC: is the abbreviation for ⇒ "remote procedure calls."

⇒ *"dynamic linking"*   **run-time dynamic linking**: is the variant of dynamic linking when a DLL is loaded not at program start-up, but only afterwards when the program started execution. Since this happens completely under program control, a not-loadable DLL doesn't cause a program halt.

segment selector: are those ugly creatures through which ⇒ "segmented memory" is made possible. They describe in which segment (or from which memory address) accesses shall happen.

⇒ *"portable executable"*   **segmented executable**: is the format of Windows EXE files under Win16. It is a complete mixed-up collection of all code, data, and resource segments of an application; these can (via the DEF file) be provided with certain attributes to control the loading process.

segmented memory: is one of the most dreadful inventions since CPUs were invented. Here the memory is not treated as a single large linear array of bytes (⇒ "flat memory model"), but rather split into 64 KB chunks (called segments). To access all the memory, two items are therefore manipulated: first the desired ⇒ "segment selector" and second the offset into the segment. The Win32 API doesn't know segmentation anymore: R.I.P.

shared memory: is a simple form of data communication, where several applications access a common memory area. Under Win16 shared memory is comparatively easy to achieve, since an area allocated from the ⇒ "global heap" can be read and written without any trouble by all applications (this can unfortunately also happen inadvertently or even with sinister intentions). Under Win32 you should use, depending on the purpose, the appropriate ⇒ IPC mechanisms. Probably most similar to shared memory in the Win16 sense are ⇒ "memory mapped files". ⇒ *"global heap"*

small memory model: is one of the memory models of 16-bit compilers. It supports one code and one data segment, both 64 KB in size (NEAR code, NEAR data). Further models: ⇒ "compact"; ⇒ "medium"; ⇒ "large"; ⇒ "huge"; also ⇒ "mixed memory model programming".

__stdcall calling convention: a newly designed calling convention for Win32, which collects the advantages of the ⇒ "C" and ⇒ "PASCAL calling convention" under one hat. For the gory details see Appendix 5. ⇒ *"calling convention"*

structure alignment (padding): describes the additional filling bytes necessary to align the components of a structure optimally to the data bus width of the CPU. Non-properly aligned structures can be problematic for RISC processors (they cause either enormous performance losses or even a program crash).

structured exception handling: is a newly defined method for Win32 in order to deal with processor exceptions or miscellaneous error conditions in a structured and coherent way. SEH is not a component itself of the Win32 API, but rather a compiler extension.

subclassing a window: with subclassing, another procedure is placed before the window procedure actually responsible for a message. This other procedure is called for all window messages before the original procedure. The new procedure can process the messages either by itself or pass them on (modified, if necessary). Therefore it can perform all sorts of tricky manipulations with the subclassed window.

symmetric multi-processing: permits supporting several CPUs in a computer. Thereby all threads or processes can be executed on all available processors; there are no special allocations of certain tasks to predetermined processors (e.g., CPU 1 only handles interrupts, etc.). This much simpler variant is called "asymmetric multiprocessing".

⇒ *"CALLBACK procedure"*

thunks: are also nasty beasts from the 16-bit world. They serve the implementation of ⇒ "callback procedures" and supply the proper data segment. Since namely the code segments for several instances are only loaded once under Win16, loading the (instance-specific) data segment into the DS register can't happen in the code itself. Therefore, before the actual call a short code sequence is called (precisely the thunk), which first loads the proper data segment and only then jumps to the start of the callback procedure. In Win32 a thunk is the general name for a transition from Win32 mode to Win16 or the other way around (⇒ universal thunks).

typesafe linking: allows a C++ compiler to make sure in the course of linking (so even crossing module boundaries) that procedures are called with the proper parameters. For this purpose further encoded information about the parameter types and the return value is attached to the procedure names (⇒ "name mangling").

universal thunks: are a comparatively transparent approach to call procedures located in 16-bit DLLs from Win32s programs. Thereby 32-bit memory areas are mapped to 16-bit segments, so that the 16-bit procedure can access them (and vice versa). Universal thunks are Win32s specific — the code does not run under Windows NT or 95!

⇒ *"locked memory"*

unlocked memory: is the opposite of "locked memory" and tells the Win16 kernel that the concerned memory area can be moved at any time. A [Global/Local]Lock() call changes the state to ⇒ "locked memory."

VDM: is the abbreviation for ⇒ "virtual DOS machine."

virtual device driver: makes sure, that hardware access from several ⇒ VDMs or Windows programs under Win16 are correctly coordinated and performed. A VxD is a 32-bit code segment.

virtual DOS machines: are based on the V86 mode of 386 CPUs. They define a quasi-complete DOS environment in a 1 MB nutshell separated from the rest of the Windows system. In a VDM a DOS application can be started as usual. The number of possible virtual DOS machines is only limited through available memory and running VDMs are activated through ⇒ "preemptive multi-tasking."

virtual memory: is making available (much) more memory than is physically installed in the computer. This illusion is reached by storing currently unneeded memory areas in a helper file (called system paging or swap file), where they can be read back when the need arises (and possibly overwrite another area, which on its part was saved in the paging file first). Virtual memory can be realized either on a segment basis (e.g., with OS/2 1.x on 80286 CPUs) or through writing and reading memory pages of equal size (⇒ "demand paging") as does Win16 in enhanced mode and, of course, all Win32 systems.

VxD: is the generic abbreviation for ⇒ "virtual device driver."

Index

This index is only one half of the possibilities to retrieve information about a specific Windows function or message. Entries here refer you to places in the main text where the underlying, often semantical and somewhat complex, problem is exactly described. Contrary to that, the entries in appendix 2 (PORT.INI: Enhanced and Clarified) are mostly dealing with simple syntactical changes (so that list is also kind of an index). The issues handled there are found in this index only if the main text has something significant to say above the information found in appendix 2. In this context I'd like to refer you to appendix 3 giving all the sorted message cracker signatures and a list of the concerned WM_* messages.

__0400H   253
__stdcall   263f, 387f
_AHINCR   210
_AHSHIFT   210
_cdecl   387f
_get_osfhandle   254
_lopen   254
_open_osfhandle   254
_pascal   387f

A

active window   273f
ANSI C prototypes   109, 140, 187
~ vs. K&R C   85f, 139f
~, advantages of using   139f
~, size of basic data types   150, 175
assembler code   177

B

base functionality, changes in the 241
bit operations 176
bitmaps, exchanging 288
BOOL 157f
Borland tools 349
bottom up porting 89f
~, advantages of 92
Button_ macros 235f

C

C compiler 60, 323f
~ and #pragmas 176
~ and warnings 178f, 379f
~, comparison of switches 324f
C pre-processor 142f, 153
~, complex macros and performance 148
~, complex macros 146f
~, simple #defines 142f
C++ 197f
~ and class libraries 199f
Cairo 15
callback procedures 47, 331
CALLBACK 211, 263f
calling sequence of window procedures 263f, 387f
capturing the mouse 274f
~ and pressing of buttons 276
casting 68, 145f, 154f, 185f, 189f, 195f, 237f
~ of pointers 174
~, erroneous 154f
changes in the base functionality (KERNEL) 241
~ in the graphics functionality (GDI) 278f
~ in the windowing (USER) 262f
~ to the sources 44f
~, syntactical vs. semantical 210f
Chicago see Windows 95
class extra bytes 264
class libraries 98f
CloseHandle 129, 254
CombineRgn 214
ComboBox_ macros 235f
communication with child windows 234f
~ other applications 269f
CompuServe, getting developer information from 104f, 203

configuration data see registry
console functions 315
control notifications 47
cooperative multitasking 10, 52
coordinates, display 284f
~, logical 284f
~, packed, table with concerned functions and messages 284
COPYDATASTRUCT 250
CPU specific functions 55, 252f
CreateFile 36
CreateProcess 29
CreateThread 75, 123
CreateWindow 39, 299
creation of Win32 GUI programs 319f
~ with Borland tools 349f
CS_GLOBALCLASS 50, 57, 298f
CVTRES 326

D

data sections 340f, 345f
~ and STRICT 106
~, alignment of 166f
~, comparison of Win16 and Win32 355f
~, problems with self-defined 153f, 164f
~, self-defined 150f, 159f
~, simple 149f
~, size of 156f
~, structured 159f
~, usage of 136
~, widening of 46, 205f, 279f
DDBs 288
DDE conversations 51, 243, 250
~, macro helpers for 268
DDE messages, packing of parameters 265f
~, table of changes 268
DDE protocol and portability 264f
DDEML 250
~ and portability 265, 268
DEF files 343
DefWindowProc 191, 212, 223
DeleteBitmap 214
DeleteBrush 214
DeleteFont 214
DeletePen 214
DestroyWindow 105

D (continued)

diagnostic compiler messages 68, 178f, 379f
DialogBox 262
DIBs 288
DispatchMessage 215
display coordinates 284
DLGTEMPLATE 278
DLL linking 343f
~ programming 290f, 339f
DLL_PROCESS_ATTACH 296
DLL_THREAD_ATTACH 296
DLLs and global window classes 297f
~ and memory management 291f
~, data sections in 50, 291f, 340f
~, difficulties in ~ programming 57f
~, dynamic memory allocations 294f, 347f
~, initialization and termination 295f
~, shared data in 292f, 345f
~, shared data sections in 345f
DOS3Call 253
DosAllocSeg 127, 128
DosClose 129
DosExecPgm 29
DosGlobalAlloc 131

E

Edit_ macros 235f
EM_GETSEL 229
EM_LINESCROLL 229
EM_SETSEL 229
EM_SETTABSTOPS 216
enhanced metafiles 288f
EXEHDR 61

F

FAR pointer 161, 171f, 194, 208f, 250
filenames, long 255f
~, conversion to MS-DOS names 258
FindWindow 50, 241, 244
focus 273f
FORWARD_WM_MOUSEMOVE 223
fread 254

FreeProcInstance 148, 331

G

GDI coordinates 54f, 279f
GDI, changes in the 278f
~, handles are private 287
~, table with changed functions 283
GdiFlush 290
GdiSetBatchLimit 290
GET_WM_COMMAND... macros 228f
GET_WM_COMMAND_MPS 233
GetActiveWindow 273f
GetAspectRatioFilter 280
GetCapture 275f
GetClassLong 264
GetClassWord 264
GetCurrentTask 269
GetDCOrg 284
GetDiskFreeSpace 55
GetFocus 53, 273f
GetForegroundWindow 274
GetInstanceData 50, 243
GetMessage 51
GetMessagePos 284
GetModuleHandle 299
GetSysModalWindow 276
GetTabbedTextExten 284
GetTextExtent 283
GetTextExtentPoint 283
GetWindowLong 146, 202, 264
GetWindowTask 269
GetWindowText 235, 243
GetWindowTextLength 235
GetWindowThreadProcessId 269
GetWindowWord 146, 202, 264
GetWinFlags 312
global heap 245f
Global... calls 246f
GlobalAlloc 248, 316, 346
GlobalHandle 258
GlobalLock 248, 250
GlobalUnlock 158
GlobalUnwire 55
GlobalWire 55
GM_ADVANCED 285
GMEM_(DDE)SHARE 249, 291, 346

G (continued)

GMEM_FIXED 248f
GMEM_MOVABLE 248
group files for Program Manager 310
GUI programs, creation of ~ with Borland tools 349f

H

HAL 23
HANDLE_MSG 220f
HANDLE_WM_COMMAND 220f
HANDLE_WM_MOUSEMOVE 222f
Handles 36
hardware accesses 253, 311
header files 334f
heap size for Win16 apps 310
  ~ Win32 apps 330
HeapAlloc 246
HeapFree 246
HIWORD 206, 218
hooks 277f
hPrevInstance 49, 203, 241f
HUGE pointer 210f
hungarian notation 113f
  ~, enhancing with self-defined mechanisms 118f
  ~, implemeting 115f
  ~, optional qualification 116f
  ~, type abbreviations 115f

I

I/O system 251
IMPLIB 61
information exchange 94
initialization files 258f, 310
  ~, non-standard access to 260f
input messages 52f
instances, communicating with preceding 241f
  ~, preceding 49, 203
INT 21 calls 252f
  ~, comparison with Win32 calls 254f
IsTask 269

K

K&R C vs. ANSI C 85f
KERNEL, changes in the 241f
keyboard input 51f, 271f

L

LIB manager 61
LibMain 290, 296f
linker 61, 327f
  ~, comparison of switches 328f
  ~, usage modes 328
ListBox_ macros 235f
LMEM_FIXED 247f
LMEM_MOVABLE 248
LoadLibrary 57, 296, 298f
local heap 245f
local input state 52f, 271f
Local... calls 246f
LocalInit 247
logical coordinates 284
long filenames 255f
  ~, conversion to MS-DOS names 258
LOWORD 206, 218
LPARAM 47, 108, 211f
LPC batching 37f, 290
lstrcmp 39
lstrlen 302
lstrlenA 302

M

macro helpers 120f, 142f, 176
  ~ for communicating with child windows 234f
  ~ for DDE 268
  ~ for message processing 227f
  ~ in WINDOWSX.H 213
make utility 332
MAKELONG 206
MAKELP 174, 210
MAKELPARAM 206
MAKELRESULT 206
MAKEPOINT 281
MakeProcInstance 148, 331

M (continued)

mapping mode 284
memory management 245f
  ~, comparison Win16 and Win32 246
message crackers 215f, 369f
  ~ and performance 219
  ~ and portability 224f
  ~ and WM_COMMAND 215f
  ~ and WM_MOUSEMOVE 221f
  ~, exceptions for 225f
message processing 227f
message queue 52f, 270f
metafiles 288f
MM_SETITEMATTR 131
modal windows 276f
Modula-2 141, 393f
mouse capture 274f
  ~ and pressing of buttons 276
mouse input 51f, 271f
MoveTo 54
MoveToEx 54, 282
MS-DOS apps under Win32 314f
MS-DOS specific functions 55, 69, 252f
MSG 215

N

name mangling 111f
naming of variables 113f
NEAR pointer 161, 171f, 194, 207f, 247
NMAKE 332
NotifyRegister 77
NTFS 256f

O

OFFSETOF 174, 209
OpenFile 316
OS/2 17f, 52
  ~, implementation on an 80286 249
  ~, porting difficult cases 131f
  ~, porting from 103, 126f
  ~, porting PM programs 130f
  ~, porting text-mode programs 129f
OS/2, technical comparison with NT 21f
  ~, tools for porting 127f

P

PackDDEIParam 265f
packed coordinates 280, 282f
  ~, table with concerned functions and messages 284
parameter packing 227f
Pascal 140f, 393f
POINT 280, 282
pointer conversions 174
PORT.INI 61, 102, 261, 277, 359f
portable executable 15
porting to Win95 or NT 16
  ~, advantages of 62f
  ~, and class libraries 98f, 199f
  ~, and keeping Win16 compatbility 87f
  ~, bottom up 89f
  ~, duration of 70
  ~, effort 66f
  ~, from OS/2 103, 126f
  ~, guidelines 85
  ~, helper libraries 95, 98
  ~, methodical approaches 93f
  ~, one-way port 86
  ~, planning 93f
  ~, top down 89f
porting tools 98f
PORTTOOL 61, 101f, 202, 359f
POSIX 12, 23
PostAppMsg 269
PostMessage 267
PostThreadMessage 269
pragmas 176
preceding instances 49, 203
  ~, communicating with 241f
preemptive multitasking 12, 57
printf 153
processes 269f
profiler 62
protected mode compatible 84f, 309
PtInRect 39

Index

R

reassembling message parameters   233f
RegisterClass   73, 157, 298, 302
registry   258f
ReleaseCapture   53, 275f
resource compiler   61, 326f
resources   94
runtime check for host system   312

S

ScrollBar_ macros   235f
segment arithmetic   173f
SelectBitmap   214
SelectBrush   214
SelectFont   214
SELECTOROF   174, 209
SelectPen   214
semantical changes   202f
SendMessage   195, 207, 238, 240, 242, 250
SetActiveWindow   273f
SetCapture   53, 272f
SetClassLong   264
SetClassWord   264
SetFocus   273f
SetForegroundWindow   274
SetGraphicsMode   285
SetMessageQueue   270
SetSelectorBase   55
SetSelectorLimit   55
SetSysModalWindow   276
SetWindowLong   146, 202, 264
SetWindowText   235, 243
SetWindowTextW   305
SetWindowWord   146, 202, 264
shared memory   249f
sign extension   176
SIZE   280
size_t   155
sizeof   151, 156f, 169, 177, 264, 306f
Software Compatibility Test   312
stack size for Win16 apps   310
   ~ Win32 apps   330
Static_ macros   235f
STRESS.DLL   56
STRICT option   68, 71, 82f, 96, 179, 184

STRICT option, explanation   105f
   ~, hints for C++ programmers   111f
   ~, implementing the   107f
   ~, redefined data types   106, 108f
strlen   155
structs   159, 162f
   ~, and memory layout   166f
structured exception handling   21, 27, 66, 75
subsystems   29, 31f, 34f, 329, 337
syntactical changes   201f
system modal windows   276f
SYSTEM.INI   see initialization files
SystemHeapInfo   208

T

TabbedTextOut   284
tasks   269f
textmode programs   315, 336f
threads   269f
TOOLHELP.DLL   56, 94, 208
top down porting   89f
   ~, advantages of   91
typedef   see data types, self-defined

U

UINT vs. WORD   205f
undocumented features   55f, 68, 310
Unicode   300f
   ~ and C compiler   304f
   ~ and macro layer   302f
   ~ and WinMain   306
   ~, advantages   308
   ~, stepwise adaption of sources   307
unions   160f
UNIX   19f
   ~, technical comparison with NT   21f
UnpackDDElParam   266f
user input   51f

V

variable names   113f

426

W

warnings   178f, 379f
WEP   290, 296
WIN.INI   see initialization files
Win16   8f
   ~, binary compatible ~ apps under Win32   309f
Win32 and binary compatible Win16 apps   309f
   ~ and MS-DOS apps   314f
   ~ and competition   17f
WIN32 constant   312, 144, 326
Win32 development   319f
   ~ development, overview of tools   322f
   ~ features and advantages for developers   65f
   ~ GUI programs, creation of ~ with Borland tools   349f
   ~ GUI programs, creation of   319f
   ~ header files   334f
   ~ SDK   58f, 76, 79, 103, 319f
   ~ SDK, differences to Win16   60f
   ~, address space   45f, 48f, 172
   ~, distinguishing ~ platforms   312f
Win32s   12, 71f, 80, 122f, 320f
   ~, advantages for developers   75f, 123f
   ~, basic archictecture   72f
   ~, disadvantages for developers   75f, 124f
   ~, stability   77
WINAPI   263
WINDBG   61
window extra bytes   264
window management, changes in the   262f
window procedures   211f
   ~, calling sequence of   263f, 387f
Windows 3.x   7f, 122f
Windows 95   14f, 79
   ~, basic architecture   40f
   ~, comparison with Win16   26f, 34f,
   ~, system DLLs   42f
   ~, thunking layer   43
   ~, virtual device drivers   42
   ~, virtual machine manager   41f
Windows NT   10f, 17f, 78f
   ~, basic architecture   22f
   ~, communication with subsystems   37f
   ~, comparison with Win16   26f, 34f
   ~, executive   23, 29
   ~, kernel   24f
   ~, MS-DOS support   32

   ~, subsystems   29, 31f, 34f, 329, 337
   ~, Win16 support   33
WINDOWS.H   334f
WINDOWSX.H   203, 212f
   ~ and helper macros   213f
   ~ and message crackers   215f, 369f
WinMain   49, 89, 96, 184, 306, 337
WinMainCRTStartup   337
WinSubclassWindow   128
WM_ACTIVATE   229
WM_ACTIVATEAPP   225
WM_CHANGECBCHAIN   233
WM_CHARTOITEM   229
WM_COMMAND   47, 131, 227f
   ~ and message crackers   215f
WM_CONTROL   131
WM_COPYDATA   244f, 250f, 271
WM_CTLCOLOR   214, 229f
WM_CTLCOLORBTN   231
WM_CTLCOLORDLG   231
WM_CTLCOLOREDIT   231
WM_CTLCOLORLISTBOX   231
WM_CTLCOLORMSGBOX   231
WM_CTLCOLORSCROLLBAR   231
WM_CTLCOLORSTATIC   231
WM_DDE_ACK   268
WM_DDE_ADVISE   265f
WM_DDE_DATA   268
WM_DDE_EXECUTE   268
WM_DDE_INITIATE   267f
WM_DDE_POKE   268
WM_DDE_REQUEST   268
WM_DDE_TERMINATE   268
WM_DDE_UNADVISE   268
WM_GET_COMMAND_ID   203
WM_GETFONT   194
WM_GETHOTKEY   56
WM_GETTEXTLENGTH   307
WM_HSCROLL   47, 229
WM_KEYDOWN   51, 216
WM_LBUTTONDOWN   284
WM_LBUTTONDOWNDBLCLK   284
WM_LBUTTONUP   284
WM_MDIACTIVATE   229
WM_MDIACTIVATE   230
WM_MEASUREITEM   216
WM_MENUCHAR   229
WM_MENUSELECT   229
WM_MOUSEMOVE   51, 280f

W (continued)

WM_MOUSEMOVE and message cracker   221f
WM_MOVE   284
WM_NCACTIVATE   226
WM_NCHITTEST   276, 284
WM_NCLBUTTONDOWN   284
WM_NCLBUTTONDOWNDBLCLK   284
WM_NCLBUTTONUP   284
WM_NCRBUTTONDOWN   284
WM_NCRBUTTONDOWNDBLCLK   284
WM_NCRBUTTONUP   284
WM_NOTIFY   131
WM_PARENTNOTIFY   229
WM_RBUTTONDOWN   284
WM_RBUTTONDOWNDBLCLK   284
WM_RBUTTONUP   284
WM_SETHOTKEY   56
WM_SIZE   216, 280, 284
WM_SYSCOMMAND   284
WM_VKEYTOITEM   229
WM_VSCROLL   47, 229
WORD vs. UINT   205f
 ~, as message parameter   47, 108f, 149f, 206
 ~, in a cast   154f
working set tuner   62
world transformation   285f
WPARAM   47, 108, 206, 211f
wsprintf   153, 187